OTHER BOOKS BY C. BRIAN KELLY AND INGRID SMYER

Best Little Stories from the American Revolution
with "Select Founding Mothers" by Ingrid Smyer

Best Little Stories: Voices of the Civil War
with "Variana: Forgotten First Lady" and "Mary Todd Lincoln:
Troubled First Lady" by Ingrid Smyer

Best Little Ironies, Oddities, and Mysteries of the Civil War
with "Mary Todd Lincoln: Troubled First Lady" by Ingrid Smyer

Best Little Stories from the White House
with "First Ladies in Review" by Ingrid Smyer

Best Little Stories of the Wild West
with "Fascinating Women of the West" by Ingrid Smyer

Best Little Stories from World War II
with "Eleanor Roosevelt: Woman for the Ages" by Ingrid Smyer

Best Little Stories from Virginia
with "The Women Who Counted" by Ingrid Smyer

Best Little Stories from the Life and Times of Winston Churchill
with "This American Mother Jennie" by Ingrid Smyer

Best Little Stories from World War I
with "Royal Couples" by Ingrid Smyer

PROUD
★ TO BE A ★
MARINE

STORIES *of* STRENGTH
and COURAGE *from*
the FEW *and the* PROUD

C. BRIAN KELLY WITH INGRID SMYER

CUMBERLAND HOUSE™

Published by Sourcebooks, Inc.
P.O. Box 4410, Naperville, Illinois 60567-4410
(630) 961-3900
Fax: (630) 961-2168
www.sourcebooks.com

Library of Congress Cataloging-in-Publication Data

Names: Kelly, C. Brian, author. | Smyer-Kelly, Ingrid, author.
Title: Proud to be a Marine : stories of strength and courage from the few
    and the proud / C. Brian Kelly with Ingrid Smyer.
Description: Naperville, Illinois : Sourcebooks, Inc., [2017] | Includes
    bibliographical references and index.
Identifiers: LCCN 2016053270 | (pbk. : alk. paper)
Subjects: LCSH: United States. Marine Corps--Biography. | Marines--United
    States--Biography.
Classification: LCC VE24 .K45 2017 | DDC 359.9/6092273--dc23 LC record available at
https://lccn.loc.gov/2016053270

Printed and bound in the United States of America.
VP 10 9 8 7 6 5 4 3 2 1

To the men and women of the U.S. Marine Corps. Bless 'em all.

And to our own latest little citizens,
Cabell, Colette, and Larkin Lee.

CONTENTS

PART III: WAR UPON WAR   207

CONTENTS

"I selected an enormous Marine Corps emblem to be tattooed across my chest. It required several sittings and hurt me like the devil, but the finished product was worth the pain. I blazed triumphantly forth, a Marine from throat to waist. The emblem is still with me. Nothing on earth but skinning will remove it."

—Major General Smedley Butler

INTRODUCTION

What a privilege and honor it is for these non-Marines to write an anecdotal history of the United States Marine Corps.

What history, what stories, and stories behind the stories, there are to tell!

For instance, we discovered the first Marine officer to fight in the Pacific theater of war—not in World War II against the Japanese, but alone against the British, against mutineers, and against hostile island natives all ranged against him as enemies.

Yet his own personal heroics would only be magnified a thousand fold by his fellow Marines of several generations later in the history-making, island-hopping Pacific campaign that contributed so much to rolling back the Japanese military monolith in the months after Pearl Harbor.

What a compelling story that was, from the courageous but hopeless defense of Wake Island to the mini-war on Guadalcanal; from the story of the first Marine to set foot on the jungled island to that of the future Episcopal bishop who earned a Silver Star and his Purple Heart at the canal the hard way.

Great college and even professional football stars, all Marines, played in a Christmas Eve regimental game that never would be forgotten among Marines.

It was in the same South Pacific area of the Solomons that John F. Kennedy, still unsteady on his feet in the wake of his PT-109 loss, went to the rescue of Marine "grunts" stranded on Japanese-occupied Choiseul Island. They had invaded the island as bait to draw off the Japanese from a real American invasion of nearby Bougainville.

But the drama, the courage, and the *esprit de corps* that mark United States Marine Corps history throughout was not limited during World War II to the expanses of the Pacific. No, not when another Marine twice was parachuted into occupied France by the Office of Strategic Services...once in full uniform.

There was surely no limit to the U.S. Marine Corps' courageous spirit at the hot spots in the same France of the First World War, nor did the Marines display any less sacrifice and courage in Korea, Vietnam, Kuwait, Iraq, or Afghanistan—even as the methods and standards of war changed. In Korea and again in Vietnam, the Marines paved the way with new helicopter technology. This advancement came after they had "borrowed" the innovative concept of bow-ramp landing barges from the Japanese on the eve of World War II and then turned the same design against the enemy himself.

In Korea, Chosin was naturally the *big* story; however, there were so many others, including that of fighter pilot Jesse Booker's stoic heroism in his ordeal as the first American Marine taken prisoner in the Korean War. And what about the escape en masse by nineteen other Marines held captive for months by the North Koreans?

Moving on to Vietnam, one of the war's most enduring heroes was the famed "Chesty" Puller's son-in-law, Bill Dabney, who with his fellow Marines manned their hilltop fortification overlooking and protecting the Khe Sanh combat base during its fabled seventy-seven days of siege by the North Vietnamese.

But was that added case of using one's own troops as bait a good strategy? Marine General Victor Krulak, who himself had led those Marines drawing off the Japanese to Choiseul Island during World War II, raised the question in his classic book, *First to Fight*.

Of course, that certainly has been the U.S. Marine Corps hallmark through the years.

First to fight!

First always, yes, but there are two more words for the Marines as well.

One is *sacrifice*. Their record of self-sacrifice is truly extraordinary, while also so moving and so overwhelming to contemplate. And finally, their *courage*, which has been on repeated display throughout all their history—again and again.

Picture two-time Medal of Honor–winner Smedley Butler and his men going headfirst through a hole in a fortified wall into a yard beyond, to fight hand to hand with the waiting enemy. Picture also the dramatic scene on the eve of the Civil War as rescuers of the fanatical John Brown's hostages dive headfirst through a splintered firehouse door at Harper's Ferry in the face of gunfire that would kill one Marine and wound another.

Or consider, as we do here, the quiet, sustained courage of Capt. Donald Cook as a captive of the Viet Cong. Month after month, he repeatedly sacrificed his own food and limited medicines for life-threatening illnesses, for use by his fellow prisoners, until finally he died, still in captivity. He would become the first Marine ever to earn the Medal of Honor as a prisoner.

Speaking of that same esteemed medal, given for both courage and willing sacrifice in actions beyond the call of duty, it was in the American Civil War that the Union's John Mackie would earn the first Medal of Honor awarded to a Marine. Sadly, his rallying cry for his compatriots to give their all came in battle against Confederate forces that included Confederate Marines. Some Confederates had in fact been former American Marines themselves.

It was the escaped slave Robert Smalls, of that same Civil War era, whose postwar legislative efforts helped pave the way for federal acquisition of land that eventually became the Marine Corps' east coast "boot camp," Parris Island. Ironically, the Marine Corps did not accept African Americans until early in World War II, and even then they took their boot camp training separately in a corner of Camp Lejeune, North Carolina, called Montford Point. Of course they have been a fully integrated, indispensable part of the Marine Corps in the years since.

Another landmark was achieved when the Marine Corps took in its first group of women in World War I, albeit just a paltry few hundred. By contrast, nearly twenty-three thousand women would serve in the Marine Corps during World War II, followed by just a few thousand during the Korean and Vietnam wars.

It was only in the Vietnam conflict that women finally were permitted to serve in the field, as historically they marched toward combat support roles, with casualties taken, in Kuwait, Iraq, and Afghanistan. In 2015, they were at last given the green light to take part in direct combat roles, alongside the men of the Marine Corps' armor, infantry, artillery, and aviation units.

The United States Marines! What a story!

We try to tell it here but can only offer the highlights, alongside the little-known personal drama. We don't go into the politics behind this or that deployment…let others debate those.

Rather, we hope to have captured at least *some* of the magnificent USMC fighting spirit, as expressed on a souvenir plaque of cardboard sold at the Marine Corps Museum just outside the Quantico Marine Corps Base in Virginia. Perhaps a bit exaggerated, but not totally, it says:

> To err is human
> To forgive divine,
> Neither of which is
> Marine Corps policy.

C. Brian Kelly, Ingrid Smyer
Charlottesville, Virginia
October 2016

PART I
EARLY WARS

A part of the scene, giving life and color to the picture, was the bright blue uniform of the Marines. They wore blue trousers then, as they do now, and a dark blue frock coat. Their belts were white, and they wore French fatigue caps.

—Marine 1st Lt. Israel Greene in "The Capture of John Brown," *The North American Review*, December, 1885

FIRST BATTLES, FIRST HEROES

HERE'S A NEWS FLASH FOR YOU: *MARINES LAND AT GUANTANAMO BAY, CUBA!*

No, not the United States Marines of today, nor even the Continental Marines of Revolutionary War days. Rather, these Marines were led by Col. William Gooch, royal lieutenant governor of colonial Virginia. They even included founding father George Washington's older half-brother, Capt. Lawrence Washington. The time was July of 1741 and these Colonial Marines were securing a forward base in Cuba for the fleet—the British fleet.

But the time was coming—barely four decades later—when Marines would be in the fight yet again. Only this time, it would be *against* the British, against their troops, against their mighty fleet. Marines would be in the fight, all right—the American Revolution fight—in the Caribbean, at Trenton, at Princeton, and on Manhattan Island at New York City, down the Mississippi River to New Orleans, on Lake Champlain, even on Mother Country England's own soil!

And here's another news flash for you: *the Continental Marines came before the Declaration of Independence.*

And another: *George Washington didn't really care for them. He felt that any decent soldier should be able to do anything and everything Marines could do. For that matter, Andrew Jackson wasn't all that crazy about them, either…even though Marines helped him win the Battle of New Orleans.*

While the *American* Marines of today proudly celebrate November 10, 1775, as the Corps' birthday, the Colonies of yesteryear had an active, ongoing Marine Corps that often served with the British fleet. Colonial Marines served both aboard British warships and in land engagements.

Thus, before there was a United States *per se*, there already was a Marine heritage well established for the future America.

Again and again ever since, the same elite and formidable military arm of the United States of America has made its presence felt, usually with dramatic success. By the end of the twentieth century, according to reliable estimates, the *American* Marines had taken part in 171 wars or expeditions, with 140,000 killed and 189,000 wounded…and still looming ahead were the twenty-first-century wars in Kuwait, Iraq, and Afghanistan. But how and why did the American Marines come into being in the first place, especially since the new nation had no real navy to speak of when the Revolutionary War broke out in 1775? Traditionally, the world's marines were the extra crewmen on warships who did the fighting with small arms from the rigging, boarded the enemy ship, and occasionally landed on enemy shore as raiding parties. And often they were the men who fired off the cannon aboard ship.

By one school of thought in fact, the Royal Navy's Marines were created to protect the Navy officers from their own sailors, who often had been plied with booze or drugs and then pressed into service, whether they liked it or not.

In any case, the American revolutionaries in 1775–1776 boasted a total fleet, if it could be called that, of only eight small ships to England's estimated 270 men-of-war.

Realizing the danger, the Continental Congress set about creating an American Navy, albeit a small one, and as part of the deal acted in November 1775 to create two battalions of Marines that would support the Navy.

And here's yet another news flash: *The first ranking officer of the two battalions—in effect the American, or Continental, Marine Corps' first commanding officer—was a Quaker, one Samuel Nicholas…also an innkeeper in Philadelphia.*

The very first official Continental Marine expedition came at today's Nassau in the Bahamas. The Revolutionary War's Continental Marines landed there twice in two years. Neither operation could compare in scope to the really stupendous amphibious assaults staged by the Marines of later generations, but like their latter-day counterparts, the Marines of the Revolution "went in" here and elsewhere, courtesy of ships or boats provided by their senior partner in war, the Continental Navy.

The Continental Marines, for their part, quite often helped out their Navy mates at sea—in the centuries-old tradition, by climbing the riggings of Navy ships and providing lethal musket fire onto the decks of close-by enemy vessels. John Paul Jones, "Father of the U.S. Navy," could thank the deadly Marines' musket fire in large part for his most famous victory at sea, against the British man-of-war *Serapis*. And he, of course, was the very sea captain who carried the war against the Mother Country to her very shores with a small-scale landing (page 9), an assault also led in part by a Marine lieutenant from New England, Samuel Wallingford.

But first, in March of 1776, came the initial Nassau expedition, led by Marines after they were carried there by the Navy. This came only weeks after that seminal date of November 10, 1775, when the Second Continental Congress assembled in Philadelphia passed its resolution creating the Continental Marines to begin with. It was just three weeks later that the Corps' first officers had been appointed, headed by Nicholas.

At their first assembly, held in Philadelphia that December, Nicholas and his lieutenant, Matthew Parke, appeared on the Philadelphia wharves in green coats, matched against off-white waistcoats, breeches, and facings. First duty for them and their new recruits: guard American ships and stores on the Philadelphia waterfront. But also awaiting them was the prosaically named *Alfred*, the converted merchantman that would be the Continental Navy's first flagship.

Captained by Navy Commodore Esek Hopkins, the same *Alfred* would soon be setting off at the lead of six additional ships, Continental Marines included, and all bound for the first of the Revolution's two Patriot raids on the British Island of New Providence (Nassau today) in the Bahamas. Two months later, in March 1776, Nicholas and 230 of his Marines, plus about 50 sailors from the small fleet, would step ashore from longboats two miles east of the island's Fort Montagu.

To be honest, the Continental Marines' first-ever landing turned out more like a game of Capture the Flag than a real harbinger of the military operations yet to come. The British spirited away most of the gunpowder the Patriots were hoping to seize, no blood was shed, and not much else was accomplished, except to capture Fort Nassau and Governor Montfort Browne.

Commodore Hopkins and his men did strip the town and forts of their cannon, and sailed off again with little hindrance.

Still, open war is not always so harmless…on their way north to the homeland, the raiding party ran into the British *Glasgow,* a twenty-gun man of war, and her tender.

The Marines on board the flagship *Alfred* turned out on deck for the nighttime action that would ensue. As the two ships exchanged fire, however, the Marines' 2nd Lt. John Fitzpatrick quickly went down, felled by a musket ball.

His Quaker commander Nicholas later bewailed the loss of "a worthy officer, sincere friend, and companion that was beloved by all the ship's company." Actually, this first *Continental* Marine officer to be killed was just one of seven Marines felled in the same action.

In addition, the *Glasgow* shot away the *Alfred*'s wheel block and lines, leaving her difficult to control. As other ships in the small American flotilla rushed up to help, the *Glasgow* withdrew for the safer waters of the British base at Newport, Rhode Island. Later, the Americans—again carried there by the *Alfred*—would mount a second raid on New Providence Island in the Bahamas, this time a bit more punitively, but nothing to change the Revolutionary War's eventual outcome.

The "Marines" taking part in Revolutionary War actions against the British often were home-grown Marines, groups raised by the individual colonies or even ship captains on their own, rather than the Congressionally authorized Continental Marines. More officially, however, the Marine Major Nicholas led three hundred Marines in support of George Washington in the twin battles of Trenton and Princeton. In contrast, militia Captain James Willing led a company of personally recruited "marines" down the Mississippi River by boat, capturing several British vessels on the way to New Orleans; some of his men then fought with George Rogers Clark in the Illinois country to help secure the future nation's western flank Later, John Paul Jones and a handful of men mounted a stunning raid against the English coastal town of Whitehaven that once was home to George Washington's paternal grandmother, Mildred Gale.

In the next hundred years, the official, organized Marines would fight the French in Haiti, the British again in the war of 1812, the Barbary pirates of North Africa, unruly natives in the "South Sea Islands" of the far-off Pacific as well as in the Mexican War, even against each other in the American Civil War. And still ahead for the USMC would be the Spanish-American War, the Great War in Europe, the "Banana Wars," World War II, Korea, Vietnam, Kuwait, Iraq, and Afghanistan, to say nothing of a myriad of smaller conflicts on the way to the big ones.

"FRIGHT" FOR ENGLAND

MOST HISTORIES TEND TO DISMISS THE AMERICAN RAID ON Whitehaven, England, during the Revolutionary War as merely a gesture, a glancing blow at best…even an oddity of sorts. But no, this rare raid on the soil of the Mother Country came so close to delivering a devastating blow that it really was a shock to England.

It was just minutes after twelve o'clock that long-ago night in April of 1778 when the Continental Navy's sloop of war *Ranger* lowered two boats off the seaport of Whitehaven on England's northwest Cumbrian coast. Ahead, hardly visible as yet, would be the nighttime lights of the wealthy Georgian town, built on shipping and coal-mining. Located on the northwest coast and facing the Irish Sea, Whitehaven was not exactly small potatoes as a target for the Patriot raiders. Before the American Revolution began, it had been England's greatest importer of Virginia tobacco. With a cross-hatch street system that may have inspired the grid system seen today in New York City's Manhattan borough, it also had deep and dangerous coal mines that extended under the sea (the Solway Firth).

It was not only the one-time home of George Washington's paternal grandmother, but even of John Paul Jones himself. To explain: Washington's widowed Virginia-born grandmother Mildred married a Whitehaven merchant and shipper, moved to the Cumbrian town, and died there of a fever just months later; John Paul Jones, Scottish-born, had spent a good part of his youth in the same town.

This was then a significant target for the American raiders pulling to shore in their longboats. Packed inside the craft were thirty sailors and Marines, led in one case by Jones and in the other by Marine Lt. Samuel Wallingford. The two boats soon separated as their crews rowed quietly for the either side of the sleeping port's harbor, tightly packed for the night with seagoing merchant ships.

The plan of the American raiders was to set fire to the British ships and to inflict all the damage they could to the adjoining port facilities in Whitehaven. The American raiders had started from two miles out, and the tide was running against them—it took the rowers three hours to reach the shore.

It was the early morning of April 23, 1778, three years to the month since British Redcoats, some of *them* marines, had fired on the American colonists gathered on the green at Lexington, Massachusetts. Fittingly enough, Wallingford himself was from rebellious New England.

That, of course—the British fusillade at Lexington and then the answering "shot heard 'round the world" both at Lexington and at nearby Concord—had been a shock. Now, England herself would be getting a return shock, with a contemporary British newspaper predicting that the people of Whitehaven "[could] never recover from their fright."

The weather this April morning on the Cumbrian coast of England was clear but frosty. As the interlopers struggled past the battery at the seaport's New Quay, their presence was as yet unnoticed, but the day's first light "was appearing over the hills behind Whitehaven," notes a Whitehaven and Western Lakeland online history. Time already was running out for Wallingford to fire the ships in the upper half of the harbor, while Jones and his men still had to raid the local fort and spike its cannon, which otherwise would cover their line of retreat through the harbor entrance. Jones, known in his youth by his shorter original name of John Paul, landed near the battlements and found the usual sentries had gone inside a guardhouse at the rear of the fort to keep warm.

Thus, he and a few of his men were unimpeded as they scaled the walls by climbing on each other's shoulders. Still undetected, they slipped through the fort, then burst into the guardhouse and quickly took the guards prisoner, all with no bloodshed.

As a result, the fledgling Continental—American, really—Navy and its partner Marines had achieved this small and momentary "beachhead" on the soil of the Mother Country.

The surprising risk this night for Jones, later to be hailed by many as "Father of the American Navy," was the possibility of mutiny among men in his crew who had no wish to engage in fighting without the prospect of earning prize money in the process. His own second in command for the raid on the Whitehaven fort, a Swede named Meijer, later said the men Jones left in the longboat by the battlement walls were laying plans to seize the boat and leave their leader behind if he didn't return soon. "In fact, it was not until John Paul Jones himself stood on the battlements, gave his men reassurance and encouraged them to become heroes that they plucked up [the] courage to join his mission," says the local online history.

By that account, he and American Midshipman Joe Green did spike the guns at the Half-Moon Battery, thirty-two-pounders located next to the fort. Even today, there is a statue at Whitehaven depicting John Paul Jones himself spiking a *real* cannon.

For Wallingford and his raiding party, however, the conflicting reports are not entirely laudatory. Some accounts accuse him and his men of simply stopping at a pub on the town's Old Quay and getting drunk.

Other accounts say they in fact secured the local public house to make sure no one could leave and give the alarm about their presence before they could fire the nearby ships: "They also later told Jones that they needed to get a light for their incendiaries, but apparently they did make very free with the liquors, etc."

In any case, history holds that the raid itself was a bungled failure, except for its electrifying shock effect on the townspeople.

But the raiding Americans did set fire to one or more ships. The merchantmen, many loaded with coal and other flammables, were packed close together at wharves adjoining warehouses also packed with flammables, and with the tide going out, the water was low—the entire merchant fleet was close to being stuck—"unable to move away from the fire," according to the Whitehaven and Western Lakeland account.

Thus the whole town and harbor came close to going up in flames, as had so much of London just a century or so beforehand, "after a simple fire in a baker's shop."

Not only did Jones and his men find a way to light up their "matches" made of sulfur-covered canvas, but they threw them into the holds of several ships. On the newly built *Thompson*, laden with coal for Dublin, someone "threw down a barrel of tar near the main mast and as the fire started to take hold they made their retreat."

The same fire ate into the ship's steerage and "burnt out the cabin." In the confusion, as Jones and his party began their retreat back to sea, one of his own men, a David Freeman, slipped away and began knocking on doors to warn the townspeople that fires had been started in their ships, "and the whole town would be consumed." (Marine officer Wallingford himself apparently complained that night about having "to destroy poor peoples' property.")

Whitehaven's own local history goes on to say that it was an alert, quickly aroused citizenry that saved the day, not by fighting the Americans, but by fighting the fire briefly flaring among the harbor's dormant ships.

Freeman's warning of the town being "consumed" might have been absolutely on target, had "the townspeople not acted so quickly." Well attuned to the dangers of fire, they had fire engines. According to the Whitehaven history, "[t]hese were immediately deployed and with valiant exertions by all classes of people working together they were able to extinguish the flames before they reached the rigging [of the *Thompson*]. From the rigging, fire could easily have spread to neighbouring vessels."

Jones later claimed he stood on the pier close to the *Thompson* while the fire took hold and held the townspeople at bay for a time.

In any case, he and his men rowed away with three prisoners, among them a ship's boy from the *Thompson* and a former sea captain seized while innocently fishing.

"As soon as Jones and his men started rowing for the ship (the American *Ranger*) people ran to the forts and started working on the guns." They managed to get two of them in working order at the half-moon battery and fired on the retreating boats "but wildly missed."

On board the awaiting *Ranger*, meanwhile, Jones's men had begun to think the raiding party had failed and been captured, until they spied the boats leaving the harbor and the smoke from the burning merchantman left behind. "The firing of shots alerted them that this was Jones, and they turned the *Ranger* around to pick up their Captain and his men."

Some would call the outcome a failure, but it's also fair to say that the raid on Whitehaven sent shock waves "throughout the country [that] were completely out of proportion with the mere few hundred pounds' worth of damage actually caused and turned John Paul Jones into an infamous pirate." Awakened to the threat of more raids, the British improved the defenses along their entire coastline.

Perhaps the *British Gazetteer and New Daily Advertiser* of May 5, 1778, overstated a bit by saying two-thirds of Whitehaven's people were left "bordering on insanity, the rest on idiotism," but certainly some, as the *Gazetteer* also said, had been given a "real fright."

A day later, the *Ranger* met, attacked, and defeated the clearly superior twenty-one-gun British warship *Drake* in a fierce firefight at sea. Typical of his tactics in such affairs, skipper Jones moved in close with his light guns busy raking the enemy ship's rigging and his Marines raking the decks with musket fire from perches in their own rigging.

The *Drake*'s captain was killed by a Marine's musket bullet, while Jones lost just three men as the British ship struck her colors. One of the three killed was his own commander of Marines on board the *Ranger*, Lt. Samuel Wallingford, age twenty-three, a native of Maine and veteran of Army campaigns against the British in North America, including the battles of Trenton and Princeton.

―――――

ADDITIONAL NOTE: IF JOHN PAUL JONES WERE "FATHER OF THE NAVY," perhaps you could argue that John Adams was father to the U.S. Marine Corps. After all, as a member of the Second Continental Congress that formally established the Continental Marines in November 1775, he was chairman of the Naval Committee that sponsored the Marine Corps resolution adopted by the Congress, which in those days always assembled in Philadelphia. The Naval Committee met, incidentally, at Tun's Tavern, and the tavern's proprietor, Robert Mullin, was appointed a Marine officer, apparently in gratitude for his enthusiastic recruiting activities for the newly established military arm.

When the Treaty of Paris officially ended the Revolutionary War in 1783 on a successful note for the former Colonies, the Continental Marines were dissolved as Congress—rashly, you might say—sold off the remaining ships of the Continental Navy.

But never fear, as the new nation's second president, John Adams (together with a new Congress), would come to the rescue in 1798 by signing into law a congressional bill re-establishing a Marine Corps—for real this time. The new measure established a Corps of 881 men commanded by a major. Adams then named William Ward Burrows as the first official Marine Corps commandant.

The early rules called upon the new Marines to operate under Navy regulations on board ship and under the general Articles of War while on shore. Their mission was to lead boarding parties and amphibious landings, to fight with muskets in close-up naval battles, to staff coastal installations, and to undertake "any other duty ashore, as the President, at his discretion shall direct."

TO THE SHORES...

"FROM THE HALLS OF MONTEZUMA TO THE SHORES OF TRIPOLI," says the well-known Marine Corps Hymn, but it really was Tripoli that came first. And there, in the Libya of today, a handful of Marines really did make history at the Battle of Derna in 1805—but only after barely completing a six-hundred-mile (some sources say five-hundred-mile), six-week desert trek simply to reach the remote site.

The battle itself, culminating in a bayonet charge, was intended to end the practice of paying "protection money," called "tribute" in those days, guaranteeing safe passage for American merchant ships often harassed by the so-called Barbary pirates infesting the North Africa coast on the Mediterranean Sea. The brief conflict is a considered a milestone in American history, but first came the nearly calamitous desert journey.

Even as such lengthy treks generally go, this was hardship duty in spades, marked by days without water, by threatened mutinies, too, among the polyglot mercenaries hired to help subdue the Tripolitan defenders at Derna.

Led by U.S. Navy Agent William Eaton, previously the U.S. consul at Tunis, and a squad of just seven Marines under Virginia-born 1st Lt. Presley Neville O'Bannon, it was an unwieldy force of 38 Greek mercenaries, 25 mostly European artillerymen, 190 camels and their drivers, a small group of Arab cavalry, and 90 men under Hamet Karamanli, who hoped to depose his brother Yusuf as the Tripolitan Pasha.

"We were very frequently twenty-four hours without water, and once forty-seven hours without a drop," wrote Pascal Paoli Peck, a U.S. Navy midshipman from the brig USS *Argus* who also was a participant in the long march from Egypt to Derna, the easternmost fortified town under Tripolitan control at the time. The column set off on March 8, 1805, "and after six weeks of mutiny, hunger, thirst, Arab intransigence, and religious tension arrived on 25 April before Derna," notes Peck.

It was weeks later that young Peck wrote a letter to a Navy colleague as a "short account" of the taxing journey across the Libyan Desert, "where we suffered almost everything possible, but in the end gained a glorious victory."

The first time they ran out of water and couldn't find a working well, he wrote, he was "almost dead with thirst," but he did have a few oranges with him that saved the day. Many more difficult days followed, with nothing green to be seen "for the space of 450 miles," but only "a melancholy desert throughout."

As the motley force struggled on, though, Peck and his fellow Americans were reunited with the *Argus* and two other U.S. Navy ships, the sloop *Hornet* and the schooner *Nautilus*, at Bomba, a reunion that meant fresh provisions—and payment for the often-mutinous mercenaries.

The column, still led by Eaton and O'Bannon, marched on eastward until reaching the fortified coastal town of Derna, which was garrisoned by a much larger force of 945 cavalry and 1,250 infantry. Eaton's request for safe passage through town was rejected by Governor Mustapha Bey, reportedly with the terse reply, "My head or yours."

Undeterred and expecting artillery support from the three U.S. warships now removed from Bomba to coastal Derna, Eaton borrowed a cannon from the Navy flotilla, split his force in two, and began his attack at 2:00 p.m. on April 27. Thus, the fort and garrison first came under fire from the naval vessels at sea, then faced assault by Hamet and his men to the southwest and from the handful of Marines, plus Eaton, and a few others at center on the land side.

Led by Eaton, O'Bannon, and another Navy midshipman from the *Argus*, George Mann, this group eventually mounted a bayonet charge on the town fort, through what Navy Commodore Isaac Hull described as "a heavy fire of musquetry [that] was constantly kept upon them from behind the Houses and the old Walls near the shore."

And then, "about a half past 3 we had the satisfaction to see Lieut O'Bannon, and Mr. Mann Midshipman of the *Argus*, with a few brave fellows with them, enter the fort," said Hull, who was on the scene as master of the sixteen-gun *Argus*. They hauled down the enemy's flag, to "plant the American Ensign on the Walls of the Battery."

Thus did the American flag fly for the first time in conquered territory of the Old World. More importantly, this small triumph served notice that newly created America could fight for its rights, even abroad…and with a deadly sting at that.

In a less satisfactory turn of events, a treaty that diplomat Tobias Lear negotiated—separately and without regard to the victory at Derna—allowed the sitting pasha of Tripoli to stay in place after all, rather than be replaced by his brother Hamet.

Also galling to Eaton and his victorious entourage: the United States would pay a ransom of $60,000 for the release of 308 Americans, more than forty of them Marines, held prisoner by the Tripolitans for nearly two years.

Obviously enough, for the U.S. Navy and its Marine partners, Derna was not a first run-in with the so-called Barbary States of Morocco, Tunis, Algiers, and Tripoli—a group described in J. Robert Moskin's exhaustive history *The U.S. Marine Corps Story* as "rapacious little political entities on the North African coast, made up in good part of Moors who had been forced out of Spain." They existed as "nations," adds Moskin, "by preying on unarmed Mediterranean shipping."

In those immediate post-Revolution years, Britain was to be no ally against the Barbary pirates for young America at all. More surprisingly, neither was former ally France. Both were busily seizing American ships at sea and pressing their sailors into service against their will. In the decade of 1801–1811, Moskin reports, "the French seized more than 500 American ships and the British more than 900."

During the same period (as of November of 1801, anyway) the fledgling Marine Corps' strength had been reduced to 23 officers and 453 enlisted Marines, and it would stay that way for the next six years.

It was the greater part (four-fifths) of the nearly 500-man Corps that sailed off with U.S. Navy ships sent to the Mediterranean to free the American frigate *Philadelphia* after it was captured by the Tripolitans on October 31, 1803—embarrassingly, it had run aground on a reef and surrendered to a fleet of small boats. That's when the 308 had been taken prisoner.

By then, Moskin adds, the United States had "paid the Barbary pirates nearly a million dollars in tribute and ransoms."

Embarrassment turned to triumph the night of February 16, 1804, when Navy Lt. Stephen Decatur and seventy-four volunteers, eight of them Marines, tied up alongside the *Philadelphia* in a commandeered ketch they had dubbed the *Intrepid*, seized the *Philadelphia,* and set it afire right under the guns of a Tripolitan castle.

The Americans got away with hardly a scratch in what Horatio Nelson would call "the most bold and daring act of the age." Of course, they did lose the prized ship in the process, but then so did the Tripolitans lose the opportunity to use the frigate themselves.

This then was the backdrop when the U.S. Consul William Eaton, Marine Lieutenant Presley O'Bannon, and their sun-baked followers took on the sitting Pasha's garrison at Derna the following year. Echoing Midshipman Peck's description, Moskin also states that their desert trek was a nightmare. "The native drivers mutinied repeatedly and the Arab warriors threatened to desert. Eaton dissuaded them by ordering O'Bannon and his seven Marines to seize the food supply."

When they persevered, reached Derna, and seized the town two Marines died in the fighting; another was wounded and recovered. Eaton suffered a wound to his wrist.

The conflict didn't end just then. "Eaton organized the defense of the city. On May 13, the Pasha's forces from Tripoli struck and were thrown back in a six-hour struggle. Almost daily skirmishes followed, until on June 10 Hamet totally defeated his brother's men," Moskin writes.

On that very day, however, the USS *Constitution* arrived with the news of State Department Agent Lear's treaty—making peace with the sitting Pasha and awarding the $60,000 ransom for the release of the *Philadelphia*'s prisoner contingent. In effect, the triumph at Derna had been to little or no effect.

Still, Eaton, O'Bannon, and their surviving Marines could go home as acclaimed heroes "from the shores of Tripoli," notes Moskin.

SELECT PERSONALITY
PRESLEY NEVILLE O'BANNON

Born in Fauquier County, Virginia, in 1776, the year the Declaration of Independence was adopted by the Continental Congress, future Marine Presley O'Bannon never knew his heroism in the First Barbary War (1801–1805) would be inspiration for the future lyricists of the official Marine Corps hymn. Even though O'Bannon lived to age seventy-four, that wouldn't be long enough ever to hear or see the official lyrics.

But he certainly would have been aware that his first name was misspelled on the ceremonial sword the Commonwealth of Virginia presented to him in honor of his heroics at the Battle of Derna, "on the shores of Tripoli."

The intention was good and absolutely fitting, but the inscription on the sword unfortunately said: "Presented by the State of Virginia to her gallant son *Priestly* N. O'Bannon [italics added]."

None of these events could have been predicted when the Virginian was appointed a second lieutenant in the Marines in 1801, nor when he advanced in rank to first lieutenant in 1802. His career in that post-Revolution era followed a standard pattern for the tiny Marine Corps of the day—shipboard duty, followed by posting at the Marine barracks in Washington, followed by more shipboard duty. Significantly, this second time, it was shipboard duty in the Mediterranean. And there he was, on board the brig *Argus* in command of its Marine complement, when a capable Marine officer was needed for an unusual mission—joining special Navy Agent William Eaton in pursuit of his scheme to replace the hostile pasha of Tripoli with his brother Hamet, off somewhere in Egypt.

For some years, three of the Barbary states—Morocco, Tunis, and Algiers—had been satisfied with the tribute money the United States paid for prevention of piratical raids on its merchant ships in the Mediterranean, but Tripoli's Pasha Yusuf Karamanli had become more and more difficult to deal with. The final straw came when he had the flagstaff in front of the U.S. consulate cut down in May 1801. That meant war, but not many months later came the embarrassment of the Tripolitan seizure of the USS *Philadelphia* and the imprisonment of 308 American hostages.

Not even a bombardment of Tripoli nor an offered ransom of $100,000 persuaded the pasha to order their release.

That was when Eaton, an Army veteran but otherwise a civilian, proposed forming an alliance with the pasha's older brother Hamet, aimed at removing Yusuf. Since contacting Hamet would be a first step, Eaton, O'Bannon, Navy Midshipman George Mann, and seven more Marines landed in Alexandria, Egypt, at the end of November 1804 in an effort to track Hamet down and enlist his cooperation.

Reaching Cairo in early January 1805, "they learned that Hamet and a few Tripolitans had joined a band of rebellious Mamelukes who were defying the rule of the Turkey viceroy," notes a Marine Corps biography of O'Bannon. Pushing on to Fiaum, Eaton finally "communicated" with Hamet and made arrangements for him to join in a punitive expedition to Derna on the Tripoli coast.

It then was March 8 when "Eaton and his motley army of

about 500 men, 100 camels, and a few mules started the long march across the Libyan desert."

All through the difficult march, it was O'Bannon and his band of Marines who often had to deal with would-be mutineers, while keeping the food and water stores safe from in-house marauders.

Reaching Derna on April 25, Eaton extended a friendly hand to its governor, but "on condition of allegiance and fidelity to Hamet," notes the Marine biography. With the governor's distinctly unfriendly reply of "My head or yours," the Americans at the doorstep to Derna prepared for battle. Meanwhile, the U.S. Navy's warships *Argus, Hornet,* and *Nautilus* all hove to in the fortified town's harbor.

With the Derna garrison still refusing to be intimidated, the ships began a bombardment on April 27, while both Hamet and the Americans attacked from two points on the landward side. A cannon moved ashore from the Navy ships with great difficulty wasn't much use after the onshore gunners carelessly fired an early shot with the ramrod still in the barrel.

Meanwhile, O'Bannon and his men led a charge in which they fought through "a shower of enemy musketry, took possession of the enemy's batteries, planted the United States flag upon its ramparts and turned the guns upon the enemy." Even so, it would be another "two hours of hand-to-hand fighting" before the fort fell.

"For many years," adds the Marine Corps biography, "memories of the dauntless Americans lingered in the songs of the women of Derna, one of which featured these words: '*Din din Mohamed U Ryas Melekan manhandi*,' which means 'Mohamed for religion and the Americans for stubbornness.'"

Disappointed in his quest to replace younger brother Yusuf as pasha, Hamet nonetheless gave O'Bannon a jeweled sword with a Mameluke hilt that Hamet had carried while he was with the Mamelukes in Egypt—thus the inspiration for the ceremonial sword that Virginia gave O'Bannon upon his return to his home state as a widely acclaimed hero. Thus, too, the modified "Mameluke" sword that became a symbolic part of the Marine officer's dress uniform for special occasions.

O'Bannon, for his part, remained a Marine until 1807, when he resigned after six years of service. He joined his brother Maj. John O'Bannon, a Revolutionary War veteran, in the frontier life of Kentucky, once a Virginia county. Presley O'Bannon served in the state legislature on behalf of Logan County from 1812 to 1820. He died in 1850 and was buried in a small rural cemetery.

In 1919, the Susan Hart Chapter of the Daughters of the American Revolution led a successful effort to have his remains removed to the more important Frankfort Cemetery in Frankfort, the capital of Kentucky.

During World War II, it should also be noted, the Fletcher Class U.S. destroyer named for Presley O'Bannon led all American destroyers of the war with seventeen service stars. Awarded a Presidential Unit Citation, the *O'Bannon* was lauded by Admiral William "Bull" Halsey, who once commented: "The history of the Pacific War can never be written without telling the story of the USS *O'Bannon*."

MEN MUTINOUS, BOAT LEAKY, NATIVES HOSTILE

OVERCOME BY MUTINEERS, HANDS AND FEET TIED, HE WAS FIRST thrown into the brig. Then, as the rebel crew set sail—under the enemy's flag, mind you—he next was shot in the left heel and placed on the open seas in a leaky boat with three still-loyal men.

You might say the outlook for 1st Lt. John Marshall Gamble, U.S. Marine Corps, the afternoon of May 7, 1814, was not too good. Not only was the boat leaky, but the nearest land was a Pacific island four miles away, torn by tribal warfare among natives who would not be friendly.

Things had looked so much better eighteen months before when Gamble, then nineteen years old, and his contingent of thirty-one Marines set sail on war patrol from the American East Coast aboard the U.S. frigate *Essex* with Capt. David Porter in command. Since this was during the War of 1812 against Great Britain, the *Essex* eventually wound up in the far Pacific taking prizes among the ships of Britain's whaling fleet in the vicinity of the Galapagos Islands.

Porter and his ship took so many prizes, in fact, that a twelve-year-old midshipman named Farragut—who would grow up to be the famous admiral David Farragut—was placed in charge of one captured ship, and Gamble in command of a second one, the *Greenwich*. With all this coming so early in Marine Corps history, Gamble probably was the first Marine officer to fight anywhere in the vast Pacific region, much less to command a ship. He would command a second prize before his adventures came to screeching halt.

First, though, as skipper of the *Greenwich*, now outfitted as a ten-gun man-of-war, the inexperienced Gamble soon faced a naval battle against the more heavily armed British warship *Seringapatam*, which had fourteen guns. By now it was July of 1813.

The confrontation between the Marine officer and skipper of the British ship took place within the sight of overall U.S. commander Porter, but too far away for him to take a hand in the fighting. As Porter noted in his journal, though, he had felt "much confidence in the discretion of this gentleman [Gamble]" at the time he placed him in charge of the *Greenwich*, albeit with two seasoned seaman as mates.

Now watching the gun battle unfold with his spyglass, Porter couldn't help but issue unheard instructions for his protégé, such as: "Now, Mr. Gamble, if you'll only stand five minutes and then tack, I'll make you a prince."

Magically enough, Gamble did exactly as Porter wished. He held his course, then tacked, then loosed a deadly broadside against the British ship—just moments after Porter had urged, "Now is your time!"

In short order, the *Seringapatam* struck her colors and joined Porter's expanding fleet of prizes, although Gamble had been wounded in the exchange of cannon fire.

Fortunately, since events would march on regardless, the wound wasn't anything disabling. The fact is, Gamble would need all his stamina and command authority very soon again.

Porter's fleet, Gamble included, sailed for the Marquesas Islands for rest, refit, and repair. Establishing a base on Nuku Hiva Island and renaming it Madison Island, Porter elected to take sides in the ongoing native wars.

Thus, with the help of his armed Americans, his side prevailed…but it would be love, not war, that would prove the undoing of the visiting sailors and Marines.

The men were fraternizing with the island women, and when Porter prepared to sail in December of 1813 in search of more war prey, many of his men dug in their heels in refusal. In *mutiny,* that is.

But luckily not all, for Porter did sail away with the *Essex,* a smaller prize ship renamed *Essex Junior,* and at least a skeletal crew for each.

That left Lieutenant Gamble on the island in charge of a dozen sailors and Marines, along with three prize ships and a contingent of prisoners of war, and all among thousands of island natives, many of them with good reason to be unfriendly.

He would be back, Porter had promised, but if not within five and a half months, Gamble would be on his own. No sooner had Porter departed than Gamble's relations with the island's natives became threatening, and it took a show of force on Christmas Eve, backed by cannon fire from the prize ships in the harbor, to quiet things down for a time.

As days, then weeks, passed, Gamble himself would sail off to obtain badly needed provisions at stops among the South Sea Islands, but of course then had to return to base. He and his men waited…and waited. They didn't yet know that Porter had been defeated and captured by the British in a battle off Chile in February. He wouldn't be coming back to newly named Madison Island anytime soon.

By April, Gamble was preparing for his own departure, as his orders allowed. But many of his men, still smitten by the native women, had turned difficult. The prisoners were troublesome. Four men had deserted outright. One of his loyal Marines had drowned.

His reliable allies were few.

While preparing the *Seringapatam* for sea on the afternoon of May 7, Gamble was attacked, bound, and placed in the ship's brig by mutinous crewmen and British prisoners. Then, with his fresh gunshot wound in the heel, came the leaky boat and the long, difficult haul back to the island harbor and the few loyal men still there.

But now the islanders turned in full fury on the handful of Americans, quickly killing four of them.

Even so, Gamble somehow managed to ready another prize ship for sailing, the *Sir Andrew Hammond*, and to hold off the attacking natives with her guns. Rescuing a sick crewman from the nearby *Greenwich* and setting her afire, Gamble immediately put to sea with three sailors and three Marines as his crew.

Running before the wind, they fetched up fifteen days later among the Hawaiian Islands, but there they were captured by one of the British ships that had defeated Porter off the coast of Chile. After many months as prisoners, Gamble and his men were dropped off in Rio de Janeiro, Brazil. Peace had been declared.

As end to the story of John Gamble, he at last returned home to his native New York in August of 1815, nearly three years after his departure aboard the *Essex*. He returned as one of the Marine Corps' first really authentic heroes. But sadly, his health apparently impaired by his long odyssey, he would die young, at age forty-six.

THIS OLD HOUSE O' MINE

THE OLD HOUSE AT 801 G STREET, SOUTHEAST, IN WASHINGTON, DC, has seen many a Marine Corps commandant come and go, but none as colorful and legendary as Archibald Henderson, who lived there so long, he allegedly forgot it was government property and left it to his heirs.

So goes the legend, well known in Marine Corps circles; however, the real historical fact is, he served as commandant and lived in the traditional commandant's quarters longer than anyone else, before or since…thirty-eight years. As an additional historical fact, the Commandant's House is considered the oldest public building in Washington in continuous use. No surprise, then, that in 1972 both the house and the neighboring Marine Barracks at Eighth and I Streets, Southeast, were entered on the National Register of Historic Places maintained by the National Park Service.

Of course, Henderson (1783–1859) was long since gone by then, but his legacy as a heroic Marine and as the Corps' longest serving commandant still lives on today in the form of boot camp history lessons for young recruits, in any self-respecting Marine Corps history book, and in the kind of stories swapped back and forth in barracks all over the world.

For one thing, a commandant who personally goes into the field of battle with the better portion of the entire Corps?

For another, an aging leader—then in his seventies—who goes up to a cannon aimed at his men and, incredibly, places his own body against the muzzle to dissuade the would-be gunners from firing?

For still another, a commandant who serves ("survives," perhaps?) a total of nine presidents and thwarts various attempts, starting with President Andrew Jackson, to disband the still small Marine Corps?

The Virginia-born Henderson, then thirty-seven, came to the commandant job on the heels of Anthony Gale, an apparent alcoholic who was the only commandant in Marine Corps history to have been cashiered from the post. It was a time of controversy and low morale among the Marines of the day—all 988 of them, both officers and men.

"The Navy Commissioners wanted the Marines broken up into small detachments," writes J. Robert Moskin in his history, *The U.S. Marine Corps Story.* President Jackson, "Old Hickory," hoped to see the Corps "absorbed" by the Army. "But after congressional hearings, these ideas died. They would pop up again—over and over—whenever the nation relaxed in peace."

Meanwhile, as time would prove, Henderson clearly was some kind of Marine, even among the pantheon of Marine Corps giants. Not only did he stay at the helm longer than anyone in Corps history, but, "Fortunately for the Corps," adds Moskin, "he became one of the Marine Corps' great commandants: able, jealous of the Corps' status and reputation, and quick to seize any opportunity to give the Marines a wider role in the nation's destiny."

Thus, in the "war" of the 1830s against Seminole and Creek Indians largely based in Florida, then Colonel Henderson "personally led his Marines into the field, fully exposed to the same dangers and discomfits as any of them." In those early days, the sight of a military commander leading on the scene wasn't completely rare, but today it would be unheard of for a Marine Corps commandant to lead his men into battle on foot, or even on horseback. In any case, Henderson was rewarded for his leadership in mitigating the Indian hostilities by being given the brevet rank of brigadier general.

Virginia-born Henderson began his Marine Corps career as a newly commissioned second lieutenant in 1806. His first taste of combat came aboard the USS *Constitution* during the War of 1812.

By then a captain, and next a brevet major, he was aboard when the famous frigate subdued the British warship *Java* off Brazil and then, as Marine commander, for the same ship's victorious gun duel with the corvettes *Cyane* and *Levant* off Portugal.

As a result, he was included in the official thanks of Congress to the men and officers of the *Constitution* for their "gallant" service, notes the Marine Corps Association & Foundation's bio sketch of the one-time commandant. He also won a "silver medal" for his part in the war, along with a jeweled sword presented to him by the Commonwealth of Virginia "in testimony of the high sense entertained by his native state for his gallantry and good conduct in the capture of the *Cyane* and *Levant*."

In the years up to the time of his appointment as Commandant in 1820 as a lieutenant colonel, he mostly pulled typical Marine Corps shore duty at posts ranging from USMC Headquarters to New Orleans, Portsmouth, New Hampshire, and Boston. The same could be said for roughly his first fifteen years at the helm of the Corps—for that entire period, except for one burst of activity suppressing piracy in the Caribbean, the Corps more or less slept quietly.

But then, in 1836, with Colonel Commandant Henderson himself taking a lead, the Marines joined the Army in fighting hostile Indians in Florida. According to Moskin, Henderson supposedly left a note tacked onto his office door saying: "Have gone to Florida to fight Indians. Will be back when war is over."

Next, once those hostilities were over in the east, came scattered Marine activity during the years of the California revolt, followed by heavy combat ("to the Halls of Montezuma") in the Mexican War.

As Henderson continued to lead, the Corps expanded and coalesced as a noteworthy and effective fighting force: Marines took part in Commodore Perry's expedition to Japan in 1852–53; were briefly deployed to Uruguay in 1855 in response to troubles at Montevideo; engaged again with rebellious Indians at Seattle, Washington Territory, in 1856; and helped in the capture of the Barrier Forts in China, also in 1856.

It was the very next year, in 1857, and right in the nation's capital, that Henderson himself once again went on the potential firing line. This came during the Know-Nothing political unrest that prompted the mayor of Washington to request Marine Corps help in controlling an armed mob of "rowdies from Baltimore." Henderson refused to be intimated by threats to fire a cannon into the Marine ranks unless they withdrew. As the story goes, his response was to go up to the artillery piece in person and stand right at the muzzle, unyielding.

Obviously the startled rowdies didn't fire, and Henderson survived, only to die suddenly of natural causes less than two years later at age seventy-five.

Whether he really forgot that the traditional commandant's home in Washington was government-owned and willed it to his heirs (he left three daughters and three sons) may be a matter of legend, but there's no doubt the historic structure has been home to every commandant to hold the leadership post since. Henderson was the Corps' fifth commandant at the time of his death in January of 1859, but was only the third Marine leader to have lived in the home.

The related legend is that one spring day in 1801, the third commandant, William Ward Burrows, accompanied President Thomas Jefferson in search for a future site for the Marine Barracks that would be within reasonable marching distance of the U.S. Capitol. Thus, they selected the quadrangle in Southeast Washington bounded by 8th and 9th Streets and G and I Streets, with the Commandant's House standing within the confines of the Marine Barracks as the official residence of every subsequent commandant.

For reasons unknown, the two-and-a-half-story house of Flemish bond brick and the Barracks were spared British retribution during the raid of 1814, which saw the Redcoats burn both the Capitol building and the White House. Another Marine Corps legend suggests the British were so impressed by the Marines' fighting spirit in the recent Battle of Bladensburg, they spared the Marine facilities as a mark of their respect.

THOSE MISLEADING LYRICS

AS PREVIOUSLY NOTED, TRIPOLI APPEARS SECOND IN THE MARINE Corps Hymn (author-composer unknown); however, in reality the storming of the "Halls of Montezuma" actually came second, at the climax of the Mexican War.

In the hymn, of course, the line goes, "From the Halls of Montezuma, to the shores of Tripoli…"

In real life, the storming of Derna in Tripoli by Lieutenant Presley O'Bannon, a squad-size group of fellow Marines, and dozens of mercenaries took place in 1803, whereas the charge up the hill at the Chapultepec citadel in Mexico City (once the veritable Halls of Montezuma) by Marines and U.S. Army soldiers—including Ulysses S. Grant—took place in 1847.

But wait…*Montezuma*? Wasn't he the Aztec Indian emperor taken hostage by the Spanish explorer Hernan Cortez in the early sixteenth century at the future site of Mexico City? But wait again…sixteenth century? No Marines around then.

As it happened, the name of the historic Aztec figure hung around…and around. By the nineteenth century it was often applied to the great citadel of Chapultepec, also a well-fortified military academy, atop a hill with a dominating view of Mexico City. The structure stood as the key fortress in the way of the U.S. Marines and Army soldiers, combined as the U.S. Fourth Brigade and led by Army Brig. Gen. John Quitman, in a final drive to seize Mexico City.

This battle came after American forces landed at Veracruz in March 1847 during the Mexican-American War. And *landed* indeed was the key word. After all, this would be the nation's largest amphibious operation until World War II—it took seventy ships carrying 12,000 soldiers, sailors, and Marines to make the landing at the doorstep of Veracruz on the eastern coast of Mexico. Taking part in the first wave of assault troops was Capt. Alvin Edson's battalion of 180 Marines drawn together from various ship detachments and patched together as a single fighting unit…a first in Marine Corps history.

The Marines landed on March 9 in special "surf boats" expressly designed for the operation—another "first"—and came ashore as part of Army Brig. Gen. William J. Worth's First Brigade.

With the invasion troops spending the day boarding their special landing craft, the fleet's gunboats didn't begin bombarding the designated landing beach with grapeshot until 6:00 p.m. The Marines first hitting the beach, proudly raced to the top of a high row of sand dunes, ready to fight…when it dawned on them that the beach was theirs for the taking. No enemy defenders appeared.

Over the next twenty days, the Americans ringed the city of Veracruz—Mexico's largest port. Digging seven miles of trenches in the process, dotted here and there with strong points, they were finally gratified to see five thousand Mexican fighters give in to the siege and surrender. Only nineteen Americans—just one of them a Marine—had been lost in sixty-year-old Army Maj. Gen. Winfield Scott's invasion operation.

As further events unfolded, Scott turned his force inland and on April 18 defeated the Mexicans in a showdown at the Cerro Gordo mountain pass. He then paused for a break in hopes of reinforcements replacing his three thousand–plus volunteer soldiers who chose against re-enlistment. Out of Scott's 3,700 volunteers, writes Moskin in his Marine Corps history, "those who re-enlisted filled only a single company."

Luckily, help was on its way. "The Secretary of the Navy and Commandant Henderson told President Polk that six companies of Marines were available," writes Moskin. "Polk gave his permission, and these Marines were organized to fight with the Army. They would write one of the most dramatic chapters in Marine Corps history."

The new Marine regiment formed to reinforce Scott in Mexico would be led by Lt. Col. Samuel E. Watson and Maj. Levi Twiggs, both veterans of the War of 1812, neither exactly a young man. The contingent arriving in Mexico consisted of 314 men, plus another 52 added Marines drawn from the ships still standing down in Veracruz harbor. As a body, the 366 Marines formed the rear guard of a column marching inland to Scott's support and headed by Brig. Gen. Franklin Pierce.

Future President Pierce's poorly disciplined column had to push through "200 miles of guerrilla-infested mountains" merely to reach Scott, whose ranks by now had swelled to 14,000 men in all (although 2,500 of them were ill with dysentery). With the Marine regiment then assigned to Army general Quitman's command, the Americans set off in

August for Mexico City, despite the fact that Mexican strongman Santa Anna's army of 30,000 would stand between them and their attempted seizure of his country's capital.

Quitman's force, Marines included, was assigned no part in the American Army's first assault on Mexico City, which halted on August 22 because Santa Anna proposed an armistice. After two weeks of inactive waiting, "Scott reopened the war," adds Moskin's account. "Worth's Regulars attacked an ancient mill, Molino del Rey, less than a mile west of the Hill of Chapultepec, the strong point dominating the plain west of the city. More than 750 Americans were killed or wounded, and that brought Quitman and the Marines to battle."

Chapultepec rose before them "lone and sheer from the plain, six hundred yards long and two hundred feet high, surrounded by a twelve-foot wall and topped by a gray-walled palace that was now a military school." It was obviously a formidable obstacle—but with Santa Anna's army massed to the south of the city, attacking from the west by way of the great Chapultepec fortress appeared the better alternative. If the Americans could breach its walls and gain control of the interior, they could then rush along two causeways to the Belén and San Cosme gates, "actually blockhouses," providing access to the city itself. Quitman's command would lead the attack on the southern side of the fortress the morning of September 13, 1847—"the most famous date in the Marine Corps' first hundred years."

Marine officers Twiggs and (Captain) John G. Reynolds each led a combined storming party of Marines and Army soldiers into heavy defending fire. At one point, Twiggs stood upright to call to Reynolds and was shot down, mortally wounded. Even so, "the Marines struggled up the steep southern side, fighting hand to hand with bayonets and clubbed rifles." Five enlisted men were also killed in the upward climb.

Meanwhile, other Army units fought their way up the tough western slopes below the citadel until, reaching "the castle simultaneously," they finally took the fortress.

But still there were the two causeways and their entrances to the city to seize. Lt. Ulysses S. Grant, the future Union general and president, and

Commandant Henderson's son 2nd Lt. Charles Henderson were among those who raced to the San Cosme gate, only to find it "too heavily defended to take frontally." Seven of Capt. George H. Terrett's Marines slipped to the left to attack from that flank, while young Henderson, already wounded in the leg, pressed the attack from the front. With Grant's twenty men also involved, the gate finally fell. The American casualties here included six Marines dead.

Also after heavy fighting, the Belen gate finally fell to the Americans in the dark early-morning hours. Thus, the Americans under Worth were prepared to fight their way into Mexico City by way of both entrances at first light on the fourteenth—but during the night, Santa Anna surprised them by quitting the ancient capital altogether. "Quitman's men raced through the thronged streets into the Grand Plaza and took possession of the National Palace, where, in ancient days, had stood the Halls of Montezuma," adds Moskin.

As for the opening words of the Marine Corps Hymn, the oldest official song of the American military services, the author of its lyrics is, surprisingly enough, unknown. Its music, on the other hand, is thought to have come from the Gendarmes' Duet in an 1867 revised version of the 1859 Offenbach opera *Geneviève de Brabant*, which in turn may have had its musical origin as a Spanish folk song.

For years the Marine Corp version's opening lines said:

> *From the Halls of Montezuma,*
> *To the Shores of Tripoli;*
> *We fight our country's battles*
> *On the Land as on the Sea;*

Since that version failed to recognize the fast-growing role of Marine aviation, Commandant Thomas Holcomb acted in 1942 to approve a new fourth line that more accurately read:

> *In the air, on land, and sea.*

BARRIERS TO OVERCOME

ON SMALL SCALE, THIS WAS A CLASSIC MARINE CORPS CHALLENGE. Faced in 1856 with an outrage to the flag, Marine detachments from three ships were looking at four Chinese river forts with walls of granite seven feet thick and topped by lethal cannon, plus thousands of enemy soldiers at hand, and all guarding the offending city.

In other parts of the world, war between England and Russia was raging in the Crimea off the Black Sea, while in the United States James Buchanan was running for president as the nation approached a heart-rending civil war just five years ahead.

In China, torn apart by the Taiping Rebellion that would kill millions, beset also by friction with Britain and France over the opium trade with the West, conditions were no less than chaotic. In Canton on the Pearl River, one of just five Chinese ports open to Western ships, Americans living, working, or visiting in the city were afraid of crazed rebels seeking vengeance against foreigners. In October, with emotions running high, the American consul there "called out for protection to Commander Andrew H. Foote of the twenty-two-gun sloop *Portsmouth,* then lying eight miles downriver at Whampoa," writes Bernard C. Nalty in the Marine Corps history, *The Barrier Forts: A Battle, A Monument, and a Mythical Marine.*

Foote sent eighty-three men into the city, nineteen Marines among them. "This little force was organized into companies and posted on the housetops and in some newly constructed fortifications around the American compound in the city."

But of course this would be too small a force to be much help in a real emergency, so the twenty-gun sloop USS *Levant* moved upstream to add twenty more Marines and a detachment of sailors to the force ashore. And finally, from Shanghai, came the thirteen-gun steam warship *San Jacinto* under Capt. James Armstrong, commodore of the U.S. East India Squadron, to add another twenty-eight Marines. At this point, Marine

Brevet Capt. John D. Simms was placed in command of the entire complement sent ashore, Marines and Bluejackets (sailors) both.

Except for a few stray shots, no real troubles developed in the city, but this moment in what is known as the Second Opium War was still a perilous one for the Americans. As Nalty notes, "From the diplomatic point of view, the presence of an American force in the midst of a fast-developing war could be taken as an insult by the sensitive Chinese."

Naturally, too, the military situation facing the Americas was "no better," because Canton, located at the apex of a wide delta, was protected by four forts halfway up the Pearl River's "tortuous" ship channel from the anchorage at Whampoa, "each of them [the forts] incorporating the latest recommendations of European military engineers."

Both Squadron Commodore Armstrong and Commander Foote from the *Portsmouth* realized that supplying a shore-based garrison against Chinese opposition "would entail either running the forts or trying to slip past them in small boats at night." Either way could mean involvement in "what was in reality an Anglo-French quarrel with the Chinese."

An offer by the Chinese to guarantee the safety of Americans in Canton seemed to solve the crisis, but not for long. As most of the Marines and sailors were returning to their ships, the largest Chinese fort inexplicably fired on the American boats, but with no resulting casualties. The next day (November 16), another fort opened fire with both round- and grapeshot on an unarmed American boat sent to sound out a channel for the ships. "The first volley screamed over the men crouched in the boat," writes Nalty. Another "harmlessly churned the muddy water astern; but a shot crashed into the boat, killing the coxswain."

That did it. "Outraged at what seemed to be a deliberate breach of faith, both Foote and Armstrong decided to avenge this insult to the American flag." Armstrong moved his command to the *Portsmouth* while two American merchant steamships attempted to tow both sloops within range of the forts in the midafternoon, but the *Levant* ran aground.

Still, the *Portsmouth* proceeded to engage the Chinese in a gun duel until dark, with one Marine aboard seriously wounded. The sloop of war was hit several times in the hull, "while grape played havoc with her rigging." She responded with 230 shells of her own, plus the occasional grapeshot.

Next came a three-day lull, during which the Americans freed the *Levant,* made repairs to the *Portsmouth,* and attempted negotiations with the Chinese. But by then it was too much for Armstrong, whose health "broke down," and he passed command of the expedition to Foote.

As Foote already knew, he not only faced four forts with granite walls seven feet thick but also their 176 guns, "some of them ten-inch caliber." Further, "there were rumored to be between five thousand and fifteen thousand Chinese troops in the Canton area." The forts might have been powerful, "the strongest in the empire," but more positively speaking, "Foote need not fear the army, a poorly equipped, half-trained rabble." Pluses and minuses aside, Foote decided to attack rather than allow the Chinese to act first.

So it was that on the morning of November 20 he personally commanded a force of 287 men landing unopposed below the walls of one fort, with the squadron's 50 or so Marines, under Captain Simms, as the spearhead. Since the sheer walls forestalled a frontal assault, the Marines chose to circle to the rear, clear out a few Chinese snipers defending the flank, and "sprint" for the interior of the fort itself.

"The defenders bolted," adds Nalty's account. Many tried to swim the river under fire from the Marines now controlling the fort's parapets. But others fleeing the fort reached the main body of Chinese troops at Canton, just four miles away. A large force then set out for the captured fort, even as the Marines under Simms were clearing out "a band of diehards" in the village to the rear of the redoubt. The Americans had chased the Chinese remnants into rice paddies to that rear when "well over" a thousand Chinese reinforcements "swarmed through the ooze of the rice paddies to engulf the Leathernecks."

But Simms waited until the Chinese were just two hundred yards away before giving the order to fire. His men responded with volley after volley, notes Nalty. "Gamely the Chinese stood their ground and returned the fire; but Marine marksmanship proved too accurate, and the enemy ran. Two other counterattacks were attempted, but both were beaten back by Leatherneck muskets and boat howitzers."

With one fort thus secured, the Americans turned the very next morning to a second barrier fort. As they moved upstream in their small boats, their own ships provided covering cannon fire, while the three remaining Chinese forts still operating "divided their fire between the pair of sloops and line of boats." A round struck one boat, killing three of its occupants and wounding five more.

"Frightening in volume," the Chinese fire overall was "for the most part inaccurate."

It wasn't long before Simms could lead his mixed force ashore, across a waist-deep creek "and over the granite walls" of fortress number two. "While a force of a thousand Chinese hovered just out of range of the tiny American howitzers," writes Nalty, "Corporal William McDougal of the *Levant* planted the Stars and Stripes on the parapet."

He soon would be planting the flag yet again.

That would be at bastion number three, located on an island in the Pearl River.

Moving swiftly, the Marines were soon hugging an embankment, "when they collided with a Chinese battery of seven guns." By Nalty's account, the surprised gun-crews fled under a storm of Marine musket fire. Mounting the top of the same embankment, Simms and his men were able to fire on the third bastion "across the water from them."

With American fire pouring down from both of the captured redoubts and from Simms's position on the shoreline, the island fort soon was shrouded with dust and smoke. "Once again Corporal McDougal broke out the American flag as the assault wave surged over the walls." Thus, by end of the second day of the American action, three forts and a potentially troublesome battery had been captured.

Next, quite obviously to all, would come an assault on the Center Fort, located on the Canton side of the Pearl. Also predictably, the action began at daybreak the next morning with a bombardment on "the squat heap of granite that was the Center Fort" from both the American guns and the captured Chinese cannon.

At first, there was no response whatsoever. The small landing force approached in small boats, three waves of them drawing closer and closer. Still, no reaction from the Center Fort.

Finally, with the boats well within range, the Chinese "cut loose'" with "clouds of grapeshot" that "whined across the river as men of the assault force leaped into waist-deep water and began wading toward the base of the walls."

When they climbed to the top, however, no more fighting: the Chinese defenders had fled. Except for destroying or spiking the captured guns and blowing up the thick fortress walls, the Battle of the Barrier Forts was over. The Chinese subsequently apologized for their initial fire on the unarmed sounding boat that had started the hostilities.

The takeaway for the Americans? "In one brief but furious campaign, Commander Foote's command had captured four powerful redoubts, killed an estimated five hundred Chinese and routed an army of thousands— all at the cost of seven killed in action, three killed in the demolition of Center Fort, and a total of thirty-two wounded or injured." None of those killed in action was a Marine, but one Marine did die of illness.

Also important, "Three days of the fiercest action proved that ships, when teamed with a strong landing force, could indeed fight forts."

FIRST UNDER THE DOOR

At an officer's wave of his cavalry hat, the squad of Marines assailed the two sets of double doors of the small fire-engine house with sledgehammers, pounding for all they were worth—the lives of hostages would depend on how fast they broke in.

A burst of shooting broke out from inside the doors, but still they didn't yield.

Desperate, 1st Lt. Israel Greene, commander of the Marine detachment, looked around for another weapon to use against the stout doors. Spotting a heavy wooden ladder lying on the ground nearby, he shouted for his Marines to pick it up and charge the doors with the ladder as a battering ram.

They assaulted the doors with an earsplitting crash. But still the doors stood strong. They delivered a second crashing blow, and at first it appeared the doors stood strong again. But no, this time, the lunging Marines had splintered a low panel to one side—an opening, small but real, presented itself.

The first to take the plunge was Lieutenant Greene himself, despite hearing a carbine shot at the opening from inside. Barely able to see in the gloomy interior, he went in, head and shoulders first, then jumped to his feet. One of the hostages pointed frantically to a bearded man kneeling close by the aperture and reloading the carbine.

Greene's chief quarry inside the barricaded engine house at Harper's Ferry that October morning of 1859 was the fanatical abolitionist John "Osawatomie" Brown (his nickname based on the colony he had once organized at Osawatomie, Kansas). Already well known, Brown was wanted for the murder of five pro-slavers in Kansas. But was it Brown himself with the carbine? All that Greene knew was the obvious fact that the stranger before him could begin shooting again any second.

As it turned out, the man hastening to reload his weapon was indeed Brown—a personification and symbol of the feelings ripping the country apart on the twin issues of slavery and states' rights. This was on the very eve of the American Civil War that would break out in 1861, with more than six hundred thousand destined to die in the conflict.

Like so many Americans, in or out of uniform, organized or individually, the Marines themselves were not really prepared for a sectional war of such magnitude. The Corps, like the nation itself, had spent the decade since the Mexican War with little action, let alone *sustained* action. Furthermore, with the death of Colonel Commandant Archibald Henderson at age seventy-five in January of that same year, Henderson's long-held baton of Corps command had been passed on to another "older" Marine, Colonel Commandant John Harris, a forty-four-year veteran aged sixty-eight.

This period of "Parade Rest" for the Corps was suddenly interrupted on Monday, October 17, by wild reports that revolting slaves had seized the federal arsenal and gun factory at Harper's Ferry on the Potomac River above Washington. Actually, it was John Brown and a gang of twenty-one followers, five black, sixteen white…and two of them his own sons (he had fathered a total of twenty children by now).

As then-President James Buchanan ordered the Marines into action, Lieutenant Greene formed his detachment of ninety Marines at the Washington Navy Yard—in dress uniform of blue frock coats, blue trousers, and white belts—before embarking on the fifty-five-mile train ride to Harper's Ferry. "It was a beautiful, clear autumn day," he said later, "and the men, exhilarated by the excitement of the occasion, which came after a long, dull season of confinement in the barracks, enjoyed the trip exceedingly."

In the meantime, Gen. Winfield Scott, the Army's ranking officer, ordered Mexican War veteran Lt. Col. Robert E. Lee to take charge of the scene, together with his aide, Capt. "Jeb" Stuart, soon to be the Confederacy's noted cavalryman. Neither Lee nor Stuart were in uniform as they rushed to the scene at Harper's Ferry, because they were on furlough and happened to be visiting General Scott's War Department when word of trouble at the federal arsenal first drifted in.

As the situation evolved that day, "Osawatomie" Brown and followers killed several people, captured the federal armory and arsenal, and took thirteen hostages with them as they holed up in the small brick building housing two fire engines. Once the shooting on October 17 stopped, Brown and four surviving followers retreated to the small structure with their hostages, one of whom was George Washington's descendant Col. Lewis Washington.

Then, for the night, stalemate.

But Lee had a plan for the next morning.

At 6:30 a.m., on October 18, as Lee watched from atop a knoll a short distance away and Greene stood by with his Marines, Stuart approached the engine house in a borrowed uniform coat with a note from Lee promising no harm to the raiders if they would surrender immediately. The future Confederate hero called out for a talk, and one of the double doors inched open.

Stuart found himself looking into the eyes of the notorious John Brown. As Stuart biographer Emory M. Thomas writes in *Bold Dragoon: The Life of J. E. B. Stuart*, the still-young Army officer also found himself looking "down the barrel of a cocked cavalry carbine."

Stuart delivered Lee's message anyway—an ultimatum, really. But Brown wasn't a bit receptive. He had many a condition to demand before any thought of surrender. Meanwhile, some of the more fearful hostages behind the double doors shouted pleas to be more lenient with Brown, in order to ensure their own safety.

One of the hostages, however, boldly shouted: "Never mind us, fire!"

It was Lewis Washington, so loud that even Lee, forty or more feet away, could hear him. "The old revolutionary blood does tell," Lee said aloud.

Meanwhile, Stuart could see that the wrangling with Brown and the pleas by the hostages were precisely what Lee hoped to avoid. That was when Stuart waved his hat as the signal for the Marine assault, then lunged to one side, out of the way.

The nearly square building, roughly thirty feet by thirty-five, presented Greene's storming party of twelve men with "two large double doors, between which was a stone abutment," Greene himself wrote in the *North American Review* of December 1885. Not so incidentally, the Marines would carry out their assault by bayonet only, to keep any stray shots from hitting one or more of the hostages inside the small building.

"Within were two old-fashioned, heavy fire engines, with a hose-cart and reel standing between them and just back of the abutment between the doors," Greene also recalled in 1885. "They were double-battened doors very strongly made, with heavy wrought-iron nails."

Greene's Marines leaped to the fore and began battering the doors with their sledgehammers, but "very little impression was made with the hammers, as the doors were tied on the inside with ropes and braced by the hand-brakes of the fire engines."

That was when Greene spied the ladder lying on the ground nearby: "I ordered my men to catch it up and use it as a battering ram... The men took hold bravely and made a tremendous assault upon the door. The second blow broke it in."

Seconds later—while Brown was reloading his carbine—Greene himself was inside. "Getting to my feet, I ran to the right of the engine which stood behind the door, passed quickly to the rear of the house, and came up between the two engines."

He saw Lewis Washington, "standing near the hose-cart, at the front of the engine-house," and then, to the left, on one knee, "a man with a carbine in his hand, just pulling the lever to reload."

"Hello, Greene," said Washington. And, pointing: "This is Osawatomie," meaning Brown.

Greene related later that as the fiery abolitionist turned to see who was behind him, "Quicker than thought I brought my saber down with all my strength upon his head."

Greene's blow knocked the abolitionist down and opened a gash on his neck, but it failed to incapacitate him. The Marine officer then tried a straight, bayonet-like thrust to the body, but the dress sword hit an obstacle, possibly a belt buckle, and bent double.

Determined to finish the job anyway, Greene rained blows on his armed adversary's head with the hilt of the sword, until the man was clearly unconscious and no further threat.

As more Marines squeezed through the hole in the door, however, more threats still remained—Brown's companions shot two of the Marines as they struggled through the opening, killing one of them. But their fellow Marines soon made short work of Brown's allies inside the engine house. Two of them were killed by bayonet on the spot, another two quickly captured.

Fortunately, none of Brown's thirteen hostages were harmed in the assault, which had taken all of three minutes' time from start with sledge-hammers to finish.

For the record, the next Marine inside after Greene was Maj. William W. Russell, the Marine Corps paymaster. The wounded Marine taking part in the final assault was Pvt. Mathew Ruppert, and the Marine killed—the first Marine fatality of the Civil War, as suggested by J. Robert Moskin in *The U.S. Marine Corps Story*—was Pvt. Luke Quinn, shot in the abdomen.

All told, eight of Brown's men had been killed the first day of his raid, and now the total was ten, including both of his sons who had gone with him. Brown himself was hanged six weeks later after being convicted of treason.

MARINES VERSUS MARINES

It doesn't get any worse than this: Marines against Marines, many of them former side-by-side comrades-in-arms—not merely once, as the fratricidal American Civil War unfolded, but repeatedly. In one historic case, it was also ironclad against shore batteries, on the James River seven miles below Richmond, the Confederate capital.

Confederate shore batteries were winning as their cannon shot and musket fire tore through the Union *Galena's* thin-skinned armor plate and gun ports. And inside that metallic skin, the decks became a bloody shambles.

Shortly after the Battle of Drewry's Bluff was over, a crew member from the Union ironclad *Monitor* found a charnel-house scene inside the shattered *Galena*. "Here was a body with the head, one arm & part of the breast torn off by a bursting shell—another with the top of his head taken off, the brains still steaming on the deck, partly across him lay one with both legs taken off at the hips & at a little distance was another completely disemboweled."

Things couldn't have looked much better just a short while before, when the Union Marine Cpl. John Mackie took charge and shouted to his fellow Marines, "Come on boys, here's a chance for the Marines!"

As related by historian Gerald S. Henig in the U.S. Naval Institute's *Naval History* magazine, "Mackie and his men removed the wounded, threw sand on the gun deck, 'which was slippery with human blood,' and got the heavy guns at work once again."

Mackie, it turns out, would be the first U.S. Marine ever to win the Medal of Honor, which itself first appeared during the Civil War as a U.S. military decoration—the very top one at that.

By definition, however, only the Americans fighting for the Union would qualify; those Americans fighting for the Confederacy would not. And like so many cases of brother against brother during the Civil War, so too the major battles and minor skirmishes often saw brother Marine fighting against brother Marine.

As one example, U.S. Marine Corps officers George H. Terrett and John G. Reynolds had fought together in the storming of the Chapultepec citadel at Mexico City in 1847 (page 28), but in 1861 they appeared on opposite sides in the Confederate rout of the Union at First Manassas (Battle of Bull Run). Here, Brevet Major Reynolds commanded a Union battalion of Marines, while Colonel Terrett commanded a Confederate brigade.

For that matter, the same John Simms seen at Mexico City and in the fight against the barrier forts in China (page 32) now turned up as a *Confederate* Marine, as did Israel Greene of Harper's Ferry arsenal fame.

In the same vein, Confederate Marines defending the James River in the Battle of Drewry's Bluff wound up firing on the flotilla of Union warships forcing their way past the Rebel fort just below the Confederate capital of Richmond. Confederate Marines posted along the river banks as sharpshooters took a significant toll among the Union sailors and Marines manning the Union craft trying to pass the sharp river bend.

As a measure of the high Union hopes, the flotilla was headed by the famous ironclad *Monitor*, which only weeks before had fought the widely feared Confederate ironclad *Merrimac* to a standstill at Hampton Roads. The federals also brought along their lightly armored ironclad *Galena*, plus the gunboats *Aroostook*, *Port Royal*, and *Naugatuck*.

From the very start of the battle at 6:00 a.m. on May 15, 1862, things went badly for the federals—the guns on their most powerful ship, the *Monitor*, could not elevate enough to reach Fort Darling and its guns atop the bluff, some ninety feet above the river surface. *Galena*'s guns could, however, and she soon became the prime target for the Confederates in a gun-duel that lasted four agonizing hours.

Galena was not only the prime target, but soon the *only* target, as the nearly useless *Monitor* retired out of range downstream, along with the vulnerable, wooden-hulled *Port Royal* and *Aroostook*. The *Naugatuck*, meanwhile, was forced out of the fight after suffering the explosion of a hundred-pound gun. "Thus the lone remaining ironclad, *Galena*, was forced to fight alone for over four hours," notes the U.S. Naval Institute's online *Naval History Blog* of May 15, 2011.

While the *Galena* was an ironclad, "its armor was still fairly thin," notes the same source. "Confederate rounds from the fort repeatedly penetrated *Galena*'s armor plating and caused a significant number of casualties. To make matters worse, Confederate Marines manning rifle pits on the nearby riverbank used sharpshooters to pick off any exposed personnel."

Then came the terrifying moment when a ten-inch round pierced the ship's thin armor skin and "smashed into one of its 100-pound Parrott guns, killing nearly its entire crew." That's when Corporal Mackie, a young silversmith from New York City and a Marine for just over a year, leaped to the fore with his clarion call to action. He and his surviving comrades quickly "manned the Parrot [sic] rifle and kept the weapon in action."

Even their heroics couldn't save the day, however, not with their *Galena* running out of ammunition by noontime and its commander John Rodgers severely wounded as of early morning. He now ordered the ironclad turned downstream again, out of range with the rest of the Union flotilla. By then *Galena* "had been hit dozens of times by solid shot," with twelve sailors and one Marine killed, plus another eleven men wounded.

Thus Richmond escaped harm, although the war continued for another three years; Mackie was promoted to sergeant, and just more than a year later (June 10, 1863) was physically bestowed with his Medal of Honor. By then he was serving as orderly sergeant in charge of the Marine detachment aboard the USS *Seminole* in waters off Texas. It was on board the same warship that he suffered his only wartime injury—an almost fatal fractured skull, courtesy of a chin hook wielded by rioting sailors aboard his own ship.

When Mackie was awarded his medal earlier at Sabine Pass, Texas, U.S. Navy Commodore Percival Drayton said, "Sergeant, I would give a stripe off my sleeves to get one of those in the manner as you got that."

━━━━━

ADDITIONAL NOTE: JUST BEFORE THE OPENING GUNS OF THE CIVIL War, the Marine Corps counted sixty-three as its officer complement, but at least twenty of them literally went South, including all three of former Commandant Henderson's sons, with nineteen of the twenty officers becoming Confederate Marines. As historian Moskin notes in *The U.S. Marine Corps Story*, the Corps began the war with 1,800 men and officers on board and never exceeded a total of 3,900 men at any one time, despite the demands for more fighting men as the fratricidal conflict wore on. A total of 148 Marines would die in the battles of the Civil War, but a greater number, 312, would die of natural causes such as disease.

For the Navy, the Civil War would be nothing short of revolutionary. "Sail gave way to steam power, rifled cannon replaced smoothbore, explosive shells shattered wooden hulls, and hastened the changeover to steel ships," Moskin adds. "The navy experimented with mines, turrets, submarines, and graduated gunsights."

The Marines, on the other hand, statistically contributed little to the war's total casualty list of more than six hundred thousand fighting men killed from both sides. Under the aging Commandant John Harris, Moskin adds, "The Civil War, on the whole, was not to be a time of distinction for the Corps."

CORNERSTONE FOR A BOOT CAMP

LITTLE KNOWN TODAY IS THE FACT THAT A FORMER SLAVE AND Union Civil War hero was a key figure in laying the groundwork for federal acquisition of a small island off the coast of South Carolina that today is the modern Marine Corps' best known boot camp, Parris Island.

Little appreciated, also, is the inescapable irony that Robert Smalls himself never could have become a Marine until the World War II era, because he was black. And even if he had been young enough to join the Marines in the early 1940s, he would have gone to a segregated boot camp that was not on Parris Island. He would have been a Montford Point Marine, rather than a Parris Island Marine.

But that part is strictly hypothetical, since Robert Smalls was born in the wrong century to join the once all-white U.S. Marine Corps. Even so, he became a Union hero during the Civil War by leading a group of fellow slaves in seizing a Confederate ammunition transport steamer off Charleston, South Carolina, and delivering it intact to the Union Navy.

In the process, he freed his own and other slave families.

He met Lincoln and helped persuade federal authorities that blacks could serve successfully in the Union armies. He later served in the postwar South Carolina legislature, helped found the Republican Party of South Carolina, and served five terms in the U.S. House of Representatives. He eventually owned his former master's house in Beaufort. Smalls even gave his master's elderly widow a home there for her final years.

As both a state and federal legislator, he also was instrumental in advancing legislation that eventually led to Parris Island, on Port Royal

Sound below Charleston, being turned into a Marine Corps recruit training post, for many years now the chief such boot camp on the East Coast.

Well worth mentioning, too: it was in part due to his legislative efforts that South Carolina acquired its first free, public, and mandatory schools.

Whoever would have guessed any such future for the slave child born one April day in 1839 in a cabin behind his master John McKee's house in Beaufort, allegedly while most of the townspeople were gathered at the local jail to witness a hanging?

Born to a "household" slave named Lydia (his father may have been McKee himself), the child Robert and his mother went with the family when they moved to Charleston in 1851. Then often taking the growing boy along on inspections of his plantations, McKee himself taught young Robert to ride a horse, hunt, swim, and sail.

At age twelve or so, the youngster was hired out as a lamplighter and stevedore on the port city's docks. Robert soon acquired expert knowledge of the coastal area and its Port Royal Sound, widely considered the finest deep-water natural harbor south of New York.

Robert became so expert that by the time of the Civil War he was serving as a pilot guiding various vessels among the reefs, shoals, and channels of Charleston harbor and nearby waters, notes an online biography by the Civil War Preservation Trust.

He certainly was also familiar with the low-lying Parris Island, just a few miles in overall size, close to both Beaufort and Port Royal on Port Royal Sound.

He was still a slave as the Civil War erupted—right at the Federal government's Fort Sumter in Charleston Harbor—on a fateful April day in 1861. He was hired to be a deckhand for the Confederate ammunition supply steamer CSS *Planter*, one of the eight slaves serving as crew. By now he had married Hannah Jones, a slave and hotel maid in Charleston fourteen years his senior.

Thus was the stage set for the great Robert Smalls Escape that electrified the North and chagrined the South.

After a two-week supply run in May 1862, the civilian captain and two shipmates in charge of the Confederate Navy's *Planter* saw no harm in breaking the rules and spending the night ashore, as Smalls and his fellow slaves had anticipated.

Seizing the vessel with no blood shed, then sailing right on past five Confederate forts and outposts in the dark, including Fort Sumter itself, Smalls and his cohorts chugged seaward until reaching the Union Navy's blockading ships. They broke out a white sheet as their signal of "surrender" and in effect won their freedom on the spot.

Smalls, by now the official "wheelman" for the small steamer, had worn the regular skipper's hat and jacket to look legitimate to anyone watching as the escape began to unfold about three o'clock that early morning. On the way to freedom, Smalls and his crew stopped to pick up others, among them his wife, her daughter, and their own two children to bring the total of slaves escaping to seventeen or eighteen.

Union Admiral Samuel DuPont, commander of the Union flotilla blocking the way in or out of Charleston Harbor, reported to his superiors that the commandeered Rebel vessel carried useful weapons and Smalls brought valuable intelligence information with him. Not only did he himself know the inland and coastal waters very well, but "he knew the locations of mines, troops and possessed a book of Confederate flag signals."

No surprise, then, that "Smalls was kept as a pilot of the *Planter* under Admiral DuPont," or that "he also piloted other vessels, including DuPont's flagship, the *Wabash*."

Suddenly, Smalls was a hero to the North who was invited to Washington to meet with President Lincoln and War Secretary Edwin Stanton. He was awarded $1,500 in prize money for capture of the *Planter*, although it was worth a good deal more.

Also, in just weeks, Northern authorities began to recruit black men as soldiers for the Union armies. Smalls himself personally took part in the recruitment effort.

Back on the war front, Smalls would take part in an estimated seventeen actions before the Civil War ended, including a stint piloting the ironclad monitor *Keokuk* in a failed Union fleet attack on April 7, 1863, on Fort Sumter and Charleston Harbor.

Wounded in the face during the attack, he was lauded for his bravery as the ironclad warship took ninety or so hits and then sank on the morning of April 8. The crew, Smalls included, was rescued only at the last possible minute.

Meanwhile, in mid-1863, his former master's house in Beaufort was to be auctioned off in a tax sale. Smalls acquired title by submitting the winning bid. In December of this same dramatic year, the captain of the *Planter* hid below deck in a coal bunker when the steamer came under heavy fire, and Smalls took charge in his place. As a result, he was appointed skipper of the vessel—"the first black U.S. Navy captain in the service of the United States."

At war's end in 1865, he piloted the *Planter* as part of the "water parade" attending the ceremonial raising of the American flag over Fort Sumter on April 14, for the first time since the beginning of the Civil War. That same night, Lincoln was fatally shot by John Wilkes Booth in Washington, DC.

It was a devastating blow, but life for the nation had to go on. For Robert Smalls in the Low Country of South Carolina, that would mean his first plunge into politics. As a first step, he and other black men formed a Beaufort Republican Club, South Carolina's first Republican organization. He then attended the state's constitutional convention of 1868 as a delegate and won election to the state legislature.

He would move on during the early Reconstruction years to win election to the U.S. House of Representatives, followed by twelve years of wins and losses as the state's largely white Old Guard gradually reasserted its traditional dominance through the Democratic Party, often by strong-arm tactics, notes a U.S. House biography of Smalls. Even so, he would serve a total of five two-year House terms.

In the end, he lost his seat to a Democrat in 1886, and finished his political career as the last Republican elected from his district until 2010. Returning to Beaufort, he served as the area's U.S. Collector of Customs, appointed to the post under two Republican presidents, Benjamin Harrison and William McKinley.

By now, Smalls had been widowed and married a second time. Serving in the state's postwar militia, he reached the rank of major general. He also developed diabetes and lost a foot to amputation. Congress awarded him another $5,000 in his autumn years as further reward for his capture of the CSS *Planter*.

In the meantime, it is fair to say that in his years as a politician Smalls had helped develop the legislation that eventually led to federal use of Parris Island as a naval facility and ultimately as the Marine Corps' first real boot camp—and, today, the oldest major base in the Marine Corps.

But assessments of just how instrumental he was in creating the boot camp tend to vary, source to source. The Robert Smalls website flatly says it was his federal legislation "that created Parris Island Marine Base."

On the other hand, the U.S. House biography of Smalls simply notes that he once as a House member "failed in a bid to make Port Royal [close to Parris Island] a coaling station for the U.S. Navy."

Landing somewhere between is an online historical note issued by the Marine Corps administration of Parris Island itself. It notes the U.S. Army established a coaling station on Parris Island during the Civil War. After the war, then-State Senator Smalls "introduced legislation calling for the state to petition the United States Congress for the creation of a naval station at Port Royal Sound."

Three years later, and by now U.S. Representative Robert Smalls, he introduced bills in the House that would establish navigation lights and authorize construction of commercial shipping facilities at Port Royal, a town that had sprung up on the coast just behind Parris Island at the point of a finger extending into Port Royal Sound. This led to examination of the area by a board of naval officers, who recommended establishment of a naval station on Parris Island itself.

In the meantime, Smalls and the rest of the South Carolina congressional delegation had cosponsored legislation that would have enlarged nearby Port Royal, a naval station on the order of New London, Newport, Key West, or New Orleans.

Instead, in 1883 Congress funded purchase of land on Parris Island for a naval station. By 1888, the island boasted an operational coaling station for the U.S. Navy. Thus, adds the Parris Island history, "Parris Island had received its first installation that would serve as the corner-stone for what eventually became Marine Corps Recruit Depot Parris Island."

SELECT PERSONALITY
JOHN PHILIP SOUSA

"Just about the sweetest music to me," John Philip Sousa once said, "is when I call, 'pull,' the old gun barks, and the referee in perfect key announces, 'dead.'"

Strange comment from a man whose worldwide fame was based on music, not trap-shooting. Strange pastime too, for a musician—shooting all the time with loudly blasting shotgun tucked into a shoulder, so close to his ear.

While his lifetime was built on music, it was also very strongly built on the Marine Corps. The son of a father who played for the Marine Band in the years before the Civil War, John Philip Sousa himself became a Marine at age thirteen (although just before he joined, he almost signed onto a circus band). He was enlisted by his father as an apprentice musician in the same Marine Band. No age barrier, no induction process, no boot camp.

Things were a bit different in those days, to be sure. But then, so was he.

Famous later in life for his lively marches, he had studied piano and most of the instruments found in any standard orchestra, but his absolute love was the violin.

Already performing on stage with that instrument at age eleven, he also was a bandleader the same year. Otherwise consisting of grown men, his private band soon folded for lack of finances, but young Sousa continued on as a member of the Marine Band until he was twenty. He spent the next six years in the civilian world playing the violin in various orchestras and composing—his first published operetta was called *The Smugglers*.

At age twenty-five, he married sixteen-year-old Jane van Middlesworth Bellis, and the following year, 1880, not quite yet twenty-six, John Philip Sousa became director of the U.S. Marine Band.

He soon made so many changes, among them strict rehearsals, that one-fourth of the band membership departed. But other changes, including a fresh repertoire and new instrumentation, were obviously effective. "Marine Band concerts began to attract discriminating audiences, and the band's reputation began to spread widely," notes the president's own Marine Band history of today. Under Sousa's leadership, the Marine Band became known as the best in the land.

Still a young man, Sousa received praise for his first well-known march, "The Gladiator," issued in 1888. Gaining "ever-increasing attention and respect as a composer," he soon composed the "Semper Fidelis" and "Washington Post" marches to real acclaim.

Dedicated to "the officers and men of the Marine Corps," his "Semper Fidelis" has traditionally been known as the "official" march of the Marine Corps.

Meanwhile, "The Washington Post" march was written in 1889 to promote an essay contest sponsored by the Washington newspaper, and was soon adapted to and identified with the 'two-step' dance. It "became the most popular tune in America and Europe, and critical response was overwhelming."

A British newsman remarked that if Johann Strauss Jr. should be known as the "Waltz King," then John Philip Sousa would be the "March King."

"With this, Sousa's regal title was coined and has remained ever since."

His Marine Band, today known as "The President's Own United States Marine Band," became an early "star" in the world of recorded music after the Columbia Phonograph Company sought an ensemble to record. The result was that sixty cylinders of the Marine Band's recorded music were released by 1890. Meanwhile, the band's "immense" popularity "made Sousa anxious to take his Marine Band on tour, and in 1891 President Benjamin Harrison gave official sanction for the first Marine Band tour, a tradition which has continued annually since that time, except in times of war."

The 1891 tour took the band to thirty-two cities and towns in New England and the Midwest, while a second tour, in 1892, would take it to thirty-seven cities across the entire country, from the East Coast to the West Coast.

The fact is, Sousa would not remain a Marine forever—in 1892, after his highly successful second tour with the Marine ensemble, he stepped down as director to form his own civilian concert band. In his twelve years at the helm of the Marine Band, he had served under five presidents—indeed, his farewell concert as leader of the Marine Band would be staged on the White House lawn.

Now, "with his own band, Sousa's fame and reputation would grow to even greater heights." He and his civilian band would perform together for the next thirty-nine years. Meanwhile, he had composed and many times conducted his famous "Stars and Stripes Forever," adopted in 1987 by the Congress as America's National March. (He composed it in 1896, in memory of his good friend and band manager David Blakely.)

Over the years, his typically Victorian heavily bearded face and high forehead became familiar worldwide. That was especially so after he was decorated by King Edward VII with the

Victorian Order, while both France and Belgium officially honored him for his work in the field of music as well.

But Sousa had other interests and talents besides music. His six hundred or so "compositions" included books—such as his best-selling *Fifth String* and his autobiography, *Marching Along: Recollections of Men, Women, and Music*—plus satiric poetry like his *The Feast of the Monkeys*, with these opening lines:

In days of old,
So I've been told,
The monkeys gave a feast
They sent out cards
With kind regards
To every bird and beast...

More *Marine-like*, one might say, was his deep love of trapshooting. Once asked what he considered life's best gifts, reports the National Trapshooting Hall of Fame, he listed a horse, a dog, a gun, "and a girl—with music on the side," in that order. He used the same list as the title of an article he wrote for the *American Shooter.*

So entranced with shooting was he that he became the first president of the organization "that was a forerunner to the present Amateur Trapshooting Association." Thus, Sousa "might well be called the father of government of the sport by amateur shooters as it exists today." In the same vein, he once wrote another article (for the *London Sketch*) in which he proclaimed: "Like love, trapshooting levels all ranks." Also a one-time chairman of the National Association of Shotgun Owners, he was an active field shooter and maintained a two-thousand-acre shooting preserve in North Carolina.

Of course, it was for his career in music that Sousa would be best known, as demonstrated by the myriad of his namesake facilities—public schools, a World War II liberty ship, various

American Legion Posts, a Sousa stage at the John F. Kennedy Center in Washington, a bridge in Washington, among others. In addition, he was honored with a U.S. postage stamp; the wrap-around sousaphone (tuba) is named after him; a John Philip Sousa annual band award is a plum sought by high school bands across the country. Fittingly, too, the Marine Band's own band hall is officially named the John Philip Sousa Band Hall.

A SHAKY START FOR MARINE AVIATION

IT WAS IN 1898, FIVE YEARS BEFORE THE WRIGHT BROTHERS BEGAN heavier-than-air aviation in general, that an assistant secretary of the U.S. Navy suggested looking specifically into the military applications of controlled flying machines.

But the bureaucrats of the Navy Department scoffed at young Theodore Roosevelt's notion, and little else of interest to the Navy's future flying fraternity happened for another twelve years. By then, the Wright Brothers had flown the world's first working airplane; they and others were developing more advanced flying machines that could measure their flights in miles rather than feet, and even the U.S. Army had acquired a Wright Brothers aircraft.

By contrast, still lagging at the start of 1910, was the U.S. Navy, to say nothing of its Marine Corps stepchild.

By year's end, though, the Navy had jumped into the world of heavier-than-air flight, with civilian test pilot Eugene Ely flying an early Curtiss airplane from a platform erected on the decks of the Navy cruiser USS *Birmingham*. When aircraft pioneer Glenn Curtiss then offered to teach flying to a naval officer for free, the Navy finally said yes, and Lt. Theodore G. Ellyson became naval aviator Number 1.

He was soon followed by others who began their flight training either at Annapolis, Maryland, home to the U.S. Naval Academy, or, during the winter months, in San Diego, California. And from that group came the very first five Marine Corps aviators, led by 1st Lt. Alfred A. Cunningham.

Cunningham, an Army veteran of the Spanish-American War, had just spent ten years selling real estate in his native Atlanta, Georgia, when he joined the Marine Corps in 1909 at the rank of second lieutenant. With the Marines and Navy only now developing the new Corps mission of occupying and defending advance bases for the fleet, he was posted for instruction at the Advanced Base School at the Philadelphia Navy Yard like any other promising Marine officer. Thanks to a onetime ascent in a balloon a few years before, however, he was more interested—fascinated, one might say—by the prospect of manned fight. He was so enthralled, in fact, that he not only joined a local group of aviation enthusiasts, but he rented a so-called airplane from its strictly amateur builder for his own private practice.

The only trouble was, it wouldn't fly.

Calling his would-be airship "Noisy Nan," he tried one test flight after another in an open field at the Navy Yard, but to no avail. "I pleaded with her, I caressed her, I prayed to her, and I cursed that flighty old maid to lift up her skirts and hike," he later complained, "but she never would."

Campaigning in the meantime for Marine Corps establishment of its own aviation wing, the affable Marine officer had made friends with some of the city's blue-blood society figures after joining the local Aero Club.

"Evidently making good use of his experience selling real estate, he sold the members of the Aero Club, many of whom were wealthy, influential Philadelphia socialites, on the idea that their city should have a Marine air base," says Marine Col. Edward C. Johnson's Marine Corps historical publication *Marine Corps Aviation* on the early years of Marine Corps Aviation.

Pressure was indeed exerted in Washington, and it was no detriment that Marine Corps Commandant Nicholas Biddle himself came from a prominent Philadelphia family. "What effect, if any, of Cunningham's unmilitary methods of advocacy had on the [subsequent] decision to detail Marine officers for pilot training is a matter of conjecture," adds Johnson.

Even so, Cunningham obviously had made himself—and the subject of aviation—known in the right places. "[H]is activities at least appear to have assured him first place on the list of potential aviators," Johnson continues.

So it was that on May 16, 1912, he received orders detaching him from the Marine barracks at Philadelphia and ordering him to report to the Navy's aviation camp at Annapolis, "for duty in connection with aviation."

When he did so, however, there was no aircraft immediately available for his flight training.

Unabashed as usual, it seems, he quickly arranged permission to do his training under civilian instructors at the Burgess Company and Curtiss factory at Marblehead, Massachusetts. There, in August, he soloed after just two hours and forty minutes of instruction…but not without some long moments of trepidation over landing on his own for the first time.

Wondering just how it would go doing it by himself, with no instructor present, according to Johnson, he later acknowledged, "Every time I decided to land I would think of some good excuse to make another circle of the bay."

Meanwhile, he kept track of his gas supply by watching a stick attached to a float in the gas tank, which was "mounted between the wings in plain view." Thus, "As the gas was used, this stick gradually disappeared within the tank." He kept flying, and flying, until the stick finally was just disappearing from view. "I got up my nerve, and made a good landing, how I don't know," Cunningham later said, adding, "This was my first solo."

After that it was back to military quarters for Cunningham, Marine aviator No. 1, but the date he originally was ordered to Annapolis for flight training, May 22, 1912, is today considered the official birthday of Marine Corps aviation.

As for the jerry-built airplane he first tried to fly in a Philadelphia field, it "probably was underpowered for its weight and might well have proved highly unstable had Cunningham managed to get it in the air," Johnson speculated in a footnote. Still, he adds that the contraption was "an excellent preliminary trainer…giving Cunningham the 'feel' of flying in its takeoff runs and occasional brief hops off the ground."

VIEW FROM TARTAR WALL

TENSION HAD BEEN BUILDING FOR WEEKS, EVEN MONTHS, THROUGH-out China. Not just tension, but rioting, church-burning, rape, and murder—often by decapitation, even dismemberment. And all aimed at Christian missionaries, their converts and, now, foreigners in general.

But the international contingent, roughly four thousand persons, crowded into the foreign-legations quarter of Peking (modern-day Beijing) at first simply hoped for the best.

Then came the day of June 13, 1900, when German Minister Baron Clemens von Kettler walked down Legation Street and encountered one of the rebellious "Boxers," signatory red sash and red hair-tie fully visible. He was sitting on the shafts of a cart while sharpening a large carving knife against his boots.

"Such presumption was too much for the Baron, who set about him with his stick," writes Julia Boyd in her 2012 book *A Dance with the Dragon: The Vanished World of Peking's Foreign Colony.*

Big mistake. Hours later, the rebellious Boxers, many clad in the same red sashes, rushed into Peking's so-called Tartar City, slashing and stabbing with swords and spears. That night, thousands of Chinese Christians were "butchered or roasted alive," as described by visiting Westerner Lenox Simpson. In addition, buildings associated with foreigners were set ablaze.

A week later, German envoy von Kettler himself was dead, assassinated on the streets of Peking, not by a Boxer but by a Chinese soldier armed with a rifle. A day later, British professor Hubert E. James was captured and murdered by decapitation, with his head afterwards hung on a gate in the Tartar Wall.

So began the climactic phase of China's Boxer Rebellion of the early twentieth century—a seminal event that would shape the extraordinary legend and legacy of the U.S. Marine Corps. Not only were the Marines part of the hodgepodge international relief force that eventually marched to the rescue of the foreign colony in Peking, but they were prominent as defenders on the scene for most of the weeks-long siege. They also fought—fought bravely and well—in the battles that preceded the final relief of the trapped foreigners in Peking.

As explained by Major Glen Butler in the October 2003 *Marine Corps Gazette*, the ordinary Chinese peasant of the late nineteenth century was already resentful of the growing influence of foreign outsiders. A long period of drought didn't help matters. At the time, the uneasiness of the masses was inflamed by aggressive secret societies, calling themselves names such as The Society of Harmonious Fists or Righteous Harmonious Fists, that took the lead in an uprising against foreigners and Christians. Westerners in the country simply called them all "Boxers" because of their physical antics resembling shadowboxing.

The more fanatical among the Boxers thought they were impervious to bullets.

With the terror spreading fast in northern China, "Many of those who escaped fled to the foreign legations in the capital city of Peking," Butler writes. "The Chinese Empress Dowager, Tzu Hsi (nicknamed 'Old Buddha'), superficially supported the calls of concern from foreign officials in Peking and Tientsin...[but took] little to no action against the Boxers."

As an estimated four thousand foreign nationals from eighteen countries jammed into the legation quarter at Peking, the U.S. Minister to China, Edwin Conger, wired the State Department on June 14 that a "rioting, murdering mob" had taken over the city beyond the legation walls, "with no visible effort being made by the Government in any way to restrain it." Indeed, there was no indication of the government's very existence, Butler added.

Meanwhile, the few military men available to protect the legation quarters, tucked against the city's ancient forty-five-foot Tartar Wall, had been quickly augmented by small military contingents sent into the capital city in late May and early June, just before the Boxers could surround the city and keep them out. As a result, the legations would be defended for an undefined future by an international force of just 429 officers and men, including about fifty U.S. Marines and two sailors, led by Capt. John Twiggs Myers.

The men making up this international force "had been rushed from 17 warships off the Taku bar to the Chinese capital to guard their countries' legations," writes J. Robert Moskin in his comprehensive history, *The U.S. Marine Corps Story*. "At Captain Myers's suggestion, the legations organized a common defense." But that didn't stop the Boxers from dismantling outlying rail tracks and cutting telegraph lines, thus isolating Peking from the outside world.

With that, the story of the Boxer Rebellion and the international response evolved into three episodes instead of one. On the one hand, there was the siege of the legation quarter in Peking, destined to last for fifty-five days, but on the other hand, there also would be fierce fighting in the city of Tientsin and all along the route of the first relief column sent to rescue the foreigners trapped in Peking...a force that never reached its destination.

All three episodes were dramatic to the end, and all three produced heroics by members of the U.S. Marine Corps. In fact, out of barely 1,100 Marines committed to battle in the three conflicts, a remarkable thirty-three men were awarded the Medal of Honor for their bravery, a number that did not include any officers since, by regulation in those days, they were not eligible.

The military and diplomatic personnel coordinating efforts to protect their nationals from the fast-growing Chinese threats came from seven different nations other than the United States—Britain, Russia, Japan, Austria-Hungary, Germany, France, and Italy.

The first relief column, intended to rescue the nationals stranded in Peking, set off from Tientsin—also a large city in northeastern China that was home to foreign nationals but much closer to the eastern coast. The relief effort owed its start to an impassioned outburst by U.S. Navy Capt. Bowman H. McCalla on June 9 at a meeting of consuls and military officers worried about their diplomats trapped in Peking.

Frustrated when the group began to break up with no plan adopted, McCalla, who had already been to Peking and back just days before, stood up and declared they had talked enough…he was going to the aid of his fellow Americans in Peking.

The others in the room could hardly ignore his added vow to start with his few men the very next day.

That's all that was needed for his companions—whether British, Austrian, Italian, Japanese, Russian, or German, all quickly signed on. The very next morning, as promised, McCalla seized two trains to transport the troops, while the others rounded up all the men they could. As Michael Miller recounts in the *Leatherneck* magazine of July 2000, the trains then "departed Tientsin carrying a 1,950-man relief force for what they all believed would be a short, two-day journey to Peking."

Not so, as events swiftly turned out.

With British Admiral Sir Edward Seymour in overall charge, the relief trains hadn't gone twenty-one miles before they struck their first problem: no tracks. The Boxers had been busy tearing up the rail roadbed.

"The advance slowed to a crawl, averaging one mile a day while working parties repaired the tracks and fought off small Boxer raids," adds the Miller account.

Four days after the expedition's start, McCalla's own train was attacked head-on by five hundred or so Boxers who already had killed all five Italians guarding the Langfang Rail Station. At McCalla's train, "Americans and British formed a rough defense and dropped the front ranks of charging enemy," writes Miller.

The fight then became hand to hand, with the attackers so fanatical "it took several rounds to kill each man."

McCalla found himself confronted by the Boxer leader, a giant man charging at the American naval officer while wielding a two-handed sword. At just thirty yards' distance, McCalla shot his would-be assailant, but it took a second rifle bullet to stop him. Meanwhile, as the fracas died down, with more than one hundred Boxers killed, their wounded comrades would not surrender but rather tried to bite those offering them help.

It soon "became obvious that the party would never reach Peking by train in time to rescue the legations," adds Miller. "The decision was made to continue by marching overland. However, the bridge crossing the large Pei Ho (river) was destroyed, leaving the expedition stalled without supplies. The construction crews turned and began to repair the track back to Tientsin."

As a result, the would-be relief force was caught "between the two cities [Peking and Tientsin] and surrounded by two armies—the Boxers and Chinese imperial soldiers." Indeed, the Chinese themselves had declared war on the foreign powers, many of which, frankly, had been taking advantage of the ancient nation's goodwill for many years.

Realizing the very survival of the relief force was in doubt, its leaders placed their wounded on sampans and started down the river shoreline. The point was led by Gunnery Sergeant Peter Stewart from the USS *Newark*'s Marine detachment and three more Marines; next, a hundred yards behind, came ten more Marines from the *Newark*.

It wasn't long before the mixed-nationality column ran into enemy fire at the villages they encountered, accompanied by constant Chinese artillery harassment. "By nightfall, the column covered nine miles, but had many casualties, and the men were dead tired." The next day was hardly better—"fighting began early and continued throughout the day."

A party of Royal Marines had joined the American Marines and sailors in the vanguard of the column shortly before they all encountered a large Chinese force. "McCalla led the men along the riverbank toward the advancing Chinese," adds Miller. "The two forces opened fire at a range of only fifty yards. The fight proved short and bloody. McCalla was hit in the shoulder by a Chinese bullet. The Chinese were repulsed with heavy losses." Still, the growing numbers of wounded slowed the advance, while the Chinese artillery fire only added to the number of casualties.

With little ammunition left, but Tientsin still a difficult seven miles away, a crucial, do-or-die day suddenly loomed. Setting out at 2:00 a.m., the would-be relief force proceeded down the left bank of the Pei Ho until coming up against an entrenched Chinese force on the opposite bank—infantry, artillery, and cavalry.

Even so, the Royal Marines finally managed to cross and to capture the Chinese strongpoint, "which turned out to be the Hsi-Ku Arsenal." Here, it also turned out, was salvation for the entire column, since the fortification held field guns, rifles, ammunition, medical supplies, and food enough to last fifty days, notes Miller's account.

But this also meant the foreign legation quarter of Peking remained under siege, without relief, while Tientsin itself had fallen to the Boxer-Chinese forces, except for a small foreign enclave…and now the vaunted relief column itself was trapped, albeit in a secure fortress for the moment.

Meanwhile, denuded of most military defenders, the foreign settlement in Tientsin was hard pressed to defend itself from the Boxers, who had "torched" the villages close to the city's defenses as early as June 15, while also attacking churches and foreign-owned properties. As they also tortured and murdered Christian Chinese who fell into their hands, "The allies could do little but watch."

Their situation only looked bleaker when a supply train sent to aid the Seymour expedition came back with word that the rail line to the north had been cut. That night, "fires lit up the sky around the walled city of Tientsin, casting an eerie glow over the [foreign] concessions." An American on the scene later reported, "The evening breeze wafted to us the howling and screeching of an immense mob."

The next morning, the Boxers attacked the Russians guarding the city's rail station and tested the American positions, only to be driven off by "well-aimed rifle fire." More trains sent to supply British Admiral

Seymour's stalled column were forced to return, but a train sent to the port of Taku (Dagu today) to coordinate with the Allied warships gathered offshore did get through. The Allies had previously conquered the Taku Forts guarding the approaches to the port city, which in normal times provided direct access to Tientsin.

Aboard the Allied ships, of course, were more fighting men, ammunition, and other supplies. Thanks to the newly opened supply corridor, five thousand or more troops pushed through the thirty-plus miles from Taku, despite a sharp firefight between a combined force of U.S. Marines and Russians fighting the Chinese just outside the Tientsin foreign settlement. The Chinese in that sector then faded away—the Allies thus could maintain their flow of men and supplies.

With the foreign enclave in Tientsin still besieged on three sides, the Allies now managed to send a force of two thousand or so to rescue the entrapped Seymour expedition. Next on the agenda would be clearance of Tientsin's walled inner city, from which the Chinese were shelling the foreign settlement section. Only then could a newly formed relief expedition go to the aid of the foreign nationals in Peking.

Fortunately, the rampaging Boxers had begun to return to the northern countryside by early July, but the inner walled city was held by a surprisingly resilient group of an estimated twelve thousand imperial Chinese troops who lobbed thousands of shells upon the nearby foreign settlement. By the time the allies had gathered sufficient forces to attack the old walled city, they numbered perhaps six thousand to seven thousand soldiers, almost half of them either Russian or Japanese.

This international force divided its assault between two gates, the east and the south, with the American contingent assigned to the South Gate and civilian engineer Herbert Hoover, the future president, acting as a guide for the U.S. Marines. The Allies suffered heavy casualties, but they prevailed in the end. And that cleared the way for a final effort to relieve the combined Boxer and Chinese siege of the legation quarter in Peking.

It was August 4, in the heat of summer, before the second relief column set off for the Chinese capital, this time as a formidable force of 18,800.

In Peking, meanwhile, the fighting had died down to a siege punctuated by occasional sniper and artillery fire into the legation quarter, hard by the Tartar Wall. The early days of the siege had been lively ones—and deadly. An area just three-fourths of a mile square in size, the legation quarters had been "under constant attack," notes Moskin in his Marine Corps history. "The Marines and the Germans, whose legations were the southernmost, took and held a section of the Tartar City Wall, on the southern side of the Quarter. By July 3, a quarter of all the foreign military professionals had been killed or wounded. At 3:00 a.m., Captain Myers led fourteen Marines, sixteen Russians, and twenty-five British Marines over the barricade and killed many Chinese in hand-to-hand fighting."

Severely wounded in the leg by a Chinese spear, his injury then quickly infected, Myers was put out of action for the duration, and his subordinate, Capt. Newt Hall, took charge. On July 13, Moskin adds, "The Japanese were shoved back; the British were severely pressed; the Germans saved their area with a bayonet charge, and the Americans fought fiercely on the wall."

Indeed, just a night later, Marine Pvt. Daniel J. Daly voluntarily manned the wall with his bayoneted rifle as his only company. Hall had gone for reinforcements. "Chinese snipers fired at him [Daly] and stormed the bastion, but he fought them off until reinforcements arrived." For his gallantry he earned the Medal of Honor. But that would be only the first of a rare two Medals of Honor to be awarded the diminutive (five-foot-six, 133-pound) native of Glen Cove, Long Island, New York.

Coincidentally, the only other Marine ever to earn two of the same esteemed award was Smedley Butler, who as a young officer was also a participant in the Boxer Rebellion. Serving courageously, even wounded fighting the Boxers and Chinese, Butler would actually earn his two Medals later, in different conflicts…but one of them was in Haiti, close to the very time and place Daly earned his second Medal.

The relief column setting out for Peking on August 4 included a Marine regiment commanded by future Corps Commandant William

P. Biddle, with Army Maj. Gen. Adna R. Chaffee in charge of the two thousand Americans taking part.

"At Yangtsun, twenty-five miles on the way," adds Moskin, "the Americans and British led the attack and stormed the Chinese earthworks." In fact, it was on this march, in the "grueling heat of the treeless plain," that the American Marines and Britain's Royal Welch Fusiliers formed a special bond of friendship that would lead, years later, to Marine Corps band leader John Philip Sousa's composition of the "Royal Welch Fusiliers" march.

In Peking, as the column came close, the Chinese attacked the legation quarter anew but soon were under attack themselves as the relief force stormed into the city by way of its gates. "The Americans, including two companies of Marines, scaled the wall south of the Tung-Pien gate," reports Moskin. Here, the legendary Smedley Butler, still a young first lieutenant, was wounded in the chest, "but saved by a button on his blouse." In just hours, by the afternoon of August 14, the siege was over.

"In the Quarter, 66 foreigners were dead, 150 wounded. The Empress Dowager Tzu Hsi and her court fled. The allies drove out the Chinese troops and plundered the city." (Some among the victorious foreign nationals had not treated the conquered precincts of Tienstin very kindly, either.)

With the siege done, most of the Marines who were rushed ashore for duty in the Boxer Rebellion would have little time for rest and relaxation. While some could look forward to dull routines aboard U.S. Navy ships again, many—the First Marine Regiment, specifically—would be going back to the bloody Philippine Insurrection that followed American victory in the Spanish-American War.

———

ADDITIONAL NOTE: TAKING STOCK ONCE THE SMOKE OF THE BOXER Rebellion of 1900 in Peking had cleared, the Marines could count not only thirty-three Medal of Honor winners in their ranks, but also the first Marine to win the coveted Medal posthumously, one Harry Fisher, a private…except it turned out he wasn't really Pvt. Harry Fisher at all.

Instead, he was Pvt. Franklin J. Phillips—that is, former *Army* Pvt. Franklin J. Phillips. As later investigation established, he had been branded a deserter and discharged (less than honorably) from the Army after he left his unit (Company M, First U.S. Infantry) in Huntsville, Alabama, and went home just before Christmas, 1898. He apparently had been refused a sickness furlough for treatment of malaria he had contracted in Cuba during the Spanish-American War.

After he appeared at a recruiting office in Pittsburgh, Pennsylvania, the following March and asked to be restored to duty, he discovered his outfit had returned to Cuba and he had been discharged, "without honor." He then enlisted in the Marine Corps under the bogus name Harry Fisher and wound up at Peking during the Boxer Rebellion. There, he was killed on July 16, 1900, while helping others erect a barricade protecting the diplomats, their dependents, and other foreigners under siege by the Chinese Boxers.

The following year, his mother, identified in the National Archives publication *Prologue* as Mrs. W. C. Means, asked Marine Corps Commandant Brigadier General Charles Heywood to use her son's real name in the official Marine Corps rolls. Inexplicably, he refused, with the excuse that "no change can be made in a man's record after his death," notes the *Prologue* publication.

As a result, on August 15, 1901, the young man's mother had to accept his Medal of Honor "under the name Pvt. Harry Fisher."

The better part of a century then elapsed. Finally, in 1988, with prodding by two Pennsylvania congressmen and others, a subsequent Corps Commandant, Gen. Albert Gray, ordered the change from "Harry Fisher" to the posthumous Medal winner's true name of Pvt. Franklin J. Phillips in the records at Headquarters Marine Corps and the National Archives.

That still left one more correction to be made—the name of the Marine Prepositioning Ship MV *Private Harry Fisher* had to be changed to the MV *Pvt. Franklin J. Phillips.* This was also done in 1988.

PART II
WORLD WARS

Well, Lieutenant, they started right out telling everyone how great they were. Pretty soon they got to believing it themselves. And they have been busy ever since proving they were right.

—Gunnery Sgt. Walter Holzworth to Lt. Victor Krulak, sometime in 1935

BRIDGE TO FOUR CONFLICTS

"Up from the sea came a line of naked men, grabbing their carbines and falling into place...," wrote an onlooking New York journalist. Still naked, they hurriedly joined their battalion formation behind a hill and then waited with their fellow Marines, "to see how much force would develop against them."

But the coastline, bristling with sniper fire moments before, now remained quiet.

Their Commanding Officer (CO), Lt. Col. Robert W. Huntington, ordered a charge. "There was no fun in this for naked men," added the correspondent for the *New York Journal*, "but they held their places and charged with the others."

Naturally, they wouldn't be unclothed for very long, nor would this be the end of the fighting at Guantanamo Bay in 1898. As Huntington's Marines were already learning, the Spaniards controlling Cuba at the time of the Spanish-American War would not easily give up their colonial territory.

Huntington's battalion, 647 men and officers strong, had come ashore from cramped quarters aboard the destroyer-transport USS *Panther* on June 10, to face an estimated 7,000 Spanish forces grouped in the area of Guantanamo City. The Marines would be supported by a relatively few Cuban rebels in the area and the guns of three more U.S. warships standing by in Guantanamo Bay: the battleship *Oregon*, the cruiser *Marblehead*, and the gunboat *Dolphin*.

The Marines splashed ashore through the surf in uniform, armed with Lee rifles, bayonets fixed.

Meeting no resistance, the advance riflemen secured "what was left of a Spanish blockhouse on a hill near Fisherman's Point," while fellow Marines and sailors from the *Panther* unloaded supplies down by their beachhead, writes R. R. Keene in *Leatherneck* magazine.

It wasn't until the next evening that the Spaniards reacted again. And now the Marines "felt the first real sting and learned to respect the 7.65 Mauser Espanol Model 1893 rifles and the Spanish sharpshooters who wielded them."

Taking a swim, naked, in the bay waters or silhouetted on the bright beach sands that evening, the Marines were easy targets for the Spanish snipers hidden in the island's "thick inland bush." Two Marine privates on picket duty "never knew what killed them."

Their hidden assailants pulled back as the Marines took to their own rifles, augmented by the occasional machine gun and helped by cannon fire from the offshore USS *Marblehead*. The snipers struck again later that night, wounding three and killing one private and the unit's assistant surgeon, John Blair Gibbs.

Undeterred, the Marines and their companion Cuban insurgents still decided they must seize the area's only freshwater well, a few miles distant. *McClure's* magazine correspondent Stephen Crane, best known today as author of the Civil War novel *The Red Badge of Courage*, was there to write a famous essay on the death of Surgeon Gibbs. Crane was with them as they toiled up hill, over rocks, down dale, in the terrible daytime heat. Their middle-aged commanding officer Huntington visibly wilted, while several much younger men making the trek to the well were sent back to the beachhead with heat prostration.

Thus the stage was set for the Battle of Cuzco Well, and the emergence of yet another legendary Marine Corps hero, this one destined to be an unintended, unwitting bridge in a total of four conflicts for the United States, up to and including World War I. Not only did Sergeant John H. Quick's USMC career span four American conflicts just before and after 1900, but he came away highly decorated for his heroics each time.

It was the morning of June 14 when Quick and fellow Marines of two companies moved out, together with about fifty Cuban insurgents, on the way to the Cuzco well. The gunboat USS *Dolphin* followed along just off shore, "ready to furnish naval gunfire support upon call… The Spanish soon discovered the movement and their main body near the well was alerted. The Marines and Cubans occupied the hill which overlooked the enemy's position, but were immediately subjected to heavy long-range rifle fire."

Captain George Elliott, later a Corps Commandant, had taken over the Marine detachment from the obviously ill Huntington, and Elliott "signaled the *Dolphin* to shell the Spanish position."

But the man sending the signals by flag was partially obscured from his counterparts aboard the ship, the signal was misinterpreted, and soon shells began falling on a small detachment of Marines en route to join the fight.

Wasting no time, Sergeant Quick "heroically placed himself in plain sight of the vessel, but in danger of falling shells, and signaled for the fire to be stopped."

Using a blue polka-dot handkerchief as a flag to wig-wag his signals in Morse Code, he "scrambled to the top of the hill where he was plainly silhouetted against the sky-blue horizon," and continued to signal. "As he calmly turned his back to the enemy and began waving his flag, he was immediately subjected to furious enemy rifle fire. While enemy bullets cut through the bushes and screamed overhead, he continued to signal the *Dolphin* as coolly as though he were on a parade ground."

It was a slow process, too.

"Letter by letter the message to the ship was spelled out in the dot-dash code. When Sgt. Quick finished this message, the ship answered. He then picked up his rifle and resumed his place on the firing line."

The *Dolphin* shifted her fire, "and by two p.m. the Spaniards had begun to retreat." The Battle of Cuzco Well fell to the Americans, as did Guantanamo, first to be used as a coaling station for the U.S. Navy, then, in more recent years, as a naval base challenging complete Communist control of Cuba and a terrorist detainment center.

The victory for Colonel Huntington's First Marine Battalion (Reinforced) contributed little materially to the overall outcome of the war with Spain, but "it took on incalculable importance for the Marine Corps," in the eyes of Marine Corps historian Allan R. Millett, circa 1980. Crane's reports from the scene pictured the battle "as an epic of bravery and professionalism that proved the military superiority of the Marines."

As one result of such glowing reports, the battalion as a group was invited to march in review before President William McKinley in Washington, where Congress reacted to the overall efforts of the Marine Corps during the war by doubling its size to 201 officers and 6,062 men.

Not only Crane, but Herman Melville of *Moby Dick* fame was among the correspondents reporting the results of the Guantanamo affair. And it didn't hurt the Marine image to have the Spanish survivors of the Cuzco Well skirmish tell their superiors they had been attacked by 10,000 Americans. Huntington, for his part, would be touted for showing off the Marines as shock troops capable of amphibious landings on hostile shores; Quick and others winning the Medal of Honor became national heroes.

At this point, many a man, even a hero like Quick, would have finished out his enlistment, gone back home, and enjoyed an easier civilian life as a local celebrity—thus Quick might have returned to his native West Virginia.

But no, Quick remained in the Marines for a total of twenty-six years and turned up next in the Philippines Insurrection that followed the Spanish-American War. Here, among other actions, he would take part in the infamous march across Samar in the Philippines…infamous for its hardship and loss of life among those taking part.

When the rebellious *insurrectos* demanding independence for the Philippines massacred members of the Ninth U.S. Infantry's C Company at Balangiga on September 28, 1901, Marine Maj. Littleton T. "Tony" Waller's Marine battalion reacted. But what a choice they made. They attacked a major rebel band holed up, literally, in the caves of the

Sohoton Cliff volcanic formations rising two hundred feet above a river. "The Marines scaled the cliffs on rickety ladders, scattered the enemy, and destroyed their camp," writes historian J. Robert Moskin in his Marine Corps history. Waller later "commended" Captains David D. Porter and Hiram I. Bearss, Gunnery Sergeant Quick, and Acting Cpl. Harry Glenn for "conspicuous conduct." (Porter and Bearss later were awarded the Medal of Honor as well.)

But soon another tragedy struck the Americans. In an effort to map a route for the Army's telegraph lines between strongpoints in southern Samar, Waller led a mixed column of Marines, soldiers, local guides, and native carriers—about a hundred in all—along the Lanang River and into jungle-covered mountains. The trek in rain and heat was so difficult, and the men were so exhausted, that the party split up. Some went ahead for help, others turned back to their starting point, and more, feverish and crippled, simply collapsed. In the end, nine Marines were counted as missing—having gone insane or died in the jungle.

When some of the native bearers were beaten off with sticks after they tried to kill a Marine officer, Gunnery Sergeant Quick carried a message from Porter to Waller recommending execution of the mutinous bearers. Waller did have eleven Filipinos shot, but was charged with murder (and then acquitted) in the storm of controversy following.

Meanwhile, the trek across Samar became such a part of Marine Corps lore, that for years, according to Moskin, "it was a tradition in the Corps to greet any Marine who had shared the hardships of the march on Samar with the command: 'Stand, gentlemen! He served on Samar.'"

John Quick, by now a sergeant major, would again be cited for bravery in the Marine landing of 1914 at Veracruz, Mexico. "He was continually exposed to fire during the first two days of the operation and showed coolness, bravery, and judgment in the prompt manner in which he performed his duties," wrote the Secretary of the Navy.

Only four years later, he would begin his heroics all over again with the Marines in France, from the Toulon Sector at Verdun and then Belleau Wood in early June to mid-October 1918, just a month before the armistice ending World War I. Thus, he survived the Battle of Soissons, the Marbache Sector near Pont-à-Mousson, the Saint-Mihiel offensive, Blanc Mont Ridge, and the Meuse-Argonne.

The new honors for gallantry he displayed at Belleau Wood included both the Navy Cross and the Distinguished Service Cross, earned by volunteering for an extremely dangerous supply run in a rickety Model T on a gunfire-swept road into the village of Bouresches (page 88).

SELECT PERSONALITY
HENRY LEWIS HULBERT

Born an Englishman, Marine Henry Lewis Hulbert earned his Medal of Honor in American Samoa and later fought at Belleau Wood, Château-Thierry, Soissons, and Blanc Mont, France. At the age of fifty-one, as the Corps' first gunner in rank, and as Commandant George Barnett's former right-hand man at Marine Corps headquarters in Washington, DC, he certainly did not have to go to France and fight…but he did.

A native of Kingston upon Hull, England, he had joined the Marine Corps in 1898 at age thirty-one in San Francisco, and in a year's time found himself fighting off a band of rebel Samoans and protecting two wounded officers by his side as their comrades retreated to a better defensive position.

Only a private at the time, Hulbert volunteered to hold up the advancing Samoans, as did two sergeants, Irishman Michael J. McNally and Bruno A. Forsterer, a former lieutenant in the German Navy. But it was Private Hulbert who would earn the Congressional Medal of Honor for his bravery that day in the Samoan Islands. "Wounded but firing coolly and methodically, Henry Hulbert took down a pair of charging rebels and speared a third on his bayonet," writes Maj. Allan C. Bevilacqua USMC (Ret.), in the December 2008 *Leatherneck* magazine.

"Then, turning to confront a sword-wielding attacker who was approaching on McNally's blind side, Hulbert shot the man at point-blank range."

All three men were part of a combined force of American and British Marines, together with sailors from both countries, who had landed on a major Samoan island to confront German-backed rebels threatening the local government. The rebels, armed with German weaponry, had already besieged the British and American consulates.

The combined Anglo-American column, hailing from warships of both countries, including Hulbert's own USS *Philadelphia*, was ambushed by a larger rebel force near the town of Faglii on April 1, 1899. "Casualties were immediate and heavy," writes Bevilacqua. "The rebels had chosen their ambush site well; the position of the Anglo-American force was all but indefensible. The only suitable defensive terrain was a low ridge-line 100 yards away. There the landing force could be supported by naval gunfire from the *Philadelphia* and HMS *Royalist*."

While the larger group successively withdrew to the defensive line behind, Hulbert remained at his forward position until both wounded officers by his side died. First Lt. Constantine M. Perkins, skipper of the *Philadelphia*, later reported he wanted especially to point out "the gallantry of Private Henry L. Hulbert, who remained behind at the fence till the last, and who was with [Lieutenant P. V.] Lonsdale and [Lieutenant J. B.] Monaghan when they both were killed."

In the years that followed, Hulbert steadily rose in rank, until serving as sergeant major at the Marine Barracks in Washington. Along the way, however, he had served with future Commandant George Barnett while on expeditionary duty in Cuba, and in 1914 the newly emplaced Commandant Barnett had Hulbert transferred to Corps headquarters.

"There was no position of sergeant major of the Marine

Corps in 1914, but by every standard Hulbert discharged that function," writes Bevilacqua also. "His office was next to Maj. Gen. Barnett's office. Anyone wishing to speak with Maj. Gen. Barnett first spoke to Sgt. Maj. Hulbert."

Then, in 1916, the Marines and the Navy established their warrant officer ranks, and in the process Hubert qualified in March of 1917 for appointment as the Corps' first Marine gunner. When America entered World War I, Hulbert didn't have to go with the much younger troops. "He was secure in his position at the right hand of the commandant. He was fifty years old, too old for combat, with a wife and infant daughter at home."

But his "strong sense of duty would not permit him to sit safely in Washington while others did the fighting," adds Bevilacqua. "He was that kind of man."

Adds an online biographical sketch from the U.S. Citizenship and Immigration Service, "He pressed his superiors to be sent into the fight."

In France, the fifty-one-year-old Gunner Hulbert was assigned as a platoon leader with the Sixty-Sixth Company, First Battalion, Fifth Marines…starting at the month-long Battle of Belleau Wood, he would be a leader of much younger men in a crucible of unrelenting combat.

As recalled by Bevilacqua, the stage for the epic battle really was set the previous fall of 1917, when czarist Russia collapsed under the weight of the war on its borders, combined with the Bolshevik revolution from within. This meant a massive number of German troops could be shifted to the fight against the Allies to the west, with the imperative of striking them a knockout blow before the newly engaged Americans arrived in strength. The Russian collapse led to the massive German offense in the spring of 1918 that pushed back the forward lines of the British and French under "an avalanche of [artillery] shells and masses of infantry."

With a million additional troops now available to their generals, the Germans overran acres of ground in their great offensive of 1918 that included the mile-square onetime hunting preserve of a wealthy Frenchman, the Bois de Belleau (Belleau Wood).

Stalling in that one sector, they set up defensives with a vengeance in the densely wooded area, most effectively with a network of machine-gun nests assuring deadly interlacing fire against any attackers.

Meanwhile, the American Expeditionary Forces (AEF) field army commanded by Army Gen. John J. Pershing "was nowhere near ready. What was on hand would have to do."

"Part of what was on hand was the Second Division United States Regular, a hybrid division composed of an Army brigade with two infantry regiments, the Ninth and Twenty-Third Infantry, a Marine brigade built around the Fifth and Sixth Marines and an engineer regiment and artillery brigade."

In the first week of June, the Marine brigade arrived at Belleau Wood, only to be greeted by discouraged French troops "streaming to the rear" and saying, "*La guerre est finie.*" Told it would be best to retreat, Marine Capt. Lloyd Williams made Corps history by his retort: "Retreat? Hell, we just got here."

The Americans dug in "while the Germans opposite caught their breath and prepared for another lunge." But the Marines made the first move.

"During the early morning hours of 6 June, elements of both Marine regiments launched an all-out attack on the key German position of Hill 142, setting off what would be a solid month of intense and sustained combat."

Gunner Hulbert, old enough to be a general, was among the wounded as the two Marine regiments suffered "what would be the bloodiest day in Marine Corps history up to that point, with more Marines falling dead and wounded than in all of the Marine Corps' previous wars combined."

Wounded or not, Hulbert never faltered in leading his men "into the teeth of murderous machine-gun fire, shooting, bayonetting, and hurling hand grenades at any unlucky Germans who tried to bar the way."

At one point, writes Bevilacqua, "he single-handedly blasted a succession of machine-gun positions, killing seven defenders, and as a subsequent Silver Star citation read, 'put the remainder to flight.'" In sum, he earned two Silver Stars and a Distinguished Service Cross for his heroism and leadership at Belleau Wood.

He then earned a third Silver Star in mid-July at Soissons, where he was both gassed and wounded. There, too, he was promoted to second and then first lieutenant.

Still ahead, though, was Blanc Mont near Reims, heavily fortified with pillboxes, concrete bunkers…and guns.

On October 4, 1918, the Germans "fought furiously to maintain possession."

But to gain possession, so did the men of the Marine Brigade, "stoutly assisted by the doughboys of the Ninth and Twenty-Third Infantry." The Americans finally wrested control of the ridgeline from the gray-clad defenders, but at heavy cost.

Of the one thousand men from Hulbert's own First Battalion, Fifth Marines, entering the battle, "only 134 would walk out under their own power." Hulbert was *not* among them. He had been cut down by a German machine-gun while trying to reorganize his decimated platoon.

Awarded a posthumous Navy Cross for his gallantry at Blanc Mont and by now recommended for promotion in the field to captain, Hulbert was without doubt a model Marine of his time. He remains so even today as namesake for the Marine Corps' Hulbert Trophy for Outstanding Leadership, awarded annually to the active-duty Marine gunner at chief warrant officer level who best exemplifies Hulbert's own leadership qualities.

The Navy also honored his heroic service by naming the

destroyer USS *Henry L. Hulbert* after the English-born Marine. "The ship's bell…now occupies a position of honor on the quarterdeck of the Infantry Officer Course at Marine Corps Base Quantico," writes Bevilacqua, himself a former Marine gunnery sergeant, retired USMC major, and author of the book *The Way It Was: A Seabag Full of Marine Humor.*

OPENING THE DOOR TO WOMEN
BY INGRID SMYER

THEY CAME BY THE THOUSANDS AS WORD SPREAD THAT THE UNITED States Marine Corps was now recruiting women. The time was in the midst of the Great War, and rather than just surprising, the response had been downright amazing. At the 23rd Street recruiting office in New York City alone, two thousand patriotic hopefuls were lined up to sign up.

All had come in response to newspaper articles simply stating that the Marine Corps was looking for "intelligent young women."

They came with enthusiasm in startling numbers to answer the call for volunteers. But only a select few would be "top notch," writes Marine Captain Linda L. Hewitt, USMCR, in her Marine Corps historical monograph, *Women Marines in World War I.*

The United States, already supportive of her Allies, declared war in April 1917, nearly three years after the conflict in Europe broke out. Hewitt also wrote, "American industry and business already had felt a tightening labor market situation even before the American war declaration that April.

"The nation was already heavily committed to the support of the Allies," she writes. "And as the thousands of young men rushed to volunteer to the Armed services, and the draft gathered in hundreds more, the labor potential for women for the first time in the history of the United States became of monumental importance."

By October of that same year, the *New Republic* wrote: "Our output of the necessities of war now must increase at the same time that we must provide for the needs of the civil populations of the countries allied with us." The same article asked, "Where are we to get the labor?"

The prospect of a crippling labor shortage receded quite a bit as women's organizations, such as the National League for Women's Services and the Woman's Committee of the Council of National Defense, rolled up their sleeves and began to direct and to coordinate activities of women all across the country. "Everyone, from housewives in Oklahoma to Park Avenue society girls, was involved in the all-out effort to support the war," writes Hewitt.

Thus, even before America entered World War I, large numbers of women had been welcomed in business offices, even in factory work to some extent.

Still, the military services were faced with a serious personnel problem by the time the United States had declared war. Most of the work that women volunteers had taken on was in the home or at women's clubs: work such as rolling bandages, knitting socks and scarfs, or planting victory gardens, even "canning a can for Uncle Sam," as the popular jingle went. Hundreds more women volunteered to hostess at canteens, organized food and clothing drives, and yet more joined together to collect books and magazines for the "boys going overseas."

Surely there was more, much more, the women could do in the emergency of war.

Josephus Daniels, the North Carolina newspaper editor/publisher turned secretary of the Navy, saw the possibility of enrolling women in military endeavors other than traditional pursuits such as nursing. He believed they could be helpful in many areas, but first he wanted to be sure there were no legal reasons women could not be enrolled in the Navy.

He put his staff to work on a study of the legal status, if any, concerning women in the Navy. His assistants turned over every stone in their search for any prohibition against the enrollment of women, but found no such laws on the books. Secretary Daniels thus could, and did, open the Navy to women!

This was a startling breath of fresh air. It gave women an opportunity to contribute hands-on to the war effort. How could other military branches say no when the Navy had already taken the plunge?

By July 1918, the war was wearing on—heavy fighting and mounting American casualties made it urgent that more troops be sent to the front in France. Loath to cut back on reinforcements for the men on the battle lines, Marine Commandant Maj. Gen. George Barnett realized there were many battle-ready Marines doing clerical work right under his nose on the home front. He was also aware of the dramatic changes being made by an unofficial but highly motivated women's "volunteer army" across the nation, usually in the name of the war effort. Although women were not new to the industrial setting, World War I was the first time women were hired in large numbers to do skilled and semiskilled labor.

Meanwhile, early predictions that women would never be put into "trousers or unbecoming uniforms," were proven wrong, as women of all stripes and in a cross section of occupations already had "donned the uniforms of elevator operators, streetcar conductors, postmen, and industrial workers, and ably carried on the Nation's business at home," writes Hewitt.

Even so, some critics put forth negative evaluations concerning the ability of women to learn the skills and routines practiced by the Marine Reserves. Calculations were "offered," wrongly again, that it would take two women to do the work of one man. The commandant was advised that if women were to be enrolled "it would not be desirable to make the change suddenly, but [rather] gradually."

The disparaging idea was that it would take inordinate amounts of time for the women to learn from the desk-bound clerks they would be replacing.

Despite such negatives and perhaps his own doubts, General Barnett recognized the urgency of the times. On August 2, 1918, he took pen to paper and wrote an unprecedented letter to Secretary Daniels asking for authority "to enroll women in the Marine Corps Reserve for clerical duty at Headquarters Marine Corps and at other Marine Corps offices in the United States where their services might be utilized to replace men who may be qualified for active field service."

On August 8, 1918, less than a week later, Navy Secretary Daniels indeed gave his official approval to enroll women as members of the Marine Corps.

Newspapers and, not too surprisingly, quite a few enthusiastic Marines themselves quickly spread the news. By August 13, women stood in long lines at recruiting offices across the country, more than ready to sign up. Some of the women had an advantage because of their stenography, typing, and office skills. And some were educated in office organization. In the end, only 305 women actually became Women Marine Corps Reserve members for the entire war.

None at that time were expected to pick up a rifle and go into combat, true…but many of the men they replaced in desk jobs would soon be shipping out to France and entering combat.

One woman who took their place would be Mrs. Opha May Johnson, already working at Marine Corps Headquarters in Washington as a civil service employee.

Acting right away, she took the honor of being America's first woman Marine. She was obviously the first "Top-Notch" on the list. Enthusiastic to the core, once she signed her name on the official document she would forevermore be the first woman to enter the exclusively male world, nothing less than a Marine Corps legend.

Opha May Johnson, née Jacob, was born in Kokomo, Indiana, on February 13, 1900, according to various sources, or some years earlier, according to others. As the *Quantico Sentry* reported on August 15, 2013, "Although some report she was in her late teenage years [when she enlisted], experts say something quite the opposite."

The *Sentry* cites Marine Corps Historian Kara Newcomer as one of those experts. "She was almost forty when she enlisted," according to Newcomer.

There is also some contention about the spelling of her middle name, which she signed as "May," but by some accounts you can find it spelled Mae. Historian Newcomer told the *Sentry*'s Lance Cpl. Samuel Ellis, "Although many spell her middle name Mae, her middle name is actually spelled May."

Newcomer added, "We also believe she probably went by her first name alone, based on how she signed her name."

Some historians even question whether she signed on as a Marine on August 12 or August 13 of 1918, but in either case it was as a clerk.

She had previously graduated from Wood's Commercial College with shorthand and typewriting as her specialty. She was chosen to be the salutatorian for her class. At the time of her enlistment, she was married to Victor H. Johnson, musical director at the Lafayette Square Opera House.

Meanwhile, on one of those suddenly busy August days in 1918, the officer in charge of Marine Corps recruiting, Col. Albert McLemore, was on hand to ensure the proper screening and processing of the women.

Five women were chosen at his recruit station that day, among them a Miss Florence Gertler who always would remember the day's excitement:

> Male noncommissioned officers went up and down the line asking questions about experiences, family responsibilities, etc., and by the process of elimination got the line down to a few hundred. Applicants were interviewed by one officer and finally given a stenographic test. Colonel McLemore conducted the shorthand test and dictated so fast, that one after another left the room. Those who remained were taken, one-by-one into Colonel McLemore's office and told to read back their notes (I remember that I made a mistake on 'Judge Advocate General,' never having heard the word, I thought it was 'Attorney General.') If the colonel was satisfied with our reading, we were required to type our notes and timed for speed and accuracy. More and more applicants dropped by the wayside, until only five were left. We were told to report back the next day for a physical examination.

These five women, obviously well trained in office skills already, were called to duty at Marine Corps Headquarters in Washington. Gentler, who wrote such a definitive description of the difficulty and stress that these "intelligent young women" endured in order to become a Marine, must have felt a great deal of pride when she learned that Colonel McLemore called these women his "100 percent girls."

RECRUIT WITH A FUTURE

The recruit from West Point, Virginia, right at the head of the York River, was just one among the four to five hundred young men who stepped off the train at the Yemassee siding in the South Carolina low country one day in August of 1918. A barge and tugboat took them from the siding to the quarantine station at Parris Island for a stay of six days.

Shucking their civvie clothes among the tents and sand dunes, they surrendered themselves to life in the Marines, some to stay, some to leave quickly; some to die in combat, others to survive.

But few would ever make a mark like the young Virginian, who already had spent a year working toward a commission by attending the Virginia Military Institute (VMI), and left thinking he might get into the fighting of World War I a lot quicker by enlisting in the Marines.

He stood out among his fellow recruits right away. Within three days, writes biographer Burke Davis, his company drill instructor, Corp. John DeSparre, had put the Virginian in charge of a platoon.

In a few more days, he was handling the platoon like a veteran of years-long standing, despite his small size and youthful looks. DeSparre was amazed. "I know he looks like he ought to be in three-cornered pants," he told his sergeant, "but by God, he's a Marine."

Was he ever! "You know I always have to tell 'em to look mean and nasty out there marching, but I never had to tell him. He's a natural. And he never makes the same mistake twice. He's already made the Company

Number One for parades, and he did it by himself." The parades were held at sunset one evening a week. Inspection by the commanding general—at the time, it was Jack Meyer of Boxer Rebellion fame, also a Medal of Honor winner—came every Saturday morning. In the Virginia recruit's opinion, though, the training base really was run by two brothers named Broadstrum. One was a major, the other a gunnery sergeant turned warrant officer. They helped shape our man's opinion "that former enlisted men as officers were superior to graduates of academies or colleges."

Meanwhile, after two months of basic training came two weeks on the rifle range, "where an instructor stood over every recruit with a swagger stick." If the recruit missed he got a hard rap on the head. For the Virginian, no raps.

"I don't know where," said his drill instructor, "but he learned it somewhere. He knows how."

Well, hunting back home in Virginia, of course.

In high school, he had also been a standout in track and basketball. He once scored five touchdowns for the school's newly formed football team despite his slight build, which was marked by a barrel-shaped chest that would provide a lifelong nickname well known today among all Marines.

The Virginian would make history.

History, especially Corps history and military history, was as important to the Marine Corps in those days as it is now. The Virginian wasn't really a great student, but he was well read. His teacher in school back home had once been displeased with his behavior and told him to take his books and go home for the day.

She meant his one or two textbooks.

So she was amazed when he opened his desk and took out two armloads of books!

Likewise, Drill Instructor DeSparre quizzed him on military history, and had to back off fast. "Hell, he gives me an inferiority complex," the DI reported to his sergeant, according to Davis. "I've read some, but that kid knows von Clausewitz backwards—and guys I've never heard of, by the dozen. He's some kid. This stuff is like a religion with him. He takes in all this stuff about the Huns [the German enemy of World War I] and their atrocities. He hates 'em like sin."

Meanwhile, the training at Parris Island proceeded. Use of the bayonet soon came up, on a field marked by big signs ordering: "ADVANCE TO KILL!"

The recruit from Virginia was too quick for his opponents and "invariably" bested them. It was thus no surprise that he would be among the five percent of his class chosen to go on to non-commissioned (non-com) officers' school and even to drill instructors' training, "under Captain Jimmy Wayt, a spectacularly profane and ungrammatical old Marine who taught minor tactics and steeped the recruits in the duties of guard troops, squad leaders, and sergeants."

Our man went through two months of intensive bayonet, rifle, boxing, judo, and infantry drill before news swept the camp that his battalion of former recruits indeed would be shipping off for France and service in the Great War "over there."

But first would come even more training in a section of the Marine Corps base in Quantico, Virginia, called "Château-Thierry." Here, the recruit and his companions trained over and over again in "miles of ditches," meant to replicate the infamous French war sector on the Western Front.

Then came word to pack up. They would travel to Hoboken, New Jersey, to ship out for France. Then came word to wait. Then came word of the Armistice that ended the Great War on the eleventh hour of the eleventh day of the eleventh month.

After all that, no combat for the young Virginian.

Others in his group were deployed to Santo Domingo to fight local rebels, but not our man. He was instead assigned to Officer Training School right there at Quantico, which meant many days that winter spent "in the wet, snow-filled pits of Château-Thierry learning the details of trench fighting."

Typically, he tended to look at the Quantico trenches "with an eye to how they might be flanked and their occupants defeated." Moreover, "His instructors found that when called upon in class he had ideas of his own, expressed them belligerently, and could not be influenced by rank or position."

By June of 1919, he had graduated from Officer Training and had earned his rank of Marine Reserve second lieutenant. He was now a Marine Corps officer!

Next came several days of machine-gun school and then…no, not another step in the career ladder, but rather, along with hundreds of others of his lowly officer rank, discharge from active Marine Corps service. Naturally, the end of the war brought about "a huge cut" of Marine Corps personnel. As a result, the Virginian was placed on inactive duty just ten days after earning his second lieutenant's bar.

What to do next? The answer that literally ignited twenty-one-year-old Chesty Puller's career as "most decorated Marine" came from Captain (and future General) William Rupertus, one of his instructors at Officer Training School. "If I were you," Rupertus said, "I'd go down to Haiti. You'll get a commission in the constabulary down there. They need men, and there's plenty of fighting. You'd see action and have some fun."

Just days later, future Lt. Gen. Lewis B. "Chesty" Puller was on his way to sign up with the *Gendarmerie d'Haiti*, the first stop on a storied career in the so-called "Banana Wars" of the 1920s and 1930s in the Caribbean and in Central America. Those sites in turn would only lead to a legendary career that took him through the island-hopping campaigns of the Pacific during World War II with Seventh Marines and then as commander of the First Marines. Further, he demonstrated heroic leadership in the Korean War again as commander of the First Marines.

As a result, this second cousin to George S. Patton (and, like Patton, a descendant of Confederate Civil War soldiers) would become the only Marine ever to win an unprecedented five Navy Crosses for heroism and gallantry in action…plus, often overlooked, a fully equivalent Distinguished Service Cross (DSC) awarded to him by the U.S. Army for his courageous service at the Chosin Reservoir in North Korea.

Among many other lesser decorations, he also earned an Army Silver Star at the Inchon, Korea, landing. In the end, he came away from his Marine Corps career leathery and wrinkled of face but still ramrod straight…and with a total of fourteen personal decorations earned in combat.

As a Marine officer or enlisted man (including his five years spent in Haiti with the *Gendarmerie*) for thirty-seven years, he won two of his Navy Crosses for heroism in Nicaragua, a third for his service at Guadalcanal, a fourth for the fighting at Camp Gloucester in the Pacific, and the fifth at the Chosin Reservoir.

As Burke Davis writes in his biography *Marine! The Life of Chesty Puller,* "His name was legend wherever Marines met in barracks and bar-rooms to swap tales, for no Marine had approached his twenty-seven years of foreign service or long exposure in combat, and no officer had become such a hero to men in the ranks."

Whenever Marines talked about legendary figures in the history of the Corps, "there were always dozens of stories to be told about Chesty Puller." Incredibly, added biographer Davis, "most of the tales were true."

A TRUCK NAMED "ELIZABERTH"

OUT OF THE THIRTY-SIX THOUSAND TO PERHAPS FORTY THOUSAND Ford-made Model T vehicles used by the Allies during World War I, exactly one was made available to the U.S. Marines deployed to France… and even that one was a donation from civilians to the Sixth Marines Regiment. Still, as a gift from three women (Mrs. Elizabeth Pearce, a Mrs. Charles Childs, and a Miss Willard—no first name available), that single Model T fast became a pet, a mascot, even a legend among the Marines fighting in France.

So writes Marine Corps Reference Historian Beth Crumley in a blog appearing January 31, 2012, on the *Huffington Post* website.

Henry Ford's Model T had made "a deep impression on officers of the

U.S. Army" after its use in the Mexican border troubles of 1916 and 1917. Meanwhile, the American Field Service, the all-volunteer organization that "provided motor ambulance service for the French Army," had decided in 1915 "to standardize on a light ambulance based on the Model T."

Later incorporated into the American Expeditionary Forces (AEF), the Field Service adopted the Ford motor for its standard ambulance and imported about twelve hundred Ford chassis as well. Even more Model Ts came along with the National Guard units fielded for the fighting in France after America entered World War I in April of 1917.

Meanwhile, the Marines were authorized "no vehicles prior to their departure to France." But, in the end, no great matter, it seems...they did have their one notable Model T, which supposedly was dubbed "The Elizabeth Ford," except that somehow, somewhere along the way, the spelling came out "Elizaberth."

Whatever it was named, the Model T belonging to the Sixth Marines soon built its reputation for reliability under fire. In a letter to Mrs. Childs, later reproduced in *Dear Folks at Home*, Marine Corps Maj. Frank E. Evans wrote that the regiment's one and only Model T "[would] go down in Marine Corps history."

The regiment's Model T, it seems, became a "hero" in connection with the Corps' historic participation in the Battle of Belleau Wood, which also incorporated the capture of the town Bouresches.

She had a "unique career," the major wrote. "Not only in Quantico [Virginia], where I drove her, but in Bordeaux, and later up in our training area, she carried everything from sick men to hardtack."

She and the regiment next spent two months in the trenches near Verdun, "and at the end of it, it seemed as though she would have to go to the scrap heap. Her top was entirely gone, and we made a mail wagon of her."

The major, it seems, just couldn't say enough about his regimental pet. "In some way the men, who have an affection for her that you can hardly comprehend, patched her together, and we brought her down to our rest billets."

But then, just a week later, they had to travel to another sector, about twenty-five miles north of Paris, "and in the long line of motor cars that made the trip, Elizaberth Ford sailed along without mishap and was the talk of the Division." But the real work was still to come, a moment when "she rose to the heights of her service and her record." A moment, too, when she became "our Joan of Arc."

That real drama came in the weeks-long campaign to dislodge four German divisions packed into the heavily forested, one-mile-square Belleau Wood close by the vital Metz-Paris Road. Here, the American Second Division struggled against the entrenched Germans from June 6 to July 1, 1918, before finally clearing them out.

In this first large-scale battle of World War I for the AEF, a Marine brigade under Army Gen. James Harbord and the Army's Third Infantry Brigade shared the burden of attack against the enemy.

On June 6 itself, "more Marines were killed or wounded on this single day than in the entire history of the Corps." Overall, the Battle of Belleau Wood cost the American Second Division 9,777 casualties, with 1,811 killed.

A little-known aspect of the battle is that the orders for the Americans were to seize both the woods and the railroad station at the nearby village of Bouresches. The Third Battalion of the Sixth Marines jumped off at 5:00 a.m. in two columns following the Lucy-Bouresches Road, until stopped less than four hours later by heavy artillery and machine-gun fire. The Marines' Ninety-Sixth Company, Second Battalion, was ordered into the fray with orders to break through and take Bouresches.

It took time and many casualties, but handfuls of Marines finally did reach the village. Lieutenant Clifton B. Cates (a future USMC commandant), briefly knocked unconscious by a machine-gun bullet that hit his helmet, organized remnants of the attacking force and began to clear the town of Germans. "Down to a handful of men, Cates managed to establish four [advantageous] positions…around the town." More Marines filtered in, despite the heavy machine-gun fire sweeping the area. In time, "sixty Marines would have to hold Bouresches."

Pinned down all night by artillery and machine-gun fire, they did receive rations and ammunition—thanks to "a Ford Model T driven by 2d Lt. William Moore and accompanied by none other than Sgt. Maj. John Quick, a Medal of Honor recipient in the Spanish-American War" (page 70). Both earned the Navy Cross for daring the German shelling and machine-gun barrages on the road from Lucy to Bouresches.

Later, in his letter to Mrs. Childs, Major Evans fleshed out details of the Model T's activities that night, saying the truck first was sent out with a load of ammunition. Later the same night, "we sent the Ford out with rations."

Not only that, but for the next five days "she made that trip night and day, and for one period ran almost every hour for thirty-six hours."

"She not only carried ammunition to the men who were less than two hundred yards from the Boches, but rations and pyrotechnics, and then, to the battalion on the left of the road, in those evil Belleau woods, she carried the same, and water, which was scarce there."

For those errands, he added, "she had to stop on the road and the stores were then carried by hand into a ravine."

Evans said he saw the Model T "just after her first trip" and counted twelve holes in her sides made by machine-gun rounds and shrapnel. In additional trips, the three privates driving her made stops for minor repairs and one time even had to change a blown-out tire. "How she and the men escaped being annihilated is a mystery," Evans commented.

Finally, on June 22, he wrote that before the battle of Belleau Wood was entirely over, he last saw the plucky Model T "resting against a stone wall in the little square of Lucy-le-Bocage, a shell-wrecked town, and she was the most battered object in the town."

One tire had been blown off and another wheel hit; the radiator was holed. In fact, "there were not less than forty hits on her." He said the Marines would cannibalize other cars if possible to restore her to driving condition again. In the meantime, the fact was that her service, "just when it was vital to get out to the fighting men [with] ammunition, food and water, can never be underestimated."

AVIATORS WITHOUT AIRPLANES

When the proud First Marine Aviation Force finally arrived in Brest, France, to join the fight against the hated Hun in 1918, they expected excitement, rejoicing, thanks. They arrived instead to a reception of total silence. "We arrived day before yesterday and found that no one here knew what we were, where we were to go, or what we were to do here," Marine Aviator No. 1 Alfred A. Cunningham reported back to his colleagues in Washington. "The trouble is that no one in Washington took interest enough in us to cable when we would arrive and what we were here for."

Then, too, no airplanes, much less any awaiting escort to their new home base in Northern France.

But where there's a will, there's often a way. In short order, the ever-resourceful Cunningham somehow secured a train "manned by Frenchmen, loaded it with the three squadrons, plus their equipment and some food and took off for Calais," noted Robert Sherrod in the May 1952 issue of the *Marine Corps Gazette.* "After three days and 400 miles the Marine entourage reached Calais. Squadrons A and B made their camp near Oyé, a town between Calais and Dunkerque [Dunkirk], Squadron C was assigned to Le Frêne, a small village about 10 miles northeast of Calais."

Then, it was sit and wait: "Despite elaborate production plans which called for 4,500 planes at the front by 30 June 1918, the American effort fell far short and caused Congressional and Presidential investigations."

The warplane assigned to the pioneer Marine outfit was the British-designed World War I De Havilland, or DH-4, often called a "flying coffin." The two-seater biplane quite normally had pilot and observer-gunner sitting front to back, but at first the main gas tank was placed between them, a potentially deadly problem corrected in the later-version DH-4B. However, as Sherrod adds, "Even worse was the overhead gravity feed, a 30-gallon tank whose contents a mild crack-up would spill onto the hot manifold pipes."

On a more positive note, "...the DH-4 could stay in the air about four hours, had a ceiling of 19,000 feet and a speed of about 124 miles per hour." It also "could climb to 10,000 feet in 14 minutes and could carry a load of about 1,200 pounds."

The first delivery of DH-4s for Cunningham and his fellow Marine pilots wouldn't come until September 23, 1918. The Army, by contrast with the Marines, had received its first American-built DH-4 as early as mid-May, but even that date had been scandalously delayed. When they did arrive in France, Sherrod writes, "the American-built planes required a major overhaul; their spruce wings were usually warped; 40 percent of the control wires were too short; the Liberty engines were carelessly or improperly assembled."

Thus, not only were the planes late reaching Army, Navy, and Marine units in France, but they needed "miracles of reconstruction and repair" performed by squadron mechanics to make them serviceable. This meant even more delay that "put a crimp in the whole World War I effort."

The situation provoked Assistant Navy Secretary Franklin D. Roosevelt, the future President, to note in August of 1918 "that no naval plane could operate offensively and only eight could take to the air."

Time was fleeting, of course, but no one in the summer of 1918 quite knew the war would be ending in November, only weeks away. In any case, the Marines naturally wanted to get into the fight.

Their waiting time wasn't a total waste, however. The pilots were given three combat missions, each with neighboring British squadrons also flying the DH-4. "This at least would introduce them to aerial combat."

Meanwhile, the American Marines had been designated the Marine Day Wing of the U.S. Navy's Northern Bomber Group. Finally, too, after the first DH-4 fighter-bomber's delivery on September 23, they began receiving more of their assigned aircraft. By October 16, the Day Wing boasted a total of seventeen planes on hand—but only eight of them were flyable, for various mechanical reasons.

Even so, they had already flown their first raid in force on October 14. Eight of the group's fighter-bombers had struck an enemy-held railway junction at Tielt, Belgium, dropping more than 2,200 pounds of bombs on it from 15,000 feet. From then on, with a fourth squadron now added to their complement, the Marine aviators spent the last weeks of the war raiding canals, rail lines, supply dumps, and airfields, usually operating in conjunction with the Royal Air Force's Fifth Group, notes Sherrod.

In early October, the Marines had also gone on a heroic "food run," a relief mission for a French regiment trapped behind German lines without food for several days. Three of the Marine DH-4s "were loaded with canned goods and bread and flown over four times at an altitude of 100 feet in the face of German heavy machine-gun, rifle, and artillery fire," writes Sherrod.

For their bravery, the three pilots were awarded the Distinguished Service Medal (DSM), while their observer-gunners won Navy Crosses. (In those days, the DSM ranked higher in the pantheon of U.S. military decorations than the Navy Cross.)

Another two of the Marine aviators were to earn the Medal of Honor before the Armistice of November 11 ended Marine Aviation's baptism of fire. One of them was Lt. Ralph Talbot, a daredevil who returned to the attack again and again when accosted by twelve German planes during the Day Wing's bombing raid of October 14. His observer, Captain Robert Guy Robinson, was wounded in the arm, stomach, and hip as Talbot pressed his attacks and shot down one of the enemy.

With his engine failing, Talbot then glided the plane homeward just fifty feet above the German trench lines and landed at an Allied hospital to get Robinson immediate medical aid. The gunner-observer's arm had been nearly shot away, but he survived.

They both earned the esteemed Medal for that action, but Talbot, fresh from studies at Yale University, had already shot down another German plane earlier in October. Taking to the air again on October 28, he unfortunately crashed on return to his home field into a pile of 1,500 newly delivered live bombs and was killed. His observer, Lt. Colgate W. Darden Jr., was thrown clear in the ensuing fire. He survived to become governor of Virginia during World War II and then president of the University of Virginia.

Remarkably, the bombs did not explode, thanks to the quick actions of 1st Sgt. John K. McGraw, who reacted as the fire spread to the wooden crates holding the bombs. He quickly pressed the nearest men into helping drag "the burning crates of bombs off the pile while other men rolled them in the mud until the fire was extinguished," says the citation for the Navy Cross he earned that day. McGraw's "presence of mind and courage undoubtedly prevented a serious explosion," the citation adds, "which would unquestionably have resulted in the destruction of the entire aerodrome and probable loss of life as well."

Another casualty of the war was popular squadron leader Maj. Douglas Roben, who was one of the three Marine officers and thirteen enlisted Marines who died as victims of the worldwide flu epidemic that struck toward the end of World War I.

In all, reports Sherrod, 282 officers and 2,180 enlisted men served in the newborn Marine Aviation ranks during World War I. Their figures are in sharp contrast to the overall Marine WWI participation of 31,315.

———

Additional Note: The famous First Five of Marine Aviation were Cunningham, Marine Aviator No. 1; Lt. Bernard L. Smith of Richmond, Virginia, Marine Aviator. No. 2, who first flew flying boats, then in WWI established the Navy's aerial gunnery school and in World War II "set up the Marine Corps Barrage Balloon Program"; Lt. W. M. McIlvain, Marine Aviator No. 3, who worked with Smith in seaplanes in "gathering data on spotting possibilities and on the ease with which a force attempting to land in small boats might be bombed from the air"; Capt. Francis T. Evans, Marine Aviator No. 4, who in 1917 stunned the nay-saying experts by flying a loop in his seaplane not once but twice, while also showing onlookers how to enter and then safely exit from a controlled spin in a float plane; and, finally, Lt. Roy Stanley Geiger, Marine Aviator No. 5, who would be not only an early Marine aviator but also a general in command of air *and* ground forces in key American Pacific island invasions of World War II.

WARTIME REUNION

As his regiment moved out, reports the weekly *Stars and Stripes* of June 14, 1918, the young Marine private thought his faithful companion Verdun Belle, and her two surviving little ones, were still with him. But she had disappeared in the grim mixing-bowl of French refugees pushing one way and troops in the other.

Her story would soon make the doughboys' weekly newspaper, although he would not—not by name, anyway.

Stars and Stripes staffer Alexander Woollcott, not yet the well-known author, actor, and literary critic he would become post-war, was brutally direct at the outset. He wrote: "This is the story of Verdun Belle, a trench dog who adopted a young leatherneck, of how she followed him to the edge of battle around Château-Thierry, and was waiting for him when they carried him out. It is a true story."

True or not, the story certainly had its dramatic ups and downs.

The unnamed Marine and his dog had met near infamous Verdun, as her full name would suggest. A setter, "shabby white with great splotches of chocolate brown on her coat," she had appeared out of nowhere, singled out her Marine Corps private and from then on stuck to him like glue. "She used to curl up at his feet when he slept, or follow silently to keep him company at the listening post," Woollcott reported. "War was no stranger to her at all." Indeed, as the shells flew overhead, they "only made her twitch and wrinkle her nose in her sleep."

Verdun Belle was so "trench-broken," she had learned to accept a specially cut-down and fitted gas mask—even to race for it at the first indication of gas rolling in. A skeptic at first, she had come to appreciate the contraption over her nose after she tried to claw it off one day, only to catch a whiff of the poison gas let loose by the German enemy.

Soon, she had surprised her young master with a brood of seven puppies, just about the time orders came down "to speed across France to stem the German tide north of the troubled Marne [River]."

Off they went on a forty-kilometer march, he weighted down with all his military gear, plus a market basket holding the seven pups, as she trotted along by his side.

Next, they endured a long advance by truck, during which "he yielded his place to the basket of wriggling pups, while he himself hung on the tailboard."

But their intertwined sagas sadden here.

As more marching loomed after the transport by truck, he simply could not carry all of her pups. He "solemnly" euthanized four of them, discarded the basket, "and slipped the other three into his shirt." Even so, a further one died, leaving Verdun with only two remaining pups.

Still, he and the trailing Verdun Belle then trudged on.

Around the Marines, streams of refugees flowed one way, while columns of troops pushed on in opposite direction. Forward they went, the Marine, his column, the surviving pups...but suddenly no Verdun Belle.

The chocolate-spotted setter was lost in the struggling tides of humanity. And the Marine had to go into battle very shortly. What could he do with the surviving pups?

Desperate, he turned to a passing ambulance attached to an American field hospital unit. He begged the medics to take the puppies, to take good care of them, too. And they tried, but it was hard to feed the unweaned pups.

Just in time came happy resolution. Verdun Belle, following another Marine outfit, arrived at the field hospital's bivouac site on a French farm, "stopped dead in her tracks, drew in her lolling tongue, sniffed inquiringly the evening air, and like a flash—a white streak along the drive—she raced to a distant tree where, on a pile of discarded dressings in the shade, the pups were sleeping."

Soon after, the hospital unit moved to the Chateau of the Guardian Angel, "which stands on the Paris-Metz road." And there the wounded from the battle of Château-Thierry arrived in ambulance after overloaded ambulance, and there too, there always was a faithful greeter...a greeter who "investigated each ambulance that turned in from the main road and backed up with its load of pain to the door of the receiving room."

Virtue sometimes is rewarded, along with devotion, love, and faith. How else could this true story end, but with the truly happy fact that one day *she* found *him*, and "the first consciousness he had of his new surroundings was the feel of her rough pink tongue licking the dust from his face," the surviving pups no doubt not far away.

ONE LAST RIVER CROSSING

ALLEGEDLY NAMED FOR A HORSE ON HIS FAMILY'S FARM IN OHIO, Marine Charley Dunbeck ran up a World War I record that *could* be summed up this way: Belleau Wood, shot in both legs; Saint-Étienne, near Mont Blanc Ridge, shot in the left temple.

As yet another injury to overcome, he was gassed somewhere along the way from his arrival in France in 1917 to crossing the Meuse River under fire just hours before the Armistice of November 11, 1918.

Or, by another set of parameters, his WWI record could be measured in hard-earned decorations that ranged from a Distinguished Service Cross and Navy Cross, to a pair of two Silver Stars, two Purple Hearts, two citations by the American Expeditionary Forces (AEF) in France, the French Croix de Guerre, and the French Fourragère.

Plus, he had been recommended for the even more rarified Medal of Honor for his gallantry at Belleau Wood.

Moreover, this little-known Marine Corps hero had begun military life in 1903 as a Marine private, and risen to first sergeant and then to Marine gunner as of June 5, 1917, but didn't stop there. In what had to have been a rapid series of promotions even for those "breakneck" World War I expansion days, wrote Maj. David N. Buckner, editor of the Maine Corps historical division's quarterly newsletter *Fortitudine* (Fall 1978), "he was commissioned a second lieutenant on 14 June

1917, promoted to first lieutenant the following day, and to captain the day after that."

As a company commanding officer assigned to the Fifth Marines, he arrived in France late that same June with the first troops of the still-mobilizing AEF. On June 11, 1918, "he led his company into Belleau Wood and was later cited in AEF general orders for 'extra-ordinary heroism and personal example set for men in the attack in the Bois de Belleau,'" writes Buckner.

Dunbeck "was recommended for the Medal of Honor by his regimental CO but the award somehow got downgraded to the Silver Star by higher headquarters."

Shot in both legs on June 12, he slowly recuperated and rejoined his men on July 24. For the next two months, his company, like John Quick's outfit (page 69), was based in the Marbache Sector near Pont-à-Mousson and then participated in the Saint-Mihiel offensive.

In early October, now coming under Marine Maj. Gen. John A. Lejeune's Second U.S. Division, the Fifth Marines took part in the campaign of Blanc Mont Ridge by taking the Germans' Essen Hook strong-point, then attacked the enemy at nearby Saint-Étienne. "During the attack, Capt. Dunbeck was felled by a gunshot wound in his left temple but refused evacuation until his XO [executive officer] could be briefed. A durable individual, he returned to his command 7 days later."

By the end of October 1918 he was his Second Battalion's senior surviving officer and thus its new commanding officer. With the arrival of November, the Marines drove toward the Meuse River in the last great Allied offensive of the war. As rumors of a possible armistice in the offing flew, then took concrete form, "The Allied command was especially keen on establishing a bridgehead across the [Meuse] river before the Armistice went into effect at 1100, 11 November," notes Buckner, as well.

"As the final guns sounded on that fateful day, Capt. Charley Dunbeck and his battalion were in place as the left half of the bridgehead."

But it had been no picnic getting there across two flimsy footbridges quickly thrown together by military engineers. They had to be crossed on foot during a foggy, inky-black night. And those few men still crossing in the morning often faced a cold rain that sometimes was sleet. And all the time under German artillery and machine-gun fire.

U.S. Army or Marine, men died during these final hours of the war with the negotiated armistice pending—and a storm of controversy quickly burst out back home in the United States. Critics said lives had been lost unnecessarily, while others argued it had been necessary to press the German enemy to the very end in order to achieve an acceptable armistice.

Meanwhile, Dunbeck and his battalion had gone across the river on their rickety footbridge—planks set on pontoons—during the night. When one of his officers fell off into the icy river waters, he shouted, "Save me, captain, I can't swim."

According to an article in the Spring 1994 issue of *Fortitudine* by Marine Corps History Director Brig. Gen. Edwin H. Simmons, "Dunbeck pulled the floundering officer to his feet and told him to wade, the water [at that point] was only waist deep… Dunbeck was soaked to the skin and it would be hours before he could get a fire going to dry out."

Dunbeck's Marines and others who had survived the river crossing, with him or at other points, did not receive final orders to stand down until the morning of November 11, and not before 11:00 a.m.

In fact, it apparently was not until 8:45 a.m. that General Lejeune's own headquarters received confirmation of the pending cease-fire. "Lejeune repeated the order to his brigade commanders," notes the Simmons account. Lejeune specifically ordered the same information sent quickly to Dunbeck and a fellow battalion commander also stranded on the German side of the river.

That very night, Simmons reports, Lejeune wrote to his wife, "Last night we fought our last battle… To me it was pitiful for men to go to their death on the evening of peace."

ADDITIONAL NOTE: AFTER A POST-ARMISTICE STINT IN GERMANY with the Army of Occupation, Dunbeck returned home to the United States and was medically retired in 1921 due to an apparent "heart ailment caused by wartime gassing," writes Buckner in the 1978 *Fortitudine*. In 1939, on the eve of World War II, he returned to active duty in command of the Marine Barracks at Hawthorne, Nevada. After added duty at Marine Corps headquarters in Washington, now promoted to lieutenant colonel, he was appointed in 1942 as CO of the Marine Guard Battalion for the Navy Department in Washington, the unit "charged with the physical security of all the Department's facilities in the Washington area."

During that period in 1942, "One of Col. Dunbeck's proudest moments came when he acted as one of General Lejeune's pallbearers at Arlington [National Cemetery]. He had been specifically chosen by Lejeune, a man he idolized."

Dunbeck held his Marine Guard Battalion command through the rest of the World War II period into 1946, before retiring again. "Four years later, with the outbreak of the Korean War, the sixty-five-year-old Devil Dog [the German nickname for the Marines they encountered at Belleau Wood] again offered his services to the Marine Corps. That war, however, we were to fight without his assistance."

Dunbeck died of natural causes in 1978, almost sixty years after he was retired "with a bad heart."

SELECT UNIT HISTORIES
FIRST MARINE DIVISION

Many times called the oldest and "most decorated" division in Marine history, and the granddaddy of all modern Marine units, the First Division came to life with its activation on February 1, 1941, on board the battleship *Texas*, just months before Pearl Harbor.

Even so, some of its regiments had already been well established, and well known, for years beforehand.

For instance, the division's First Regiment was formed at Guantanamo Bay, Cuba, in 1911. Its Fifth Marine Regiment was created in 1914 at Veracruz, Mexico. Its Seventh Marines was activated in 1917, only to be disbanded after World War I, then reactivated in 1941 just months before Pearl Harbor and the Japanese invasion of the Philippines.

In addition, as the regiments came and went before the Marines had a division all their own, the year 1918 saw the formation of the Eleventh Marines at Quantico, Virginia, as a light artillery unit that was then deployed to France. Once in France, however, the regiment was employed as an infantry outfit instead of artillery. During World War I, of course, the Marines of various regiments famously fought in the great battles of Belleau Wood, Château-Thierry and Saint-Mihiel, often alongside their U.S. Army comrades-in-arms, among others.

Between the Great War in Europe and World War II, the Eleventh Marines was decommissioned but twice reactivated for brief duties, such as serving in Nicaragua as infantry. Formed again as an artillery unit in 1940, the Eleventh Marines then became a part of the newly created First Division just in time for World War II.

The newly formed First Division first saw combat in the hellish, six-month "mini war" of Guadalcanal, during which it earned the first of its three Presidential Unit Citations of WWII. Then it joined in the "island-hopping" Pacific campaign that followed its success against the Japanese at Guadalcanal. The division was also noted for its amphibious landing assaults on Peleliu and Okinawa against fanatical, suicide-bent Japanese defenders.

Following the war came a relatively quiet period of occupation duty for the Division in North China, but a period still marked by the turbulence of civil war between Communist and Nationalist Chinese forces.

But soon after, with the invasion of South Korea by the Communist North, came a sudden, frantic rebirth of the division's many fighting elements that had been disbanded after WWII. As events rapidly unfolded, elements of the First Marine Division were rushed into the battle to hold the Pusan Perimeter at bottom of the Korean "thumb," before being thrown into the famously successful amphibious landing by American-led United Nations forces at Inchon, halfway up the western coast of the Korean peninsula. This fray led to the Division's role as part of the UN's X Corps as it charged up the east side of the Korean peninsula almost as far as the border of Red China.

The Division's own website says the Chinese Communists "suffered more than 37,500 casualties trying to stop the Marines' march out of the 'Frozen Chosin'" as the Division conducted a fighting withdrawal from the Chosin mountains and plateau in North Korea.

Calling itself the "Old Breed," the Division furnished standby Marines for possible action during the Cuban Missile Crisis of 1962. But its next real combat came in Vietnam, where the entire Division had been deployed by June of 1966. In its first three years there, the Division conducted forty-four named and unnamed operations. "It successfully beat back and decimated every enemy assault in its area of operations, pursuing the enemy into his sanctuaries."

Moving on to Middle Eastern battles with an entirely fresh generation populating its ranks, the Division in 1990 "formed the core of the force sent to Southwest Asia in response to Iraq's invasion of Kuwait." In early 1991, the First and Second Marine divisions fought side by side in the hundred-hour Operation Desert Storm, ousting the Iraq forces as the First Marine Expeditionary Force. The First Division led the breakthrough to Kuwait City.

Then taking a leading role in disaster and famine relief operations in Bangladesh, the Philippines, and Somalia, the Division returned to combat again in the war against Iraq in 2003. Here, allied with the British and the Third U.S. Army Infantry Division troops, the Marines (led by President Donald Trump's defense secretary James "Mad Dog" Mattis) and sailors conducted the deepest penetrating ground operation in Marine Corps history.

Not only joining in the seizure of Baghdad, Division elements captured Iraqi leader Saddam Hussein's hometown of Tikrit before fighting insurgents in Anbar Province and taking part in the liberation of Fallujah.

Elements of the Division also fought in Afghanistan on and off after 2006. Deploying to Helmand Province in force in 2010, "the Division served as the ground combat element for Task Force Leatherneck, leading a multinational coalition working alongside Afghan National Security Forces…[in] large-scale offensives throughout Helmand Province, including Sangin and Musa Oal'eh districts." In 2012, as leading element of Task Force Leatherneck, the Division focused primarily on training and advising Afghans to take over security and stability operations.

SELECT PERSONALITY
DAN DALY

Retired from active duty and then the Fleet Marine Corps Reserve, Dan Daly spent a good part of the Depression years working as a bank guard on Wall Street, not too far from his original home of Glen Cove on Long Island.

A single man all his life, he once opined: "I don't see how a single man could spend his time to better advantage than in the Marines." He himself joined the Marines in 1899 with the hope of fighting in the Spanish-American War; he was not officially retired until 1929, serving thirty years in all.

He was too late for combat in that war, and his wasn't the longest serving record of all time by any means, but still Sgt. Maj. Daniel "Dan" Joseph Daly was one unique Marine—"the outstanding Marine of all time," Commandant John A. Lejeune once called him.

And to Maj. Gen. Smedley Butler, Dan Daly, only five-foot-six in his stocking feet, was "the fightingest Marine I ever knew."

No Marine alive today fails to know why Dan Daly was so venerated: Other than his admirer Smedley Butler, Daly was the only Marine to win two Medals of Honor. One came for his heroic actions during the Boxer Rebellion and the other for action in Haiti.

Both honors are well known, but not so well known is his series of actions at Belleau Wood, France, during World War I, that for many another man quite possibly would have qualified for the same great distinction.

For Dan Daly, the first Medal of Honor came after he was carried to northeastern China's Taku Bay in May 1900 aboard the USS *Newark* and was marched with other Marines to the defense of the Legation Quarter in the Chinese capital of Peking when it came under siege by rebellious Chinese Boxers. As the siege wore on for the foreigners trapped in the diplomatic enclave, Daly and his fellow Marines often stood duty on the neighboring Tartar Wall, despite intense enemy fire and outright attacks.

On the night of August 14, 1900, Daly was alone on the wall for a period of time while his commanding officer, Marine Capt. Newt Hall, went to round up reinforcements. Daly was left with only his rifle and bayonet to defend himself and his position while under repeated sniper fire. When the Chinese stormed his position, he fought them off alone until Hall and the reinforcements came to his aid.

Fifteen years later, by now a gunnery sergeant instead of a private, he earned a second Medal of Honor for fighting rebels (*cacos*) in Haiti. This time, Daly was one of forty mounted Marines led on a deep reconnaissance patrol by the same Smedley Butler, now a major, in the mountains of northern Haiti on October 24, 1915.

Ambushed in the dark of night at a river crossing in a ravine, the Marines rallied at a defensive position a mile away after losing twelve of their horses. They had also lost their only machine gun at the river. That was a crucial item for the besieged patrol—but how to retrieve it?

"Fighting Dan" Daly had the answer. "Daly stole back on his own and, under fire, recovered the gun from the back of a dead horse," writes J. Robert Moskin in his history of the Marines. The next morning Sergeant Daly led one of three Marine squads that moved out and scattered the attacking *cacos*.

For his work that night and early morning, Daly, plus the leaders of the remaining two squads, Capt. William P. Upshur and 1st Lt. Edward A. Ostermann, all received the Medal of Honor, Daly for the rare second time.

On a related point, it was during the same Haitian campaign in the fall of 1915 that Smedley Butler won the second of *his* two Medals of Honor. The first had come for his gallantry at Veracruz, Mexico, the year before. Now, in November of 1915, he was with a force of Marines that surprised a band of *cacos* holed up in an old French masonry fort. One company of Marines taking part in the attack on the old fort reached a tunnel-like opening in the masonry wall, so narrow it could only accommodate one man at a time.

Undeterred, Sergeant Ross L. Iams, plus Butler's orderly, Pvt. Samuel Gross (real name Samuel Marguiles, says Moskin) and then Butler himself all squirmed through as the first three in, followed by others. They found themselves in "a wild, hand-to-hand struggle...with rifles, bayonets, machetes, clubs, and rocks," writes Moskin. "In 15 minutes, more than 50 *cacos* were killed. Butler blew up the fort. Iams, Gross, and Butler received the Medal of Honor."

Daly was a newsboy early in life, and etched out a career that would have been fulfilling for any career Marine even without his all-but-unique two Medals of Honor. He served sea duty aboard the Navy ships *Newark, Panther, Cleveland, Marietta, Mississippi, Ohio,* and *Machias*; he served in combat in China, Haiti, and France; other service took him to Panama, Cuba, Mexico, and Puerto Rico, and he served at eight duty posts in the United States.

He was "a fine military figure, erect and well-proportioned" despite his small size," says Moskin also. "A 'natural' for publicity, he disdained it and disliked all the fuss made over him. He termed medals 'a lot of foolishness.'"

Among his pleasures, he favored a pipe "crammed with cut plug tobacco." He did not drink; he was a "strict disciplinarian, yet fair-minded and very popular among both officers and enlisted men." He could be recklessly daring, but he was always attentive to the needs of his men. "Offered a commission on several occasions, he is said to have declined on the grounds that he would rather be 'an outstanding sergeant than just another officer.'"

He is well-remembered for his battle cry during the bloody World War I fight to oust the Germans from Belleau Wood in France in June of 1918. The Marines had taken "a terrific pounding" on the outskirts of Lucy-le-Bocage on the edge of the woods. "They were outnumbered, outgunned, and pinned down" when their first sergeant, Dan Daly, ordered an attack, leaped forward, and shouted, "Come on, you sons of bitches, do you want to live forever?"

It was here, you could argue, that Dan Daly once again went beyond the call of duty as he risked his life putting out a fire in an ammunition dump. He also visited a string of his own machine-gun crews to cheer and encourage his men while their sector was under especially heavy bombardment. Further, in heroic storybook fashion, he did not leave the legendary Belleau Wood before attacking a German machine-gun nest single-handedly with hand grenades and his automatic pistol—and capturing it. That was on June 10, 1918, and on that same day he found time to help recover wounded men from the heavily fought-over village of Bouresches.

Also a veteran of the earlier fighting in the Toulon Sector of France, Daly moved on from Belleau Wood to take part in the Allied Saint-Mihiel and Champagne Offensives. Wounded once in June, he was also twice wounded in October during the latter campaign.

World War I would be his last combat service. For his service overall, he not only won his two Medals of Honor, but also the Navy Cross, the Distinguished Service Cross, and the Croix de Guerre, plus many lesser awards and campaign medals for the China Relief Expedition, the Philippines Campaign, Mexico, the Haitian Campaign, and World War I.

The armistice ending World War I came on the eleventh of November in 1918, as is well known. Somewhat coincidentally, one might say, Daly was born on another November 11, but in 1873. He died in April 1937, at the age of 63—with "his record as a fighting man…unequalled in the annals of Marine Corps history," notes his official online bio.

AVIATION RECORD-HOLDER

IN HOW MANY NON-AMERICAN WARS CAN A SINGLE MARINE FIGHT? First Sgt. Peter P. Tolusciak made it two: two *Polish* wars between two world wars, although he wasn't then a Marine—and he wasn't even born in Poland. He was a native of Pittsburgh, Pennsylvania.

Tolusciak was attending the prep school for Duquesne University when, at age sixteen, his parents gave him permission to join the Polish "Blue Army," formed in France toward the end of World War I in support of the Triple Entente, notes Marine Corps Historian Annette Amerman in the 2010 issue of the history division's *Fortitudine* newsletter. "After the war ended," his units "were transferred to Poland, where they took part in the Polish-Ukrainian War and the Polish-Bolshevik War."

After more than one hundred years of domination by Germany, Russia, and Austria, the immediate postwar period was a turbulent one for a re-emerging Poland. As it sought to re-establish itself as an independent nation, both Soviets and Ukrainians resisted. After all, the Poles "were eager to reclaim all the land that had been lost, and more, if possible."

As a young Polish-American, Tolusciak was fully sympathetic with Poland's best hopes and willing to join the fight for their achievement. At war's end, he opted to remain in Europe and enter the fledgling Polish Air Force. Trained in France in 1919, he then began training aspiring Polish military aviators himself.

Next assigned to a tactical aviation unit based at Krakow and flying the French-made Brequet, XIV (A2), he bucked orders calling for the discharge of Americans serving in his new unit. Two fellow Americans did leave, but Tolusciak begged to stay on.

"I cannot go home at this moment, when the Motherland is being threatened," he wrote to his squadron CO, Capt. Franciszek Rudnicki. "I came to defend the Motherland, and will carry out my task and the order given to me by my parents."

And defend he did, with permission granted by no less than the chief of the Polish Air Force. In no time Sergeant Tolusciak and Sub-Lt. Lucjusz Moszczynski were leading the squadron's first combat mission, in support of the Thirteenth Infantry Division.

But they faced a few drawbacks, answered by a few creative solutions.

"Due to the lack of ammunition—particularly bombs—the squadron could not operate fully against the enemy," writes Amerman. "To compensate, the squadron began adding wooden fins to artillery shells and found that the makeshift bombs worked quite well."

Indeed, in Polish attacks on Bolshevik lines near Czudow on April 19, 1920, "seven bombs were dropped, destroying three railway cars and damaging a platform and steam locomotive."

From then to June 10, Tolusciak flew in another fourteen combat missions of bombing, strafing, and reconnaissance. Meanwhile, with the squadron ordered to move on from its latest base near Kiev, the young Polish-American volunteered to stay behind on the ground to help explode leftover bombs and destroy the hangars. "He and eight other soldiers carried out the task during the night; they burned the hangars, filled the cistern with gasoline, and exploded two train-wagon's worth of bombs."

Perhaps a bit more than they expected, the explosion that followed came close to destroying an entire train, "as well as a bridge that was above the railway."

Meanwhile, Tolusciak and his cohorts still had to catch up with their aviation outfit, but without the luxury of transport by air. "In the two weeks it took to catch up with the squadron, the group gathered more than 100 stragglers and others who had been left behind, with Tolusciak leading the cobbled-together army by his aerial map."

Reunited with his old outfit, Tolusciak discovered it didn't have an operational airplane for him to fly, so he transferred into a sister organization, the Third Squadron. There, newcomer Tolusciak "continued his admirable flying—often volunteering for the most dangerous assignments and returning [with] the aircraft nearly shot out from under him."

He survived a crash-landing in a shot-up plane in late July, but continued flying dangerous combat missions through the rest of the summer and much of the fall. He was awarded Poland's highest military decoration, the Order of Virtuti Militari, for his actions in April through June, with a second "Virtuti" to be recommended at later date, quite possibly making him the only Marine to have been nominated twice and awarded once with Poland's highest military decoration.

And he wasn't even a Marine yet!

Sailing for home in January 1921, he boarded the ship alone, without the young woman he had married in Poland just three days before—explanations unknown.

He at least did have the company of "a large number of Polish-Americans who had fought in World War I and in the Polish-Bolshevik War." However, few (if any) could have matched his record. He had taken part in "nearly 40 separate actions in Poland, accumulated more than 208 hours in the air, was twice recommended for Poland's highest military decoration, and was barely 19 years old."

It was hardly a year later that he joined the Marine Corps and graduated from basic training at Parris Island, just in time to join two thousand Marines in a realistic reenactment of Pickett's Charge at Gettysburg. But aviation was in his blood, and soon enough he was a member of the Marines' VO Squadron 2 out of Port-au-Prince, Haiti, though not yet as a pilot himself.

With no major war coming for almost another two decades, he might have been kept busy by the intermittent "Banana Wars" of the Caribbean basin that resulted in Marine Corps intercession from time to time.

As fate would have it, the previously obscure Tolusciak would make *his* contribution to Marine Corps history when tapped to take part with three other Marines—1st Lt. Ford O. Rogers, 2nd Lt. Horace D. Palmer, and 1st Sgt. Benjamin F. Belcher—in attempting to fly the longest airplane flight in the history of American aviation.

As explained by USMC historian Amerman: "The pair of pilots and their mechanics/relief pilots flew from Santo Domingo City, Dominican Republic, to San Francisco and back over a three-month, 10,953-mile journey that began simply as a flight to St. Louis, Missouri, in order to observe the Pulitzer Air Races. The Marines quickly drew attention and turned their journey into a contest to complete the longest flight in American history."

Given brand-new, two-seater DH-4B aircrafts, the four fliers took off from Santo Domingo City in September 1923 for Port-au-Prince as the first leg of their long journey to San Francisco. On just the second day of their flight, however, they ran into the first of many obstacles—due to heavy rains slowing his takeoff at Guantanamo Bay, Palmer's right wing-tip snagged a small tree just as he lifted off for the team's planned hop to Havana, but he flew on anyway.

At Havana, they found that leading-edge ribs of the wing were smashed, fabric was torn…and Palmer had flown the hop across Cuba with a three-foot, inch-thick branch hanging off the end of the wing.

After Tolusciak and Belcher made necessary repairs, on they all flew into the Continental United States, on to St. Louis, on to San Francisco via Texas and Arizona, before proceeding on to Reno, Nevada.

By now it was late October. The weather in California had been warm, "so we did not think to provide ourselves with gloves or even sweaters," Rogers reported. "[We] soon found our mistakes. Crossed the 'hump' [the Rocky Mountains] at 12,000 feet and discovered what Arctic exploration in an undershirt is like."

For the next five days, the fliers fought their way eastward through sleet, snow, fog, winds, and clouds to Salt Lake City, to Cheyenne, Wyoming…then the weather began to clear.

Now following their earlier path in reverse, they alighted on October 31 at old McCook Field, Dayton, Ohio, today a part of Wright-Patterson Air Force Base, where an inspection showed that their planes remained in excellent mechanical shape. Still needing "engine work," however, they laid over for three weeks, then headed south and east.

After the group split up—briefly, they thought—Rogers landed in South Carolina while Palmer and Tolusciak plowed on for Miami.

But when Rogers reached Miami himself, no Palmer!

Then, a telegram: Running low on fuel, Palmer and Tolusciak had "made a quick landing on the Palm Beach Country Club Golf Course and in so doing had badly damaged [their] plane."

Despite a bent axle, they made it to Miami the next day, December 3. There, they straightened the axle by "putting an auto chain jack under the center of the bend and standing three men on each wheel while the jack was being taken up."

Thus was the historic flight able to resume and come to a triumphant end on December 9, 1923, after the final hops in reverse to Havana, Guantanamo Bay, Port-au-Prince, and finally Santo Domingo City. There, they were welcomed with great public fanfare and congratulatory messages from Maj. Gen. Commandant John A. Lejeune, among others of note.

By year's end, Tolusciak was appointed a naval aviation pilot; he soon would be promoted from sergeant to first sergeant as well. Still based in Haiti, he survived the crash of a plane that caught fire in the air on February 4, 1924, when a hose from the fuel tank to the carburetor broke, and the spilled gasoline was ignited by the hot exhaust pipe.

Just weeks later, he ran another aircraft into a group of small trees and a hut while taxiing, with minor damage ensuing. Meanwhile, he had heard his wife back in Poland wanted a divorce and was heartbroken at the news. A final denouement in his now deeply saddening story came on December 12, 1925.

Testing the engine of a newly repaired DH-4B together with Gunnery Sgt. Merle V. Slocum at an altitude of 150 feet, Tolusciak was suddenly presented with a seized-up engine. He tried to return to his airfield "by attempting a 'side-slip' landing, but the maneuver failed, and the airplane burst into flames upon impact. Both Marines were killed instantly."

PEARL HARBOR PREDICTION

FOR THE MARINES, THE JAPANESE ATTACK ON PEARL HARBOR actually began at the Ewa Mooring Mast Field just four miles west of the naval base itself. The raiding Japanese aircraft shot up the Marine air facility and all forty-seven warplanes parked wing to wing on the runway *before* hitting the Navy ships at Pearl itself.

Then, they swept back and struck at Ewa Field again.

Looking down from his Zero fighter above, Japanese Lt. Yoshio Shiga saw a lone Marine standing by his disabled plane and dived at him, "all guns blazing," reported Walter Lord in *Day of Infamy,* his blow-by-blow account of the sneak attack on the U.S. Pacific Fleet headquarters in Hawaii, on December 7, 1941.

"The man refused to budge," said Zero pilot Shiga later. The Marine was firing back at the onrushing airplane with nothing but a pistol.

"Shiga still considers him the bravest American he ever met."

Taken totally by surprise, the Marines at Ewa lost all their own fighter planes because they had been purposefully parked close together to prevent sabotage by infiltrators on the ground. Likewise for the Navy and Army personnel over at Pearl Harbor that same Sunday morning. All were totally surprised and unprepared to fight back.

The result was more than 2,400 U.S. servicemen killed, seven out of the eight battleships in port sunk or heavily damaged, among a total of seventy-odd naval vessels struck. Scores of aircraft also caught close together on airfields surrounding the naval moorings were destroyed, along with Army, Navy, and Marine barracks, ammunition stores, or supply facilities.

The only saving grace was the absence of the American aircraft carriers, safely out at sea at the time, one of them having just delivered twelve Grumman F4F Wildcats to isolated Wake Island two thousand miles to the west of Hawaii (page 131).

The news flash behind the well-known Pearl Harbor story is that so much of the same scenario, and the nation's step-by-step response to it, had been predicted by a lone wolf, alcoholic Marine Corps officer Lt. Col. Earl "Pete" Ellis, a good *twenty years beforehand.*

Or, as once summed up by Lt Col. P. N. Pierce in *Leatherneck* magazine (February 1962): "Twenty years before Pearl Harbor, the Marine officer who predicted the attack disappeared mysteriously, somewhere in the 'forbidden islands' of the Pacific. Behind him he left one of the most amazing documents ever written—a secret study which forecast the events of World War II, still two decades in the future."

To which Marine Corps combat veteran, savant, and innovator Victor

Krulak added in his highly regarded book *First to Fight: An Inside View of the U.S. Marine Corps*: "As early as 1912, still a lieutenant, he [Ellis] began a messianic exploration of the strategic confrontation between the United States and Japan, with whom he was convinced we would eventually go to war."

Moreover, said Krulak: "He predicted that the Japanese would initiate hostilities and that the United States would have to fight its way back across the Pacific in a series of hard amphibious assaults to capture the necessary bases. In some cases, the amphibious attacks of 1942–45 took place exactly as he had presaged."

Ellis, seen as brilliant and a loner from the start, "served in France [during World War I] as a staff officer, and [for] the five years thereafter, he inspired great confidence on the part of his superiors."

But he also was seen as "a gravely flawed personality."

General Krulak, himself a Marine battalion leader in the island-hopping Pacific campaigns of World War II, minced no words in his assessment of the mystery man who predicted that very same strategy for defeating Japan. "He was moody, often contentious, and impatient with slow thinkers. He had a firecracker temper. He sometimes disappeared for days without explanation."

Probably worst of all: "And he drank. He drank a great deal—more and more as years passed. His alcoholism caused him to move in and out of hospitals continually, usually receiving such euphemistic diagnoses as 'nephritis,' 'neurasthenia,' 'psychasthenia,' and 'exhaustion.'"

How could he get away with such behavior? Said Krulak: "His superiors, including the ascetic General Lejeune [John A., commandant, 1920–1929], always protected him because of his sheer ability and his total loyalty to the Corps."

Before disappearing in Japanese-controlled Micronesia in 1923, apparently on an intelligence-gathering mission of his own or perhaps even of Lejeune's making, Ellis left behind "a precious legacy"—an "extraordinary thirty-thousand-word study entitled *Advanced Base Operations in Micronesia*."

Basically, here was the American strategy for a Pacific war with Japan, the very framework of the so-called "Orange Plan" adopted by the Joint Board of the Army and Navy in 1924.

"Written in 1920–21, and based on lectures he had prepared in 1916, it was less a true study than a portrait of the future—the fruit of an incredible prescience." In his "uncanny forecast of things to come," Ellis had outlined "the step-by-step drive westward across the Pacific to meet the need, as he saw it, for 'bases to support the Fleet, both during its projection and afterward.'"

He traced the American route through the Marshall and Caroline islands "much as it actually happened." Going beyond strategy, Ellis even discussed "the full range of tactical, technical, and practical problems that would ultimately confront our forces as they drove across the Pacific from island to island."

He warned of the problems that could be caused by reefs and man-made obstacles. He foresaw the need for coordinated naval gunfire and air support; the logistics of combat loading of equipment and supplies; the need for specially designed transport ships; the organization of newly taken beachheads; the use of underwater demolition teams or "frogmen"; the tactical use of smoke and darkness; and the usefulness of "reconnaissance, raids, and feints."

Coincidently or not, Krulak himself led his own Marine parachutist battalion in a fake attack on a small and obscure Japanese-held island to distract the Japanese from U.S. preparations for the very real invasion of Bougainville (page 154).

Ellis, unfortunately, never lived to see his predictions so closely borne out in the 1940s. Visiting Japan itself before he disappeared in Micronesia, he was last reported to have been seen alive, but very ill, in Koror in the Japanese-controlled Palaus, in 1923.

Rumors as to the circumstances of his death flew for years, even including the possibility of murder by the Japanese in their zeal to hide their preparations for war in that part of the Pacific. But Krulak offered a different tack. "The bottle finally killed him, at Koror..." he wrote, "during a secret reconnaissance of Micronesia, the area where he was convinced critical battles would be fought in the war with Japan."

A finishing news flash here from Krulak: "What he learned in his extensive explorations of the southern islands was not that the Japanese had fortified the area, as was suspected, but that they had done very little—at that time—in the way of fortification, and it was their weakness they were striving to keep secret, not evidences of strength."

MARINE CORPS WOMEN IN WORLD WAR II

By Ingrid Smyer

HOLLYWOOD IN ITS GOLDEN DAYS SHOULD HAVE WRITTEN THIS story. A success story, without a doubt, for it had everything a dramatic, colorful movie should: brave, bright-eyed uniformed women not only marching in parades, but proving over and over again their intelligence, their strength, and yes, their *power* as they did their part and more for the war effort in World War II.

Don't forget that some twenty years beforehand during World War I, it had taken only 305 "Marinettes" to win acclaim for freeing up just a relative handful of men from their desks and typewriters at Marine Corps Headquarters to go "over there."

So now, by contrast, nearly twenty thousand women Marines were in actual service…and in many jobs beyond clerical or administrative desk work.

However, bringing the women on board was not necessarily a popular idea at the higher levels of the Marine Corps hierarchy for a while, not even as late as the fall of 1942.

Faced with high war losses suffered during the campaign for Guadalcanal—and the potential of even more losses in upcoming

117

operations—a fast-mounting need for manpower was more than merely apparent, it was critical.

How to fill the need for manpower? With womanpower, of course.

On October 12, 1942, the news came up under inauspicious circumstance at a bon-voyage dinner party given for Col. William A. Eddy, and the commandant's son, Marine Lt. Franklin Holcomb. The dinner in the Commandant Thomas Holcomb's Quarters that evening caused quite a bit of excitement in more ways than one.

It seems the portrait of early Commandant Archibald Henderson, the longest serving commandant of all time, had been hanging over the buffet at the commandant's quarters without incident for many years. Someone asked, "General Holcomb, what do you think about having women in the Marine Corps?"

Before Holcomb could reply, the painting of Commandant Archibald Henderson fell from the wall to the buffet below with a startling crash.

One can imagine the moment of stunned silence that must have followed!

Was this just another Marine Corps "sea story," or legend? Perhaps not, since Colonel Eddy's onlooking child Mary, would later verify the story.

In any case, what the commandant in the portrait would have answered is beyond imagining, since a question of this nature would have been unthinkable back in his day.

The crashed painting was just a coincidence, wasn't it?

It was well-known that General Holcomb was strongly opposed to having women relieve Marines—men, of course—for combat duty. He, along with many other Marines, was not happy at the prospect. But he had run out of options—women in the Marines it would be!

Having women in power was not a new idea. It was unpopular with many military men, but not among the women who were already serving with the Army, in the Navy, and in the Coast Guard, all as volunteers.

In the years between World War I and World II, a range of military and congressional leaders had publicly, if only from time to time, thought out loud about the feasibility of a women's adjunct in the Marine Corps.

They were prodded by leaders such as Army Chief of Staff Gen. George C. Marshall and Congresswoman Edith Nourse Rogers. Rogers, who had been a Red Cross volunteer in France in 1917, discovered that women who had been wounded and disabled during that war were not entitled to health care or veterans' benefits. She worked diligently to provide such benefits for future servicewomen. In addition, by May 1941 she had introduced H.R. 4906, the bill establishing the Women's Army Auxiliary Corps (WAAC).

Though soon a reality, the auxiliary corps turned out to have been doomed from the start. The women who aspired to join up found that, since it was only an auxiliary organization, they were neither fish nor fowl—that is, they were neither in the Army nor of the Army.

Fortunately, the WAAC would be reorganized and converted to full military status as the Women's Army Corps (WAC) in the late summer of 1943.

With the proponents rectifying mistakes encountered in the formation of earlier women's military organizations, and with the support of First Lady Eleanor Roosevelt, the "Navy bill," Public Law 289, was signed on July 30, 1942. The bill established the Navy Women's Reserve (WAVES), and the same congressional edict authorized a Marine Corps Women's Reserve (MCWR).

In the meantime, the Coast Guard also was authorized a women's reserve, the SPARS.

As President Franklin D. Roosevelt, yielding to pressure from the Congress and the Secretary of Navy Frank Knox, signed the legislative measures into law on November 7, 1942, the matter was settled for the Marine Corps at last.

On November 5, Commandant Gen. Holcomb wrote to the commanding officers of all Marine posts and procurement districts to prepare them for the forthcoming MCWR and to ask for their best estimates of the number of Women Reservists ("WRs," as they came to be called) they would need to replace their enlisted men and male officers. As an early goal, the Corps hoped to take in five hundred women officers and six thousand enlisted women, then shoot for a total of one thousand officers and eighteen thousand enlisted women by June of 1944.

The public, excited about the news of women in the Marine Corps, expected a catchy name similar to those of the other women's additions to the military: WACS, WAVES, and SPARS. Marine Headquarters was bombarded with suggestions for charming and cute nicknames, among them: MARS, Femarines, WAMS, Dainty Devil-Dogs, Glamarines, and even Sub-Marines.

General Holcomb adamantly ruled out cute names—somewhat later, in March 1944, according to the Marine Corps historical monograph *Free a Marine to Fight: Women Marines in World War II*. In that publication by Colonel Mary V. Stremlow, USMCR (Ret.), he was quoted in an article for *Life* magazine as saying flat out: "They are Marines. They don't have a nickname and they don't need one. They get their training in a Marine atmosphere at a Marine post. They inherit the traditions of Marines. They are Marines."

And indeed they were Marines, these women of World War II. When the call finally came for women to join the Marine Corps, they came, they joined, they proved their mettle, not only at the desk jobs handed out to the World War I "Marinettes," but at roughly two hundred additional military specialties—really important tasks such as weather-forecasting, parachute-rigging, or decoding.

To organize the MCWR was a natural follow-up that had to be done efficiently. As might be expected, however, an organization created within the Marine Corps, the Women's Reserve section, was staffed to handle the new activity.

Everything seemed all well and good, but somebody—presumably a woman—had to be put in charge as director of the newly created MCWR. The surprise choice, a newcomer to America's military world, much less to the Marine Corps, was Ruth Cheney Streeter. As events turned out, she proved a wise choice.

Commissioned a major and sworn in by the Secretary of the Navy on January 29, 1943, Streeter, forty-seven, had an outstanding résumé to offer, even though she had never held a paying job. Popular and respected by her peers even in her college days, she had been selected president of her class at Bryn Mawr, despite completing only two years of study. After her university career, she was actively involved for twenty years as a volunteer in New Jersey health and welfare work. She was the wife of a prominent lawyer and businessman and a mother of four—three sons in military service and a fifteen-year-old daughter still in school.

She had been selected from a field of twelve outstanding women recommended by Dean Virginia C. Gildersleeve of Barnard College. No advocate for bringing women into the Corps, Commandant Holcomb nonetheless firmly believed the success of the MCWR would depend largely on the character and capabilities of its director. He sent the Director Col. Littleton W. T. Waller, a once-controversial veteran of the Philippines Insurrection, and his assistant, Maj. C. Brewster Rhoads, around the country to interview each candidate for the job.

In her Marine Corps historical monograph, Stremlow, USMCR (Ret.) describes Mrs. Streeter as confident, spirited, fiercely patriotic, and highly principled. Stremlow goes on to suggest Streeter must have seemed an obvious choice.

Yet Streeter herself offered a different reading of the situation years later as she remembered the circumstances of her final interview for the post: "As nearly as I can make out, General Holcomb said, 'If I've got to have women, I've got to have somebody in charge in whom I've got complete confidence.' So he called on General Waller, who said, 'If I've got to be responsible for the women, I've got to have somebody in whom I have complete confidence.' And he called on Major Rhoads. So then the two of them came out to see me."

The next step for Streeter was an interview with General Holcomb himself. As she faced him with a bit of trepidation, he repeatedly asked if she knew any Marines. At first she skirted the answer, but finally she truthfully responded that she did not know any Marines.

As the interview continued, she was dismayed to think she probably would be rejected because she didn't know the "right people."

In the end, however, Holcomb told her the unexpected—her replies had been just what he wanted to hear; if she had high-ranking friends in the Corps, she might circumvent the chain of command when she couldn't get her way.

After her conversation with Holcomb, Waller reassured her that the interview had gone well, but warned that her appointment still had to be approved by the secretary of the Navy. Now, she *did* have a possible ally in high place: Secretary Knox was a close friend of her mother and even her in-laws, since her lawyer-husband had been the secretary's personal counsel. But that happenstance proved no barrier in the end.

Indeed, throughout the rest of her life, Ruth Streeter would remain devoted to the Marine Corps, Stremlow also notes; however, before she received the call to lead the WRs, she had joined another part of the war effort even before the United States had been at war. Witnessing the fall of France in 1940 from afar, she realized even then that her country would likely be drawn into the war, and she wanted to be ready to serve.

The fact that British, Russian, and other women around the world were flying planes early in the war led Streeter to think that American women could organize and ferry planes to Europe. Surely her male Marine Corps interviewers must have been impressed to learn that this society woman from Montclair, New Jersey, then in her midforties, had learned to fly, had even earned a commercial pilot's license, had bought her own plane, and had joined the Civil Air Patrol, all on her own initiative.

Although her own plane was used to fly missions spotting German submarines off the coast of New Jersey, to her enormous frustration she was relegated to the position of adjutant in her Civil Air Patrol unit, organizing schedules and doing, as she once called it, "all the dirty work."

When the quasi-military Women Air Service Pilots (WASPs) was formed under the leadership of the legendary aviatrix Jackie Cochran, Streeter was forty-seven years old—twelve years beyond the age limit. But that didn't stop her from trying to join the WASPS at least four times. She was turned down at each attempt, and when she tried to meet Jackie Cochran personally, she only met with another rejection.

In 1943, just weeks before learning the Marines would come calling, she inquired about flying with the WAVES, only to be told she could be a ground instructor. "She declined and a month later found herself in Washington, the first director of the MCWR," writes Stremlow.

As the new director filled key billets for the new organization, one of her first choices was Capt. Lillian O'Malley Daly, who had been a World War I "Marinette" and a personal secretary to the commandants of that era. Another rare "leftover" from World War I service would be Martrese Thek Ferguson (page 203), soon to emerge as commander of the Second Headquarters Battalion (Henderson Hall) in Arlington, Virginia, home base for 2,500 women Marines during World War II.

Training for the women inductees was first held at colleges campuses in New York and Massachusetts, but then all MCWR training was moved to Camp Lejeune late in 1943. It was there that the women Marines, one of them former Commandant Lejeune's own daughter Eugenia, would be the nation's only military women to receive actual combat training, although the thorny issue of sending women into real combat was an argument still to emerge in the years ahead.

For her first six months as director, Streeter was given the services of Marine Major Rhoads, fresh from his duties in her own selection process, as her so-called "running mate." He had been assigned to acquaint her with Marine Corps lore and customs.

Not relinquishing her post until December 1945, months after the end of World War II, Colonel Streeter would be succeeded by her assistant, Lt. Col. Katherine A. Towle, formerly a dean at the University of California, Berkeley.

Meanwhile, Stremlow reports that by the end of World War II, "22,199 women were ordered to recruit training and, of these, 21,597 graduated." During that time, usually far behind the front lines, they had served in supply warehouses, aviation control towers, at radio consoles, even as aviation mechanics, among other specialties. One of the first WRs to be sworn in was Captain Anne Adams Lentz, a former clothing retailer who oversaw the design of the basic forest green WR service uniform.

"When the war finally ended with the abrupt surrender of the Japanese," writes Stremlow, "women Marines were working in 225 specialties…and comprising one-half to two-thirds of the permanent personnel at all large Marine Corps posts and stations."

In the interim, a highlight for the WRs and their memories would be the sprightly Marine Corps Women's Reserve Band. It was formed in November 1943, trained by members of the Marine Band and led by Master Sgt. Charlotte Plummer, former head of the Portland, Oregon public school system and a member of that city's municipal band. Based at Camp Lejeune, the women's band gave concerts on national radio programs; entertained both the male and female troops at Parris Island, Henderson Hall, and other USMC bases; and visited hospitals where Marines were recuperating from combat wounds.

At those stops, the band always played its very own *March of the Women Marines*, composed for it by Marine Band Musician First Class Louis Saverino.

———

ADDITIONAL NOTE: WHEN TODAY'S WOMEN MARINES LOOK BACK AT their own history, what they might see in the story of both World Wars are just two baby steps, except for the significant jump in numbers serving in the second go-round. But the women's world in general was changing and changing fast.

The Women Reserves of World War II vintage had hardly put away their forest greens before Harry S. Truman signed the congressional legislation of 1948 that opened the door for women to serve as *regular* members of all military branches—Marines included. These were primarily in nursing and noncombat slots.

Just two years later, the Korean War erupted with 120,000 American women, 2,787 of them Marines, serving on active duty before the hostilities ended in an uneasy ceasefire in 1953. The Army, Air Force, and

Navy all sent nurses to the faraway battleground itself, while the Marine women largely remained home in leadership and administrative jobs that once again freed up their male counterparts for combat duty, notes the *Korean War Educator* website. For instance, in 1952, "Hazel A. Lindahl, a reservist from Boston, was Camp Sergeant Major of more than 40,000 Marines at Camp Lejeune—the top enlisted post."

It would take yet another war, Vietnam, a decade or so later, before the women Marines finally would serve in the field, close to if not quite thrust directly into combat…but they were creeping up to their combat roles of the modern-day Marine Corps.

While thousands of women served in the Marine Corps during the Vietnam War, only twenty-eight of them actually reached the shores of Vietnam itself, according to the Women Marines Association website.

There, they filled desk billets with the Military Assistance Command, Vietnam (MACV). They were based in Saigon, working for the most part in the Marine Corps Personnel Section and providing administrative support to Marines as far north as the Demilitarized Zone (DMZ). In addition, two women, each at the rank of lieutenant colonel, served as historians for the Military History Branch joint staff of the MACV. At colonel, private, corporal, or whatever rank—the lives of women Marines on station in Vietnam were not totally without risk, and sometimes they were close enough to combat to hear and see nearby gunfire.

Even then, the women Marines were not exposed to anything like the warfare they would see up close in the Middle East as the twentieth century evolved into the twenty-first century. Not authorized to serve in actual combat—armor, artillery, or infantry—until late 2015, they nonetheless often came under fire in support roles close to or even on-site with the Corps' male combat personnel in the Kuwait, Iraq, and Afghanistan conflicts (pages 329 and 349).

As America and the world rushed, it often seems, into the twenty-first century, the women Marines already could boast the first female African American combat pilot of any branch of the armed forces in their midst, Vernice Armour (page 314). In addition, Lt. Col. Sarah Deal

Burrow served in both Iraq and Afghanistan as the Corps' first female pilot of any kind. Like Armour, she flew helicopters, often on ten- to eleven-hour missions, and carried cargo ranging from Humvees to prisoners to troops.

Many of the women serving in support roles in the Middle East, whether officer rank or enlisted, were so close to the fighting in the Kuwait-Iraq-Afghanistan conflicts that they were taking casualties.

In other areas or roles, however, so much a part of the Marine Corps were the women by then that there was hardly a ripple of notice when Lt. Col. Lauren Edwards took command of the Eighth Engineer Support Battalion at Marine Corps Base Camp Lejeune, as the first female leader of any Marine engineers support battalion; when Maj. Christine Houser, a backseat weapons systems operator, became operations officer for the USMC All-Weather Fighter Attack Squadron 225 at Miramir MC Air Station in California; when Margaret A. ("Meg") Ryan, twelve-year Marine Corps veteran (Philippines, Desert Storm/Desert Shield), and a former clerk to Supreme Court Justice Clarence Thomas, was appointed a judge on the U.S. Court of Appeals for the Armed Forces; or when Colonel Mary H. Reinwald (USMC Ret.) took over as the first female editor of the iconic Marines magazine *Leatherneck*.

SELECT UNIT HISTORIES
FOURTH ("CHINA") MARINES

Assembled in 1914 for possible use in Mexico before briefly fighting rebels in the Dominican Republic, the Fourth Marines would actually be known best for its years in China and its subsequent ordeal on Corregidor and Bataan in the Philippines, followed by nearly two years of regimental extinction during World War II.

For the Fourth Marines, deployment to China, specifically to super-sophisticated Shanghai between the world wars, meant soft duty and easy living, but only for a while. It was assigned to protect the Americans and their interests in the International Settlement at Shanghai, an enclave consisting of an estimated forty-five thousand foreigners, with sixteen thousand more located in the nearby French concession.

The exotic mix included thousands of Russians who had fled the Communist takeover of their country. The ballerinas, musicians, and performers among them "transformed Shanghai into one of Asia's premier artistic centers," the PBS program *History Detectives* once pointed out.

"With a currency exchange rate of about 20 to 1," noted PBS, "the troops lived well. Chinese labor was cheap, so the servicemen were well taken care of. They spent their earnings on silk, ivory, and other goods, which they often shipped home. They even had their own club, fitted out with several bars, a bowling alley, library, and ballroom."

During this time, with the help of the Royal Marines also based at Shanghai, they formed the Corps' only fife and drum corps, the Fessenden Fifes, named for Sterling Fessenden, the American chairing the Shanghai Municipal Council.

The Japanese invasion of Manchuria in 1931 increased tensions for a time, and then wider war between China and Japan broke out in 1937. Pressure on the foreign settlements at Shanghai increased as the Japanese seized the surrounding territory. With the European powers then at war as of late 1939, with Japan allying itself to Nazi Germany and Fascist Italy, the Fourth Marines prepared for the day when its personnel must leave Shanghai.

That day finally came in November of 1941, just two weeks before Pearl Harbor.

"The United States seriously began considering the evacuation of its forces from China following the growth of Japanese power and hegemony in the country," notes Marine historian James S. Santelli in the USMC reference pamphlet, *A Brief History of the*

4th Marines. "Admiral Thomas C. Hart, commander in chief of the Asiatic Fleet, felt that war was inevitable and began pulling out those units under his command that were in exposed positions along the Chinese coast."

With the French garrison at Shanghai under Vichy Government control as early as 1940 and the Settlement's British forces sent to more pressing hot spots, the Fourth Marines "became the only obstacle in Japanese designs on the International Settlement." In 1941, intelligence sources warned that the Japanese were planning "incidents," that would provide an excuse to march their troops into the enclave.

As Washington finally consented to the regiment's withdrawal on November 10, one battalion-sized element sailed for the Philippines aboard the liner *President Madison* on November 27, with the remainder of the Fourth Marines following aboard the *President Harrison* a day later. "The era of the 'China Marines' thus came to an end," adds Santelli.

But not to a good end, unhappily enough.

Immediately assigned to the defense of the Olongapo Naval Station and the Mariveles naval base in the Philippines, the Fourth Marines, at this time consisting of 44 officers and 728 enlisted men, plunged into "frantic" preparations for the widely anticipated hostilities. "Although war was expected, it broke out earlier than had been anticipated. Japan launched a sneak attack on the Philippines on 8 December 1941 to coincide with its strike at Pearl Harbor."

As at Pearl Harbor, the attacks took the form of bombing and strafing by Japanese airplanes. The Fourth Marines at Olongapo were spared at first, but on the fourth day of the new war, December 12, the naval station itself joined the list of air raid targets. The Marines responded with rifles and .30-caliber machine guns, "the only weapons available to the regiment."

As bad news became worse, invading Japanese ground troops

threatened to seize Manila any day; the Fourth Marines, now under U.S. Army command, were ordered to help destroy potentially useful facilities and equipment at Olongapo—starting on Christmas Eve. They were next ordered to concentrate at Mariveles and then at Corregidor, the island fortress at the tip end of the Bataan Peninsula.

There, "The Marines were immediately given the task of preparing beach defenses on the island, a mission originally entrusted to the Army. As the enemy bombed Corregidor, its Marines worked day and night strengthening its defensive installations. Antiboat booms were constructed, mines laid, tank traps and trenches dug, and barbed wire strung at potential landing sites."

During, and because of, all the turmoil, the Fourth Marines was becoming almost unrecognizable as a unit. Marine detachments from various naval installations in the Philippines were added to the regiment's two-battalion complement as an entirely new battalion. Additionally, as the Japanese incursion continued for the next four months, the Fourth Marines took in allied personnel from the Army, the Navy, and Filipino units. Eventually, the regiment's size swelled to five battalions in total. It now counted personnel from "all segments of the U.S. and Philippine military services," and thus had become "one of the strangest military organizations in Marine Corps history."

The final and inevitable outcome, sadly, was surrender to the overwhelmingly superior numbers of invading Japanese. Fearing a possible massacre of his one thousand sick and wounded, his own defenders running out of ammunition, Army Lt. Gen. Jonathan Wainwright saw no option but to surrender his forces, including the Fourth Marines, on May 6, 1942.

Col. Samuel L. Howard, CO of the regiment, "ordered the national and regimental colors of the Fourth Marines burned to prevent their capture," writes Santelli. "He then led his men into captivity. As of noon on 6 May 1942, the Fourth Marines temporarily ceased to exist."

It is said that Howard wept as he lamented, "My God, and I had to be the first Marine officer ever to surrender a regiment."

In defending Corregidor, wrote naval historian Samuel Elliot Morrison: "Colonel Howard's 4th Marine Regiment…lived up to the great traditions of the Corps in the last bitter days. The backbone of Corregidor's beach defense, it set an example of courage for those who began to give under the strain."

In the meantime, many soldiers and Marines were to be forgotten heroes as the new war roared on. Among the latter, two sergeants held in a reserve unit at Corregidor joined in an attack on Japanese machine guns at the base of a stone water tower. "Sgt. Major Thomas F. Sweeney and Quartermaster Sgt. John E. Haskin, two old-timers and close friends, personally attacked the machine-gunners," writes historian Moskin. "Haskin was killed bringing more grenades up to Sweeney on top of the water tower. Sweeney destroyed one of the guns before he too died."

More hard times were ahead for the 1,283 Marines taken prisoner at Corregidor—from the Fourth Regiment alone, 239 officers and men would die in Japanese captivity, Moskin adds. All told, the Fourth Marines had 330 killed in defense of the Philippines and 357 wounded.

But just two years later, the Fourth Marines would live again, reborn from a combination of the four Marine Raider battalions. The First, Second, Third, and Fourth Marine Raiders were redesignated as the new Fourth Marines, still bearing the name and honors of the old. As such, the new Fourth, together with the Twenty-Second and Twenty-Ninth Marines, took part as elements of the Sixth Marine Division in the invasions of Guam and Okinawa.

At war's end, members of the new Fourth became the first American occupation forces in mainland Japan. While securing the Yokosuka Naval Base, their freed scores of Allied prisoners held at the naval base and at Yokohama, more than one hundred of them still-surviving men from the "old" Fourth Marines.

Some of the newly freed prisoners of war still had pieces of the old unit's battalion colors, which they had kept hidden from their captors ever since Wainwright's surrender. With the Sixth Division dissolved soon after, the Fourth Marines was once again reactivated in 1951, its men then serving in Korea with the Third Marine Division.

Reappearing in Vietnam, the Fourth Marines again served under the Third Marine Division, in operations in Quang Tri Province from the Laotian border to the beaches on the South China Seas below the Demilitarized Zone. Leaving Vietnam in late 1969, after five years of deployment, the Fourth Marines could boast a total of eleven Medal of Honor winners, one of them a hospital corpsman. Later, various of its member battalions served individually in Kuwait, Iraq, and Afghanistan.

STILL ABLE TO STING

HERE THEY CAME, A REAL NAVAL PARADE, AS THE HANDFUL OF MARINE and Navy defenders of tiny Wake Island looked on and began counting.

Let's see now, cruisers, yes, and then a bunch of destroyers and transports… none of them friendly.

After four days of bombing and strafing by Japanese aircraft, the military and civilian personnel at Wake Island had known even more unpleasantness would be on the way shortly. And now the hour of invasion was upon them…or was it?

Incredibly, Marine 1st Lt. Clarence A. Barninger Jr.'s Battery A of five-inch guns at Wake's Peacock Point opened up and scored three quick hits on the Japanese light cruiser *Yubari*, which turned away in a trail of smoke.

Even better, from the battered atoll Wilke's Island, 2nd Lt. John A. McAlister's Battery L, also five-inchers, opened up and actually sank the small parade's lead destroyer, *Hayate*. (Historical note: The *Hayate* would be Japan's first loss of a surface warship to U.S. naval forces in World War II...and just four days after Pearl Harbor.)

The battle continued, unequally for the losing Japanese. The shore-based Marine guns found more targets in the flotilla, as did the Marines' four Grumman Wildcats on hand. In the end, writes J. Robert Moskin in his Marine Corps history, on December 11, 1941, the Marines at Wake Island sank two destroyers, and damaged a cruiser and "several other ships." They also shot down three Japanese bombers and damaged four more.

The Japanese had suffered at least five hundred dead and the Marines none.

Most important, the Japanese turned away altogether, for that day anyway.

In his *History of United States Naval Operations*, Vol. 3, Naval historian Samuel Eliot Morison summed up: "The eleventh day of December 1941 should always be a proud day in the history of the Corps. Never again, in this Pacific War, did coast defense guns beat off an amphibious landing."

Coming within hours of the surprise Japanese attack on Pearl Harbor, the first aerial bombardment of Wake Island had come as no surprise to any of the roughly 2,000 Americans, military and civilian, busily preparing for war on the tiny, 2.5-square-mile bit of U.S. territory in the Pacific Ocean, 2,000 miles west of Hawaii. They had been expecting an attack for quite some time—that's why most of them were there.

Even that morning, the three islets making up the atoll had "hummed with activity," wrote James W. Wensyel in *World War II* magazine (November 2001). For months, Wake had been the site of construction work. "Working feverishly to complete an airstrip and defensive fortifications were 449 U.S. Marines of the 1st Defense Battalion, commanded by Major James P. S. Devereux; Marine Fighter Squadron 211, equipped with 12 Grumman Wildcats, led by Major Paul A Putnam; 71 Naval personnel; a five-man Army radio detachment, commanded by Captain

Henry S. Wilson, and 1,146 American civilian construction workers of the Contractors Pacific Naval Air Bases Company, managed by Dan Teters—all under the overall command of [U.S. Navy] Commander Winfield S. Cunningham."

Also on hand were maintenance staff for the Pan American Airways trans-Pacific Clipper flying boats that made refueling stops on Wake.

The fact is, "war with Japan was imminent." An airstrip on Wake "would allow American heavy bombers to strike the Japanese-controlled Marshall Islands." If, as was expected, lightly defended Guam was lost to the rampaging Japanese, "Wake would be one of the closest American outposts to the Japanese mainland. Each day work began early and finished late."

Of course, the Japanese were well aware of the same geography and its strategy potential.

At 7:00 a.m. local time on December 8, the Army radio personnel on Wake picked up the radio alert from Hawaii that Hickham Field at Pearl Harbor was under attack by "Jap dive bombers."

Marine Major Devereux quickly ordered Bugler Alvin J. Waronker to sound the General Alarm. However, with no further developments yet coming, the Marines prepared for their traditional morning raising of the flag at 8:50. In the past, Waronker had tended to have trouble getting the "To the Colors" just right, "but this time he did not miss a note, and for several minutes all activity stopped as each man stood at attention and saluted the flag."

Devereux himself later recalled, "The flag went up, and every note was proud and clear. It made a man's throat tighten just to hear it."

It wasn't long after that the Japanese struck—in the form of thirty-six Mitsubishi G3M2 Nell bombers. Their fragmentation bombs and machine-gun fire killed thirty or more Americans that first day. "For Wake's defenders, the war had begun."

Not only that, but for many who survived the pending weeks-long onslaught, the war really wouldn't end until 1945.

Predictably, after their first attempt at seizing Wake Island failed, the

Japanese came back two weeks later, on December 23, this time in greater strength—four heavy cruisers took part in this naval parade, plus the usual transports and landing craft needed for an amphibious operation. The first of nine hundred or so tough infantrymen from their Special Naval Landing Force came ashore at 2:35 a.m.

This followed days of aerial bombardment and strafing, virtually at will in the final hours, since the last of the Marine Wildcats had been lost in dogfights with the Japanese by December 21. The surviving Marine aviators and their crewmen now became riflemen.

With the Japanese troops ashore, the Americans, civilian and military, fought desperately "with rifles, bayonets, grenades, and fists." But as more troops landed, "there were simply too many Japanese and too few Americans."

Navy Commander Cunningham informed Pacific Fleet headquarters at Pearl Harbor, which itself was still recovering from its December 7 battering: "Enemy on island. Issue in doubt."

From off shore, beyond the range of the remaining Marine guns, Japanese warships pounded the last pockets of resistance, while from overhead Japanese aircraft continued to bomb and strafe with no opposing planes available to interfere.

"I tried to think of something," Devereux said later, "but there wasn't anything... We could keep on expending lives, but we could not buy anything with them."

Ranking officer Cunningham finally "made the inevitable decision to surrender." He phoned Devereux on Wake's only phone line to issue the order. "The major gulped, then quietly agreed, 'I'll pass the word.'"

He and Sgt. Donald R. Malleck, "who carried a white cloth tied to a mop handle," walked across the island telling their compatriot Americans to lay down their arms. "Stunned defenders threw away rifle bolts, destroyed delicate range-finding instruments, drained hydraulic fluid from recoil cylinders, and then surrendered."

By now, their casualty count was eighty-one Marines, eight sailors, and eighty-two civilian contractors killed or wounded...with many more to come before the Wake Island saga would end. For the Japanese, the surrender by a relative handful of Americans was no proud "victory," since it had cost two destroyers and a submarine sunk, seven other ships damaged, twenty-one aircraft lost, and nearly one thousand men killed.

Well aware of the price they had paid, the Japanese took revenge by treating their prisoners, civilian or military, with equal brutality.

"Some were stripped naked, others to their underwear. Most had their hands tied behind their backs with telephone wire, with a second wire looped tightly from their necks to their wrists, so that if they lowered their arms they would strangle themselves. Personal valuables were taken and wounds ignored."

First jammed into two concrete ammunition bunkers, they next were taken out and forced to sit naked on the "blistering hot concrete" of their own airstrip. "That night, bone-chilling winds replaced the heat. The prisoners sat there, still waiting for food, water, or medical treatment. The unfortunate prisoners remained sitting on the airstrip for two days."

Finally given largely spoiled food and told to grab items from a pile of confiscated clothes, some bloody, the prisoners were formed up and addressed by the flotilla's commander himself, Admiral Sadamichi Kajioka.

An interpreter translated for him as he said, "The Emperor [has] graciously presented you with your lives."

"Well, thank the son of a bitch for me," replied an irreverent Marine.

Truly brave words, but the life-threatening conditions for the captured Americans only continued. As *Stars and Stripes* reported on January 22, 2012, "Most of the prisoners were spread throughout the expanding Japanese empire and forced to work in deplorable conditions."

Gary Rogde, originally from Idaho, had been among the young men enticed to work on Wake Island "by adventure and U.S. government contractor dollars," despite the risk of war.

"Rogde was taken to Sasebo, where he helped to build Soto Dam. He was injured in a rockslide, [his daughter] Sherie Rogde said, and without medical care, was saved only by the maggots that helped keep the infection down on his wound until he was rescued. It was here, in Nagasaki prefecture, that he saw the mushroom cloud of the atomic bomb from afar."

But Rogde, who would live into his nineties, was one of the luckiest among the Wake Island survivors, military or civilian.

By being taken to Japan, he missed the mass execution on October 7, 1943, of ninety-seven civilian contract workers who had been kept on the atoll as forced laborers. The ninety-seven "were bound, blindfolded, and forced to the ground, facing the majestic turquoise water that surrounds the coral atoll," notes Matthew W. Burke in *Stars and Stripes*. "Then the machine guns sounded."

The massacre came after U.S. fighters had attacked Wake and its Japanese occupiers that October, among the nation's first steps on the long Pacific Ocean path to the Japanese homeland.

Previously, on January 12, 1942, the prisoners sent to Japanese prison and labor camps were jammed into the hold of a merchant ship with little light, buckets for toilets, and continued brutal treatment.

Reaching Yokohama, about twenty American officers and enlisted men were transferred to a prison in Japan, while the others would continue on to Shanghai, where some would end up working in area coal mines.

On the way to Shanghai, however, three sailors and two Marines were taken on deck, blindfolded and brutally beheaded on the spot. Most of their comrades spent the rest of the war at the Woosung war prisoners camp near Shanghai. "The Americans would never forget Woosung," writes Wensyel in *World War II* magazine. "The bleak loneliness, bitter cold winds whistling through their flimsy huts, wormy stone-studded rice, and dawn-to-dusk work made a lasting impression." So did the never-ending brutal treatment.

They were joined there by captured personnel from the Marine detachment assigned to the U.S. Legation at Tianjin, China. Its two ranking officers, Col. William H. Ashurst, CO, and Maj. Luther A. Brown, executive officer, joined with Devereux in efforts to see that their fellow Marines "would never succumb to their captors."

Devereux, for his part, "insisted on the same military discipline found at a stateside Marine base," adds Wensyel's account. "He also insisted that the Marines exercise every day, despite their weakening bodies." Then, too, "Despite the terrible conditions inflicted on them, American prisoners saluted their officers, maintained their chain of command, and walked with pride and dignity."

Sometimes, albeit in small ways, they could strike back at their captors. "Put to work repairing roads, the prisoners instead widened or deepened potholes or loose-packed the dirt so the holes would soon get worse. Assigned to clean weapons, they polished the metal until it was too thin to be safely fired, lost parts, hid bearings, loosened bolts, or substituted incorrect parts."

But all were losing weight and weakened by malnutrition—many were dying from illness, untreated battle injuries, and lack of proper food.

Meanwhile, nearly a year after their arrival at Woosung, they were moved to a prison camp at Qiang Wang, still in occupied China—Devereux called it the "worst hellhole" yet. This would be followed in 1945, last year of the war, by a series of moves. As it became more evident they were losing the war, the Japanese now alternated between kindness and brutality in reaction to the obvious American successes.

One move took the Wake Island prisoners and others by train to Fengtai on the outskirts of Beijing. On the way, four Marines and an aviator managed to escape their train. With the help of Chinese Communists, they reached friendly hands and freedom after a forty-two-day trek.

Soon after, Devereux and company were sent to Pusan in occupied Korea, and from there to Honshu, Japan, and then on to Sendai or Hakodate, also in Japan proper. "They were in Osaka during a B-29 raid," writes Wensyel, "and while changing trains in Tokyo, narrowly escaped death or injury when an angry civilian mob attacked them as the Japanese guards looked the other way." Even at Hakodate, the final stop for most of the Wake captives, they were subject to beatings by the guards until the very last days of the war.

"Today," writes Burke in *Stars and Stripes*, "Wake Island, which sits between Hawaii and Guam in the North Pacific, is a virtual ghost town, partially unclaimed by thick jungle brush, littered with pillboxes and abandoned Japanese fortifications. It's home only to a small contingent of contractors and members of the U.S. military."

Meanwhile, Wake's commanding officer of the World War II era, Winfield Scott Cunningham, died a rear admiral at age eighty-six in 1986. After Wake Island's surrender, he, like so many of his compatriots at Wake, spent the rest of the war as a prisoner of the Japanese. He later was awarded the Navy Cross and collaborated on the book *Wake Island Command*.

Devereux, retired from the Marines with the rank of brigadier general in 1948, died at age eighty-five in 1988 after he served four terms in the U.S. House as a Republican from Maryland and ran, unsuccessfully, for governor of the state. He also was awarded a Navy Cross. His Marine battalion that defended Wake Island was awarded a presidential unit citation by order of Franklin Delano Roosevelt.

FIRST TO LAND

THE U.S. NAVY STRUCK BACK AT JAPAN WITH A VICTORY IN THE Battle of Midway in early June 1942. Beyond that start on an American comeback in the Pacific, the Marines for their part still had many giant steps ahead of them. The first would be the invasion of Guadalcanal, and the first Marine to step ashore there may have been an obscure company commander, Fifth Marines, from Bridgeport, Connecticut, named Bill (William) Hawkins.

"My company was part of the first assault group," he once wrote, "and the boat I was in was the first to unload. I guess I was the first Marine ashore on the 'Canal. Thank God we met no resistance; every Jap in the area would have been firing at my head."

As he added in his first-person account in the book *Semper Fi, Mac* edited by Henry Berry: "The landing itself was perfection. Our intelligence reports were way off base on the number of Japs originally on the island. There were nowhere near as many of them there as we originally thought. Our real combat was to come from reinforcements the enemy sent to the 'Canal."

And what reinforcements they did send, and what support they did give them!

The battle for control of the jungle-covered island in the Solomon Sea was to last for half a year. As America's first ground counteroffensive against the Japanese in World War II, it assumed monumental proportions both in the scope of forces committed and in the shared psychological goal of emerging as the winner rather than loser.

The initial objective for the invading First Marine Division (and two Marine Raider battalions) on August 7 was the capture of the airfield the Japanese were building on Guadalcanal—once operational, it would be a serious threat to the U.S. supply routes in the southwest Pacific.

The first waves of the sixteen thousand Marines coming ashore behind Bill Hawkins quickly captured the airfield, now to become their own Henderson Field, and dug into a defensive perimeter around the airstrip of roughly seven miles by four miles. And there they largely stayed for weeks that became months as they fought off banzai attack after banzai attack, underwent bombing, and endured nightly shelling by Japanese warships. Before it was all over, the Japanese would land thirty-six thousand troops on the island, and the Americans fifty thousand.

Never content to sit and wait for the enemy to come to them, the Marines carried out repeated search-and-destroy patrols from the start, Bill Hawkins's B Company included. One time, Hawkins writes, while leading his B Company on a probe against the Japanese with two other companies and the ocean close to his flank, they ran into "tremendous machine-gun fire and couldn't move."

He started shifting his company back toward its command post, all the while "hugging close to the water." As they came around a point, however, he was "thunderstruck" to see a Japanese cruiser "right in front of us."

It was so close, "A couple of the Nip sailors actually waved."

The sight of the big warship was totally unexpected…and terrifying. "My immediate thoughts were how in the hell did it get in so far and how damn big its guns were."

He and his men "took off for the jungle as fast as we could," he added. "Thank God they didn't fire a shot, but seeing that cruiser as if it had come out of nowhere was something I'll never forget."

For Hawkins and many of his fellow Marines, life on Guadalcanal usually meant "constant patrol action," often around the Matanikau River west of Henderson Field. "Sometimes the fight would break off suddenly, and other times we'd run into too many Japs to handle. Then we'd break off the action, which is exactly what happened in one of those fights when I came very close to becoming a battlefield statistic—the fire we received on this occasion was just too overwhelming."

He made the "snap decision" to get his men out of there and back to their defensive perimeter.

"The next thing I knew, General Vandegrift [Alexander Archer Vandegrift, CO of the First Division] called me into his command post.

"'Hawkins,' he said, 'I understand you have reported that you were pinned down by tremendous fire. Just what the hell does that mean?'

"'Well, sir,' I told him, 'this is what I mean by pinned down!'

"Then I showed him where Jap machine-gun bullets had creased both sides of my helmet. To make sure he knew what I meant, I also showed him where another bullet had taken off part of my Tommy gun's stock.

"Vandegrift looked at me for a minute or so.

"'Captain, that's being pinned down!'"

Close calls or no, Hawkins endured the horrors of war on Guadalcanal—the stink of the jungle, the killing of men from both warring sides right in front of him, the helpless-feeling fears of the nightly shellings—all for ten weeks without suffering a scratch. Still, he recalled the impact on the newly landed Marines of the disastrous Allied loss of four cruisers in the Battle of Savo Island off the 'Canal, three of them American, two nights after the Marines first came ashore. The Marines then had to defend their perimeter with their supplies cut off for a time.

"The next thing we knew the Marines were orphans," he wrote. "After the cruisers went down, the Navy pulled the transports out. Hell, I don't think they were half unloaded. Before long we were on one meal a day."

Luckily the Marines, when they landed unopposed at first, had been able to seize large stores of Japanese food—a mixed blessing, it seems. "The rice wasn't bad, but I never cottoned to the raw fish heads."

Meanwhile, fate had another Marine career in store for Hawkins.

Not long after his session with Vandegrift, the general decided that the troop and cargo transports once again serving the combat area should have Marine officers aboard. "I ended up being one of those officers," wrote Hawkins.

That's how the first Marine landed on Guadalcanal and would go on to survive two ship sinkings off Guadalcanal.

By October 1942 he was serving aboard the transport *Alchiba* and sailing out of Noumea, New Caledonia, for Guadalcanal. They were "loaded" with supplies and even towing a loaded barge. No sooner had they reached the "Iron Bottom" bay between Savo Island and the canal itself, than someone spotted a Japanese two-man midget submarine on one side of the ship. "Naturally all eyes are on her."

However, at the same time, "a full-size Jap sub is coming in on the other side of the *Alchiba*. But no one knows this."

In seconds, "Wham! We take a torpedo on the other side of our ship—the side no one is paying any attention to."

With the transport sinking, it appeared the vital supplies it carried would join the sunken ships at bottom of Iron Bottom Bay.

But no! Its skipper, Jim Freeman from Alabama, rallied quickly. "Head for the shore!" he yelled. "Maybe we can beach her and not lose the cargo. The men ashore really need this gear."

"So we headed for the beach, the very spot where I had landed on August 7."

And there she safely stayed for several days while being unloaded—more to the point, while the aviation gasoline and bombs aboard were unloaded. No sooner had the last hundred-pound bomb been taken ashore, then "another two-man submarine showed up and stuck a torpedo into our ship."

Not only that, but "it hit exactly where the bombs and gas had been stowed. If it had hit us an hour or so earlier, we would have all gone to kingdom come."

As a result, Hawkins and his companions abandoned ship—the same ship—for a second time.

He was placed on board the USS *McCawley*, "one of the most famous transports in the fleet." She was famous largely because her captain, William Rodgers, did all he could to make the troops he carried, Marine or Army, as comfortable as possible. The *McCawley* also served as the flagship for Rear Adm. Richard Kelly Turner as it plied the dangerous waters between New Caledonia and the Solomons until June 30, 1943.

On that morning, as part of the U.S. New Georgia campaign, "We landed our troops at Rendova, which is only seven miles from the all-important Munda airstrip." At noon, the Japanese struck. "Submarines, Mitsubishis [bombers], and dive bombers came at our transports. We took a torpedo early, and Admiral Turner quickly transferred his flag to a destroyer."

The attack lasted six hours, during which the *McCawley*'s own guns downed three of the Japanese aircraft, one of them by Hawkins himself. The ship itself was left "dead in the water," as her skipper Rodgers lamented. By then he, Hawkins, and the crew had abandoned the stricken transport and were looking on from the nearby destroyer and similarly named *McCalla*.

Why not go back and put her under tow, Rodgers asked the startled destroyer captain, who quite reasonably refused at first. "But Rodgers was one smooth talker. Finally, he convinced the destroyer's captain we should chance it. So, six of us, including Captain Rodgers, got in a launch and headed back toward the transport."

They had gotten to within one hundred yards when their ship suddenly blew up in front of them, "definitely finished" this time.

Days later, rumors floated around Guadalcanal that an American PT boat had mistakenly torpedoed the transport in the dark after all naval personnel were told that any ships they came across would be Japanese. Since no one was killed as a result and the abandoned ship might have sunk anyway, "the blunder was hushed up."

Years later, Hawkins was in San Francisco on business. He stopped in a bar, struck up a conversation with a fellow customer, "and we got talking about the war."

"Oh," said the stranger, "I was in the Pacific all right. But I'm afraid I was on a PT boat that sank an American ship."

Not the *McCawley*! Hawkins wanted to know.

"That's right. Do you know about it? I was a lieutenant JG [junior grade] at the time. Thank God there was no one aboard her. I think it was pretty much hushed up."

"Well, you SOB," Hawkins laughed. "You sank *my* ship!"

Then, added Hawkins, they both had another drink.

———

ADDITIONAL NOTE: FIRST DIVISION COMMANDER VANDEGRIFT, NOT so incidentally, would become a rarity even for the elite Marine Corps and its "First to Fight" spirit: a general awarded the Medal of Honor—in his case, for his role as CO of the Division during the months-long battle for control of Guadalcanal itself. Then a major general in rank, he later became the eighteenth commandant of the Marine Corps and a full general, the first active-duty Marine officer to reach four-star rank. A native of Charlottesville, Virginia, the son of a local architect, and a University of Virginia graduate, the general previously had served in China, Haiti, and Nicaragua, and at stateside USMC duty posts. After Guadalcanal, he commanded the I Marine Amphibious Corps during the invasion of Bougainville in the Northern Solomons, then returned to Washington as commandant-designate.

For the Marines in World War II, a long, often tortuous but ultimately victorious island-hopping campaign across the Pacific still lay ahead after the warfare on Guadalcanal. They would be called upon to subdue often fanatical Japanese defenders on one island after another, islands that would also become as well-known as Tripoli or the Halls of Montezuma. Among the World War II island invasions still to come for the Marines, always with the essential help of the Navy and often with crucial Army and Air Force support as well, were Tarawa, Iwo Jima, Peleliu and Angaur, Saipan, Guam, and Okinawa.

GUADALCANAL LOGBOOK

DETERMINED TO GET INTO MARINE AVIATION FROM THE START, determined to seek out the Japanese Zeroes every day at Guadalcanal, fighter pilot J. Hunter Reinburg considered a day without action a day lost. Still, in his Grumman Wildcat (FHF-4) and then aboard his more advanced bent-wing Chance Vaught Corsair (F4U-1), he saw plenty of action and wound up a WWII ace with seven "kills" to his credit.

Typical of a *good* day at the job was the time he led a formation of eight Wildcats and four Army P-39s to Savo Island, the volcanic atoll thirty miles east of the Marines' Henderson Field airstrip on Guadalcanal itself.

The Marine fighters were to rendezvous there with fifteen Douglas Dauntless dive bombers (SBDs) on their way to the newly built Japanese airfield at Munda Point on New Georgia Island, 170 nautical miles from Savo.

Typically, too, Reinburg was delighted. "This mission appeared most attractive as it seemed reasonable the Japs would surely send up some fighters after such easy targets as the SBDs," he wrote later. "Conversely, we looked upon the bombers as Zero-bait. My flight had yet to see a Jap plane in the air, much to our consternation."

But not all wartime missions go according to the best laid plans.

As time passed and the dive-bombers still had not shown up for the bombing run on Munda, with Reinburg and company as escort, he and his fighter-pilot compatriots naturally became a bit impatient.

It would be a shame, squadron leader Reinburg thought, "not to complete some sort of useful mission" while airborne and partway to the Japanese air base anyway.

"A thought flashed through my mind to invent an alternate mission." So it was that Reinburg and his fighters attacked the Japanese air field by themselves, surprising a number of Zeroes (and a few machine-gun nests) on the ground and strafing them. It was, he later said, "like shooting fish in a barrel."

In fact, the dive-bombers never did show up that particular day, but Reinburg and his fellow fighters made their mark on Munda anyway, by destroying at least nine Zeroes before they could take off. In addition, as the Americans ran out of ammunition and turned for home, one of two Zeroes giving chase but flying too low, caught a wing tip in the water and crashed. His companion turned tail and disappeared in the direction of his own home field.

The Marine aviator who told his own story in his self-published book, *Aerial Combat Escapades: A Pilot's Logbook*, originally couldn't get into the U.S. Naval Academy or the Marine Corps itself because of "failing eyesight." Trying more than once and passing all other requirements in 1937, he failed the eye dilation test, with warnings of contracting myopia and glaucoma. "My dreams from childhood appeared to be forever shattered because I wanted to have a career as an officer/aviator in the United States Marines Corps," he wrote. Worth noting, also, is that his own stepfather, later Lt. Gen. Clayton C. Jerome, would be a World War II and Korean War Marine Corps combat pilot.

In 1940, Reinburg learned the Navy was so desperate for combat fliers it had waived the eye dilation test, and by February 1941 he had completed flight school and won his commission as a second lieutenant in the Marine Corps Aviation Reserve. By the time all was said and done, he had flown 287 combat sorties in World War II and even more as a Marine Corps night fighter in Korea. "For night air action over Korea," he added, "I was awarded the Silver Star to add to my twelve Air Medals and six DFCs [Distinguished Flying Crosses] from WWII." In addition to his seven kills in air-to-air combat during WWII, he also was credited with seven planes destroyed on the ground.

Meanwhile, even at hard-fought-over Guadalcanal, not every day brought action. Some days, he complained, were outright boring. For a time, he and his fellow fighter pilots amused themselves and made their ground support personnel happy by creating gallons of "high octane" ice cream on high-altitude flights.

They and their cooks figured out that by filling large, sanitized containers with water, cocoa, and powdered milk, then flying in the chilled altitudes of thirty thousand feet or more, they could come back with palatable "ice cream" to be enjoyed by all. But since even a short flight to those freezing altitudes could consume one hundred gallons of fuel or more, was it a waste of government money and resources?

Not really, Reinburg argues in his book. They would fly over Japanese-occupied territory just above the range of the enemy antiaircraft batteries (which invariably fired on them anyway, but in vain). Thus, for the price of 100 or so gallons of gas, the Marine aviators made the Japanese waste their own precious ammunition. And still the ice cream, nicely frozen, came back with the Marine fighters—for all, ground crews, infantry "Grunts" or pilots, to enjoy.

Perhaps naturally, the day came when it all wasn't quite so easy for aggressive warrior Reinburg. He was in fact shot down.

"The one-man pararaft...is just long enough to allow me to stretch my legs while sitting up," he would write. And yes, "The sea was rough," he would say. Moreover, "The flexible rubberized bottom of the raft rippled with the waves against my buttocks."

Yes, this time Reinburg was in the drink, four miles east of Japanese-occupied Rendova Island and drifting in the ocean toward Munda, another enclave bristling with the enemy just nine miles away.

Whenever he crested a swell, he could see the masts of ships in the distance…friendly ships at that.

Steady paddling did not seem to close the gap.

A pair of American Navy torpedo bombers flew past overhead.

Frantic waving did not attract their attention.

After a while, darkness fell and the wind continued to blow him parallel to the Rendova shoreline and toward Munda Point.

It was June 30, 1943, and just short hours before dark, he had led a flight of eight Marine Corsairs aloft from Strip Number 1 on Guadalcanal to fly combat air patrol over American landings on Rendova.

The recently acquired Corsairs sometimes tended to lose engine power at altitude, and of course they also could be shot down by the enemy. Reinburg was unlucky enough that afternoon to encounter both misfortunes. First, the engine did fail him. He was able to fly lower and get it started up again, but he almost immediately ran into Japanese Zeroes. He shot down one or two himself, but had to bail out when his Corsair was shot up and became engulfed in flames.

Next thing he knew, he was in the water and far from home base. It wasn't clear if anyone had really noticed him go down. Officially speaking, he was MIA—Missing in Action.

Reinburg managed to reach Rendova itself during the night, slept on a beach, and then set off again in his pararaft the next morning for fear of running into Japanese troops if he remained ashore.

In the distance again were ships—destroyers. Whether enemy or friendly, he couldn't tell. Whipped and buffeted by the wind and waves, he did his best to keep paddling, to make an approach, until suddenly one of them veered off course and came at him with trainlike speed.

Someone threw over a line with big, knobby knots and he clung on for dear life as they hauled him aboard.

As he lay "panting" on the deck, he was elated to hear a distinctly American voice say, "Where the hell did this flyboy come from?"

ADDITIONAL NOTE: AT ONE TIME DURING HIS SOUTH PACIFIC TOUR, Reinburg would be assigned to VMF-122, the Wildcat squadron on Guadalcanal briefly commanded by Maj. Gregory "Pappy" Boyington, already an ace from his prewar days with the Flying Tigers in China. As the squadron's officer, Reinburg said, he spent considerable time with Boyington, who was known as "Black Sheep" because of his drinking.

"I never saw him sober as CO of VMF-122," writes Reinburg, describing himself as a teetotaler, "and I was continually flabbergasted how he could fly so well."

Even so, they were good friends, and Boyington "never missed a mission assigned to him."

When Boyington broke a leg in a friendly wrestling match one night and was hospitalized in New Zealand, Reinburg moved up to squadron leader. Boyington recovered three months later, and was first given a desk job because of his rank and seniority. However, because of his drinking, it didn't work out, and he was placed in command of VMF-214. "The squadron became known as the 'Black Sheep' because their CO had long been known as the 'Black Sheep' of Marine Corps Aviation," wrote Reinburg.

Later in Korea, as commanding officer of the VMF(AW) (N)-513 Night Fighter Squadron, Reinburg would earn the Silver Star on the night of August 21, 1950, by spotting the gun flashes of hidden enemy artillery nests in mountainous terrain, then bombing and strafing them until his ammunition was expended. At that point, he repeatedly faked his bombing runs while the friendly troops he was covering could move out of danger from the North Korean artillery units.

After engaging in two wars, WWII and Korea, Reinburg was a test pilot for jet aircraft for a time, and afterwards ran an airplane charter service. He died in 1997 at his home in Coronado, California.

FUTURE BISHOP BATTLE TESTED

ONCE A NEW ENGLAND PREPPIE AND STUDENT AT YALE, AND LATER a bishop of the Episcopal Church, Paul Moore Jr., was also a young Marine platoon leader in the Tulagi-Guadalcanal Campaign. As he himself would write years later, seeing his first dead Japanese soldier was traumatic, as was seeing his first dead Marine. And then there was the long moment when he had to report his platoon's retreat to the storied Lt. Col. Lewis "Chesty" Puller.

It was at Guadalcanal that the Marines carried out in America's first major amphibious landing of World War II. There, the First Marine Division (and supporting elements such as Marine Air and Marine Raider units) took on the occupying Japanese forces in what turned out to be a bloody, often horrifying mini-war of six months. Before the Japanese were finally subdued, both the Second Marine Division and the Army's Americal Division had joined the fight, which often boiled down to hand-to-hand and bayonet fighting.

Back and forth the tide went. On the one hand the Americans defended the approaches to their key possession, Henderson (Air) Field; on the other, they attacked entrenched Japanese in the jungle, on the high ridges or along the rivers of Guadalcanal.

Both air and naval battles raged throughout the Solomons as the Japanese constantly sought to reinforce their troops on the island and the Americans resisted every such attempt.

Among those thousands of young Marines caught up in the fighting on Guadalcanal proper was New Jersey native Paul Moore Jr. Admittedly not "very good at the things you do in basic training," the tall young Ivy Leaguer was actually good at handling a rifle. Thus, after officer training, he arrived in the Solomon Islands a rifle platoon leader, landing first at Tulagi Island and then moving on to neighboring Guadalcanal.

Here he would come to know all the usual (and unpleasant) 'Canal experiences: the bugs, like malaria-carrying mosquitoes; the jungle vegetation; the humid, cloying heat; the stickum mud; the rain, rain, and rain; plus the ever-present enemy threat. One thing he hated especially was shelling by Japanese battleships.

"They had these huge guns," he recalled in the book *Pacific War Remembered: An Oral History Collection*, edited by John T. Mason Jr. "Being shelled by naval gunfire to me was far more terrifying than being bombed or being shelled by artillery. You would hear those shells going overhead just like a subway, with an enormous roar and rattle, and you would just roll out of bed and cling to the floor."

Other threats when not actually in combat were the frequent Japanese bombings. "Every day at noon a flight of high-flying Japanese bombers would come over." The aerial dogfights taking place "right over your head" between the American Wildcats (Grumman F4Fs) and the Japanese fighters escorting the bombers were easily seen from the ground.

Despite the air defense, "They'd drop these bombs, not very accurately, but when they hit the ground the whole island would just shake up and down."

Among the frequent ground-level frays, large and small, at Guadalcanal was the Battle of the Matanikau River, "a jungle river," as Moore said, about two hundred yards wide where it emptied into a bay. "The Matanikau was outside our lines, and for a long time there was a sort of seesaw between the Japanese troops and our own—sometimes the Matanikau was ours, sometimes it was theirs. So from time to time troops would be sent out to try to secure the river."

One of those times, it was Moore himself at the lead of a company. "I was responsible for leading seven hundred men single-file through this impenetrable jungle, with machetes and a compass." He was sent to approach the river mouth from inland while another unit approached the defending Japanese right up the beach.

As Moore and his men drew near the Japanese on the far banks of the river, they could hear firing between the Americans on the beach and the enemy opposite. And so far, the Americans were being "thrown back."

Enter "Chesty" Puller, who "was in charge of this operation."

According to Moore's account, Puller's "tactics were to send one platoon after another across a totally exposed sand spit which closed off one end of the river." Further, "The order given to each of these platoons was to run across the sand spit until they were opposite the bank, wade across the river, and attack the Japanese battalion, which was dug in with automatic weapons and hand grenades and mortars in the [river] bank."

Naturally, the attacking Marines "would get support fire from machine guns and mortars from our own troops." But, perhaps also naturally, one platoon after another "went over and got annihilated." He listed three platoons, then four, in a row.

"We were lined up just behind the shore, ready to go. Ours was the fifth platoon to go over, and you know we all realized it was insane. We heard what had happened to the other platoons. But if you're a Marine, you're ordered across the goddamn beach and you go."

Indeed they went and running at a zigzag across the beach, they wound up on the ocean side of the sand spit, "peeking over the top, with our weapons trained on the embankment across this little river." The idea now was to send scouts "to draw fire and show where the weapons were." Next, with heavy supporting fire, the platoon would attack across the river.

The intelligence was that they could wade across, but the two scouts found the water was over their heads. They had to swim.

"Art Beres, one of my corporals, got to the opposite bank. I remember him holding on to a root, with the bank about a foot over him, and when he turned around I saw his whole face had been shot away. Two other guys had been killed at that particular moment, and I went across to get Art so he could be brought back."

By that time, Moore added, "I'd called for us to attack (even though we were swimming we were told to attack, so we attacked)."

He got the wounded corporal back behind the spit, then turned to continue swimming across the river with the rest of his platoon. Meanwhile, mortars and hand grenades were "going over my head" and so many bullets were hitting the surface of the water it looked like showers of raindrops were hitting it all around them.

"I guess we got almost to the opposite bank and at that point realized two or three people had been killed, two or three others wounded, and there was just no way we could do it, so I called for retreat."

Back at the American side of the river, they found two men who looked unconscious, but on closer examination they turned out to be dead.

"So we just left them there and ran back to the protection of the sand spit. I remember when I was leaning over trying to bring one of my men to safety seeing bullet marks in the sand around my feet and thinking, you know, if I get out of this, maybe it means I should do something special. There was a feeling—I don't know if it's very good theology, whether it's superstition or what, but certainly I felt that I had been very fortunate, and that I was, in a sense, living on borrowed time, and that this was another good reason to give my life to the Lord, and it seemed being a priest was the way."

Still, the future Episcopal bishop felt he had better go see "Chesty" Puller, "just to report to him what had happened."

Said Moore also: "I wasn't particularly proud of the fact that we had retreated, but it seemed to me the necessary thing to do." He was convinced they all could have sacrificed themselves, and still "the emplacement would not have been taken."

He found Puller sitting under a coconut tree.

"I came up to him and said, 'Lieutenant Moore reporting, sir.' I saluted and told him that I just started the platoon across and what had happened, what I saw of the Japanese emplacements."

No answer. No response, according to Moore's account. "He not only didn't answer me, he didn't even turn his head to speak to me. It's as if I hadn't been there. After a while I just left."

The attacking Marines fell back overnight to their defensive perimeter around Henderson Field (named for dive-bomber pilot Maj. Lofton R. Henderson, killed at Midway). The next morning, they moved out again against the Matanikau River positions of the Japanese, but this time they crossed up river near its headwaters, outflanked the Japanese by the beaches, and attacked them from the rear.

In the process, the tall (six foot four inches) Ivy Leaguer got up and threw a hand grenade at a Japanese machine-gun nest, "though obviously it made me very vulnerable."

The day before, he had spent a while spotting for the U.S. artillery. The friendly artillery would fire, Moore related, and he would spot where the shell landed on either side of a Japanese artillery piece just 250 yards or so down a rough road.

"I'd wait until the shell landed, jump out of the foxhole to see where the explosion was, and then jump back in again and relay through word of mouth, all the way up to where the observation post for the artillery was, that it had landed to the right or the left, or whether it was short or what."

Trouble was, "As soon as I popped back down in the hole, there would be an explosion just where I'd been standing, because the Japanese artillery would have fired on me."

That was on November 2, 1942. The next day, "We got ready for a full-fledged attack to establish a beachhead rather than just coming down and withdrawing…" He and his platoon ran into machine-gun fire—they were "lacerated" by it. "I lost four or five men and two or three others were wounded, so the platoon was down to about seven men at this point, and the platoon sergeant and I were still going."

That's when, realizing they had to do something about the machine guns, Moore stood up and threw a grenade into the machine-gun nest. But as he ducked back, he took a 25-caliber rifle bullet in the chest, between two ribs, that just barely missed his heart and his backbone "as it went through the other side of my body about an inch."

Naturally, he was evacuated while his compatriot Marines "went on down to the beach and wound up in a bayonet fight with the Japanese, whom they finally pushed back into the sea." More Americans were killed, and "there was a terrible slaughter of the Japanese" before the battle was finally concluded.

Moore, winner of a Navy Cross for his actions at Guadalcanal, would soon be on his way to recuperation from his severe wound. He was allowed to return home to the United States, where he entered a seminary and became an Episcopal priest on his way to appointment as thirteenth bishop of the New York Episcopal Diocese.

He became noted as an outspoken moralist and spokesman for liberal causes both within the Church and outside its normal boundaries. As such, he was an early advocate of ordaining women as Episcopal priests; he also defended the right of homosexuals to serve as Episcopal bishops. He marched with the Reverend Martin Luther King Jr., during the Civil Rights demonstrations of the 1960s, protested the Vietnam War, and spoke out against the Iraq War.

He and his first wife, the former Jenny McKean, had nine children, and after her death he married again, this time to Brenda Hughes. He died in 2003 at the age of eighty-three.

JFK TO THE RESCUE

"WIND 'ER UP," SAID YOUNG NAVY LIEUTENANT JOHN F. KENNEDY as he and his heavily armed gunboat—unrelated to his famous PT-109—set off to rescue a band of Marines recently landed on a little-known Pacific Island. They had been sent there as bait intended to divert Japanese forces from the U.S. landings on Bougainville in the first days of November 1943, and now they were in trouble.

Diversion had been the strategy as 658 men from Lt. Col. Victor H. Krulak's Second Marine Parachute Battalion, First Marine Parachute Regiment, stealthily came ashore on Choiseul Island's deserted southwest coast near a spot on the map called Voza. At that moment in time, the still-black early morning of October 28, no one knew that a good many of those same young Marines would be depending on a future president for rescue from the suddenly swarming Japanese.

After concealing four landing craft on the islet of Zinoa, two thousand yards offshore from Voza, the Marines landing on Choiseul broke up in groups pursuing specific assignments. As one party established a base camp on a height one thousand yards above Voza, another would attack a Japanese barge-staging base at Sangigai to the southeast, and still others would search for a possible PT boat base on behalf of their U.S. Navy comrades.

The Navy would do its part in the deception plan by announcing that twenty thousand troops had landed on the small island fifty miles from Bougainville, the real target for invasion on November 1.

Japanese reconnaissance pilots unwittingly did their part also by discovering and reporting the Marine landing. Once it was daylight, the Japanese obligingly bombed a phony supply dump the Marines had built with empty boxes. Krulak sent his headquarters a deliberately uncoded message—"in the clear," so the Japanese would be sure to pick it up—falsely stating that his entire "division" of twenty thousand Marines had landed safely and were moving into planned positions.

In reality, he sent just two companies to attack the barge base, located a ten-mile march down the coast. While Company E would attack the barge site, already freshly bombed, Krulak and his Company F were to take up an ambush position to the Japanese rear, blocking their likely escape route to inland mountains.

The double-edged plan worked well. Of an estimated 150 to 200 Japanese thought to have been at the barge base, 72 were killed and another 40 fled. The Marines lost six, one went missing, and 12 were wounded. Meanwhile, the remnants of the Japanese facility yielded valuable documents. The Marines also destroyed a landing barge and 180 tons of enemy supplies.

So far, so good, it appeared.

But they soon ran into problems. As they had already known from the beginning, their own four landing craft hidden off Voza had been attacked by U.S. fighter planes whose pilots mistook them for enemy boats. Three landing craft were damaged, hence the overland march to Sangigai instead of a fast ride by boat.

Another snag came after companies E and F met at their planned rendezvous point following the action at Sangigai, once a quiet fishing village. As planned, Company E was picked up by a landing craft and taken back to the "Mountain Camp" above Voza; but Krulak and his Company F were left to fend for themselves overnight. Meanwhile, notes Greg Bradsher in the National Archives' magazine *Protocol* (Fall 2010), "natives informed Krulak that the Japanese were sending reinforcements to Sangigai—just as the Allied command hoped they would."

The next morning, October 31, Krulak and his men were picked up by a landing craft for a fast return to their temporary home base up the coast. The Marine party then moved inland to its mountain camp behind Voza.

Krulak sent out protective patrols, and arrangements were made for a Navy PBY flying boat to come for the wounded and for the Japanese documents seized from the wreckage at Sangigai. Next, the trouble-making Marines would turn northward and strike at Japanese facilities at Choiseul Bay, "to keep the Japanese guessing and to do as much damage as possible before their true strength was perceived." Maj. Warren T. Bigger and Company G were dispatched for this job and would strike on November 1—the very day that the Third Marine Division and Second Raider Battalion landed at Bougainville's Empress Augusta Bay.

As Bigger and his men headed northward in three landing craft, the enlarged Japanese forces were moving up toward Voza from the direction of Sangigai. And then Bigger's party literally "ran into problems"—at the mouth of the Warrior River and two hundred yards from shore, his boats ran aground on a shallow coral reef.

Their engines strained so loudly they might have been heard by the Japanese before he ordered his men to offload and slog ashore. Now bogged down in jungle and swampy ground, they fell behind schedule—there was no way to complete their mission and return in time to be picked up at the river-landing site by dusk. They would have to spend the night in the swamp and carry out their planned raid the following day, November 2.

With his own party's radio failing, Bigger sent several men back to the river to get in touch with Krulak by radio from there…but that radio didn't work either. Meanwhile, the Japanese had realized this was only a small force of Marines and were deploying eight hundred to one thousand fresh troops both above and below Voza.

Bigger could guess the enemy were stirred up, but had no certain knowledge of what was coming. Still, on November 2, he attacked a Japanese fuel dump with mortars, his number two planned objective. Meanwhile, at the river, his scattered men were engaged with the enemy.

The larger Japanese forces dispatched to Choiseul Island were in fact hunting down the Marines with grim intent. It wasn't long before two captured Marines were tied to trees, in one case bayonetted to death, and in the other, cut up with knives.

By radio, Krulak had asked for an evening PT-boat pickup of Bigger's men at the Warrior River. He was not yet fully aware of the pressure his men faced at or near the river as time approached for rendezvous and pickup. With the failure of their landing barge's engine, one group of surviving Marines was left drifting toward shore and under fire from the Japanese troops waiting for them.

About this time, personnel of Kennedy's PT Squadron 19, based at Lambu Lambu, seventy-five miles distant, were rushing to respond to Krulak's request for help. Only two PT boats—gunboats, really, rather than torpedo boats—were on hand, and one of them, Kennedy's PT-59, was in the midst of refueling. His fuel tank was only a third full, enough to get him to Choiseul's Warrior River but not all the way back.

Still underweight, gaunt, and sometimes unsteady on his feet in the aftermath of his nearly fatal adventure in August as skipper of the sunken PT-109, the future president didn't hesitate in responding to the plight of the stranded Marines. And never mind that his gunboat didn't have enough fuel to make the round trip all the way back to home base. He could always get a tow from his squadron's companion PT-236, which luckily was fully refueled. The PT-236 could accompany him part way, stand by while he dashed in for the Marines, and then give him a tow back home. The real issue would be getting there in time to help. Even then, could Kennedy's PT-59, only seventy-seven feet in length and with its own crew of eighteen, squeeze aboard sixty more men?

In fact, by the time JFK could draw close, the stranded Marines found that their still drifting landing craft was actually holed after scraping across a coral reef, and slowly sinking. The engine had quit because it was flooded out. To make matters worse, they had a totally helpless, critically wounded man with them.

Having reached the coastline off Voza about 6:00 p.m., JFK found Krulak himself and another PT-boat officer aboard a boat, and with their guidance set off to find Bigger and his men—"with the fuel gauge reading almost empty and only thirty minutes of daylight remaining."

Ahead, while under Japanese mortar fire, more of Bigger's Marines had left a landing craft with a bent rudder, only to pile aboard the very vessel that developed a hole in its hull upon striking the coral reef. Luckily, JFK's PT-59 came along just then and began taking on the Marines.

Dangerously overloaded, JFK's gunboat began the return dash to the American-held sanctuary at Vella Lavella. "Kennedy's crew gave the Marines canned peaches, the first real food they had had in six days. Up to that point, they had lived on one D bar and one K-ration per day. The men had lost an average of fifteen pounds each during their week on Choiseul." Refueled by PT-236 on the way, Kennedy's PT-59 arrived at his Lambu Lambu Cove base about dawn. Unfortunately, his critically wounded passenger, given JFK's own bunk, had died.

Meanwhile, with the Bougainville invasion an obvious, but hard-fought, success, there was no need for the remaining Marines to stay on at Choiseul. Fighting the Japanese until the last possible moment, they were extracted by Kennedy's same PT squadron early on November 4.

Thus, the small Marine force landing on Choiseul had succeeded in misdirecting the Japanese at a critical moment just before the Bougainville invasion, and had even drawn off some of the enemy's potential reaction forces. In addition, Krulak's Marines destroyed enemy facilities and captured helpful documents for Navy intelligence. Thanks to the stolen documents, the Navy was able to mine areas the Japanese considered safe and thus sink two Japanese warships.

Meanwhile, the physically exhausted Kennedy went on to more action against the Japanese in the same waters, but was ordered hospitalized at Tulagi on November 18. Kennedy was afterwards sent home in December for eventual discharge from the Navy on grounds of physical disability.

He would go on to serve in the U.S. House, in the U.S. Senate, and in the White House as President, until assassinated in 1963 by Lee Harvey Oswald, a former Marine.

SELECT UNIT HISTORIES
SEVENTH MARINES

Activated in 1917, the year the United States entered World War I, the Seventh Marine Regiment was immediately sent in search of Germans in Cuba, thanks to Cuba's production of sugar, considered a vital commodity even in wartime.

With the cooperation of the Cuban government, the idea was to protect sugarcane plantations and sugar mills owned by Americans and others from possible sabotage by German agents thought to be operating in Cuba.

Fifteen sugar mills were located in the area of Guantanamo Bay alone, and that is where the Seventh Marines were based at first. In time, however, elements of the regiment spread to posts at various locales throughout the Caribbean island. In an effort to show the flag without resorting to force that might upset the local populace, the Marines made themselves evident by marches and patrols, very much like a police force.

Without using their weaponry, or needing to, the Marines patrolled largely on horseback—at their peak number in Cuba, the Seventh Marines employed an estimated five hundred horses. They also were equipped with a few motor vehicles, but those all too easily bogged down on Cuba's primitive and often muddy roads.

The only fights threatening the Seventh Marines personnel were of the individual, barroom variety, it seems. In that vein, many a regimental veteran would return home still talking about a major such fight one night in June of 1918 that began as a barroom fistfight in Santiago's red-light district and then became a rock-throwing fracas with local men outside the establishment. "Reportedly, the Cubans pulled knives and attacked the Marines," says *A Brief History of the 7th Marines* by James S. Santelli. "A few of the Cubans then fired on the Americans with handguns and rifles[,] causing the unarmed Marines to scatter. The fight ended with three Leathernecks being injured, one seriously."

As a result, Santiago's red-light district was declared "off limits to the Seventh Regiment."

Meanwhile, the Great War in Europe came and went without any engagement by the "old boys" of the original regiment. Still, two decades later an entirely new generation, making up a reactivated Seventh Marines, would see plenty of action in the Pacific during World War II, starting with a four-month combat stint on Guadalcanal and continuing with landings on New Guinea, New Britain, Peleliu, and Okinawa in the long and bloody American march to Japan itself.

The Seventh, as part of the First Marine Division, then went on to thankless Marine Corps duty in Northern China, where Division units underwent repeated harassment, testing, and probing—albeit on small scale—by the Communists fighting the Nationalists in their longstanding civil war for control of China. The regiment briefly deactivated, then quickly reactivated; it would in fact be the last element of the Fleet Marine Force to leave China.

But then came the Korean War and fresh activation for the

Seventh, which took part in the Inchon Landing, the incursion into North Korea, the fighting withdrawal from the frozen Chosin Reservoir, and continued duty in South Korea until the signing of the 1953 armistice that ended the fighting.

Less than ten years later, during the Cuban Missile Crisis of 1962, major elements of the Seventh were aboard ship in the Caribbean and ready to land in Cuba again. At the last minute, the Soviet Union agreed to stand down and withdraw its missiles in Communist Cuba. Just three years later, the Seventh Marines was off to real war for a third time. The regiment was redeployed in Vietnam, where it would remain for five years fighting in one campaign after another, among them the Tet Offensive.

After a respite of twenty years, the regiment was thrown into the mix of wars in the Middle East from the 1990s and on into the twenty-first century. It was deployed once in the rescue of Kuwait from the Iraqi invasion of that small country, then three times in the Iraq War that began in 2003 and again in the Afghanistan conflict that began in response to the September 11, 2001, terrorist attacks on the Pentagon and World Trade Center.

One of the Seventh Marines' best known personalities was "Chesty" Puller, whose five Navy Crosses and other decorations—earned in the Corps' so-called "Banana Wars," in World War II, and in Korea—resulted in his reputation as one of the most decorated Marines ever.

Among many others of note was a fellow Guadalcanal veteran, Sgt. John ("Manila John") Basilone of the Seventh's First Battalion. Sergeant Basilone goes down in history, notes Marine historian Santelli, with the "double distinction" of being both the first enlisted Marine in World War II and the first Seventh Regiment Marine to be awarded the Medal of Honor.

He earned his medal for the courage he displayed on October 25, 1942, during a nighttime *banzai* charge against the Marine defensive lines by large numbers of Japanese. Basilone was credited with staying at his machine-gun post after bringing up fresh ammunition despite the intense enemy fire.

"I was very near Johnny that night," wrote First Marine Division veteran Ed Fee in the February–March 1998 *Guadalcanal Echoes* newsletter published by the Guadalcanal Campaign Veterans Association. Again and again, "His machine gun chattered ones, twos, and threes and then went full automatic for the balance of the belt when the Japanese charged."

The battle went on for "four straight hours," Fee added. During that time, "star shells fired from beach naval anti-aircraft fluttered, whistled, careened and exploded at tree height, illuminated [sic] him, front and above. When the battle quieted eighty Japanese lay within fifteen feet of his gun-nest."

Unfortunately, Basilone was killed on Saipan just months later, and fellow 'Canal veteran Fee asked why "the most celebrated enlisted man in the Marine Corps" had been allowed to go overseas again for a second tour.

The very next night after Basilone's medal-winning performance on Guadalcanal, the Second Battalion's platoon Sgt. Mitchell Paige earned the Seventh Regiment's second Medal of Honor. The impressive Sergeant Paige single-handedly manned his section's two machine guns after their supporting crews were killed or disabled during another Japanese attack, and afterwards led a bayonet charge that "drove the enemy off and prevented a breakthrough in Marine lines."

A "CLASSIC" FOOTBALL GAME

NEVER IN ALL THE ANNALS OF THE SOLOMON ISLANDS WOULD there be anything quite like it—a Christmas Eve All-Star football classic played by All Americans, the nation's premier running back of 1943, even pro football stars from back home as the Fourth and Twenty-Ninth Marine Regiments met for the 'Canal championship of '44.

No pads. No grassy field of play, either—just a rock-hard parade ground of baked earth and coral.

But, yes, there would be regimental band music before, after, and during halftime, and greetings at midfield to start the game by both regimental commanders. Plus, a switch at halftime from one side of the field to the other by Sixth Division CO, Maj. Gen. Lemuel C. Shepherd.

Kick-off at 1415 (4:15 p.m.), December 24, 1944.

The big game for the Marines occupying Guadalcanal after the departure of the vanquished Japanese began as two-handed touch football, but soon disintegrated into something a good deal rougher. People came away with bloodied knees and elbows as a matter of course.

For the men stuck at Christmastime on an alien jungle island in the middle of nowhere with plenty of combat lying ahead, there was a lot of steam to blow off.

And these were high-caliber players. "Both teams were made up entirely of former college football standouts who could have made any all-star team assembled in the States," writes Marine Maj. Allan C. Bevilacqua USMC (Ret.) in the December 2015 issue of *Leatherneck* magazine. Thus, the players included such stars as Notre Dame's 2nd Lt. "Irish George" Murphy, captain of the school's 1942 team, playing at the 'Canal as an end (called a "wide receiver" these days).

The day's rosters also included All-American Tony Butkovich of Purdue, the nation's leading ground-gainer in 1943, at fullback. Once the Big Ten's single-season rushing record-holder, Butkovich was a mere corporal in the Marines.

Both played for the Twenty-Ninth Marines, while the Fourth Marines could boast Wisconsin's former tackles Dave Schriener and Bob Bauman, both Marine Corps officers in 1944. Others fielded for the game included a scattering of professional players and host of additional college stars. The Fourth's running back John McLaughry, a standout at Brown and veteran of professional play with the New York Giants, later wrote to his parents, "It was really a lulu, and as rough hitting and hard playing as I've ever seen." He also said, "My dungarees were torn to hell in no time, and by the game's end, my knees and elbows were a bloody mess."

Bloody noses were also frequent, Major Bevilacqua writes, but still, "There were no cheap shots, no taunting, and no insults, just hard, clean, legal hitting on a rock-hard field."

As background for his account of the "Football Classic," or "Mosquito Bowl," Bevilacqua also recalls "a backwater of the war, far removed from the climatic battles fought in its jungles and swamps two years before, Guadalcanal [by now, in late 1944] was the staging area for Major General Lemuel C. Shepherd Jr.'s Sixth Marine Division."

For many of those playing and the hundreds more merely watching the Guadalcanal "Classic" on Christmas Eve of 1944, the words "staging area" meant many more months still ahead of absence from home and family, of primitive living conditions, of unfamiliar disease, of deprivation, and of more combat.

Even so, the "Football Classic" certainly was the "most ballyhooed football game west of Pasadena, California," Bevilacqua writes, but "in the glamour department," he adds, "it fell somewhat short of the New Year's Day Rose Bowl Classic and the Rose Parade that precedes it."

Somewhat? "Actually it was a bit more than that, a good bit more than that. In point of fact, the Football Classic was football at its most primitive."

No stadium, of course. But the hard-packed parade ground hosting the game had a name: "Pritchard Field, in honor of Corporal Thomas Pritchard, an explosive ordnance disposal specialist, who only the day before had died in an accidental detonation there."

Spectators? Oh, yes, by some (perhaps exaggerated) accounts, possibly as many as ten thousand—"perched and roosted wherever they could to watch the action."

It seems there was one football, elderly and somewhat worn.

No helmets, no cleats, no uniforms.

Running back Butkovich wore cutoff dungaree shorts and a T-shirt.

But that was by pregame design. To tell the players apart, he and his fellow Twenty-Ninth Marines wore shorts, and the Fourth Marines wore dungaree trousers.

"There were a few amenities," reports Bevilacqua. "Hundreds of programs had been printed, although with the players' uniforms bare of numbers, it was a bit difficult for spectators to know exactly who was who."

Beer was available—warm and tepid, to be sure, but beer still. The Communications people had rigged up a public address system. What more could anyone want?

Especially once the two-handed touch above-the-waist rule fell by the wayside. "After only a few opening possessions by each team, the game quickly evolved into football as full of hard blocking and tackling as any game played on college or professional gridirons thousands of miles away."

While a good time apparently was had by all, looming over everyone present was "the baleful unknown."

However, for the record, there were no miffed feelings, no complaints of running up the score. With a last-minute interception ending a threatened touchdown drive, the game between the two illustrious Marine regiments closed out in a tie, and a scoreless tie at that!

Since there was still a war going on, the story doesn't end there. As fate would have it, twelve of the game's players would be killed in the invasion of Okinawa in the months ahead, among them Notre Dame's "Irish George" Murphy, Purdue's rushing star Tony Butkovich, and Wisconsin's pair of tackles, Bob Baumann and Dave Schreiner.

"They say certain guys are heroes because they did this or that," commented Colorado A&M's onetime captain Walter "Bus" Bergman, himself a player in the 'Canal Classic. Looking back years later, he added: "I say the heroes are those guys who never came back. I've thought about that a lot. I think about the sixty or seventy extra years I got on them. I know I was lucky."

As cited by Denver *Post* sports writer Terry Frei in a Memorial Day piece published on May 26, 2014, Bergman's Twenty-Ninth Marines team for the game included his own tentmates Murphy and former Boston University tackle Dave Mears, all of them young lieutenants and platoon leaders in D Company, Second Battalion.

Another noted player in the 'Canal Classic was the Twenty-Ninth Regiment's player-coach and captain Chuck Behan, formerly of the Detroit Lions. The Fourth Marines' roll call included Sgt. Bob Spicer at quarterback and his occasional substitute, future major-league *baseball* celebrity Hank Bauer. Unfortunately, both Behan and Murphy died on Okinawa.

Some of Bergmann's heroes—and fellow game participants—would come back, as he did. They would even come back, whole in body in some cases—but in others, badly nicked.

As sports writer Frei also notes, Spicer was wounded by shrapnel in the arm, but returned to the battle for control of Okinawa. "I jumped over a ditch and found a bunch of Japanese soldiers lying there," he explained. "I guess somebody threw a grenade at me. That's how I lost my eye."

Returning home to Boulder, Colorado, he lettered at guard for the Colorado Buffaloes for three more football seasons and served as team captain in 1948.

"Incredibly," writes Frei, "he did it with one eye. After a long career in the banking business, he retired in 1989."

Bergmann, after a postwar lifetime spent as a football coach, died in 2010 as one of the last living participants in the 1944 Guadalcanal Football Classic—"a forgotten football game played long ago on a far-away island…unheard of by most Americans," says retired Marine Major Bevilacqua in his account for *Leatherneck* magazine. "For Marines, though, the island of Guadalcanal occupies a special niche in our history," he also writes, "and the Football Classic is woven into the cloth of our traditions."

MARINES OUT OF UNIFORM

WHILE MOST MARINES SERVED OPENLY, BRAVELY, EVEN BRASHLY AT times in the Pacific all through World War II, the Corps also had a man or two out of the enemy's sight in Europe and North Africa. Well, make that a few hundred out of the enemy's sight, but still relatively few, relatively unsung…and often even out of uniform.

These surreptitious Marines of World War II were the mere handful of carefully picked men, enlisted and officer-rank, fighting the Germans in Europe and North Africa as operatives for the Office of Strategic Services (OSS). And in this amazing group was one Peter J. Ortiz, USMC, who parachuted into occupied France to fight the Germans, first in civvies and a second time in full Marine Corps uniform.

The ironic fact is that Ortiz took his place in the boot camp ranks at Parris Island in a uniform already bedecked with combat ribbons marking his five years of service in the French Foreign Legion. It was almost no time before the chief of staff at Parris Island was writing Marine headquarters to say the newcomer's "knowledge of military matters was far beyond that of the normal recruit instructor."

His recommendation: Give this man a direct commission in the Marine Corps Reserve.

And no wonder, since Ortiz, born in New York City in 1913 to an American mother and a French father, had traveled extensively and attended school in France before quitting his studies at the University of Grenoble to enlist in the Foreign Legion several years before Nazi Germany invaded Poland in 1939. He fought with the Legion against the Rif rebels in Morroco, but after rising to acting lieutenant's rank and being wounded, he left the region and returned to America a decorated (two Croix de Guerre) combat veteran while still in his early twenties.

He briefly worked in Hollywood as a technical adviser on military movies, but re-enlisted in the Foreign Legion within weeks of the opening World War II hostilities in Europe. He won a battlefield commission in the massive Battle of France in May of 1940, but was wounded and captured the next month.

"Ortiz was taken when he learned that some gasoline had not been destroyed before his men had withdrawn," Marine historian Benis Frank writes in an online article for the California-based Military Museum (*Colonel Peter Julien Ortiz: OSS Marine, Actor, Californian*). "He returned to that area on a motorcycle, drove through the German camp, blew up the gasoline dump, and was on his way back to his lines when he was shot in the hip, the bullet exiting his body, but hitting his spine on the way out. He was temporarily paralyzed and easily taken."

Now came fifteen months as a prisoner of the Third Reich, a fallow period except for his repeated escape attempts. However, the last attempt in October 1941 finally paid off and enabled him to return to the United States by way of neutral Portugal on December 8, the day after Pearl Harbor.

Interrogated by Army and Navy intelligence officers, Ortiz waited several months for a promised commission. When nothing happened, he enlisted in the Marines in June of 1942. "He had been offered commissions by the Free French and the British in Portugal, but he wanted to wear an American uniform," says Frank.

He would indeed be yanked out of boot camp, and even though he already had made dozens of jumps with the Foreign Legion, he was sent first to parachute training. "I never minded jumping," he once quipped. "Airplane travel made me sick, so I was happy to jump out."

Meanwhile, word of this tall, debonair, unusually handsome, and multilingual combat veteran gradually filtered up through the higher echelons of American military circles. By now a captain, he was dispatched to nearby Morocco as an assistant naval attaché on the heels of the 1942 Operation Torch Allied landings in North Africa. But that was strictly a cover: he was *really* working for "Wild Bill" Donovan's OSS in coordination with British SOE (Special Operatives Executive) operations along the Tunisian border, as the OSS embarked on its first hit-and-run missions of the war against the Germans and their allies.

Thus, in early 1943, he was at hand for the Battle of Kasserine Pass.

"During the action Ortiz literally found himself traveling all across the battlefield," reports Dwight Jon Zimmerman in an online piece on July 20, 2014, for the Defense Media Network, titled *The Incredible Saga of OSS Col. Peter J. Ortiz in World War II: A Marine in the OSS.* "He witnessed the panicked flight of American soldiers during the opening hours of the German offensive, briefly fought with an armored reconnaissance unit from the British Derbyshire Yeomanry, then linked up and fought with elements of the American First Armored Division."

Himself once a member of a Foreign Legion armored unit, he ran across an "old Legionnaire friend," adds Zimmerman. "Ortiz attached himself to his friend's unit and fought a desperate action near Pichon."

A severe wound to his right hand—suffered while dispersing a German patrol with grenades—sent him to a hospital in Algiers. In May 1943 he was reassigned to OSS headquarters in London in preparation for jumping into Southern France to work with the Resistance there against the German occupiers, including the dreaded Gestapo.

He was then parachuted into the Haute-Savoie region of southeastern France in January 1943 as part of a three-man SOE team also consisting of British schoolmaster and Colonel H. H. A. Thackwaite, and a French radio operator known as "Monnier."

They were to link up with the Resistance movement against the Germans in the area of the Vercors Plateau to assess its numbers, weaponry needs, and prospects for the day the Allies would mount their widely expected invasion of occupied France.

"Not only were there some 3,000 Free French maquisards in the area, but it was planned to turn Vercors into a redoubt against which the Germans would attack in vain and which would be a major center of French resistance in the area to be called upon when D-Day arrived," Zimmerman writes.

The trio parachuted into France on a moonless night dressed in civilian clothing but carrying their uniforms—and now, as the team made contact with the local Maquis and gathered intelligence, the Ortiz legends were born.

For one, Thackwaite later reported: "Ortiz, who knew not fear, did not hesitate to wear his U.S. Marine captain's uniform in town and country; this cheered the French but alerted the Germans and the mission was constantly on the move."

According to a variation of the story that later emerged, Ortiz was present one time in a cafe when he heard several German patrons curse the Maquis, then mention the American "swine" in the area—himself, apparently. By most accounts, he threw aside his cape, guns in hand, to reveal the Marine uniform beneath, then made his escape from the café before the startled Germans could stop him.

By some versions, shooting did take place, and Ortiz was *not* among the wounded.

One of his favorite but bold tactics was to help himself to German staff cars from the enemy's motor pools. As mentioned in his citation for Most Favourable Order of the British Empire: "he ran great risks in looking after four RAF officers who had been brought down in the neighborhood and accompanied them to the Spanish border. In the course of his efforts to obtain the release of these officers, he raided a German military garage and took ten German motors which he used frequently."

In addition, he somehow "procured a Gestapo pass for his own use in spite of the fact that he was well known to the enemy."

Safely returning to England in May 1944, just days before the Normandy invasion of June 6, Ortiz was awarded the Navy Cross for his months-long undercover work in occupied France. Noting that he (usually) operated in civilian clothes and thus could be "subject to execution in the event of his capture," his Navy Cross citation also noted he led repeated raids on the German enemy, helped organize equipage drops for the Maquis and related Resistance groups, while inflicting "heavy casualties on enemy forces greatly superior in number, with small losses to his own forces."

Unsurprisingly, Ortiz was not done, for the war was far from over yet. On August 1, 1944, he parachuted into southern France again, this time at head of an OSS team consisting of an Air Force officer, five Marine sergeants, and a Free French officer with papers falsely saying the latter was also a U.S. Marine. The team boldly dropped by daylight near the town of Les Saisies in the Haute-Savoie region, accompanied by nearly nine hundred containers of weaponry, ammunition, and other supplies for the Resistance fighters.

One of the Marines, Sgt. Charles Perry, was killed when his parachute assembly failed, and he was buried with full military honors. In surviving photos, Ortiz can be seen attending the burial in full Marine Corps uniform. The team, meanwhile, carried on with its assigned contacts among the Maquis and their local allies in the common fight against the Germans.

All this came about just before the second great Allied invasion of France, this time on August 15 and from the Mediterranean Sea rather than the English Channel. Thus, the newly landed Allies would be driving hard for German-held territory close to where Ortiz, by now a major in rank, and company were operating in Southern France, primarily with the French Bulle Battalion.

But as events turned out, Ortiz and his men would not prove invincible. Coming under artillery fire in the town of Montgirod and driven into hiding in nearby mountains on August 14, the Ortiz team unexpectedly encountered a convoy of German troop trucks two days later at little Centron on the Isère River. As the Germans poured out of the trucks and began shooting, the six interlopers put up a stiff fight while splitting up into two sections of three each. Ortiz and the two Marine sergeants with him took the heaviest German fire as they retreated from house to house. But now the local residents begged them to give up, to avoid reprisals that would be imposed on the whole village—everybody was aware of the German "massacre"s at two small French towns and "the destruction of the town of Oradour-sur-Glane and all its inhabitants."

Ortiz agreed, although he expected that "we would not be treated as ordinary prisoners of war."

For his own part, he later wrote in an action report: "personally the decision to surrender was not too difficult. I had been involved in dangerous activities for many years and was mentally prepared for my number to turn up."

But he wasn't alone. Still with him were Marines John P. Bodnar and Jack R. Riser. "Sergeant Bodnar was next to me and I explained the situation to him and what I intended to do. He looked me in the eye and replied, 'Major, we are Marines, what you think is right goes for me too.'"

Shouting to the Germans that he wanted to surrender, Ortiz stepped out of cover during a brief lull in the firing. "[H]e stepped forward and calmly walked toward the Germans as machine-gun bullets kicked up dust around him. Finally, the firing stopped, and Ortiz was able to speak to the German officer in charge. The [German] major agreed to accept the surrender of the Americans and not harm the townspeople. When only two more Marines appeared, the major became suspicious and demanded to know where the rest of his enemy were. After a search of the town, the Germans accepted the fact that only three men had held off a battalion."

With Ortiz and three of his team—Bodnar, Risler, and the Frenchman Joseph Arcelin—all soon sent to the "loosely controlled" Marlag und Milag Nord naval POW camp near Bremen, the story only goes on.

Held at Marlag/Milag from the end of September 1944 to April 1945, the four "OSS Marines" and most of their fellow POWs were suddenly ordered to evacuate, to avoid liberation by the advancing Allied forces.

As the prisoner column marched along, it mistakenly came under attack by British Spitfires. In the confusion, Ortiz and three companions dashed into a nearby woods and hid. The column moved on without them.

"We spent ten days hiding, roving at night, blundering into enemy positions hoping to find our way into British lines," Ortiz himself later reported. "Luck was with us. Once we were discovered but managed to get away, and several other times we narrowly escaped detection…"

The surprise is, he and his companions finally decided they would be better off in the same POW camp they had left less than two weeks before, rather than hiding in the wilderness. It now seemed to be under control of the remaining POWs themselves and was likely to be liberated soon. In fact, it was, by the British Seventh Guards Armoured Division on April 29.

Returning to London with his fellow Marine POWs, Ortiz was awarded a rare second Navy Cross, in part for surrendering to the Germans in order to spare the villagers of Centron from Gestapo reprisals and then refusing to divulge harmful information when frequently interrogated by his captors. But the citation also goes on to say: "The story of this intrepid Marine Major and his team has become a brilliant legend in that section of France where acts of bravery were considered commonplace."

Remaining in the Marine Corps Reserve for some years and eventually retiring as a full colonel, Ortiz returned to Hollywood after World War II as both a technical adviser and occasional actor. "So dramatic were his adventures…that two movies were made about his accomplishments. One was not too bad a movie, *13 Rue Madeleine*, with James Cagney, and the second, a not-too-good one. This was *Operation Secret* with Cornell Wilde," adds Zimmerman also. Ortiz volunteered to return to active duty as an official observer for the Marines in French Indochina in 1954—the very year the insurgent Vietnamese won the Battle of Dien Phen Pu as prelude to the Vietnam War of the 1960s and 1970s—but he was turned down.

In addition to his two Navy Crosses, Legion of Merit with Combat V, and two Purple Hearts, Ortiz also held the French Croix de Guerre with five citations and the *Médaille des Blessés, Médaille des Évadés,* and *Médaille Coloniale* and was honored by the French as a Chevalier of the Legion of Honor. He died of cancer in 1988 at age seventy-four.

———

Additional Note: As noted by Marines historian J. Robert Moskin *(The U.S. Marine Corps Story)*, few Marines served in the European theater of war other than the handful with the OSS such as Ortiz and his fellow team members operating in southern France. Another "OSS" Marine was one Capt. John Hamilton, known better in later days as the movie actor Sterling Hayden—he jumped into Yugoslavia with Gunnery Sgt. John Harnicker and a Navy radio operator to work with the anti-German partisans, Moskin notes. Further, 306 other Marines did take part in the D-Day landings at Normandy, "including four officers on Eisenhower's staff and enlisted men who acted as riflemen on shipboard [that original Marines role!] and exploded floating mines in their ships' paths."

Moskin also writes that others fired 5-inch batteries during the North Africa and Normandy landings, while still more Marines from two U.S. cruisers "landed on the islands of Ratonneau and If near Marseilles and disarmed 700 Germans." But that was about it for the European and North African spheres of World War II.

MARINES WITH BODYGUARDS

TO A UNIQUE GROUP OF MARINES SERVING IN THE PACIFIC DURING World War II, destroyers were "sharks," tanks were "turtles," amphibious vehicles were "frogs" (what else?), and dive-bombers were "chicken hawks." One of these unique Marines was Samuel Billison, and like all the others in his special group, even as a mere private, he went into combat situations—Iwo Jima, for one—with a personal bodyguard.

The holder of a doctorate in education later in life, among other achievements, he was, in the words of the *Los Angeles Times*, "born on the floor of a humble hogan, destined to be a sheepherder."

But instead of a sheepherder on a Navajo Indian reservation, he first became a Marine, and then one of that super-exclusive cadre, a Navajo "Code Talker."

As one of America's "secret weapons" engaged in World War II, the Marine Corps trained 421 Indian Code Talkers, most of them Navajos, to use a largely Navajo-language code preventing the Japanese from understanding Marine radio and telephone talk in the combat zones of the Pacific.

Having always wanted to be a Marine, young Billison enlisted in the Corps the very day he graduated from high school in 1943. Just the year before, as he once explained, Japan's code experts were breaking into the American military codes almost at will. But then came the brilliant suggestion of American engineer (and World War I veteran) Philip Johnston, a missionary couple's son who had grown up on a Navajo reservation and knew the tribe's impenetrable, unwritten language. Why not use Navajo as the basis of a code the Japanese could not break, he proposed.

Realizing the possibilities, the Marine Corps quickly recruited an initial class of twenty-nine young Navajos "and told them to come up with a code incomprehensible even to other Navajos outside the program," says the *L.A. Times* account.

"They gave aircraft the names of birds, naval vessels the names of fish, and land vehicles that of animals," adds *Times* staff writer Myrna Oliver. The Japanese never did decipher all the Marine Corps "chatter" about "birds," " fish," and "animals."

The new code was used "in every Marine assault in the Pacific from 1942 to 1945," wrote Will Jones in the Richmond (Virginia) *Times-Dispatch* on the heels of a talk by Billison at the McGuire Veterans Affairs Medical Center in Richmond in November 2003.

"If you say it wrong, you might be cussing your father-in-law," Billison said on that occasion. "You really have to be careful." Just one word in Navajo could mean twenty things, depending on how it is spoken.

In the code developed by the cadre's first twenty-nine members in 1942, each letter in the English language was assigned several Navajo words. For example, writes newsman Jones, the letter A was assigned "wolachse," which means *ant*, "tsennill," which means *ax*, and "belasana," which means *apple*.

"For the many words with no Navajo equivalent," adds the Oliver account, such as foreign place-names such as Guadalcanal, the Code Talkers spelled them out using a Navajo word for each letter—*ant* for A and so on. To keep the Japanese from guessing the meanings behind repeated sounds, "each letter of the alphabet was represented by an accepted set of three alternating Navajo words."

Hence the letter A's *ant, ax,* or *apple.*

"The code was very difficult," Billison himself said at that same Richmond meeting, "but, after you learned it, it was very easy."

Interestingly, the Marines almost balked at adopting the Navajo code, for fear it was difficult to learn and too time-consuming for use in the field. But experiments at the Navajos' training ground at Camp Pendleton, California, "showed that older U.S. codes required two hours to encrypt, transmit, and decipher while the Navajo code took only 2.5 minutes," writes Oliver in the *L.A. Times.*

Even so, those passing through the tough training at Pendleton "had to memorize the difficult code without written notes."

During the Iwo Jima landing, she adds, Billison was one of six Code Talkers who transmitted more than 800 error-free coded messages in a key 48 hours of the fierce 36-day battle for control of the island and its badly needed airstrips. Two of the Navajo Code Talkers landing on Iwo Jima were among the 6,821 Marines killed or fatally wounded on Iwo. At same time, 20,000 Japanese defenders also died.

According to Major Howard Connor, signals officer for Billison's Fifth Marine Division, "Were it not for the Navajos, the Marines would never have taken Iwo Jima." So precious to the Marines Corps were the Navajos, in fact, that they were assigned a bodyguard in combat situations to protect them from capture and possible disclosure of the code if tortured.

The bodyguards were even ordered to kill their Navajo wards if their capture appeared certain, but luckily that never did happen.

Billison did survive the war, and before earning his doctorate in education, studied law at the University of New Mexico, notes Oliver in the *L.A. Times.* He became a teacher, school principal, and administrator who helped reorganize reservation education systems under the Bureau of Indian Affairs.

Once the highly secret Navajo Code Talker program became known in the late 1960s, Billison "served on the Navajo Nation Council and, in 1971—three years after their highly secretive work was finally declassified—helped organize the Navajo Code Talkers Assn., serving for years as president," adds Oliver.

With the secret finally out, books, articles, even a movie (*Windtalkers*, starring Nicholas Cage as a Navajo Code Talker's bodyguard) gave the Code Talkers some well-deserved credit for their brave work on behalf of their country. The never-broken code, Billison liked to say before his death in 2004, was quite a credit to "a bunch of 16-year-old kids who were sheepherders."

Meanwhile, long after the Code Talker secret became known, Congress jumped into the act in 2002 by awarding gold medals to the surviving five members of the original twenty-nine Code Talkers and silver medals to all the rest still surviving, Billison included.

As he also said that time in Richmond, however, people often asked how he felt fighting for America after its largely white early settlers, immigrants all, basically took it away from Native Americans. "It's very simple,'" he said at the time. "All the native Americans, we still think of North America as our country."

SELECT PERSONALITY
VICTOR H. KRULAK

He was dubbed "Brute" when he arrived at the Naval Academy at five-foot-four and 116 pounds, but that didn't stop him from earning a Navy Cross during World War II. Nor from persuading his own Marine Corps to adopt amphibious landing boats with drop-down ramps up front. Nor from paving the way for helicopter warfare, even before Korea became the conclusive proving ground.

Nor from serving brilliantly in three wars all told, WWII through Vietnam.

All this, and Victor H. Krulak never made commandant of the Marine Corps…although his own son Charles did.

While acknowledging his subject's propensity to embellish, even to deny, elements of his life story, the elder Krulak's biographer nonetheless calls him "the most important officer in the history of the Marine Corps."

Indeed, "his contributions accrued not just to the Marine Corps, not just to the U.S. military, but to America," argued Robert Coram, author of the biography *Brute: The Life of Victor Krulak, U.S. Marine,* in an interview by Maureen Cavanaugh of San Diego's KPBS public television station in December 2010.

Moreover, says Coram, General Krulak was a major buffer against efforts to diminish or disband the Marine Corps after World War II and victory for the Allies.

"Not many people know the constant unrelenting efforts of the Army over the years to diminish or to do away with the Marine Corps," Coram argued, adding that "basically the plan would have reduced the Marine Corps to a state of servitude, to a small 50–60,000 people whose job would essentially [be] to be a Navy police force."

That never would have suited the diminutive but always aggressive Krulak, who carried his personal "war" against U.S. strategy in Vietnam all the way to Lyndon B. Johnson's Oval Office.

He certainly looked a dim prospect for future command of all Marine Forces in the Pacific when he entered the Naval Academy—on a physical waiver—as a bantam-sized teenager. According to biographer Coram, a midshipman took one look at him and said, "Well, Brute."

It was meant sarcastically, of course. But "Brute" loved the name, Coram added, "and forever after that, he introduced himself as Brute Krulak." The smallest man ever to graduate from the Naval Academy at the time, he nevertheless cut a wide swath. Typical of his personality, it seems, one of his favorite expressions was, "This place needs an enema."

After a while, people forgot the origins of the name "Brute." They thought it had to be because he was one tough Marine, and he was.

Make that *resourceful* and tough. He was barely out of Annapolis and past Basic School at the Philadelphia Navy Yard in the mid-to-late 1930s when he was deployed to Shanghai, China, with the Fourth Marines as a company commander. That's when he found the solution to the problem the Marines— supposedly the nation's real experts at amphibious landings— had been having with their landing craft for years.

Until that time, the Marines and most other troops assault- ing an enemy beach by small boat had to climb, jump, or fall over the gunwales to get out, and all too often in deep water, sometimes even in water over their heads. But Krulak found the Japanese had developed the solution to that very problem. He simply adopted their solution—swiped it, really—from the Japanese themselves.

When they began invading China by landing troops on beaches, he cruised among the offshore Japanese vessels in a tug- boat as an observer—gunfire all around, bombs dropping, says biographer Coram—and immediately noticed that the Japanese landing craft had a mobile ramp at the bow that lowered down and eased the troops right onto the sand, while the propellers at the stern were protected in shallow water from grinding into the bottom by their housing in a concave chamber. In the shallow water, a pair of skids kept the craft upright.

He submitted his notes and photographs to headquarters…and nothing happened. Later, he discovered his report was filed away at Navy headquarters in Washington and forgotten as the work of "some nut out in China."

Undeterred, he made a two-foot model of the Japanese

landing craft from balsam wood and took it to his Marine Corps superiors. "And the short version is, he stole the design of the Japanese landing craft and put the drop bow on the Higgins Boat, which General [Dwight D.] Eisenhower later said won the war for America," adds Corum in the television interview. In addition, Krulak's flag-ranked son Charles once said, "There would not have been a Normandy or an Okinawa or an Iwo Jima without that boat."

For the Marines, it was sweet irony in the years after Pearl Harbor to be using the Japanese-designed drop-bow land-ing craft, built by Andrew Higgins's boat-building company, throughout their highly successful amphibious invasions of one Japanese-held island after another in the Pacific.

But Victor Krulak, still in his twenties and soon to be com-mander of a World War II Marine parachute battalion, wasn't done yet.

As his best-known combat experience—for which he won the coveted Navy Cross—he led a Marine raiding party of just 628 men onto the small island of Choiseul in the Solomons as bait intended to draw large Japanese forces, while a Marine division invaded strategically important Bougainville Island nearby (page 154). As his citation for the award states, "Although wounded during the assault on 30 October [1943], he repeatedly refused to relinquish his command and with courage and tenacious devotion to duty, continued to lead his battalion against the numerically superior Japanese forces."

Not yet a full colonel and serving out the war in major staff positions both stateside and in the Pacific, Krulak then took part in negotiations leading to the surrender of Japanese forces in the Tsingtao, China, area.

With the war over, he began looking at the primitive helicop-ters of the era with considerable interest—and foresight. In those days, Coram reminds that in those days, helicopters were "flimsy, slow, low performance, and a bit treacherous." They were more like toys than "serious military pieces of equipment."

But Krulak, at a time when choppers could fly at only eighty miles an hour, had the vision to "see the day when they could travel 200 miles an hour." And further, "At a time when helicopters could carry two people, he could see the day when they could carry 20, 40, 50 people."

And those people could be troops.

"He pushed the Marine Corps to create an experimental helicopter squadron." As a result, the Korean War, which erupted in 1950, played host to the world's first helicopter war, rather than Vietnam as many Americans may think. "That's nonsense," says Coram. "The Marines did it in Korea 15 years earlier, and they did it because of Victor Krulak."

At the time the Korean War broke out, General Krulak was serving in a high staff position with the Fleet Marine Force, but it wasn't long before he joined the fight in Korea as chief of staff for the First Marine Division. He flew so many reconnaissance and other flights in the first year of the war, often in helicopters, he earned an Air Medal.

By the time the Vietnam War heated up in the mid-1960s, he was directly involved as commander of the Pacific Fleet Marine Force with the rank of lieutenant general—and doing so with his customarily strong views on strategy and counterinsurgency warfare.

"And it was his belief that pacification—it was called combined action platoons or combined action program at the time—was better than the army program of attrition—of standing toe to toe, and slugging it out, and the last man standing wins," Coran explained in the TV interview.

Right or wrong in his views, Krulak was not in charge of the whole war, and his aggressive advocacy of his views may have cost him the office of Marine Corps commandant. With Vietnam still a major struggle for the United States in 1968, "when he had everything in the world to lose and absolutely nothing to gain, General Krulak went to Washington and went to the Oval Office and in effect said to Lyndon Johnson, if you don't release these stultifying restraints that you've placed on the military, if you don't let us do our job, bomb the harbor at Haiphong or take away the sanctuaries of the North Vietnamese, you're going to lose both the war and the [next presidential] election."

As a result, Krulak was firmly dismissed from the president's presence. By his own account: "As soon as he heard me speak of mining and unrestrained bombing of the ports [in North Vietnam], Mr. Johnson got to his feet, put his arm around my shoulder, and propelled me firmly toward the door."

The speculation is that his encounter with LBJ may well have been the reason he never was elevated to commandant—as many thought he fully deserved—and never was given a fourth general's star.

Former Defense Secretary Robert Gates once acknowledged Krulak's penchant for "overcoming conventional wisdom and bureaucratic obstacles thrown in one's path," while Marines writer-historian Bing West, a former assistant defense secretary, once said Krulak was legendary "for the depth of his intelligence."

A success in civilian life as well, Krulak joined the Copley Newspapers in San Diego, California, as both an executive and columnist once he retired from the Marine Corps in 1968. He also produced his well-received book on the history and culture of the Corps, *First to Fight: An Inside View of the U.S. Marine Corps.*

At the time of his death at age ninety-five in late 2008, the *Los Angeles Times* said of his book: "It remains on the official reading list for Marines and has been said to carry the DNA of the organization that prides itself on being the worst enemy that a foe of the United States can imagine."

======

ADDITIONAL NOTE: HIS THREE SONS, MARINE INFANTRY OFFI-cers Charles and William, and Navy Chaplain Victor Jr., all served in Vietnam. Remarkably, Charles, after a distinguished career of his own, became a commandant of the Marine Corps that his father loved so much. Charles, also a Naval Academy graduate, served two tours of duty in Vietnam as a platoon rifle company and battalion commander. He was later commanding general of the Tenth Marine Expeditionary Brigade and the Sixth Marine Expeditionary Brigade, Fleet Marine Force, Atlantic, before becoming commanding general, Fleet Marine Forces Pacific, a command his father held during the Vietnam War.

He was appointed the thirty-first commandant of the Marine Corps in 1995 and served in that capacity for four years before retiring to pursue civilian interests with the rank of full general. Among those interests, he served without salary as president of Birmingham-Southern University for four years before retiring from that post in the spring of 2015.

Among his many decorations earned as a Marine officer and leader, he was awarded the Navy's Distinguished Service Medal for his command of the logistical support system for the large First Marine Expeditionary Force engaged in the successful Desert Storm operations against the Iraqi invaders of Kuwait. "His 'nothing is impossible' attitude and resourcefulness provided the flexibility need to develop a Force operation plan which took advantage of the enemy weaknesses," his citation says. In the process, he created two of the largest combat service support areas in Marine Corps history. In a matter of days he turned empty desert into support facilities large enough to support two Marine divisions in combat.

Fighting men are vital, true, but so are the support systems and planners behind them.

THE UNHERALDED PEOPLE

BUT LET US HEAR ALSO OF OTHERS WHO SERVED ON THE FRONT lines often unnoticed, without clear and obvious glory…like World War II Marine Bert Clendenin. He was listed as a tail-gunner and radio operator, but in reality was a glorified crew chief (aviation mechanic) once left on a Japanese-occupied Pacific island to fix his wounded DC-3 aircraft all by himself. That is, left alone for weeks with needed airplane parts and life-giving supplies occasionally provided to him by air.

If it sounds a bit unusual, it was—even for a Marine. And yet it was not totally unique, writes Robert Akers in the Huntingdon (West Virginia) *Herald-Dispatch* of July 11, 2014. "Bert's experience on the islands of New Caledonia, Bougainville, Tarawa, and Green…was essentially the same and no different than the thousands of Marines deployed to the South Pacific. The temperature was extremely hot, wet, and slimy. The islands stink like rotten compost; they were covered in unbelievably deep mud and covered with huge mosquitoes."

These were no ordinary stateside mosquitos. These insects "were the size of a fly and moved in swarms so large that the joke was that it would take a shotgun to kill them."

Always hungry, never feeling adequately fed, Clendenin and his fellow Marines found an endless supply of coffee was their only real comfort. "The only problem with coffee was that the green flies loved the coffee. If a Marine became distracted, he would look back at his cup to find several flies swimming in the black drink."

Clendenin himself once said, "All you could do was toss the coffee out, bang the cup a couple times to knock the flies out, and get another cup."

Of course, the real point here is not the coffee, the flies, or the mosquitos, but rather the dangerous duty that unheralded people like Bert Clendenin performed day after day, in his case as a flying crew chief aboard a lumbering DC-3 transport delivering supplies to far-flung Marine detachments and picking up wounded for transport back to the rear.

Akers, himself an airline pilot, cites a passage from the book *Fighter Squadron at Guadalcanal* in which the author, Max Brand, writes: "I watched some big transport planes, DC-3s load up with the wounded and take off to carry them back to safety. It took extra armor-plated nerve to be the pilot of a DC-3 in a combat zone. Those planes will take a lot of tonnage, but they're slow, they make a big target, and there's not even a popgun for defense."

And right there, as crew chief, sitting in the copilot seat of one such transport, day after day, was Bert Clendenin. "His job was to make sure the aircraft was in top shape and to assist the pilot with flying and navigating duties," adds Akers. "Their first missions were supply runs to all of the islands, including Guadalcanal. As the war progressed, Bert and his squadron continued to fly farther north, always dangerously close to the Japanese battle lines."

On one "memorable" day, however, they flew out of the canal to avoid sniper fire so hurriedly that the plane was taxiing "before Bert was on board." Luckily, the radio operator pulled him aboard, "and away they flew."

Just moments before, Clendenin had been refueling the plane, and soon the pilot noticed they were losing fuel. They probably had been for quite a while, too. "Bert looked out the window and saw the cause of the fuel leak. The gas cap was bouncing on top of the wing attached by the metal lanyard."

In his hurry to avoid the expected sniper fire back at Guadalcanal, he had forgotten to secure the gas cap.

Dangerously low on fuel at this point, the pilot "made a bid for Russell Island, where there was an emergency airfield carved out of the jungle."

But then, more trouble. The pilot came in too fast, "because he was worried the engines would flame out at any second."

Then, still more problems. Quickly running out of space on the short emergency runway, "the pilot intentionally stood on the right rudder to aim for a clearing." But the plane "cartwheeled."

"Everyone survived the crash, but the airplane was a mess."

Thankfully, the Marines maintained a real, functioning airstrip across the small island; in fact, it was temporary home to the VF-214 "Black Sheep" squadron led by Major Gregory "Pappy" Boyington.

But elsewhere on Russell Island were Japanese troops, as well.

Regardless, "Bert sat with the plane while the pilot went to find help. The next day another DC-3 landed and took off with the pilot and radio operator."

That meant "Bert was left behind to fix the wrecked plane." Left behind for six weeks, as events turned out—but not totally alone or forgotten, exactly.

"Once a week for six weeks, an airplane brought aircraft parts, tools, mail and pay to Bert. It left with a list of supplies that Bert needed to complete the project. For six weeks, Bert slept in the back of the airplane, with both of his Thompson machine guns on his lap and his hand on the .45 [pistol] in the shoulder holster."

In addition, he crossed the small island just about every day to visit his new aircraft-mechanic friends at the "Black Sheep" airfield. "They shared everything with him, even when they didn't have it to share."

Meanwhile, as usual during his time in the South Pacific, he was always hungry. "Like all Marines in the South Pacific, he survived on local fruit, biscuits, and water."

The day finally came when his DC-3 appeared to be ready. He borrowed a Jeep that was the "Black Sheep" squadron's "main form of transportation," even though it was "riddled with bullet holes" and lacking its entire floorboard. Still, it would be useful in pulling his wrecked aircraft free from the jungle growth it had crashed into. So, he drove back through the island's aggressive foliage, holding his feet off the ground as he went.

With his plane soon standing free and looking good to go, his squadron flew in a pilot, a "crusty twenty-seven-year-old major," to try getting the DC-3 off the ground. "The major walked around the airplane without saying a word. He wasn't satisfied until he ordered Bert to get into the right [copilot's] seat. When Bert hopped up on the airplane the major smiled because he knew that if Bert would fly in it, then it would fly."

In short order, they took off and flew to Bougainville without incident. There, the plane "spent a single day in the hangar before the depot mechanics determined that not only was it ready to return to service but that it was one of the best airplanes in the fleet."

Still, "Bert never got a medal, commendation, thank-you, or a pat on the back" for his brave and lonely repair job. "The Marines were too busy fighting a war to take the time to give each other a medal."

In fact, Akers writes, Bert Clendenin would return to San Diego two years after he began his Pacific War tour with only sixteen of his original hundred-man company walking off his troop-carrier ship with him: "The rest of his Company was killed in action serving as radio operators in the SBD-3 Dauntless Dive-Bombers, tail gunners in the Grumman Torpedo Bomber TBF Avenger, or flying as crew chiefs in the DC-3. Very few survived to be sent home as a wounded Marine. He never learned how his friends died, just that they took off in the morning and never returned."

───────

ADDITIONAL NOTE: AIRLINE PILOT AND FREELANCE WRITER AKERS, AN officer in the West Virginia Air National Guard, served abroad himself. He was deployed to Bosnia, Iraq, and Afghanistan, among other foreign duty posts, earning three Air Medals, four Aerial Achievement Medals, and two Meritorious Service Medals in the process.

BIRTHING AN "ALLIGATOR"

EVEN THOUGH VICTOR "BRUTE" KRULAK DESERVES MAJOR CREDIT FOR development of the Marine Corps' landing craft used so extensively in the island-hopping campaigns of World War II, he himself credited boat-builder Andrew Jackson Higgins for much of the same landing boat's great success.

As Krulak wrote in his book *First to Fight*, "As far back as 1900, when the concept of the Advanced Base Forces [i.e., amphibious striking forces] was born, the Marines were obliged to face the problem of moving their heavy equipment and supplies ashore over undeveloped, often surf-pounded beaches."

Progress in that regard was slow, with few real solutions found almost until the last days of peace before Pearl Harbor. Credit Krulak for the discovery of the front-end landing ramp used by the Japanese in the assault he "observed" on the Chinese Coast at the mouth of the Yangtze River in 1937. Meanwhile, American boat-builder Higgins had developed a boat, the *Eureka* "with a novel underwater hull, for use by rum-runners in the Mississippi Delta during Prohibition." Ideal for beach landings, the special hull design "protected the propeller from striking the bottom and facilitated retraction from the beach."

In March of 1941, at the behest of Maj. Gen. Holland M. ("Howling Mad") Smith, Krulak traveled to New Orleans to have Higgins redesign the *Eureka* with a landing ramp up front. After fast work by Higgins and fast approval by a combined Navy–Marine evaluation board, "The Navy then ordered two hundred of the Higgins ramp-type boats and, at long last, the LCVP (Landing Craft, Vehicle, and Personnel)—workhorse of World War II—was a reality."

Even so, for organizers of Marine amphibious operations, supposedly the Marine Corps' specialty, there was yet another challenge ahead—how to cross a coral reef, with or without accompanying surf. This was crucial, since so many of the Pacific islands soon to be occupied by the Japanese were surrounded by coral reefs. As pointed out by the mysterious Major "Pete" Ellis in "his forecast of the Great Pacific War" back in 1920, the water covering the coral reefs often would be too shallow to accommodate a boat, or heavy surf could be breaking right at the reef. Either condition could be a threat to a landing craft.

"While Ellis had no answers to the coral reef problem, he did his successors a favor by illuminating its magnitude," wrote Krulak. Obviously enough, not even the innovative Higgins Boat would solve the coral reef problem.

Enter now a second civilian patriot and entrepreneur, Donald Roebling, son of John Roebling, "the steel and wire rope magnate" of the same family that built the Brooklyn Bridge.

His creation, hand-built in the 1930s, was a rugged rescue vehicle on tanklike tracks, "equally at home in the water and on the land, one capable of crawling over any forbidding Everglade terrain—over mangrove and irregular coral, through mud and shoal water—and one with respectable cargo capacity."

His latest, much improved version of the Roebling *Alligator* generated nationwide publicity in 1937, and that brought it to the attention of the Navy and the Marine Corps. By the spring of 1940, with the war clouds fast gathering, "the first version of a military amphibian tractor, built by hand in Roebling's shop in Dunedin, Florida, was completed."

As with the last-minute acceptance of the Higgins Boat: "There was no great bureaucratic delay in the process. The Marines saw something they believed would help them fight the upcoming war. They persisted in their effort to get it. Donald Roebling, once he was convinced the idea was important, willingly gave his time and later his design. The Navy cooperated and, in twelve months, from decision to launch, it all happened."

Perhaps no surprise, before the Marines ordered the tracked amphibian vehicle in quantity, the ubiquitous Krulak himself was placed in charge of the testing program...with near-disaster encountered at one point.

With the machine doing well, the day came—at exercises at Culebra, Puerto Rico—when General Smith directed Krulak to "put it through its paces for Admiral Ernest J. King, who had just assumed command of the Atlantic Fleet."

King, later to be the Navy's top admiral during World War II, was not exactly known for an affable manner.

"Following General Smith's instructions," Krulak writes in his book, "I brought the amphibian alongside the flagship, the old battleship *Wyoming*, where General Smith had his headquarters, went on board and explained the machine's capabilities to the admiral. He did not seem particularly interested, but when General Smith offered him a ride, he agreed, more as a courtesy than anything else. He specified, however, that his time was short and that the ride must be brief. Along with an aide, he boarded the amphibian and observed its operation as we cruised around the flagship."

All was going well enough, but Krulak then made a fateful decision. On impulse, "I headed the craft toward the nearby coral reef that fringed the harbor and told the admiral that I intended to show him how it behaved in crossing the rough coral surface. He did not want to go, saying that time was short, that he was due back in the flagship."

But Krulak assured him it would take "only a few moments." After all, they were in a protected harbor, the water was calm, no large waves were breaking at the reef, which was covered with three feet of water—no challenges in sight whatsoever.

However, as fate would have it, a coral head knocked off one of the tracks. "There we were, helplessly immobilized some fifty to one hundred yards from dry land, unable to go one way or another, inaccessible." And Krulak knew from experience in these matters it would take at least two hours to fix the track problem.

Of course, King directed "a few plain words" to Krulak, "words not intended to contribute to my long-term peace of mind." Then he departed, with his aide hurrying after. "He clambered over the side— starched white uniform and all… [T]hey waded ashore to the accompaniment of the admiral's cursing, thumbed a ride to the dock two miles away, and finally made their way back to the *Wyoming*."

Fast forward a few years to New Caledonia in May of 1943. Now CO of the Second Parachute Battalion, Krulak was once again ordered to test the new LVT (Landing Vehicle, Tracked), but this time on a coral reef being battered by heavy surf. With still more Japanese-held islands to be assaulted at that point in the Pacific War, it would be important to know if the LVT could handle large waves and a coral reef at the same time.

Until then, the LVT had been considered a supply vehicle "because of its thin skin and slow speed." But as events turned out, the LVT did so well that 125 of them were assigned to the expectedly tough Tarawa landing "in an altogether new role—as a conveyance for troops in the initial assault."

In the assault at Tarawa, a bitter fight from the start, "Troops were disembarked from transport ships into landing craft and then transferred to LVTs for the final run across the reef to the beach." The hard-earned Marine victory there came "replete" with testimonials to the decisive contribution of the LVTs, Krulak asserted.

Even so, "It was a bloody time for the LVT crews and their passengers," he conceded. "Some sixty-one tractors were disabled by enemy defensive fire either at sea or as they repeatedly crossed the reef with successive loads of men and supplies. The remainder of the tractors succeeded in making numerous trips with their precious cargo of assault troops intact. At the shoreline, eleven more were knocked out by direct fire weapons or land mines. All things considered, however, they served their purpose well."

Sadly, this was at the cost of a 60 percent casualty rate for the personnel of the Second Amphibian Tractor Battalion.

Still, the LVT had proven its worth. At the urging of General Smith, it would henceforth be given a ramp like the "pure" landing craft developed earlier, along with more armor, more speed, and better communications equipment.

By the time of the Marines landings at Cape Gloucester, Guam, Saipan, Tinian, Iwo Jima, and Okinawa, many of the LVTs would even be armed with a 37-millimeter gun or a 75-millimeter howitzer. At Okinawa, moreover, "once ashore, the LVT weapons were integrated into the structure of Marine division artillery and fired in close support of the advancing forces."

As Krulak summed up, by war's end more than fifteen thousand LVTs "had been built and had served in every theater of war." Roebling's *Alligator* has done its job.

IWO PHOTO REVISITED

AFTER YEARS OF CONFUSION, CLAIM, AND COUNTERCLAIM OVER THE Marine flag-raising at Iwo Jima, a new official study has resulted in a new ruling…and still a mystery remains. A few mysteries, actually.

However, some issues *have* been resolved. First of all, and long ago, it was established that not one but two flag-raisings took place on the fanatically defended Pacific island. As it turns out, the one flag-raising that produced the world-famous photo, which in turn inspired the iconic Marine War Memorial statue next to Arlington National Cemetery across the Potomac River from Washington, DC, was actually the *second* flag-raising on Iwo's dominant Mount Suribachi. That came at about 12:20 a.m. on February 1, 1945, the fourth day of battle following the costly Marine landings on Iwo Jima.

But first, with real whoops and hollers among hundreds if not thousands of spectators watching, there had been the raising of a smaller American flag on the high mountain slope. *Leatherneck* magazine photographer Ssgt. Louis R. "Lou" Lowery photographed that flag-raising. "Shouts and celebrations were heard from the Marines on the beach as ships in the surrounding waters sounded their horns," writes *Leatherneck* editor Col. Mary H. Reinwald, USMC (Ret.) in the July 2016 issue of the magazine.

But that wasn't the flag-raising nor the photo that would inspire a distant national audience—and fellow Marines everywhere.

Reporting on the latest official panel to rule on longstanding "issues" dogging historical accounts of how it all happened that day on Iwo Jima, Reinwald explains that soon after the first flag went up, "a resupply patrol, tasked with replacing the first flag with a larger one, was sent to the top of Suribachi."

Among the patrol members were Sgt. Michael Strank, Cpl. Harlon H. Block, Pfc. Ira H. Hayes, and Pfc. Franklin R. Sousley. "Joe Rosenthal, an Associated Press photographer, joined them as they made their way up the mountain." Also climbing the mountain slope with the patrol were Fifth Marine Division combat correspondents Sgt. William H. Genaust and Pfc. Robert R. Campbell.

"The second flag was raised at approximately 1220 as the first flag was lowered," relates Reinwald, herself a member of the latest Marine Corps panel convened—after seventy-plus years—to identify and correctly credit the flag-raisers. This was a major point to resolve, even so long after the fact, although there still was no question that "Joe Rosenthal photographed the second flag-raising, and one of his shots became the iconic photo."

Meanwhile, relatively few Marines on the ground at Iwo Jima or in the nearby waters took much notice of the second flag-raising, even though the flag this time was larger. First Lt. Harold G. Schrier of the E Company (Second Battalion, Twenty-Eighth Marines), the officer who led the patrol raising the first flag that morning, didn't see the second one go up—he was busy tending to the lowering of the first flag.

Meanwhile, "When Rosenthal's photograph was sent back to the States, the sensation it created led to a decision to bring the flag raisers home to take part in a war bond tour," adds Reinwald. "Pfc. Rene A. Gagnon returned to the United States in April 1945 and identified the flag raisers as Sgt. Hansen, PhM2c (Pharmacist's mate, second class). [John H.] Bradley, Sgt. Shrank, Pfc. Sousley, Pfc. Hayes and himself. Bradley and Hayes also were brought to Washington, DC, that month, and they confirmed Gagnon's identification of the flag raisers."

Now it seems they were wrong, not only in terms of who was where, but also who was there…and who was not there at all. For starters, Hayes, a Pima Indian from Arizona by background, confirmed a year later that Harlon Block, rather than Hansen, was the Marine in what's called position #1 in the Rosenthal photo.

Then, too, the latest panel investigating the iconic flag-raising, headed by Lt. Gen. Jan C. Huly, USMC (Ret.), determined that both Block and Gagnon were there in positions #1 and #2 as previously thought. But it turns out in the closest forensic examination yet that

Sousley was in position #3, rather than at #5, as previously thought, and rather than Bradley.

Strank, meanwhile, still was placed at position #4 by the Huly panel, and Hayes still looked good at #6.

So, who was at #5 rather than Sousley, now thought to have been at #3?

With photographic evidence of a broken helmet liner strap as a key to his identity, the Huly panel determined it was Pfc. Harold H. Schultz of Detroit, a member of Lieutenant Schrier's Company E. As further evidence of his presence, the panel said, the sling of his rifle could be seen attached to the stacking swivel, rather than to the upper-hand guard sling swivel, as would have been appropriate. He apparently was the only Marine seen in the photos with both the broken helmet liner strap and inappropriate sling attachment.

Oddly enough, adds the Reinwald account of 2016, "no previous identification or claim that Pfc. Schultz was a flag raiser has ever been found."

At same time, the addition of Schultz to the famous photograph seems to eliminate Bradley. Ironically, Bradley's son James and co-author Ron Powers collaborated on the bestselling book about the flag raisers, *Flags of Our Fathers*. The book later was the basis for a movie directed by Clint Eastwood.

The double-edged point regarding Bradley and Schultz first was raised by the *Omaha World-Herald* in late 2014 under the headline: "New Mystery Arises from Iconic Iwo Jima Image." Explains Reinwald: "The story detailed the efforts of two history buffs, Stephen Foley and Eric Krelle, to prove that Pharmacist's Mate Second Class John H. Bradley, the corpsman who was awarded the Navy Cross for his actions in the initial days of fighting during the Battle of Iwo Jima, is not in Joe Rosenthal's iconic photograph of the flag raising on February 23, 1945, as had been believed for almost seventy years."

It should also be noted that since Iwo Jima was a real firestorm for the invading Marines, there were casualties among those associated with the second flag-raising.

"The fighting on Iwo Jima took a huge toll on the Marines involved in the second flag raising," Reinwald writes. "Both Cpl. Block and Sgt. Strank were killed in action on March 1, as was Sgt. Hansen. Pfc. Bradley was wounded on March 12 and evacuated the next day. Pfc. Sousley was killed on March 21."

In the wake of the Huly panel's findings, some questions are resolved, but several are not. The Marines plan more analysis, and among the questions yet to be answered, adds Reinwald:

"Why weren't the flag raisers identified clearly from the beginning? Why did John Bradley, Ira Hayes, and Rene Gagnon identify Bradley as the individual in Position #3?… Why did no one notice the absence of a corpsman's gear on anyone depicted in the photograph and the memorial [statue]? And perhaps most puzzling, why did Schultz never say anything?"

In partial reply to some of the issues, Reinwald also points out that no one on the scene that terrible day realized the inspiring impact that Rosenthal's photo would have. Meanwhile, the life-and-death struggle on Iwo Jima raged on for days, even five weeks, with nearly 6,000 of the 70,000 Marines taking part killed and another 17,400 wounded. With four of the original flag raisers killed and Bradley wounded, "only Ganon and Hayes emerged from their time on Iwo Jima physically unscathed."

As for Schultz, it appears he was also seriously wounded at Iwo Jima, recovered, and then spent three decades working for the U.S. Postal Service in the Los Angeles area. A quiet, self-effacing man, according to news accounts, he first married at age sixty-three.

A stepdaughter, Dezreen MacDowell, was quoted as saying he once, at dinner in the 1990s, did mention that he was one of the flag-raisers. "Harold, you are a hero," she apparently responded. But he said, "Not really. I was a Marine."

In the same vein, both *Leatherneck* editor Reinwald and former Marine Corps Commandant Gen. Robert Neller agree that it's the spirit and symbolism of the iconic photo that really matter. "Simply stated," Neller said in 2016, "our fighting spirit is captured in that frame and it remains a symbol of the tremendous accomplishments of our Corps—what they did together and what they represent remains most important. That doesn't change."

———

ADDITIONAL NOTE: IWO JIMA IS A VOLCANIC ISLAND ONLY EIGHT square miles in size, and lies just seven hundred miles south of Tokyo. Before the Fourth and Fifth Marine Divisions landed on the heavily defended island's southeast beaches in February 1945, it gave the Japanese an important radar and fighter-plane base from which to harass American B-29 Superfortresses flying from the Marianas Islands to bomb the Japanese homeland. Securing the island would eliminate that constant threat and provide fighter protection for the big bombers. Seizure of the island would also give them an emergency landing strip for use on their way home to bases at Saipan and Tinian.

Unfortunately for the attacking Marines, Iwo Jima also offered possibly the strongest Japanese defenses and heaviest enemy firepower of any island in the Pacific. The 20,000 to 21,000 defenders fought back—usually to the death—from an estimated 1,500 fortified caves, scores of ferroconcrete pillboxes, blockhouses, trenches, and miles of interconnecting tunnels.

SCULPTURE FOR THE AGES

SOON AFTER THE U.S. NAVY COMBAT ARTIST FELIX DE WELDON FIRST saw Associated Press photographer Joe Rosenthal's photograph of the Iwo Jima flag-raising, he set to work for three straight days creating a model sculpture made from a mix of Johnson's soft floor wax and some hard sealing wax.

The first result was so impressive, the Austrian-born de Weldon was immediately pressed into doing larger and larger models for both the Marine Corps and the Treasury Department's war bond drives. Today, the final result is the seventy-eight-foot U.S. Marine Corps War Memorial statue overlooking Washington, DC, from a key site close to the war-veteran graves lining Arlington National Cemetery.

The late de Weldon was not only the sculptor behind that imposing sculpture but also the creator of more than two thousand public sculptures around the world, including busts of Presidents Truman, Eisenhower, and Kennedy at their respective presidential libraries.

The U.S. Navy enlisted man previously had "done" kings, statesmen, political, and military figures of note, but he would become best known for his Marine Corps War Memorial in Arlington, Virginia, honoring the more than six thousand Americans killed and twenty-five thousand wounded in the Battle of Iwo Jima in 1945, as Douglas Martin noted in his *New York Times* obituary of de Weldon. As of that time, the *Times* had also said, "More than 100 million people have visited it since it was dedicated in 1954."

It is, overall, quite a piece of work. "The memorial weighs more than 100 tons and is one of the largest bronze-cast statues in the world," added Martin in the *Times* obituary for de Weldon, who had died on June 2, 2003, at the age of ninety-six. "The M-1 rifle carried by one of the figures is sixteen feet long." The carbines, for that matter, stretch to twelve feet each.

Originally taking shape in plaster, the gigantic memorial statue was then sent in 108 pieces to the Bedi-Rassy Art Foundry in Brooklyn, New York, to be cast in bronze, a process taking three years, according to the Semper Fi Parents website. "After the parts had been cast, cleaned, finished, and chased, they were reassembled into approximately a dozen pieces and brought back to Washington by a three truck convoy." Once raised, six human figures towered up to thirty-two feet and stood on Swedish granite.

The sculpture was dedicated by President Eisenhower on a Marine Corps birthday, November 10, 1954. The inscriptions on the War

Memorial, really intended as a symbol honoring *all* Marine Corps dead, include the tribute by Fleet Admiral Chester Nimitz for the Marines who fought at Iwo Jima: "Uncommon valor was a common virtue."

De Weldon's painstaking approach to his sculpture process included modeling the faces of the three flag-raising survivors in clay. For the other Marines taking part, all three then erroneously presumed dead (page 195), the sculptor used all the pictures and physical details available. He also first molded all six figures in the nude "so that the strain of muscles would be prominently shown after clothing was modeled on the struggling figures," adds Semper Fi Parents.

In addition, "Steel framework, roughly duplicating the bone structure of the human body, was assembled to support the huge figures under construction."

Meanwhile, a nine-foot model of the future memorial toured war bond rallies across the nation under Treasury Department auspices.

The Austrian-born combat artist de Weldon had grown up in Vienna as the son of a textile manufacturer during World War I. After studies in Rome, Paris, and Madrid, he settled in London between the world wars and was known for his busts of England's leading royal figures. He came to the United States by way of Canada in the 1930s.

According to *Times* writer Martin, as a civilian, de Weldon always worked in a coat and tie.

While he often relied on the help of hired mechanics and moldmakers for his larger works, Martin added, the sculptor insisted his own ten fingers were the only other "sculptors" he employed.

BLACK MARINES FINALLY WELCOME

IT IS HARD TO BELIEVE THESE DAYS, BUT UNTIL WORLD WAR II, BLACK personnel were not welcome, nor even found, in the U.S. Marine Corps. That's the reason a young *white* Marine was startled to see *black* Marines trucking ammunition from the beach to the front lines on the embattled island of Peleliu one day in 1944.

Not only did Edward Andrusko of Company I, Seventh Marines, see his first black Leathernecks on the beach at Peleliu, writes Marine Corps historian Bernard Nalty in the Marine Corps' historical monograph *The Right to Fight: African-Americans in World War II*, but he accepted the offer of a ride inland from one of the African American truck drivers. With a load of high explosives sitting right behind his seat up front in the truck and the noise of battle soon sounding ahead, Andrusko thought maybe he hadn't made a good choice of transportation. But he did reach his unit safely, Nalty notes.

In fact, Andrusko ran into the black Marines again not long after as his company, "advancing through the island's rugged terrain, encountered concealed Japanese positions and came under fire that pinned the men down."

Andrusko and his first sergeant went to "find riflemen to take the place of casualties and stretcher-bearers to carry off the wounded and dead."

The first Marines they encountered proved to be of the very unit he had met on the beach, and the [black Marines] immediately volunteered to help, Nalty also notes. Andrusko's first sergeant also had no idea that black Americans were serving in the Marine Corps, "so complete was the segregation of the races, but he welcomed their aid."

In further fact, the black Marines on Peleliu that day moved up the ridges where Company I was fighting, carried off casualties, and manned empty foxholes "to help beat back a nighttime Japanese counterattack." One of the wounded they carried off compared them to "black angels sent by God."

At the time, noted Nalty, "few white Marines knew that African Americans had been serving in the Corps for more than two years." And no wonder: "The leadership of the Marine Corps had shown scant enthusiasm for accepting African Americans, who had to overcome the barrier of racial prejudice as they struggled for the right to serve. But serve they did, ably and gallantly."

As an example cited by Nalty: the Marine Corps' own commandant going into World War II, Maj. Gen. Thomas Holcomb, once said blacks had no place in his organization. "If it were a question of having a Marine Corps of 5,000 whites or 250,000 Negroes, I would rather have the whites," he apparently declared.

But the pressure for acceptance of black personnel into the Navy, and thus the Marines, was strong both from America's leaders of color and from President Franklin Delano Roosevelt, himself once an assistant secretary of the Navy. As a first step, the Navy took in black sailors as messmen or stewards.

However, as late as the summer of 1941, Navy Secretary Frank Knox "opposed the recruiting of African Americans except as stewards in officers' messes," Nalty reports. But Knox subsequently and "reluctantly" suggested accepting five thousand black men for general service in the Navy.

Even so, Commandant Holcomb still "voiced his deeply felt misgivings" and complained that black Americans seeking Marine Corps billets were "trying to break into a club that doesn't want them." The Army, by contrast, "had maintained four regular regiments of black soldiers since shortly after the Civil War."

Without demanding full integration of black men with their white counterparts in the armed services, FDR kept pushing the issue of black military service until finally, on April 7, 1942, weeks *after* Pearl Harbor, Knox told the Navy, Marine Corps, and Coast Guard they must take in black recruits for general service. After another six weeks passed, the Navy announced that those same services would take in one thousand of the newcomers a month and the Marines, specifically, "would organize a racially segregated 900-man defense battalion, training the 'blacks' recruited for it from the beginning of boot camp onward."

As of June 1, 1942, the Marine Corps began recruiting "colored male citizens of the United States between the ages of seventeen and twenty-nine, inclusive, for service in a combat organization." What this meant would be segregated, all-black units commanded by white officers, starting with a brand-new "boot camp" in North Carolina, entirely separate from the Corps' longstanding Parris Island boot camp to the south in South Carolina.

Thus were born the so-called Montford Point Marines.

At first, however, the black recruitment campaign went slowly. "By the end of September about half of the 1,200 recruits needed to man the [Fifty-First Defense] battalion and render administrative, housekeeping, and transportation support had enlisted." More happily, a new draft provision of January 1943 for all services assured the Marines of 1,000 black recruits every month.

Meanwhile, "Segregation prevailed at the Marine Barracks, New River, North Carolina—soon redesignated Camp Lejeune—where the African Americans would train, and in the nearby town of Jacksonville. For the black recruits, the Marine Corps established a separate cantonment, the Montford Point Camp, in westernmost Camp Lejeune."

The recruits at Montford Point not only found strictly white officers in charge, but at first a special staff of all-white enlistees, as well, filling jobs ranging from clerk to typist or even drill instructor. These were replaced as quickly as possible with the newly trained black Marines.

Thanks to the draft-generated influx of black Marine recruits pouring into the ranks every month, Secretary Knox authorized the creation of a Marine Messman Branch (later the Stewards' Branch) "and the first of sixty-three combat support companies—either depot or ammunition units—as well as a second defense battalion, the Fifty-Second."

Still, both fears and prejudices against black Marines remained. When the Fifty-First Defense Battalion was considered ready for deployment to the Pacific, the Marine major general in command of American forces on Samoa warned that the presence of a black battalion would "infuse enough Negro blood into the population to make the island predominantly Negro."

Even while traveling across the United States by train for embarkation at San Diego, the men of the unit occasionally ran into hostility or had brushes with local Jim Crow laws on segregation.

After weathering those problems at home, the pioneer black battalion spent six months in the Ellice Islands upon first reaching the Pacific theater of war. In September 1944, it transferred to Eniwetok Atoll, "a vast anchorage kept under sporadic surveillance, and occasionally harassed, by Japanese aircraft."

By now equipped with anti-aircraft guns, searchlights, and radar, "the battalion stood ready to meet the threat from the skies." But no real action ever did transpire for these early black Marines.

It was much the same story for the second battalion of blacks emerging from Montford Point. It was deployed to the Marshall Islands, again as an antiaircraft unit, with one half based on Majuro Atoll to protect the locally based Marine Aircraft Group 13, while the other half "helped defend Roi and the adjacent island of Namur in Kwajalein Atoll, where Marine Aircraft Group 31 was located."

While little action was seen by either group, the black recruits on Majuro did form reconnaissance parties that boarded landing craft "to search the smaller islands for Japanese and [to] remove the natives from harm's way." The two battalion groups then were reunited on newly recaptured Guam to become part of the island garrison.

Meanwhile, the Marine Corps had formed its new black depot and ammunition companies from the new wealth of manpower provided by the draft.

While the two black defense battalions deployed to the Pacific saw little action, the story was quite different for the men of the depot and ammunition companies, originally considered akin to stevedores. Far from safe in their jobs, they "saw savage fighting in the battlefields of Saipan, Tinian, Guam, Peleliu, Iwo Jima, and Okinawa." All told, the Corps fielded fifty-one depot companies and twelve ammunition. Their black Marine personnel normally were equipped with rifles, carbines, or submachine guns. They appeared for the most part in both the South and Central Pacific islands.

Typically of the action they sometimes experienced during the invasion of Saipan in June 1944, a squad from a depot company "fought as infantry to reinforce a thinly held line about a hundred yards from the water's edge." Many of the same men next helped "eliminate Japanese infiltrators who had penetrated along the boundary between the Twenty-Third Marines and the Eighth Marines."

At another landing point on Saipan, a depot company's Pvt. Kenneth J. Tibbs became the first black Marine killed in combat in World War II.

In the end, the black support units performed so well in the Saipan invasion, newly installed Commandant Lt. Gen. Alexander A. Vandegrift (who replaced Holcomb on January 1, 1944) was moved to say: "The Negro Marines are no longer on trial. They are Marines, period."

—————

ADDITIONAL NOTE: THE INTRODUCTION OF BLACK PERSONNEL INTO the Marine Corps during World War II didn't signal an end to segregation or to racism within or outside the Corps, by any means; however, it did end a long drought of Marine Corps service by black men that had been in effect since the Revolutionary War. In the eighteenth century, slavery was still a fact of life. However, Nalty also writes that several black Continental Marines were among the estimated five thousand blacks, freemen and slaves, who served the American cause, illustrating the irony that they would seek independence for a country that, for a time, denied it to others.

"HOW THOSE MARINE GIRLS COULD DANCE!"

BY INGRID SMYER

RAISED IN BROOKLYN, NEW YORK, MARIA THERESA ("TESS") THEK was destined to "out-Marine" most male Marines, since she would marry a Marine, have a son who became a Marine, and become a pioneering Marine herself.

Not only would she be one of the early female Marines of the World War I era, she would later make history as one of only two women to serve as Marines in both world wars of the twentieth century.

Just for good measure, she also managed to rise from her start in World War I as a private to the rank of lieutenant colonel by the time she finished her service in the World War II era. At her final colonel's rank, Maria Theresa Thek Shine Ferguson had served as commanding offi-cer of Henderson Hall in Arlington, Virginia, with nearly 2,500 women under her command there. This was the only military post in the United States designated exclusively for women Marine reservists.

It was years before, just prior to her twentieth birthday, that she began her Marine Corps life as a private on September 7, 1918, during World War I. Promoted to private first class in January of 1919, she served in Washington, DC, as a clerk in the Adjutant and Inspector Department at the USMC headquarters.

Before joining the Corps, Thek had already changed her name to Martrese Theque—her brother George once said she wanted it to sound more French, according to Wheeler Ponder Genealogy.

The girl "most likely lived the typical life of a child of a large Catholic family living in Brooklyn at the time," the same website notes. "When the family lived in a home backing St. Leonard's [Catholic] Church, the priest would frequently knock on the boys' window in the morning when he needed an altar boy for Mass. A Thek boy was always available to fill in."

Apparently, the young Martrese almost became a nun instead of a Marine. Her aunt Margaret, herself a nun in the religious order of St. Agnes, tried to convince her, but without success.

Later, while in Washington serving the Marines, the young woman joined several other women who organized a basketball team to play against their counterparts from the Army and Navy. They wore Navy blue turtle-neck sweaters with "USMC" embossed across the front in white lettering.

Another highlight of her first Marine Corps stint came when she joined twelve fellow "lady" Marines on a pioneer trip to the Marine Corps base at Quantico, Virginia, for a "mixer" dance, thanks to an invitation from the staff of the *Leatherneck* newspaper.

This first Friday-night dance and weekend, just before Thanksgiving 1918, was such a success it became a regular feature, since the women based in Washington could take the train down from the city's easily accessible Union Station.

As *Leatherneck* reported on the heels of this first visit, the women left quite an impression. "They lined up in a column of twos and marched behind the band to the parade grounds where they watched the O.T.C. (Officer Training Class) men parade. They saluted [the ceremonies of] Colors and Retreat. Then they made the offices of the *Leatherneck* their headquarters."

"Boys," added the obviously enthused *Leatherneck* writer, "they are just like any other girls in some respects, for they carry mirrors with Marine emblems on them, but they are regular Marines, for they are very proud of their personal appearance and carry their own powder.

"And how those Marines girls can dance!"

After the war and her initial enlistment, Martrese lived with her family in Brooklyn for a time and worked as a stenographer for a brokerage firm. In 1922, she married Frank J. Shine, a Marine Corps veteran of World War I. As of 1930, they lived in Brooklyn, they had a son (also named Frank), and the elder Frank worked for an insurance company as a clerk. She was a secretary in a law firm; the Shine couple kept lodgers in their home, one of them her own sister Marie.

However, Frank Senior died young, and by 1940 Martrese was remarried to John Ferguson and living in Jamaica, Queens. They had four children between them and were joined in this household by a brother from each of their families.

It was just a month after the formation of the Marine Corps Women's Reserve for World War II that Martrese once again enlisted in the Marines. This time she was accepted for officer's candidate school, even though she lacked the college degree normally required.

Arriving at Massachusetts' U.S. Midshipmen School (Women's Reserve) at Mount Holyoke College as part of the initial group of seventy-one candidates, Martrese finished first in her class and was commissioned a second lieutenant in April of 1943, with orders to report to Camp Lejeune, North Carolina. By May, she was a first lieutenant.

As one step quickly followed another, she rose to her final rank of lieutenant colonel and held her command of Henderson Hall before the end of the war.

Returning to civilian life again after World War II, Martrese bought the "Tower House" in Southampton, Long Island, and operated it as a summer guesthouse. Later passing it on to the Southampton Hospital, she died on August 1, 1988, at the Veterans Administration Hospital in Northport, Long Island, just short of her ninetieth birthday.

PART III
WAR UPON WAR

There was an undeniable mystique about the Marine Corps, a feeling of being vastly superior to the soldiers of the U.S. Army (Marines never refer to themselves as soldiers), alongside whom they were sometimes forced to campaign.

—Martin Russ, a Marine in Korea and author of *Breakout: The Chosin Reservoir Campaign, Korea* and *The Last Parallel: A Marine's War Journal*, based on his own post-Armistice service along the 38th parallel dividing North and South Korea

MEDIUM TRANSPORT HELICOPTER SQUADRON 161

By the time of the surprise start of the Korean War in mid-1950, the Marine Corps already had been thinking about helicopters—and planning for their soon-to-be crucial battlefield role. The first American troops were rushed to the scene in support of the beleaguered South Koreans; however, only a handful of American choppers were available.

In the hard-fought Pusan Perimeter at the toe of the Korean peninsula that same summer, the challenge so often met by the few "whirlybirds" and pilots arriving on the scene was negotiating the rough, poorly developed Korean terrain. "It was hot and dusty, the road network was very poor, and the country very mountainous," recalled Marine aerial observer 2nd Lt. Patrick G. Sivert in Marine Historian Lt. Col. Ronald J. Brown's monograph *Whirlybirds: U.S. Marine Helicopters in Korea.* "There was no apparent pattern of any sort to the mountains...no particular ranges or draws, compartments or corridors."

"Korea's river valleys were the only flat space available for easily built roadways, but they also were prone to flash floods," Brown adds. Furthermore, "The lack of reliable telephone communications was also a problem because the short-ranged infantry radios of the day did not function well when out of the line of sight." The cumulative effect of these and related problems made Korea "an operational nightmare."

But there was one solution—the choppers, even the small ones of the era, were "unrestrained by the terrain." They could relay radio signals, they could overfly traffic jams or countryside lacking any roads whatsoever—and they could lay wire for land-line communication at unprecedented high speed.

No wonder they were pressed into duty from day one by the commanders of widely dispersed fighting units for transportation or aerial reconnaissance.

In short time also, they proved indispensable for medical evacuation, search and rescue of downed pilots, artillery spotting, and emergency supply drops. Finally—the ultimate goal, to the extent allowed by size and capacity—they could be troop-carriers.

Arguably, it was the Marine Corps' Medium Transport Helicopter Squadron 161 that set the standard for chopper warfare of the future with a slew of operational and combat "firsts" achieved in Korea. As the late Marine Corps History and Museums director (Brig. Gen.) Edward H. Simmons wrote in an introduction to Brown's monograph, HMR-161 "is noted for its work in developing the helicopter as a tactical tool for the Marine Corps and its ability to accomplish its mission regardless of the circumstances."

To which, former squadron member Lt. Col. Gary W. Parker adds in an official squadron history: "As a neophyte in Korea, HMR-161 tested the Marine Corps' newly developed concept of vertical assault during many landing exercises while continuing to support the First Marine Division." Its choppers ducking in and out of the rugged mountains of Korea for months on end, "HMR-161 proved that helicopters could survive in combat and effectively carry out their mission of supporting the ground troops."

Indeed, by the time the fledgling helicopter unit finished its Korean tour after the uneasy armistice of 1953 stopped the fighting, HMR-161 could boast of really striking success. "As the first transport helicopter squadron in combat, it had flown over 30,000 hours and completed more than 32,000 flights," Parker notes. Moreover, HMR-161's pilots, crewmen, support personnel, and truly newfangled machines "had tested and proven the vertical assault concept for employing troops in combat."

To go back a bit, the post-World War II atomic bomb tests at Bikini Lagoon convinced Lt. Gen Roy S. Geiger, himself an early Marine Corps aviator and now commander of the Fleet Marine Force, Pacific, that amphibious operations of the future should be reviewed and updated for the atomic age. Another leading Marine Corps seer who also predicted the still-primitive "whirlybird" would become a major weapons system for the Corps was Gen. Victor Krulak, the WWII veteran who foresaw the usefulness of the Higgins-boat type of landing craft.

The Marine Corps' first helicopter squadron, HMX-1, was established in late 1947 to develop and evaluate possible uses of the helicopter, "in particular the possibility of transporting combat troops in an amphibious assault," writes Parker.

The Marine leadership made plans for possibly developing several helicopter transport squadrons, but lack of money and lack of widespread helicopter expertise delayed their creation—until the Korean War erupted in mid-1950. "Marine Helicopter Transport Squadron 161 was born from the urgent need of that time," adds Parker's squadron history.

Commissioned in January 1951, the helicopter outfit began life at El Toro, California, with "only four officers, no enlisted men, and no helicopters or aircraft of any kind—not a very auspicious beginning."

But then Sikorsky HRS-1 transport helicopters, flying all the way from the East Coast, slowly began to make their appearance two or three at a time. The squadron's HRS-1 transport could cruise at 90 knots and carry 1,500 pounds of cargo or lift four to six fully equipped combat troops under field conditions. The new machines began arriving a few weeks after the unit moved to the USMC air facility at Santa Ana, California.

The unit's first HRS-1 was flown across the country by two pilots from the virgin HMX-1 chopper squadron, based at Quantico, but all the rest of the Sikorsky transports were flown to California by the Korea-bound squadron's own, newly acquired aircrews, with only a couple of minor accidents reported.

As both personnel and their "birds" built in numbers, aircrews began training in the nearby Santa Ana mountains…but now one of the squadron's authorized complement of fifteen HR-1s was lost in attempting "a rough landing," luckily with no one injured. Just twelve days later that same May (1951), squadron CO Lt. Col. George W. Herring and Maj. William P. Mitchell were on a routine training flight in the mountains when they came across the wreckage of a downed Marine OY-1 spotter plane.

Landing on a nearby road, Mitchell and Cpl. T. L. Foster pulled out the pilot while Herring flew to El Toro to pick up a doctor and return. The injured pilot later was transported by chopper to El Toro for treatment.

The end result was the squadron's first rescue mission, the Parker historical account notes. In the Korean War just ahead, there would be many more, to say nothing of troop lifts.

It was on September 2, 1951, that the first elements of Transport Squadron 161 arrived in Korea, where the need for helicopter support still was "acute." Just eleven days after its arrival at Pusan, the squadron was up to its metaphorical neck in "the first mass helicopter resupply operation in history" by airlifting a day's supplies to the Second Battalion, First Marines, while the latter was attacking the enemy along a nearby ridgeline.

"Our supply and evacuation route was four miles of mountainous foot trails," the Second Battalion's CO, Col. F. B. Nihart, said later. "The only way to keep supplies moving over these trails was by Korean Service Corps porters. The 400 Koreans could not keep up with the logistical demands imposed by heavy casualties and high ammunition expenditure."

The freshly arrived choppers, relieving the Korean porters, "performed admirably." Just another six days later, the new normal for the neophyte outfit resumed with a hurry-up supply call from the Fifth Marines zone. In eighteen flights flown in just an hour, ten of the squadron's choppers carried in more than twelve thousand pounds of supplies to their comrades on the ground.

As another indication of the repeated demands to be made upon the helicopter unit, both in Korea and in Vietnam a decade later, HMR-161 next launched its first tactical airlift—delivering a reinforced reconnaissance company in support of a Republic of Korea (ROK) unit on the front. This meant landing an assault squad, followed by Shore Party Battalion Marines who would clear a landing zone. "The assault squad had to disembark from the helicopters while they were hovering, using thirty-foot knotted ropes, and then cover the shore party members while the landing zone was being prepared."

The first fighting troops were airlifted in just an hour later. After another twenty minutes, "a second landing point was opened, and from this time a steady flow of troops and supplies moved into the area."

As a result, in a mere four hours total, "some 224 fully equipped troops and 17,772 pounds of cargo were lifted to Hill 884, which later became known as 'Mount Helicopter.'" In addition, the choppers laid eight miles of wire in the short time of fifteen minutes, "to connect the reconnaissance company on Hill 884 with the First Marines command post." Called "Operation Summit," the action "received front-page headlines throughout the United States and gave the American public its first knowledge of Marine helicopters in combat."

So began the squadron's years of combat operations in Korea—one rescue mission after another, one tactical troop airlift after another, medical evacuations, supply run after supply run, and for an amazing seventeen straight months, a steady diet of combat operations without the loss of a single pilot or crew-man. Unfortunately, that record ended on February 12, 1953, with a pilot and crew chief lost when their helicopter crashed into the sea south of Pusan while trying to rendezvous with an aircraft carrier.

Meanwhile, HMR-161's personnel awakened every day in Korea on call for who-knew-what in advance. On April 5, 1952, it was a sudden call from their parent First Marine Division ordering an immediate lift of 662 troops from the Second Battalion, Seventh Marines, together with 10,000 pounds of rations to the Kimpo Peninsula—and starting at 5:45 a.m. that very day. Consisting of a fifty-seven-mile round trip flight on average, the job was done with a record ninety-nine flights by the squadron (115.9 hours of flight time).

The result by day's end, another "first" for the squadron, was "the longest round-trip distance of a large-scale helicopter troop movement up to that time," notes unit historian Parker. In addition, Parker's history notes that Squadron Commander Col. Keith B. McCutcheon said at the time that "this airlift, more than any other in which HMR-161 has participated, proved that a Marine transport helicopter squadron can successfully operate as an 'on-call' tactical tool."

Staying on well beyond the 1953 truce that stopped the overt fighting, the squadron marked 1,000 days in Korea on May 29, 1954. Barely a year later, HMR-161, now equipped with the more advanced HRS-3 chopper, was rotated back home to the United States, for a stay of several years in Hawaii. By then it had flown more than 16,500 hours in 18,607 sorties, carried more than 7,500 million pounds of cargo, and moved thousands of troops from one place to another.

During its long break from combat, the unit and its men trained on the beaches, in the mountains, and in the waters of the Hawaiian Islands, all to improve their proficiency in the various aspects of helicopter operations integrated with amphibious operations. They practiced nighttime tactical airlifts along with daytime exercises, plus carrier-based troop airlifts to landing sites. Their helicopters and personnel also took part in the recovery of astronaut Wally Schirra when he splashed down in the Pacific after a brief sojourn in space aboard his *Mercury* "Friendship Seven" capsule in 1962.

The training would stand the squadron in good stead when it was deployed to Vietnam in time for the massive U.S. buildup of 1965. Now flying the Sikorsky UH-34D Seahorse, previously designated the HUS-1, the squadron's personnel once again hardly had arrived on station that May before they were in combat. This time, just off the beach at Chu Lai, they conducted the first amphibious helicopter assault of the Vietnam War under combat conditions by moving assault teams of Marines from a Navy aircraft carrier to shore.

Unfortunately, less than a month later the then-carrier-based squadron lost two choppers and eight of its men to a nighttime mid-air collision off the coast of Vietnam.

Next, moving ashore at Phu Bai, near the city of Hue, HMR-161 began its more normal daily operations—resupply and medical evacuation missions for the most part. As one of the two northernmost Marine units based in South Vietnam, the squadron, called the "Pineapples" because of its Hawaiian background between wars, often would operate in support of the First Division South Vietnamese Army (ARVN) and a battalion of the Fourth Marines, both located in the northern Quang Tri Province.

In August of 1965, the 161st joined four other chopper squadrons in Operation Starlite south of Chu Lai, "the first major battle employing the Marine Corps doctrine of vertical envelopment," notes Parker.

The result, after five days and four days of combat, was

destruction of an entire Viet Cong regiment—but also a grudging respect for the guerrilla movement's fighting prowess. For their part, the helicopters engaged had "hauled troops, ammunition, rations, wounded Marines, and even prisoners."

Not long after, the HMR-161 "whirlybirds" were once again demonstrating their versatility by operating from a carrier in Operation Piranha—"first carrying the initial wave ashore, and then providing logistical support." And soon after that, they once more were ferrying supplies—even live chickens, ducks, pigs, and goats—to remote ARVN outposts in the north.

Meanwhile, when seven HMR-161 choppers joined the Army's 101st Airborne Brigade in Operation Gibraltar, "all seven received numerous hits from enemy automatic weapons fire in the landing zone." After one of the choppers was actually shot down, "Sergeant Dante S. Romeo, the crew chief, evacuated the helicopter carrying his M-60 machine gun and covered the rest of the crew while they scrambled for safety." Pilot (Capt.) Billy G. Phillips, Romeo, and the rest were quickly picked up "in the mist of heavy enemy fire" by Capt. Manuel O. Martinez, who had been piloting another chopper as wingman. A total of fifty-eight enemy rounds hit the seven choppers, some of which barely staggered back to a nearby village for quick emergency repairs before returning to base. Martinez was awarded the Silver Star for his heroism and Romeo a Bronze Star with Combat V for his.

As days became weeks, weeks became months, and then the years of warfare continued, such was the new norm for the 161st of the Vietnam era: troop lifts, supply runs, rescues. One time the squadron picked up a soldier mauled by a tiger…and the slain tiger itself.

In one especially dramatic supply operation, two ARVN outposts in the rugged terrain of Ba Long Valley were entirely dependent on the squadron for their supplies. In the always-threatening monsoon weather of any December, the call came one day for emergency resupply—eight choppers with an escort of six fixed-wing aircraft—jets—braved the weather in response. "Six trips were made into the valley; each time a different approach entry was used as the weather was constantly changing. At times the flights of four [choppers] had to fly in column formation to enter and leave the valley through a small break in the weather, while the second flight of four helicopters orbited outside of the valley."

Meanwhile, the jets voluntarily swept through with suppressive fire, again and again, against Viet Cong positions on the ridges overlooking the valley. "This was extremely dangerous for the jets because at times they had to operate at altitudes of 300 feet or less in a valley which gave them little room to maneuver."

As a final upshot, "The eight helicopters flew 95 sorties, carried 51,950 pounds of much needed cargo, and transported 119 troops into the valley."

With periodic rotations for three-month stays in Okinawa, this was life for the helicopter crews providing dangerous support of the ground troops in Vietnam, or rescuing airmen shot down to the ground. "Hardly a day passed that the squadron was not involved in some sort of tactical operation," writes Parker. Sometimes that meant "inserting and extracting reconnaissance teams."

That is to say, they were quite often behind enemy lines.

One day, though, the unit history concerned Parker himself.

With his squadron by now flying the larger CH-46 "Sea Knight" chopper (capable of carrying seventeen to twenty-five fully equipped troops), Parker was wounded when the helicopter he was flying was downed on September 2, 1968. "In the face of intense fire," Parker himself writes, his wingman (and squadron executive officer) Maj. Joseph L. Felter and crew chief Cpl. Rodney E. Weiss daringly landed next to Parker's wrecked chopper.

"Corporal Weiss jumped out of his aircraft and, under heavy enemy fire, helped the wounded pilot, Captain Gary W. Parker, into his helicopter. Major Felter patiently held his aircraft in the zone until all of the downed crew were on board and then evacuated the wounded to the emergency hospital at Quang Tri."

Obviously enough, Parker survived the episode, typical of his unit's daily and dangerous drama both in Vietnam and Korea.

———

ADDITIONAL NOTE: THE 161ST WAS HONORED WITH Presidential Unit Citations both in Korea and in Vietnam. Historically known for its achievements as the world's first helicopter transport squadron, its personnel decades later were also repeatedly deployed for the U.S. actions in Kuwait and Iraq. While in Iraq in 2006 and flying forty-year-old CH-46 Sea Knight choppers, the unit celebrated an amazing fifty thousand flying hours, or eleven years, free of any Class-A mishaps, meaning accidents resulting in deaths or more than $1 million in damage to the aircraft.

FIRST CAPTIVE

HE HAD NO INTENTION OF MAKING HISTORY THIS WAY, BUT WHAT else to expect if you fly your F4U-5 Corsair three times *under* the target bridge on a photo reconnaissance mission in enemy-held territory at the start of a new war.

If you're shot down in the process, you could become an early captive of the enemy.

Marine Captain Jesse V. "Davy" Booker, a decorated World War II

veteran, actually *did* fly his Corsair under the bridge in enemy-held territory at the start of the Korean War to get better photos of the supporting
beams. He *was* shot down, and he thus became the *first* U.S. serviceman
to be held as a Korean War Prisoner of War.

"Talk about doing dumb things," he later said, "I made three passes—
under the bridge—lifting the wing each time to let the oblique cameras
shoot the supporting members. The trouble was on my third pass they
were waiting for me. I was hit with something big which tore off half my
right wing and the oil cooler system."

A carrier-based pilot described by his Navy buddies as "hard as nails,"
Marine aviator Booker had been ordered on August 7, 1950, to get
close-up photos of an unusually sturdy bridge near Seoul, South Korea,
that had withstood three separate bombing attacks.

According to the Marine Corps History and Museums Division
monograph *The Problems of U.S. Marine Corps Prisoners of War in Korea*
by Colonel James A. MacDonald, Jr., USMC (Ret.), the Corsair lost all
of its oil in less than two minutes and simply wouldn't fly. Rather than
bail out, Booker "elected to ride the plane down."

His two wingmates, both fellow Marines, saw that he landed safely
and ran for cover in a wooded area. But the trees hid the sight of his
capture and severe beating as "the first of 221 Marines known to have
been taken prisoner of war by the enemy during the hostilities in Korea,"
adds MacDonald.

This was of course an historical "first" no Marine or any other U.S.
serviceman would want. Especially since it came about abruptly and
brutally. "He barely cleared his aircraft and reached the concealment of
nearby trees when a group of North Korean soldiers surrounded him,"
writes MacDonald, himself a Korean War veteran.

Booker realized his service revolver would be no real use against so
many men armed with powerful rifles. He didn't really have time to
think, since "they denied him any freedom of choice by rushing in and
overwhelming him."

Nor was there any chance of escape. "He was some 200 miles from the nearest friendly ground troops, and helicopter rescue operations were not highly developed at that stage in [the] hostilities, so rescue by that means was virtually impossible."

As soon as he was disarmed, Booker's captors "struck him repeatedly across the chest and body with their rifles until they beat him senseless." He then was dragged and pushed off to a temporary cell in a nearby village.

Reunited some time later with other American officers held in a facility near the North Korean capital of Pyongyang, Booker found them in as pitiful condition as he himself—"beaten, half starved, and filthy." Many had "foul-smelling, septic wounds."

An online 2010 newsletter issued by the Marine Corps Aviation Reconnaissance Association (MCARA) adds that Texas-born Captain Booker was put in a cage labeled "Capitalist Warmonger" and beaten so badly he was partially paralyzed. After the Inchon landing that relieved the hard-pressed United Nations forces defending the Pusan Perimeter, Booker "was taken North, thrown into a ditch with over 100 other POWs who were then machine-gunned with only nineteen surviving to go into the 'death camps.'"

The MacDonald account also notes that Booker, along with other captured American officers, was occasionally lined up before a firing squad. "Sometimes they went through all the motions of an execution without actually firing the fatal shots," writes MacDonald. "At other times the tableau ended with the sharp crack of rifles and one or two American officers fell dead."

Booker was among those who "faced the firing squads several times."

Held prisoner for the duration of the war, more than three years, Booker was finally released in September 1953 as the "longest surviving Marine Corps POW," adds the same source. Weighing a healthy 162 pounds at the time of his capture, he came home weighing just eighty-seven pounds and was hospitalized for four months.

He then "moved on with life," wrote David Lauderdale, columnist for the Hilton Head and Beaufort Island pocket in South Carolina *Packet*

(March 26, 2011). He went by the words of a chaplain in his POW camp who advised, "Take it, accept it, forget it."

Moving on, though, wouldn't be easy, thanks to the physical abuse he had suffered as a prisoner. He did serve another fifteen years on active duty, then represented the Marines for ten more years "by setting up JROTC programs in high schools," Lauderdale also reported.

For most of the time, he didn't talk much about the POW experience. "He'd say they 'weren't very kind to any of us.' He'd say he did a job he was paid to do. He'd also say he held many POWs who died in his arms, a smile on their faces because that was the easy way out."

After Booker died in the spring of 1993, his wife Lil revealed what he had gone through even after his release in 1953. "He did have to have a portion of his intestines removed after damage from beatings with gun butts in his abdomen," she wrote to a POW veterans organization, "and he continued to have dysentery through the years; then back surgery to try to correct the problems from bayonets in the back, then lung surgery as a portion of it was collapsed due to beatings, etc. He passed away during a final 'corrective surgery' on 13 April 1993."

Once he retired in 1976, the couple returned to Beaufort, "where he'd once been stationed and where Lil spent part of her childhood on Parris Island," Lauderdale writes. "Her father was a Marine Corps general, and both his brothers were admirals."

Lil then sold real estate for thirty years while the retired Marine aviator "fished and volunteered for everything," such as heading up the local Red Cross and United Way. Appearing in the 1987 documentary *POW— Americans in Enemy Hands, World War II, Korea and Vietnam*, Booker said three things kept him going as a prisoner: knowing he had a loving wife, having lived long enough to appreciate his country, and his faith. A year later, no surprise, he was invited to the Reagan White House as one of the first U.S. servicemen to receive the newly authorized POW Medal.

Lauderdale reported that Booker then told the *Boot* newspaper at Parris Island: "It wasn't just me who received that award. It's a tribute to everyone who was ever a POW—whether they came home or not."

He also had this advice for his fellow POWs: "Too many people relive the hatred the rest of their lives. I've never had time for hatred. I have plenty of time to fish, plenty of time to spend on my boat, cherish the time I spend with my wife—but I don't have time to hate."

———

ADDITIONAL NOTE: WHEN MOST OF THE AMERICAN POWs WERE FINALLY released in August of 1953, Captain Jesse V. Booker, first man captured by the enemy in Korea, was one of the first Marine officers returned to welcoming American arms—more than three years after his original seizure. All told, 7,140 American fighting men of all services were captured in Korea, notes the MacDonald paper. "Of this number 2,701 or about 38 percent died while interned, and 4,418 were recovered. Marine Corps statistics show that 221 Marines were captured, 194 were recovered, and 27 or about 12 percent died." This was the war in which Americans POWs, notoriously, were "brainwashed" in the enemy's strenuous propaganda effort to turn them against their own country. But, notes MacDonald, out of the nearly 5,000 surviving their captivity, only 21 Americans refused repatriation…and none was a Marine.

PRELUDE TO MARINE LANDING

ONE OF THE MOST DRAMATIC EPISODES OF THE KOREAN WAR WAS A briefing rather than a battle that took place in a Japanese office building before a group of high-ranking "brass" from the Pentagon, including two members of the Joint Chiefs of Staff: the Navy's Forrest Sherman and the Army's J. Lawton Collins.

The strategy session on August 23, 1950, was held in Douglas MacArthur's headquarters in Tokyo, in the Dai Ichi building. It was to be a crucial meeting during which the seventy-year-old Army general of World War II fame must win over the doubters wary of his proposed Inchon landing. Phenomenally successful in his Pacific campaigns of the recent world war, considered imperious by some, godlike by others, this was a man who often referred to himself in the third person, but who was sensitive enough to have once vomited on the White House steps after a quarrel with President Franklin Delano Roosevelt.

The briefing by MacArthur just a month before the proposed landing on the Korean west coast really was his bid for approval of the bold plan by the Joint Chiefs, with Admiral Sherman and General Collins expected to recommend yea or nay when they returned to Washington. It was obviously a moment of high tension for the veteran strategist MacArthur, who would argue the case as his own chief advocate.

As the briefing unfolded, the Navy first explained all the problems posed by the high tides at Inchon, the wide mud flats, the narrow Flying Fish shipping channel—all elements conspiring to protect Inchon from invasion by sea.

"If every possible geographical and naval handicap were listed," said Admiral Sherman, according to MacArthur biographer D. Clayton James. "Inchon has 'em all."

Next, argued Collins on behalf of the Army, Inchon was too far to the rear of the besieged Pusan Perimeter at the foot of South Korea to have any great effect on the distant enemy forces threatening to push the American defenders and their allies into the sea. Further, with little manpower available for the invasion of Seoul's port city of Inchon, troops must be taken from the already hard-pressed Pusan line. Finally, the South Korean port Kunsan, south of Inchon, was more suitable physically and would be far easier to seize.

Also to be considered, the doubters noted, was the fact that Inchon presented no beaches. There were only seawalls, city streets, and easily fortified buildings to confront the landing troops.

"More than an hour passed during the presentations," writes James in his three-volume biography *The Years of MacArthur*. "Except for making some one-sentence remarks, MacArthur had sat quietly puffing on his pipe. When everyone was finished, the group looked at the general for his reaction, but he continued to sit and smoke in silence for an estimated minute or longer."

MacArthur himself later would write in his memoir *Reminiscences*: "I waited a moment or so to collect my thoughts. I could feel the tension rising in the room… If ever a silence was pregnant, this one was." He recalled his own father's advice: "Doug, councils of war breed timidity and defeatism."

At last, with one of his chief aides by now shifting uneasily in his seat, MacArthur rose to his feet. He walked back and forth, "gesturing with his pipe and speaking at first in a low voice," James writes.

Using no notes, he spoke for forty-five minutes. He began slowly, but gradually built his case, and in the end, he achieved perhaps the best "dramatic presentation and eloquence" of his entire career.

He began with reference to British General James Wolfe's bold attack on French Quebec in 1759 by way of the walled city's highest, most difficult—and therefore undermanned—heights. "On the Plains of Abraham, Wolfe won a stunning victory," recalled MacArthur in his briefing two centuries later.

"Like [French commander] Montcalm," McArthur argued, "the North Koreans would regard an Inchon landing as impossible. Like Wolfe, I would take them by surprise."

Then addressing the Navy's physical problems with Inchon, MacArthur agreed they were "indeed substantial," but added they were "not insuperable." Stating that he had complete confidence in the Navy, MacArthur wryly suggested, "In fact, I seem to have more confidence in the navy than the navy has in itself."

Turning to the Army argument, he agreed a landing at Kunsan to the south would be less hazardous. But he said also that it would be "largely ineffective and indecisive." It would not cut the enemy's supply line nor envelop the enemy from above. "Better no flank movement than one such as this," he insisted. Better, even, to add the invading manpower to the forces holding out in the Pusan Perimeter.

Noting that seizure of Inchon had the South Korean capital of Seoul, just twenty miles away, as its real objective, MacArthur argued that was the step needed to cut the enemy's supply line and to seal off the southern peninsula altogether.

"The vulnerability of the enemy is his supply position," MacArthur added. "Every step southward extends his transport lines and renders them more frail and subject to dislocation. The several major lines of enemy supply from the north converge on Seoul, and from Seoul they radiate to the several sectors of the front."

The seizure of Seoul, he said, would "paralyze" the North Korean supply system.

The alternative to his proposed bold stroke, the World War II commander insisted, would be continued "savage" sacrifice by the men fighting in the Pusan Perimeter.

"Are you content to let our troops stay in that bloody perimeter like beef cattle in a slaughterhouse?" he asked.

After MacArthur finished, he sat down to another "pregnant" silence, his listeners apparently stunned. Finally, Admiral Sherman rose.

"Thank you," he said. "A great voice in a great cause."

According to biographer James, members of the Joint Chiefs still had their reservations in the days following. Nonetheless, recalled MacArthur in his memoir, he received a wire from that body six days after the tense briefing session: "We concur, after reviewing the information brought back by General Collins and Admiral Sherman, in making preparations and executing a turning movement by amphibious forces on the west coast of Korea—at Inchon."

And Inchon it would be, the aging MacArthur's last masterstroke. But prelude also to an agonizing period of trial and glory for the First Marine Division, itself of recent World War II fame.

MASTERSTROKE ACHIEVED

ANOTHER DAY, ANOTHER MEETING BETWEEN GENERALS AT MacArthur's Tokyo headquarters.

However, this one was in early July, just days after the North Korean Communists invaded democratic South Korea; this time, it was Marine Corps Lt. Gen. Lemuel C. Shepherd Jr., commanding general of the Fleet Marine Forces, meeting with MacArthur.

MacArthur tapped on the wall map in his office with his corncob pipe. The spot he indicated was Inchon, on the west coast of Korea. "If I had the First Marine Division," he said, "I would land them there."

Barely two months later, it indeed was the First Marine Division largely leading the way for the amphibious landing at Inchon, with the recapture of nearby Seoul the true objective. Going ashore with the so-called "grunts" of the Marine infantry was World War II veteran Maj. Edwin H. Simmons, a company commander who would later be director of the Marine Corps History Center as a brigadier general.

Simmons was well aware of the limitations under which the division would be attempting its landing at Inchon. "The amphibious forces were in atrophy," he recalled in an interview with Alexander S. Cochran Jr. that appeared in the December 1985 issue of *Military History* magazine. "There were virtually no amphibious ships available. Plus terrible hydrographic conditions on the west coast of Korea—thirty-foot tides which made the timing of the whole thing very critical. Plus, the availability of troops to execute it. There were none in Japan, and the understrength First Marine Division was one-half in the Pusan Perimeter and one-half in Camp Pendleton [California]."

What exactly were the hydrographic problems for the incoming Marines? "To get to Inchon port, you had to go through what was called 'Flying Fish Channel.' The actual channel was quite narrow, and there were mudflats on both sides of it, which was an invitation to grounding. And then there were these very high tides, twenty-nine-plus feet, which were unbelievable—you have to see them to believe it—there was only one time every month when the tides would accommodate the landings."

The Marines themselves had some reservations about going ashore at Inchon, and for good reason. "There really weren't any beaches to land on, though the actual plan designated Blue, Green, Yellow, and Red Beaches as landing sites," recalled Simmons. "They really were seawalls. We would have to use scaling ladders or find breaks in the seawalls. And we were not at all sure that we could get our amphibious tractors up through the breaks in the seawall."

There was more adversity at play than simple physical obstacles. Just five years after the truly gargantuan effort expended on World War II, to say nothing of the thousands of casualties, the nation simply wasn't ready for another war. The Marines themselves weren't ready for another war.

"You have to remember that the nation's state of readiness was at an appalling low," says Simmons. "There just wasn't any shipping available. Paradoxically, the First Marine Division was never in worse logistical shape than it was before we first landed in Korea. But, from a tactical point of view, it was the best division I ever served in. The quality of the men was superb. I sometimes think the very fact that we had so little in the way of materiel made us more efficient. We didn't have the great super-abundance that Americans are [now] used to going to combat with."

Meanwhile, Army Gen. MacArthur had appointed his own chief of staff, Army Maj. Gen. Edward M. Almond, as commander of the X Corps, incorporating both the First Marine Division and the Army's Seventh Infantry Division as the officially designated landing force.

Simmons had been assigned as a member of the reconstituted First Marine Regiment just days after the Korean War call-up of the reserves. "We were only at Camp Pendleton for ten days, coming up to strength, drawing our war reserves," he recalls. "We had been promised good equipment, but it didn't turn out that way. This stuff had been packed up hurriedly at the end of World War II, and, when you opened a box marked 'bayonets,' you would find gas masks. It has been said by others that Korea was fought with World War II surplus, and that is essentially accurate."

He and his men sailed from San Diego, California, late in August with no inkling that they would be invading the South Korean west coast on September 15—but they did know their new regimental commander was the well-known Col. Lewis B. "Chesty" Puller, who had fought at Guadalcanal and led the old First Regiment ("First Marines") at Peleliu during the Pacific island-hopping campaigns of World War II. Characteristically, he had been "bombarding" Washington with messages asking for command of the newly formed First Marines since the outbreak of the Korean War.

Simmons was on hand the day Chesty Puller rose and characteristically "growled" at his men, "You young people are lucky. We used to have to wait every ten or fifteen years for a war. You get one every five years!"

And more to the point: "You people have been living by the sword. By God, you better be ready to die by it."

"With those inspirational remarks," adds Simmons, "he sent us off to battle." Off to battle, that is, with no rehearsals and little training beyond calisthenics and other exercise.

When they set sail from California, Simmons and his companions knew they were going to Korea, of course, but they thought they would be reinforcing the Marines in the Pusan Perimeter. Instead, in the late afternoon of September 15, he and his company emerged from an LST (Landing Ship, Tank) aboard amphibious tractors bound for Blue Beach Two on the south side of Inchon. Enemy resistance would prove to be light—in fact, the defense of all Inchon was fairly ineffective, largely because North Korea's first-line troops were down south assaulting the Pusan Perimeter.

Still, for Simmons and his men, finding their assigned beach landing site in the darkening twilight and the black smoke of combat would not be easy. When the young officer asked the tractor driver about it, he said, "I don't know. A couple of weeks ago I was driving a bus in San Francisco."

In any case, Simmons and his Marines eventually found their way to Blue Beach Two, made their way through a break in the seawall, and joined the Army units and Marines already comprising a firm and secure beachhead at Inchon. "The first wave was made up of Army armored amphibian tractors manned by Army troops," explains Simmons. "These were gun tractors. The second and third wave[s] were the Marine rifle companies. This was a matter of expediency. We had had armored amphibian tractors during World War II, but we no longer had them in postwar organizations. The Army amphibian tractors were available. It was a manning-level problem. We probably had the tractors in depot. But we didn't have the units to man them."

Aside from such detail, the battle for Inchon went quickly and easily for the Americans, along with the recapture of Seoul. Then came the drive northward into North Korea that led, on the east side of the divided nation, to the X Corps' ordeal at the Chosin Reservoir in late November and early December of 1950 as the Red Chinese entered the war.

In the meantime, MacArthur's masterstroke of Inchon "turned the war. It changed the war. It changed defeat into victory." Turned the war, that is, until the Red Chinese jumped in and made Chosin a household word throughout America and the Marine Corps World.

SELECT PERSONALITY
CLAYTON C. JEROME

This Marine's last combat assignment was as a Marine Corps general in Korea, where his own Marine aviator stepson would earn a Silver Star. In the beginning, however, Clayton C. Jerome embarked upon his military career at the tail end of World War I as an obscure midshipman at the U.S. Naval Academy in Annapolis.

Later, even as a general, he was also typical of so many who served the nation and the Corps with distinction, and yet were little known to the public at large.

Jerome would twice win accolades for his heroic actions that had nothing to do with combat, although he also earned decorations as a fighter pilot and squadron leader for his participation in five World War II campaigns against the Japanese in the Pacific. He was decorated for his service in Korea as well.

Born in Hutchinson, Kansas, in 1901, he graduated from the Naval Academy in 1922 and began his flight training in 1924. Spending time in China and at various stateside postings, he achieved a remarkable aviation feat in 1930 while practicing aerobatics above the city of San Diego, California.

Flying at the low altitude of two thousand feet, he was startled when his control stick broke off right at the socket—somewhat comparable to a car driver having the steering wheel come loose from its base.

Jerome had engine power, but no real control—not even for a glide to safety. He could bail out and leave the airplane to its own devices, but then it could crash in a busy, heavily populated area and kill innocent persons on the ground.

Therefore, he stayed with his craft. He brought his plane back to normal level position by maneuvering the socket itself with his hand. Then, once his aircraft was on an even keel, he somehow managed to lash the stick back into place with a handkerchief, his belt, and his necktie stuffed into the socket all before landing safely. He received no decoration for the feat, but he did receive a letter of commendation from the chief of the Navy's Bureau of Aeronautics.

After obtaining a master of science degree in aeronautical engineering from the California Institute of Technology at Pasadena, Jerome spent much of the 1930s as a naval attaché at several Central and South American embassy posts.

Jerome briefly came to public attention for his exploits in the wake of an airplane crash in a remote area of Venezuela in 1937. Assigned to the U.S. Embassy in Venezuela at the time as Naval Attaché for Air, he joined the search for the crash site in a seaplane and found the wreck in the jungles of Cuyuni. He made two dangerous landings on the nearby Cuyuni River and flew out four survivors, for which he was awarded the Distinguished Flying Cross.

Moving up rapidly in rank, he was a full colonel by the time he fought against the Japanese in the Pacific Theater campaigns. He first flew in the Solomons, where his stepson, Hunter J. Reinburg, was to become a Marine Corps ace with seven kills. Jerome then participated in the Treasury-Bougainville, Bismarck Archipelago, and Philippines campaigns, earning three Legion of Merit awards, an Army Bronze Star, and the Air Medal in the process.

During that time, he had served as operations officer for his unit in the Northern Solomons, as aircraft and island commander at Emirau on the Bismarck Archipelago, and finally as commander of the Mangalden airstrip in Luzon and of the Marine Air Groups at Dagupan, both in the Philippines. "During that [latter] time he directed Marine air support on all the Luzon battlefronts," notes a Marine Corps History Division online biography. He won additional accolades for encouraging his subordinate, Lt. Col. Keith B. McCutcheon, in the development of *his* vital theories on close air support. Jerome asked McCutcheon to support the left flank of the Army's First Cavalry Division during the U.S. invasion of Luzon in the Philippines, with the result that McCutcheon became known as "Father of Modern Close Air Support" for his development and use of ALPs (Air Liaison Parties). These were specially trained Marines who used their radios and smoke markers from forward, ground-level positions to direct air strikes.

"McCutcheon himself as head of Marine Air Group 24 flew combat missions in the Douglas SBD Dauntless [dive-bombers, which]…had their targets called in by ALPs in radio-equipped Jeeps moving with ground units," notes a January 2015 profile of McCutcheon at the *Tails through Time* website. "As a result, during the battles on Luzon, McCutcheon's SBD pilots quickly gained a reputation for lethal accuracy in the battlefield."

Meanwhile, like so many other World War II Marine veterans, Jerome, his stepson Hunter Reinburg, and McCutcheon all moved on in just five years to the new war in Korea. But first, Brigadier General Jerome was named commander of the Marine Air Station at Quantico, then chief of staff for the Quantico Marine Base schools in general. He next was moved to Corps Headquarters in Washington, where he would serve simultaneously as director of Public Information, of Recruiting, and of Marine Corps History. In September of 1950, soon after the Korean War broke out, he was named director of Marine Corps Aviation and assistant commandant of the Marine Corps for Air.

Not yet permanently tied to desk work, he was soon in Korea as commander of the First Marine Aircraft Wing. Promoted to major general, he returned afterwards to the United States to become commanding general of the Second Marine Aircraft Wing and of aircraft in the Atlantic Fleet's Marine Force. His final posting, coming in August 1955, was as commanding general of aircraft in the Pacific Fleet Marine Force. He retired in 1959 with the rank of lieutenant general.

While in Korea, he received the Distinguished Service Medal and his fourth Legion of Merit award for his leadership of the Marines' First Wing. His other career decorations ranged from the Distinguished Flying Cross to various campaign ribbons, to World War I and World War II Victory medals.

BRIDGE DROP URGENT

IT WAS IN THE FIRST WEEK OF DECEMBER 1950 THAT A LONG TRAIN of a thousand vehicles and many thousands of troops from the United Nations' X Corps came inching down the narrow, convoluted road clawed into mountainsides. From Koto-ri, about fifteen miles below the plateau holding the Chosin Reservoir, to safe haven in the valley below, it was an ugly drop of another sixty or so miles.

To make matters really tough, a Siberian cold front had moved into the Chosin Reservoir sector of northeastern North Korea, along with nine divisions of fresh Red Chinese soldiers in their padded, quilt-like uniforms and sneaker-like shoes. They had appeared in late November in overwhelming numbers, suddenly rushing out of the night with bugles blaring, and catching the United Nations forces totally by surprise.

Pushed back and pushed back, the men of the X Corps—largely consisting of the First Marine Division and the U.S. Army's Seventh Infantry Division—were now resigned to a fighting retreat down the winding mountain road that everybody called the MSR (Main Supply Route). Just fighting in a different direction, their leaders would say. But it was a withdrawal, and it was brutal.

The destination, seemingly so simple, was sanctuary at a UN-held (read: *American*-held) port at the foot of the narrow, snakelike road running down from the mountainous plateau. Yet, it was not so simple in reality, because negotiating the MSR meant fighting back the Chinese lining the ridgetops on either side of the road, enduring their nighttime attacks, and sometimes encountering the occasional daytime attack. The Chinese were also noted for coming up unnoticed from behind and picking off the wounded in the backs of the X Corps trucks. A stream of North Korean refugees also floated close behind the troops, certain to hide infiltrating Chinese solders among the truly pitiful civilian ranks.

The Marines responded to the human enemy the only way practical: Attack, attack, and attack, all the way up to the enemy-held ridgetops alongside the road and even a bit beyond. However, in the numbers game, the Red Chinese were winning hands down. While the X Corps had the finite number of fourteen thousand men to extricate, the Chinese had seemingly infinite numbers. In fact, they had flooded the area with more than one hundred thousand troops.

Meanwhile, both sides faced the weather enemy: the cold that froze over the reservoir above, that created treacherous ice slicks on the MSR, froze the oil in the mechanisms of Marine rifles, and welded the fingers of captured Chinese to their rifles.

To make matters worse for the withdrawing X Corps, the Chinese had blown away the only bridge at the Funchilin Pass, a span covering a deep, two-thousand-foot chasm next to a hydroelectric facility just a few miles down the pathway to safety from Koto-ri and halfway to the village of Chinhung-ni.

With the gap yawning menacingly, it had to be bridged somehow.

Indeed, as Korean War Army veteran Roy E. Appleman wrote in his 1990 book, *Escaping the Trap: The U.S. Army X Corps in Northeast Korea, 1950,* "Each side knew the eight miles from Koto-ri through Funchilin Pass was the showdown. For the…[Chinese] it was their last chance to destroy the X Corps in North Korea. For the UN Troops in the Chosin Reservoir area, it was simply a case of their survival."

While most physical damage to the MSR could be repaired fairly easily, the gap at the pass was the real problem. The Chinese had already twice destroyed bridges across the chasm, which was located next to a gatehouse and to four huge pipes—steel penstocks—carrying water from the reservoir to Power Plant No. 4 in the American-held valley below.

In all the planning to get his division, its vehicles, its wounded, and its dead out of the trap, the First Marines Division's commanding officer, Maj. Gen. Oliver P. Smith, once explained that the gap at Funchilin Pass presented a "serious catch." The Chinese "could not have picked a better spot to cause us serious trouble," he added in a post-action report to Washington. "The drop down the mountain was sheer," he went on to say. And further, "There was no possibility of a bypass."

What was needed now was another portable span like the last one the Chinese had destroyed—an M-2 Treadway bridge consisting of prefabricated parts. Two days was the timeline to fix the bridge suddenly thrust upon Marine Lt. Col. John H. Partridge, commander of the division's First Engineer Battalion. He had only two days to gather the ponderous pieces needed and to put them into place.

It would be no job for amateurs, either. The Treadway project called for meticulous placement of big, eighteen-foot steel beams weighing more than two thousand pounds each. The MSR crossing-point would need four such sections.

Up at Koto-ri, men of the Army's Fifty-Eighth Engineer Treadway Bridge Company were among the troops awaiting evacuation. They had with them four of the Brockway trucks needed to transport and to join up the cumbersome bridge sections. Of the four trucks, two were actually in operating condition.

However, of the four steel girders needed, exactly none was to be found up on the plateau. They were down in the valley, below the Chinese-controlled heights.

What would be the solution? Well, again, it was simple enough in concept: just airdrop the big steel girders to the trapped troops above the gap in the road and let them build a new bridge, albeit under enemy fire. Simple—except that in a practice run by U.S. Air Force personnel at Yonpo, near the port of Wonsan on the coast below, one of the air-dropped steel girders plunged deep into the frozen ground. "One source said twenty feet deep," Appleman writes.

They had used a G-1 twenty-four-foot parachute, and then watched in dismay as the steel beam "buried itself." As a result, the word immediately went out to supply depots in Japan: forty-eight-foot parachutes, please.

With no time to waste—men were dying on the MSR—the 801st Army Quartermaster Airborne Supply and Packaging Company's Capt. Cecil W. Hospelhorn flew to Yonpo with the forty-eight-footers. An all-night stint by the supply men and aircrews produced a total of eight Treadway sections rigged for airborne drop by Fairchild C-119 "Flying Boxcar" cargo planes, flying at eight hundred feet above Koto-ri the next morning, December 7.

The first three sections came to ground at 9:30 a.m. on Pearl Harbor Day, and were recovered intact.

At intervals until noon, the C-119s brought in the remaining five, with one damaged and another mistakenly delivered to surprised Chinese troops hovering outside the defensive perimeter.

Now it became the turn of the Brockway trucks, soon jolting down the washboard road, often under hostile fire from the ridges above.

It would be the morning of December 9 before the bridge-builders could creep close to the gap in the road—a feat accomplished only after the Marines cleared out nearby ridge crests and the bridge area, often at high cost in personnel, although they did have the help of airstrikes and artillery fire.

The Treadway sections were put into place between noon and 3:30 p.m. that same day, and traffic began to roll at six o'clock that evening with the attacking Chinese still doing their best to halt the withdrawal. A tractor hauling an earthmover almost did the job for them when it broke through the plywood flooring of the new span and blocked the downhill flow. Luckily, the Americans managed to back it out and realign the Treadway beams to suit the axle widths of remaining vehicles.

Through the night that followed, the drivers rode the steel sections railroad-style, coaxed along by men pointing flashlight beams, and the withdrawal went on…and on, through the entire next day. Finally, early on December 11, the X Corps' last survivors, plus those tanks and trucks still mobile, were thought to be safely across the Treadway span. A Marine Corps demolition team did its job too—by destroying the life-saving span.

"I had a sense of well-being," Partridge said later, "after everyone had crossed over and I'd blown the bridge."

———

ADDITIONAL NOTE: COL. LEWIS "CHESTY" PULLER'S FIRST MARINES were the last to pull out of Koto-ri and cross the bridge before it was blown. Typically, Puller insisted on proudly walking out after giving over his personal Jeep to a handful of the dead and wounded.

In the days before the final breakout, it should also be noted, many hundreds of wounded men and even some of the dead had been flown out by C-47 transport planes. Some were even transported by small observation aircraft whose crews braved the constant Chinese fire in the area—and the constantly bad weather. They had to rely upon a barely usable airstrip that Partridge's engineers had scraped out of the frozen terrain above Koto-ri.

As the Marines finished crossing their new Treadway girders at Funchilin Pass, at least one able-bodied man was left behind. According to a Marine Corps history of the confrontation at Chosin by Brig. Gen. Simmons, the overlooked Marine was Pfc. Robert D. DeMott, and he had been "blown off the road by a Chinese explosive charge."

When he regained consciousness, he climbed back to the MSR and joined the refugees. "He heard the detonation that blew the bridge, but figured he could make his way on foot through the gatehouse above the penstocks. This he did, as did many of the following refugees."

SHEPHERD TO THE PRESS

WHAT IS GLORY? FOR FLEDGLING NEWSMAN—AND MARINE CORPS reservist—Michael C. Capraro, it was Chosin, where quite suddenly his first duty one night was no longer playing shepherd to the press, but instead taking charge of a hundred or so Marines ambushed on the road from Koto-ri to Hagaru by the Red Chinese.

"He proved public information officers can do more than arrange Jeep rides for correspondents," Warrant Officer D. R. Yancey, a fellow Marine, told the United Press later. "It took more than three Chinese regiments to scare Captain Michael C. Capraro, information officer of the First Marine Division."

He took command, Yancey related, and "emphatically" rejected demands to surrender his force, made up mostly of Marines but also including a handful of South Koreans, U.S. Army soldiers, and British Royal Marines. "Showing no excitement at all, he quieted the men and personally set up a defense. All the time he was under machine-gun and small-arms fire."

By morning, the fighting stopped, and the "ambushed force was able to rejoin its column," added Yancey, who was wounded and evacuated to Tokyo before he and Capraro could meet personally.

"I never got a chance to meet and thank him," wrote Capraro himself years later. "Also, it was the Lord's work that saved us. Not mine."

Capraro's First Marine Division spent one horror-filled day after another in late November and early December 1950 on that same road to Haguru. They were faced the whole time "with annihilation, trapped in subzero cold in North Korea by overwhelming forces of Chinese," the newsman-turned-Marine would also write.

In reality, Capraro had been a Marine prior to becoming a newspaper man. His combat experience in the Pacific during World War II—with stops at Guadalcanal, Cape Gloucester, Iwo Jima, and Okinawa—came before he landed a job as a newspaper reporter at the San Francisco *Chronicle*. Even then, as Capraro recalled in the April 1994 issue of *Military History* magazine, he continued to moonlight as "a press officer for a Marine Reserve unit across the bay," before the call came to serve in Korea.

"The day suddenly came when my presence was requested, post-haste, at Camp Pendleton, California. The famed First Marine Division, in mothballs since World War II, was pumping up for combat in war-stricken, bleeding South Korea. And I was going with it."

It was mid-summer of 1950. After first crossing the border in late June, the invading North Koreans had already captured the South Korean capital of Seoul and its nearby port city of Inchon, and now were moving upon Pusan at the far south end of the Korean peninsula.

At first, Capraro was less than enthusiastic, but then…he was only twenty-seven, single, and a captain, which paid better than his newspaper job. In short time, he found the "call was not one that a still young, gung-ho Marine could ignore."

The decision, for others, was not quite so easy. For many fellow reservists, especially the enlisted men who were married, "with children, mortgages, auto loans, and other financial burdens peculiar to civilian life," the recall caused serious hardship and sacrifice.

If the Korean War was the forgotten war, "Marine reservists—and their families—were its forgotten heroes." Of course, add the reservists of the Army, Navy, and Air Force.

In any case, he and his fellow Marine reservists rushing to Camp Pendleton found it "had the air of a huge, hastily assembled job fair" as thousands of Leathernecks vied for the plum assignments. Naturally, "career-enhancing billets went to regulars, and those left over went to reservists."

In his case, logic reigned—newsman Capraro was given the billet of PIO, Public Information Officer, for the First Marine Division. But that didn't excuse him from his first order of business, and any Marine's first order: being prepared to fight the enemy at the drop of a hat.

In the weeks just ahead, the Korean War was almost lost, as American, South Korean, and a mix of fellow United Nations forces with their backs to the sea barely fought off the rampaging North Koreans in the steadily shrinking bubble called the Pusan Perimeter. Yet, as Capraro wrote for *Military History*, "The Communist invasion of South Korea suffered a stunning reversal on September 15, 1950, when the First Marine Division stormed ashore at Inchon and within three weeks liberated Seoul [with a little U.S. Army help, of course]. The end-around sweep conceived by General Douglas MacArthur had been brilliant."

As another result, neophyte journalist Capraro suddenly became almost as well known to the journalistic fraternity covering the war as MacArthur himself.

"Television had not yet emerged as the nation's preferred media," he noted. "News coverage was left to swarms of print and radio journalists and photographers. Ensuing Marine successes dominated headlines and front pages stateside. Marine Corps Commandant Clifton Cates once called the explosion of publicity 'almost embarrassing.' He did not, however, order it to be stopped."

A bit gleefully, Capraro also wrote that all this began a "love affair" between the First Marine Division and the press "that continued unabated throughout the war, much to the envy and frustration of U.S. Army public relations experts in Korea and Japan." The Army lavished the press with fancy accommodations, food, communication facilities, transportation, and four-star briefings at the drop of a hat, he also said, "yet the leathernecks got all the headlines."

For good reason, too. "The Marines had *esprit de corps* in spades; they were pros. They showed no fear in combat. All these traits added up to good copy. Stories slugged 'With the Marines in Korea' instantly captured readers' attention."

Not that Capraro spoiled visiting correspondents with fancy amenities—not by a long shot. "I did not patronize or curry favors. At best, the division's accommodations for press visitors were spartan—a cot in our PI tent, which for some reason always sagged badly. Showers were cold and communal. Chow was strictly GI. And booze, even beer, was rationed if and when available, and that was not often. BYO [Bring Your Own] was the rule. Few complained, though."

Capraro argued that his fellow Marines, whether "grunts" or generals, made his job easy. All were combat veterans, some were even "stars," but one in particular was special. "The legendary Lewis Puller, 'Chesty' as he was known, epitomized the old, old Corps, with service in Nicaragua, Haiti, China, and World War II. Cocky as a bantam rooster, he was outspoken and a source of salty, memorable quotes."

Many of the visiting press were well known, too—among them were the *New York Herald Tribune*'s Marguerite Higgins "and her frequent companion from the *Chicago Daily News*, Keeyes Beech, a former Marine war correspondent," plus, from the *New York Times*, Homer Bigart, and *New York Post* columnist Jimmy Cannon, among many others.

The war in Korea, even for journalists, of course, was serious business. "I…personally witnessed, helplessly, the capture of Frank 'Pappy' Noel, an Associated Press photographer and Pulitzer Prize winner," Capraro wrote in *Military History*.

Also running the risks of combat situations were Capraro's eighteen

Marine combat correspondents (CCs), who carried rifles and considered themselves "fighters first and specialists thereafter." One of these men, Sam Jaffee, was later widely recognized as an ABC television correspondent. Another, Ted Sell, "went on to a brilliant newspaper career." Moreover, Capraro's CCs suffered their own occasional casualties: "Our first…was Norman Kingsley, a Los Angeles reservist who was severely wounded storming the seawalls at Inchon." Worse, both Tech. Sgt. Shannon Means and Cpl. Bill Lourin, each a Marine combat correspondent under Capraro, would be killed in action before the fighting in Korea ended.

Capraro himself barely escaped with a whole skin from his night at Chosin surrounded by the Red Chinese. He had been riding as a passenger in a convoy that evening of November 28, 1950, "when the Chinese struck." As Warrant Officer D. R. Yancey later said, Capraro "took command" of the hundred or so personnel with them in the ambush near the Chosin Reservoir, "emphatically rejecting Chinese demands that he surrender."

Instead, Capraro "quieted the men and set up a defense." He did so while "all the time he was under machine-gun and small-arms fire." The fighting continued until daybreak, at which time "the ambushed force was able to rejoin its column."

Capraro, shepherd to the press covering the Korean War, was later awarded a Bronze Star with V (for Valor) for his actions in combat that night. "I'd have gladly exchanged it for a bottle of Jack Daniels," was his wry remark.

Still, he argued, there was glory in what happened at Chosin. For thirteen days, from late November to early December, "The First Marine Division was faced with annihilation, trapped in subzero cold in North Korea by overwhelming forces of Chinese." America and the world watched helplessly from afar in painful suspense, all the while wondering, "Could the Marines break out of the trap and withdraw to the sea, where U.S. Navy ships waited to evacuate them?"

They could and they would. "After thirteen frigid days and nights of fighting in trying terrain against a foe determined to have our pride as well as our hides, we marched free from the trap, with our wounded, our equipment and most of our dead."

It was, as Division Commander Oliver P. Smith proclaimed, no retreat, but an orderly withdrawal, even an attack "in a different direction." The way his rejoinder came out, though, was this:

Retreat, Hell! We're just attacking in a different direction!

But was he the sole author of the famous bit of defiance? In an article for the monthly publication *Military* out of Sacramento, California (March 1991), Capraro acknowledged that Smith made such a remark to him, and he, Capraro, relayed it on to the news media.

"I established a radio link with UP [United Press] correspondent Charles Moore in Hungnam and got out the account of General Smith's interview with a newsman—me—during which he rejected any notions of retreat and declared the division was attacking in a different direction, as part of an orderly withdrawal."

It was the *Retreat, Hell!* version that then made headlines throughout America, and across the world.

"Over the years," Capraro acknowledged, "some journalists have speculated over the story's origin, and Frank Conniff, chief Hearst correspondent and executive, editorialized [that] Smith may have made the remark, but he felt certain I had provided the punctuation. I admit only to the release of the statement."

But Capraro also said that at Chosin, the Marines, *his* Marines, achieved glory. "There is an exhilaration in knowing you've given all that you've got, surmounting incredible odds, for a cause in which you believe," he wrote in *Military History* magazine. "This, I believe, was glory."

————

ADDITIONAL NOTE: ON THE SAME DATE OF NOVEMBER 28, 1950, that Capraro and his assorted one hundred survived their trap up in the North Korean mountains around the Chosin Reservoir, former semipro football player Hector Cafferata Jr. and a semi-blinded companion also spent hours under a human-wave attack by the Red Chinese in the same area, completely alone.

It was about 1:30 a.m. when they were awakened by the attack. In the fighting that followed, most in his squad were killed or badly wounded. That left just Cafferata and fellow Marine Kenneth Benson on their own, and Benson had been temporarily blinded by a grenade that destroyed his glasses.

"I told Benson, 'Hang on to my foot. We're going to crawl,'" he once told an interviewer for the Charlotte (Florida) *Sun*. "We crawled up to a wash, where rainwater cut a shallow trench into the side of the hill. I told him, 'This is where we're going to stay.'"

Stay they did, but not quietly. For one thing, Cafferata, New York City born but raised in rural New Jersey, happened to be a good shot.

As the Marine Corps *Times* tells the story, Cafferata lobbed hand grenades at the Chinese troops while Benson reloaded his rifle. The former football player fired eight shots, "dropping eight enemy soldiers."

This went on for a total of about five hours. Cafferata, in his stocking feet despite the freezing temperatures, continued to do the shooting, and Benson took charge of the reloading. All the time, Cafferata's feet were literally freezing. Cafferata fired his M1 rifle so repeatedly, he later said, "that thing turned to charcoal—I had to put snow on it to cool it off."

Nor were the attacking Chinese exactly idle. As they lobbed grenades of their own, he lobbed them back. "For the rest of the night," he related, "I was batting hand grenades away with my entrenching tool while firing my rifle at them. I must have whacked a dozen grenades that night with my tool. And you know what, I was the world's worst baseball player."

Of course, few could get through a night like that unscathed, including Cafferata. He lost part of a finger and came away with a piece of shrapnel in one arm. And at daybreak, he was seriously wounded by a sniper, just before rescue by fellow Marines.

The medics who first tended him reported his feet were blue from frostbite. But he would survive and, after eighteen months of hospital treatment for his wounds, was able to attend a White House ceremony in which Present Harry S. Truman presented him with the Medal of Honor.

The citation said he had killed fifteen Chinese, wounded others, and forced even more to back off. But author Peter Collier said in his book, *Medal of Honor: Portraits of Valor Beyond the Call of Duty*, that Cafferata's commanding officers counted about one hundred Chinese dead around the ditch where he and Benson took refuge that night.

They didn't report that real number, "because they thought that no one would believe it."

Meanwhile, Cafferata returned home to New Jersey after his recovery to work for the state's Fish and Wildlife Service. He also operated a bar in Alpha, New Jersey, before retiring to Florida, where he died in 2016 at the age of eighty-six. "I did my duty," he once said. "I protected my fellow Marines. They protected me. And I'm prouder of that than the fact that the government decided to give me the Medal of Honor."

Michael Capraro, in the meantime, became an operations officer with the Central Intelligence Agency for twenty years. After retiring and going into the commercial real estate business, he died of cancer in Charlottesville, Virginia, on November 28, 1995, at the age of seventy-three.

MASS BREAKOUT

NOT MANY U.S. SERVICEMEN TAKEN PRISONER BY THE RED CHINESE during the Korean War ever escaped. Not even Marines. Many Americans never came back at all. But one group of Marines, nearly two dozen strong, did come back. They escaped captivity after months as POWs, and they did it all together in one mass breakout.

It's hard to say where, or with whom, their shared saga begins. One relevant place is the "Frozen Chosin," that epic battle in North Korea where overwhelming numbers of Red Chinese overran the United

Nations' X Corps, consisting of the First Marine Division and the Army's Seventh Infantry Division, right after Thanksgiving of 1950.

For the Americans pushing northward toward the Chosin Reservoir up on the plateau above the North Korean east coast on November 28, the day began normally for a combat operation. But not for Pfc. Charles M. "Bud" Kaylor, a Marine machine-gunner who thought he would be getting home to Hopkins, Minnesota, in time for Christmas. Naturally, he was thrilled at the prospect as he climbed aboard the lead truck in a convoy of five heading down the long MSR (Main Supply Route) from Koto-ri to the valley below.

Thoroughly elated, he just had been told his dependency discharge had come through, notes author John G. Hubbell in his story "The Long Way Home," appearing in the 1977 Reader's Digest book, *True Stories of Great Escapes*. Told he would have to find his own way down the mountain range, Kaylor joined mail clerk Art Foley in hitching a ride aboard a truck driven by Cpl. Fred Holcomb of Hamden, New York. Two more Marines rode in the back as fellow passengers, while a third "was riding shotgun" up front next to the driver. And off they went, unremarkably at first, on the seventy-mile trip down the MSR to real safety at the bottom.

Reaching a small, quiet-looking roadside village, the Marines were surprised to see a crowd of excited Koreans emerge from their huts shouting and pointing down the road. Misinterpreting the excitement, the Marines laughed and threw them candy and cigarettes.

But then, coming around a sharp curve, they found the road was blocked by a Jeep piled high with heavy logs. They came upon it so suddenly, driver Holcomb couldn't stop in time to avoid hitting it. When he did, his vehicle careened off the road, and he just "bulled his way on."

Worse yet, they now were surrounded by Red Chinese soldiers six and seven feet deep in the ditches alongside the MSR, with more "running down the hill on both sides of the road, shooting as they came."

The Marines, of course, reacted aggressively. Kaylor emptied his carbine, firing blindly into the mass of soldiers in the ditches, but his ammunition was spent in just seconds. "He dropped flat on his back and saw two bullets sing past, within an inch of his nose. He saw them go by, because they had come right through the steel side of the truck, and it had slowed them down." About this time another "came through and got Art Foley, the mail clerk."

Then "something yellow" sailed into the truck—a grenade shaped like a potato masher. Kaylor managed to pick it up and throw it out the back of the truck before it went off.

Meanwhile, the driver had been wounded; with only two good tires left, the truck veered all over the road. The Marine riding shotgun was blasting away at the driver's side of the road to protect him.

Taking Foley's carbine, Kaylor sat up to begin firing again when he saw a Chinese soldier lob another yellow grenade at the truck, a perfect throw from the ditch. Luckily, Kaylor was able to grab it by the handle and throw it right back. "It hit at the Communist's feet and instantly exploded. The Red died with unbelieving surprise on his face."

Still, there was no time to congratulate himself. The truck itself swerved and crashed into one of the two ditches alongside. "Kaylor went over the side and ran to some thin bushes." He watched as truck driver Holcomb and his shotgun man ran toward a frozen river a good five football fields away. The gunner went down as the Chinese kept firing, but Holcomb reached the edge of a thick wood and disappeared among the trees.

Alone now, Kaylor was knocked down and wounded in a leg by yet another grenade thrown his way. It went off just five feet from him, and seconds later he was taken prisoner.

Bleeding "fast," he was escorted to a command post, where he lost his parka to a Chinese officer who then sent him on to a Chinese aid station for treatment of his leg wound. In the meantime, he was weak from the loss of blood. "He kept falling down, and the Reds kept pushing him along. Every step seemed colder than the last. It was −15 Fahrenheit, and all he wore now was his field cap, a shirt, pants, shoes, and long underwear."

As events unfolded, most of them unwelcome, Kaylor was cheered to be reunited with truck driver Holcomb the next day. They were interrogated together, in perfect English, by a friendly-seeming, smooth-talking Chinese lieutenant named Fung. He contended the Chinese would not kill them and didn't even want to keep them as prisoners. "All we want to do with you guys is get you get out of Korea so you can't fight us anymore."

Claiming the Chinese would put them on a neutral ship and send them back to the United States, he took their home addresses. "I'd like to write you fellows after the war and see how things turn out for each of us," he asserted.

The next day, though, Fung was gone, and they were ordered to start walking northward through the heavy snow in a group of about 250 POWs, including 43 more Marines. Kaylor limped along with the column for eleven days, until they reached a village near the Yalu River. Exhausted and malnourished, most of the prisoners were happy to lie on bare floors in cold North Korean houses "in a sleeping stupor" for days.

When the prisoners finally rallied, the Chinese made them swap their uniforms for Chinese. And then began long interrogations by English-speaking Chinese officers.

"It was kept mostly on a personal plane, and the officers kept it up until they got the answers they wanted." What they wanted were denouncements of the American way of life under capitalism.

"When the prisoners realized what the Reds wanted to hear, they told them tales of wretched, hungry childhoods that had been lived in antic-ipation of joining the Marine Corps, where they could at least get some food and clothing. They told of aged parents who lived as best they could on the infrequent and niggardly charity of the Wall Street bosses. The Chinese seemed to like this."

Meanwhile, Christmas came and went, followed by lectures every other day in a bleak, cold barn the prisoners called the "Big House." After the lectures, came roundtable "discussions with an English-speaking offi-cer busily taking notes on what was being said. He sometimes would interject a comment, and the Marines would all nod solemn approval."

The passing weeks soon stretched into months under the same

enforced regime, and then came a deadly outbreak of dysentery. "It hit everyone, and the ones it hit the worst died. Sometimes only one would die in a week, sometimes three, four, or five." Kaylor, for his part, suffered more from malnutrition that racked his legs with pain. At one point, he was left flat on his back for twenty-eight days, often delirious. Finally, the torment stopped and he was able to walk again.

And just as well, since another move was in store for the prisoners— all the way down from their winter quarters near the Yalu, it turned out, to a town by the 38th parallel that had divided the two Koreas.

First, though, sixty prisoners were divided into two groups of thirty each at the Big House. A ranking officer spoke at length, then announced one group would be released, while the other would be held longer to help instruct incoming prisoners.

Toying with the POWs, the Chinese officer asked, "Which group is it? Who is going home?" Looking around at the men in his group, Kaylor could take satisfaction in knowing they all "were barracks bull-session artists, and all had given the Reds master snow jobs." In fact, Kaylor, Holcomb, and the rest of their thirty *were* the choice to leave. "The thirty Marines took the news with stone-faced joy, for they wanted the Reds to feel they would just as soon stay there and be Communists as return home and be Communists. The other thirty also remained stone-faced, but they had trouble fighting back the tears."

That very night, the first thirty were loaded into trucks and started on their way to the Chunchon area just below the 38th parallel. The trip took five nights, and when they arrived, the officer in charge, a Lieutenant Pan, announced a delay in plans. "There has been an American offensive," he said. "It is too dangerous to let you go now. You might be killed."

The Marines were marched into a prison camp, where they lingered for another six weeks with no further action. It was May 1951. Kaylor and many of his buddies had been POWs since November or December of 1950.

However, on the night of May 15, nineteen of them, Kaylor

included, were marched to a river, given razors and soap to clean up with, and then fed real pork and rice instead of the usual sorghum seed and millet. Some of them were made sick by the unaccustomed food.

Best of all, Pan told them that word had come to release them.

Another journey of three nights by truck took them to the Imjin River, where the Chinese were retreating across the river by the thousands. A field commander on the scene took charge of the group in place of Pan and said they would be shipped north—no release.

Tech Sgt. Charley Harrison of Tulsa, Oklahoma, was visibly outraged, and declared he would not go back north to resume captivity. Meanwhile, with UN artillery coming close, the Chinese guards had retreated into foxholes. All nineteen Marines just walked off, waded across the shallow river, and ran for their lives through woods on the other side.

Escape? Not quite. Falling asleep in a wheat field before dawn, they awoke to find four Chinese soldiers "pointing guns at them and jabbering to each other."

Harrison, who had learned some Chinese, smiled at the soldiers and told them he and his buddies were newly released prisoners of war "and that the high command would be displeased if they were shot or taken back."

He could see the Chinese were not buying his story. Instead, they were debating among themselves whether to shoot the Marines out of hand or to take them back to the Chinese lines as prisoners again. Harrison kept on talking in Chinese to the four enemy soldiers, but also with asides in English telling various members of the group which Chinese soldier they should jump at his signal.

Finally, he gave the signal in English—"Let's get them."

Faced with the choice of kill or likely be killed, they overpowered the four in seconds and killed them by strangulation and rifle butts to the head. Then, it was time to run again.

They came upon a Korean village, where a friendly resident, old and bearded, sent them to a former mayor's house on top of a hill with a promise to alert the American forces, then only miles away. Soon, a low-flying U.S. Army L-5 artillery spotter plane appeared. Rushing outside with strips of wallpaper ripped from the walls of the Korean house, some of the Marines spelled out the words POW 19 RESCUE in a rice paddy.

Truck-driver Holcomb was so excited, he remained standing in the rice paddy despite enemy fire. "Snipers fired at him from the hills occasionally, but they weren't coming close and Holcomb was much too excited to care."

Then the L-5 dropped a message: "Come out to the letters so you can be counted. We are sending tanks in to pick you up."

The tanks did come, just half an hour later, and that would be the end of the story, except for one thing. As the tanks approached, Lt. Frank Cold of Tampa, Florida, the only officer among the Marines, spoke up. "But this is the Army coming in to get us," he said, "and we're still Marines. So let's be rescued like Marines, in formation."

And that's the way the Army found them, all nineteen Marines lined up in columns of twos, with tears streaming down every face.

SHOWBIZ FOLKS

Tooling along in his little Cessna OE Bird Dog, on one artillery-spotting mission after another, for a total of eighty-five in less than a year's time, was Ed McMahon, a former Corsair training instructor who never made it to the Big Show of World War II. But still, a sitting duck plane flying above very resentful people in Korea was dangerous enough, wasn't it?

Then, there was Lee Marvin. Fast-pedal back to the Big Show itself, and there he was, shot in a very posterior area of his body while taking part in the invasion of Saipan. With a no-nonsense wound of nine by three inches in size, he was destined for hospitalization and rehabilitation for a long thirteen months.

Also in the Pacific, Brian Keith repeatedly saw the air attacks on the Japanese naval base at Rabaul, and no wonder—he was rear gunner in a two-seater SBD Douglas Dauntless dive-bomber repeatedly attacking Rabaul.

Whereas, far away, on the other side of the world, Sterling Hayden parachuted into occupied Yugoslavia to join local partisans in their guerrilla operations against the common German enemy…

All combat veterans, all showbiz people—Ed McMahon, Lee Marvin, Brian Keith, Sterling Hayden, and so many more—and all Marines, as well.

As were so many other names from the ranks of show business. Tyrone Power flew transport planes in the Pacific; Steve McQueen was a tank crewman. Others who served in World War II or Korea included Robert Ryan, Cesar Romero, George Peppard, Gene Hackman, Bradford Dillman…

The list just goes on and on.

Few of them made real history as Marines, but all did serve, often in combat. Yet, what history these citizen-Marines made when they returned to their civilian lives in showbiz.

Consider Ed McMahon. As *Stars and Stripes Central* said in its obituary of June 23, 2009: "He volunteered for service during World War II. He went through flight training at various bases, but the end of the war came before he was deployed overseas." But then, of course, he had his chance in Korea, where he flew eighty-five combat missions in his butterfly-like Cessna, bouncing along on the air currents as he spotted for the artillery crews below.

Of course, he's not so well remembered for his military service. He made his real mark as Johnny Carson's sidekick—through the 6,583 *Tonight Show* programs that he introduced, he became as much an institution as did Carson himself. Who in modern American life isn't familiar with his "Heeeere's Johnny" opener? In addition, notes *Stars and Stripes,* MacMahon "announced for Jerry Lewis's Labor Day telethons and pitched for television's Publishers Clearing House sweepstakes."

Fittingly, after his birth in Detroit, Michigan, McMahon grew up hoping to become a radio announcer. He also wanted to be a Marine Corps fighter pilot, and he did become one in early 1945. After winning his wings and commission, "McMahon was sent to the Corsair Operational Training Unit at Lee Field, Green Cove Springs, Florida," writes M. L. Shettle, Jr. in *United States Marine Corps Air Stations of World War II*. But instead of being deployed into combat, he was assigned to be an instructor at the same fighter-training school.

He finally did receive orders to "join the Marine carrier program on the West Coast," possibly meaning a chance to join the fight in the Pacific, but the United States dropped the first of its two atomic bombs on Japan on that very day. The orders were cancelled. Returning to civilian life and college studies, McMahon began his television career at a Philadelphia station, and "in two years he had become Philadelphia's top TV personality," writes Shettle.

But the Korean War came in 1950, and with it a recall to active duty. This time, his specialty would be artillery spotting from the highly vulnerable, single-engine Cessna.

Returning again to civilian life once the hostilities were over, McMahon resumed his television career in Philadelphia, until he was named the announcer for Johnny Carson's show *Who Do You Trust?* in 1958. He went along as Carson became host of *The Tonight Show* in 1962, thus beginning a joint stint that kept them together for thirty years. Meanwhile, McMahon retired from the Marine Corps Reserves in 1966 with full colonel's rank.

Lee Marvin came from a boyhood marked by expulsion from a series of Eastern prep schools. Even earlier, at age four, he had run away from home for two days. In fact, according to his *New York Times* obituary, he was kicked out of one boarding school for throwing a roommate out of a second-floor window. He eventually dropped out of a school in Florida to join the Marines. "After a sheltered life, I went the other way," he once said. "I wanted to prove how tough I was."

Before his wounding in the 1945 invasion of Saipan, scout sniper Marvin took part in twenty landings on Pacific Islands held by the Japanese, also according to the *Times*.

When he recovered from his Saipan wound more than a year later,

Marvin "drifted aimlessly" through various menial jobs, until his work as a plumber's apprentice digging septic tanks near his family's home in Woodstock, New York, "took him to a local summer-stock playhouse." There, "as a lark," he auditioned and was given an acting job.

A series of small roles led to a Broadway stint in *Billy Budd*, followed in the early 1950s "by more than 200 featured roles in television dramas." Those, in turn, led to a bit part in the movie *You're in the Navy Now*.

After moving to the West Coast and Hollywood, "he played the widely acclaimed part of a psychopathic multiple murderer in an early episode of *Dragnet*" and briefly overcame the bad-guy image as the tough but kind-hearted police lieutenant in the TV series *M Squad*.

In 1966 Marvin entered Hollywood's history books by winning the Oscar for Best Actor for his two roles in the movie *Cat Ballou,* in which he played both a drunk gunfighter and his brother, a sober gunfighter. This victory was quickly followed by perhaps his best known, most fitting role: the hard-bitten commander leading a group of Army misfits on a suicide mission behind Nazi lines in *The Dirty Dozen*. Another of the former Marine's best film acting jobs came in the 1968 movie *Hell in the Pacific*. All told, he acted in fifty-six movies up to his final role in the 1983 film *Gorky Park*.

Marvin died of a heart attack on August 29, 1987, at the age of sixty-three in Tucson, Arizona, with his childhood friend Pamela Feeley Marvin by his hospital bedside. Reunited on one of his trips back to Woodstock to visit his ailing father, they had married in 1970.

Among other "movie star Marines," Macdonald Carey and fellow cast members were so moved by the experience of making the 1942 film *Wake Island*, they *joined* the Marines as a result and thus served in the South Pacific. Others of some note would include director George Roy Hill (*The Sting, Butch Cassidy and the Sundance Kid*), a transport pilot during WWII and an F4F Panther fighter-jet pilot in Korea; Hugh O'Brian (legally named Hugh Charles Krampe), a drill instructor at age eighteen; comedian Jonathan Winters, a member of the postwar occupation forces in Japan; and many, many more.

THE FIGHTING "MUSIC"

So many people would at last know this Marine bugler's name—more than fifty years later. Officially, he was a Marine Corps "Music," or musician, but by the time they heard his name, most people didn't really catch on to that part. Most didn't know who or what he was, period.

Still, they suddenly knew his name: Darrell Cole.

Hailing from Park Hills, Missouri, he became a Marine in 1941, just months before Pearl Harbor. After boot camp at Parris Island, he was assigned as a bugler to the First Marine Regiment, First Marine Division. Although he had played the French horn with real verve in high school, he didn't want to be a Music. He wanted combat. He wanted it so badly that he kept requesting a change in rating. But the Marine Corps was short on buglers, so his request was denied. However, it wasn't long before he saw combat, after all.

What kind of combat, you may ask, can a bugler expect, even in a hard-fought-over place like Guadalcanal?

Especially in a place like Guadalcanal, it might be said.

But not to worry: when a machine-gunner was suddenly needed, he stepped in and filled the slot. Indeed, that was exactly what he had hoped for.

So, he survived Guadalcanal. He was returned stateside in early 1943 with the 'Canal behind him, and was assigned to the First Battalion, Twenty-Third Marines, Fourth Marine Division. Then came Kwajalein Atoll, another bloody stop for the Marines in the far-off Pacific.

There, again, he dropped his bugle long enough to take up a machine-gunner's job, and this time the Corps did pay a bit more attention. Arriving next on Saipan with his Fourth Division, he was now an assigned member of a machine-gun unit. Good—but more to the point, he did so well in the invasion of Saipan that he was made a machine-gun section leader. When his squad leader was killed, the young Missourian took over the squad, despite wounds of his own, and led it so bravely and effectively that he received the Bronze Star for valor, in addition to his Purple Heart.

Just three days later, notes a Navy biography, he led his squad ashore in the invasion of Tinian, the island from which two atomic bombs would later be delivered on Hiroshima and Nagasaki, Japan. At Tinian, says the same biographical sketch, "he continued to live up to his growing reputation as the 'The Fighting Field Music.'"

Meanwhile, it was only after Saipan that the Marine Corps bugler finally won official changes in rating and rank, first to line corporal and then to sergeant. Both promotions came just in time for Iwo Jima.

He and his men went ashore with the initial assault wave on February 19, 1945. Held up by a pair of Japanese gun emplacements, the onetime Music took care of them with hand grenades. But then came another deadly impediment to the advance—three enemy gun emplacements.

His section's machine guns knocked out one of the three, but two were still in action as the former bugler first attacked them both single-handedly while armed with just one hand grenade and a pistol.

"Twice he…returned to his own lines for additional grenades," says the official Navy biography. It further states that he continued his one-man assault "under fierce enemy fire until he had succeeded in destroying the enemy strong point."

He was just returning to his own squad's position when a Japanese grenade rolled too close, and that terrible misfortune made the bugler's Medal of Honor a posthumous one.

The ship—for there would be a ship—was named after the Marine bugler fifty-one years later. The Arleigh Burke (or Aegis) class guided-missile destroyer was nicknamed "The Determined Warrior" in memory of her namesake and assigned to Norfolk, Virginia, as home port.

Then, five years later, the destroyer carrying the hero's name was off to the Persian Gulf region and to the wars against terrorism.

The bugler's family felt close to the ship and crew. They had been at both her launch and her commissioning. A nephew and others were aboard for the shakedown cruise, and they visited the ship again in 1999. "We feel it is a family member," the bugler's nephew Vincent once remarked. Family members were even sent copies of the ship's magazine, *The Bugler*.

One October morning in the year 2000, Vincent was sitting at his desk when the soft sounds of a radio playing in the background suddenly changed to a news report. He heard the name "Cole." The rest "was a blur."

Even so, he said, "It got my attention."

It was about his deceased uncle Darrell Samuel Cole's ship, "The Determined Warrior" (officially known as the USS *Cole*), struck by terrorists that October day in the harbor at Aden, Yemen, with seventeen of her crew killed by the bomb blast that had blown a huge hole in the destroyer's Navy-gray hull right at the waterline.

Worse, photos of the deceased began to come forth. On a happier, earlier day, one of them had sat right across from visiting Cole family members at a table in the ship's mess. Vincent recognized the face of Rodrick McDaniels of Norfolk when it appeared in the papers. For that matter, he remembered "more than one face" among all the photos of the dead.

As he and the rest of America soon learned, the damage to the USS *Cole* was caused by explosives carried in a small boat that had pulled up alongside the *Cole*. The bomb damage was so extensive, the hardworking survivors barely saved the ship, which weeks later was carried "piggyback" across the seas by the Norwegian heavy-lift salvage ship MV *Blue Marlin* for repairs at the same Ingalls shipbuilding shipyard in Pascagoula, Mississippi, where she had been built. Said B. C. Lee, a carpenter at the shipyard: "It makes me feel good the Navy chose us to repair it."

ADDITIONAL NOTE: THE COMPOUND FAILURES OF ALERTNESS THAT allowed a small boat to approach the *Cole* undeterred on October 12, 2000, led to significant reforms in U.S. Navy security precautions. Reportedly, only two sailors armed with two pistols containing two rounds each were patrolling the decks of the billion-dollar guided-missile destroyer when it was approached in the Aden harbor by the harmless looking boat. Meanwhile, the al Qaeda terrorist network headed by Osama bin Laden claimed "credit" for the attack, but in the years after the attack, various other terrorist leaders were identified as masterminds of the plot that resulted in the detonation of an estimated five hundred to seven hundred pounds of explosives carried in the boat.

MARINE "ARMY" IN VIETNAM

ARRIVING IN IMMENSE NUMBERS BY SEA AND BY AIR IN VIETNAM, the Marines were there to stay the course—but often as infantrymen fighting inland against the homegrown Viet Cong or the invading North Vietnamese. That meant one mean firefight after another, some big and many small, but fought fiercely nonetheless.

Take the night of June 15, 1966, when Ssgt. Jimmie Howard's platoon of C Company, First Reconnaissance Battalion, was holding an observation post on a bump in the terrain called "Hill 488," out in enemy-dominated territory twenty-five miles west of Chu Lai. Howard, from Burlington, Iowa, had already earned the Purple Heart in Korea—three times—plus a Silver Star. Now the big guy was about to earn the Medal of Honor in one of those small-unit actions so typical of the frustrating U.S. experience in Vietnam.

That night, he and the eighteen men of his platoon were attacked about ten o'clock by a full North Vietnamese battalion, recalled J. Robert Moskin in his exhaustive history, *The U.S. Marine Corps Story.* As only a mere sign of what was to come, the first assault hit Lance Cpl. Ricardo

Binns's team of four "out front." In the melee that ensued, the Marines threw their hand grenades, and Binns shot the nearest attacker. Lance Cpl. John T. Adams of Portland, Oregon, his ammo used up, used his empty rifle as a club to kill two more of the attackers before he was shot and killed. In addition, Cpl. Jerrald R. Thompson, of Palmer, California, would die from a fatal wound, but not before he killed two more assailants with his knife.

But this was only the beginning for Howard and his sixteen Marines still remaining.

Forming a tight perimeter at the crest of their hill, they would hold all night long against "assault after assault." Severely wounded in a grenade blast and unable to use his legs, the Korean War vet still directed his platoon's defense. "He distributed his ammunition to the other men, maintained radio communication, and called in artillery fire and air strikes. The enemy taunted them: 'Marines, you die!' Flares lighting the bare mountainside revealed hordes of the enemy."

As the air strikes continued, Howard's men used up their grenades. Their rifle ammunition running low, "they squeezed off single shots and threw back rocks."

With the breaking dawn, a total of five Marines were dead, and all the others but one were wounded. "Corpsman Billie D. Holmes, badly hurt himself, cared for the wounded."

Still, in the great Marine tradition, they had held their position.

Even so, their ordeal was not yet over. As evacuation helicopters now approached, Howard waved them off and called for more air strikes in the immediate area. The North Vietnamese were not yet gone, by any means.

First Lt. Marshall Darling's C Company, Fifth Marines, landed on Hill 488's southern slopes by chopper and swept up the high ground, "wiping out enemy positions as they went." Finally reaching the trapped platoon at the crest, they found Howard and his men had just eight rounds of ammunition left.

Meanwhile, as Maj. William J. Goodsell brought in his airship and hovered ten feet off the ground, it drew fire, and he was killed. Then, when a second chopper came in to extricate Howard's hard-hit platoon, its crew chief was killed by ground fire.

As the battle went on, there would be more casualties on both sides. Among the Americans, four more Marines died, including 2nd Lt. Ronald Meyer, a year out of the Naval Academy at Annapolis, Maryland. Both Darling and Lance Cpl. James Brown crawled into the fire zone to retrieve Meyer's body. Later, Lance Cpl. Binns and Corpsman Holmes were recommended for the Navy Cross, while Sergeant Howard earned the esteemed Medal of Honor, "for saving his platoon from annihilation."

The intense but small-unit battle was all over by noon, significant only to those directly involved. Yet, it was just one, figuratively speaking, of a thousand and one intense, small-unit actions the Marines fought in Vietnam—as did, for that matter, the U.S. Army. To many, this sort of activity did not seem the traditional Marine Corps mission.

By the end of 1967, the Corps had more than seventy-seven thousand men in Vietnam, largely coming under what was known as the III Marine Amphibious Force (III MAF) and based for the most part in the country's three northern provinces.

This war was not like World War II or Korea. For the Marines, it was more like occupation duty in a thoroughly hostile environment. "There were those who believed the Marines were in the wrong place—that they should have been posted in the Mekong Delta, where they could have utilized their thirty-year-old amphibious capability [perfected during World War II's island-hopping campaign in the Pacific]," Moskin writes.

Based in the north of the country, they were "in the ambiguous situation of serving quite like an army force." Moreover, "they were in Vietnam—and stayed in Vietnam—not because they were specialists but because they existed. They were needed and they wanted a piece of the action."

While not in their traditional role, the Marines were certainly getting action. In 1967 alone, they killed an estimated 17,876 of the enemy, while in that one year they themselves suffered 3,452 killed and nearly

26,000 wounded. According to Moskin, this meant a total of 5,479 Marines killed since 1962 and another 37,784 wounded. "Only in World War II," he noted, "had the Corps suffered more."

SELECT UNIT HISTORIES
NINTH ENGINEERS

These Marines built their own forty-seven-mile stretch of road, then kept it up, guarded it, checked it every day for newly planted mines, and fought off the occasional Viet Cong or North Vietnamese Army attack for four long years, but not without the occasional casualty as well.

Heavy equipment operator—twelve-ton, rubber-tire mobile crane operator—Fred DuPont writes online that the Ninth Engineer Battalion's 47.6-mile stretch of Vietnam's coastal Route 1 included the "longest fixed-span bridge ever built by the Marine Corps," a 722-foot span across the Ba Ren River. He also writes about the time Capt. Reno Rizzo, CO of Delta Company, took a round in the chest in a North Vietnamese-mounted ambush just south of the village of Dien Ban.

That was just the beginning of the surprise attack by an estimated one hundred North Vietnamese against Rizzo's convoy of seven vehicles loaded with bridge-building materials from the big U.S. base at Da Nang and manned by thirty Marines from the Battalion's Delta and Service companies.

Actually, after two years on station at Chu Lai and environs, hostile action in this part of northern South Vietnam was not a total surprise to the men of the Ninth Engineers. In May of 1968, they had marked the two-year anniversary of their arrival "in country" from stateside. Their thousand-man battalion had been created in late 1965 for the specific purpose of joining the defense of the democratic-leaning South against the

Communist insurgency that was aided and abetted every step of the way by the North.

In their first two years on station, notes a Ninth Engineers website maintained by the late Mike Cummings Sr. and his son Michael Cummings, the Marine engineers had turned Vietnam's Route 1 "from an impassable road into nearly 50 miles of two-lane, gravel-based highway." Their stretch ran from home base at Chu Lai north to the Cau Lau River. In the process of turning "a virtual towpath" into a Vietnamese "super highway," they built or repaired forty-one bridges and ninety-seven culverts. Their trucks hauled more than eight thousand cubic yards of crushed rock and earth a month.

Located in coastal flatlands in the Republic of Vietnam's five northernmost provinces and running through rice paddies, their road looked like "a 47.6-mile stretch of bridge across a sea of water" during the monsoon rains that came every year. Naturally, too, the new road improved the flow of commerce among its villages and towns. However, if the road was the battalion's to maintain, it was also the battalion's to guard and to clear of mines during the daytime, because the nights often belonged to the Viet Cong.

Eight mine-sweep teams were sent out daily from the Ninth Engineers company base camps located at various positions along the road. Once the sweeps were finished, the road was open for business—and the Ninth's grade engineers, dump trucks, and other heavy road equipment went into their daily action.

The mine-sweeping operation was no mere training exercise—it was an absolute necessity, because mines can kill or maim for life. The Viet Cong repeatedly hid mines along the road, especially above the metal culverts, where the mine detectors wouldn't be able to distinguish the extra metal of a mine.

Striking at night, the enemy also blew bridges and culverts with explosives. During the battalion's first two years in Vietnam, its Marines repeatedly had to repair and even rebuild the roadway's bridges. There were so many bridges, it was impossible to provide night security for them all. Thus, smaller, unguarded spans were prime targets for the Viet Cong. One was blown and then rebuilt six times in two years.

"We can replace destroyed culverts in about two hours," First Lieutenant Rick Ericson, CO of the battalion's Charlie Company, once said. "The blown bridges usually take about one week to rebuild."

At the same time, the engineer Marines mounted their own combat patrols and operated a civilian dispensary for the local Vietnamese. As specialists, though, they also provided water purification units, built schools, and once constructed a float-raft ferry crossing for allied Korean Marines, to say nothing of building their own base camp at the very start of their Vietnam tour.

And, like any other combat Marines, they came under occasional fire and took casualties. The reminder comes from former Ninth Engineers member DuPont, who once wryly noted, "A mine sweep is a very exciting way to start your day." He detailed the dangerous procedure:

"Every morning two sweep teams would leave from each outpost, one north and one south, to clear the roads of mines before any work on the road could commence. Our teams usually consisted of two Marines with metal detectors, two with K-bar knives to probe any suspected spots in the road, two with grappling hooks out ahead in the rice paddies to snag any wires running to explosives planted in the road..."

It took a brave man to drive the truck idling behind the sweep teams. One day it did hit a mine. DuPont's company corpsman (medics) were killed and seven Marines were wounded. "The driver of the truck, Cpl. Paul Kozak, was so severely wounded and burnt, it took twenty-seven separate operations to put him back together. He now runs Vet Works, a nationwide service to help homeless veterans get their lives back together."

Another episode producing casualties came that day in August 1968 when Delta Company's Captain Rizzo was hit in the chest in the opening fusillade by hidden North Vietnamese Army (NVA) ambushers. The bullet passed through his right lung and lodged next to his spine, DuPont writes in an online article for WarStories.com, "A Bad Day at Dien Ban" (July 2011). This was on the battalion's stretch of Vietnam Route 1, just south of the village of Dien Ban.

Rizzo's Jeep driver sought cover by running their vehicle off the road into the lower ground alongside, but in the process Rizzo and two non-coms traveling with him were spilled unceremoniously into the mud by the side of the road.

Almost instantly, the convoy's "gun truck"—a six-by-six "stacked with sand bags and some armor-plating," but armed with a .50-caliber machine gun mounted on the back—charged on through the gap left by the lead Jeep. By standing plan, its driver, Lance Cpl. Ruley, blew on through the ambush site with Lance Cpl. Pete Triosi "blasting away with the 50 cal."

They themselves came under a hail of small-arms fire. Triosi was hit in the arm as the gun truck careened ahead, "but [he] never quit." His machine-gun fire was joined by a stream of rounds from truck passenger Pfc. Paul Ricard's standard M-16, "giving their CO as much covering fire as they could."

In minutes, the gun truck reached a Korean Marines compound just ahead, near the village of My Hat, and U.S. Marine personnel there began organizing for a fast rescue mission. But the damaged gun track overheated on the way back, and the handful of Marines aboard took to their feet, still pressing forward.

Meanwhile, Major Caleb Wall, executive officer of the Ninth Engineers, flew into a nearby Allied base by helicopter to establish contact with Australian Army advisers to a South Vietnamese unit and to organize an even stronger response.

After an hour's engagement with the enemy at the ambush

site, the Marines of the rescue party were ordered to pull back—helicopter gunships were on the way.

Back at the Jeep, it had been a long hour for Rizzo and company. His Staff Sgt. Charlie Edwards "caught three rounds in the stomach" from an NVA soldier "standing over them." Edwards struggled to reach an M-16, then "emptied the whole twenty-round magazine into him." Meanwhile, the other noncom in the Jeep, a Sergeant Nehila, was wounded in the back and legs.

Still lacking any cover and "desperately wounded," Rizzo and Edwards crawled about one hundred yards to a well surrounded by a dirt berm. There, Edwards stuffed mud into Rizzo's bullet holes to stop the bleeding. "The surgeon told him [Rizzo] later it was the action that saved his life."

As for Nehila, he "lay wounded and dazed during the entire ambush and could not be found in the confusion." He was recovered, though, after "he wandered into the PF [Popular Forces] compound at Trung Phu' the next day and was taken to Da Nang by Medevac."

However, that was not the entire story. With Rizzo's command vehicle off the road and the protective gun truck bulling its way through up ahead, Lance Cpl. Ray Cummings's tractor/trailer "was now the lead vehicle [in the column and] taking the brunt of the NVA punishment." In addition, Lance Cpl. Bill Lee's tractor/trailer was behind Cummings's. "Everyone on those two trucks bailed out and began returning fire." So did men from the remaining vehicles even farther behind.

Meanwhile, "The automatic fire from the NVA had died down as they started walking mortars in on the Marines." The first round hit the Jeep, and it exploded, "taking their only radio with it." Another round struck next to the well, "wounding SSgt. Edwards again, this time in the head." He pulled out a piece of shrapnel stuck in his forehead and put it in his flak jacket.

By now, the Marines from the rest of the convoy were leaving their cover and advancing to help protect Rizzo and Edwards at the well site. Lance Cpl. Lee was dispatched in search of a radio at the nearby ARVN base at Hoi An and "was hit in his flak jacket by a round that knocked him face down in a rice paddy. Shaking that off, he again proceeded to carry out his orders."

After contacting the Delta Company headquarters, Lee started back for the well, thus again exposing himself to enemy fire, and coordinated a retreat from the well under covering fire provided by ARVN soldiers and their Australian advisers.

But as the Marines stood up to carry the wounded to a place of safety, one of them, a Lance Cpl. Moore, was shot in the shoulder, and Lee yet again exposed himself to enemy fire by carrying Captain Rizzo to safety.

Medevac helicopters called in from Da Nang had to hold off while four U.S. Army gunships arrived and raked over the NVA positions with deadly effect. One of the Army choppers was then able to swoop in and lift off Rizzo, Edwards, and the other wounded.

In all, says DuPont's account, seven Marines were wounded in the brief battle on Route 1, one of them the same Mike Cummings who later maintained the Ninth Engineers website until his death in early 2016. He had suffered a minor wound in the leg from a ricocheting bullet and was treated at the scene. Meanwhile, both Rizzo and Edwards later recovered from their wounds, DuPont writes.

HAZARDOUS DUTY PACIFYING

ARRIVING AT THE DA NANG AIR BASE COMPLEX IN SOUTH VIETNAM on May 1, 1969, second-generation Marine Rocky Jay flew in aboard a civilian airliner along with a Navy corpsman and two Marine "grunts" returning for a second tour of duty in the nasty war. As they knew, he was a first-timer.

"Well, Boot, where are you headed?" asked one of the trio.

"I said I had orders to III Marine Amphibious Force [III MAF] to a CAG unit.

"They all hollered, 'CAG unit!'"

Jay then asked if they knew about the Marine Corps–sponsored Community Action program that stationed small groups of Marines in Vietnamese villages as CAPs—Community Action Platoons, answering to a regional supervising CAG or Community Action Group—in what basically was a pacification effort.

To this, the corpsman said, "Yeah, we're always going out and picking up what's left of 'em."

Later, as they all flew on to Quang Tri, this time aboard a military C-130, Jay later wrote, "We couldn't land because the airstrip was catching rockets, so we flew farther north into Dong Ha."

He finally arrived at Fourth CAG headquarters at Quang Tri by truck. As night fell he could see artillery flashes and explosions in the mountains to the west, "but I was so tired I found a rack and went to sleep."

Welcome to Vietnam! And there would be more shocks ahead.

The next morning, six young Marines, Jay included, met the colonel in charge. "A corporal took pictures of us shaking the colonel's hand, and later we were saying how nice it was that the colonel had taken the time out of his busy schedule to have his picture taken with us."

That was not quite the case. "The corporal just laughed and told us they were for body identification if we got blown away."

The next day, reporting to his CAP village for the first time...age nineteen, and weighing a fit 185 pounds, Jay was surprised first to meet a fellow Marine "wearing a pair of cutoff shorts and a couple bandoliers of ammunition, carrying an M-16, with sandals on his feet!" Moreover, he couldn't have weighed more than 130 pounds.

"He said he was from Oklahoma and he was with the CAP. The other guys also weighed maybe 130 pounds. I thought to myself, I got to fight a war with these guys?" And true, they sure didn't look like any Marines he had ever seen before.

A week later, Jay was sent to CAP school in Da Nang, as he relates in the 1994 book *Our War Was Different*, a collection of oral histories gathered by fellow Marine and Vietnam veteran Al Hemingway. Here, Jay ran into old buddies from boot camp and other assignments that came before his deployment to Vietnam. "There must have been 200 of us there."

But already there had been casualties, especially in the First and Second CAG sectors.

"I think we had six killed that first week. It was reality."

As another reality for Jay, he would be the "new boy" among the nine Marines assigned to his particular CAP, which was located just south of the Cua Viet River and north of Quang Tri in one of the largest areas of operation (AOs) in the northern I Corps sector. "The southern border of the AO was a dirt path and the northern boundary was the Cua Viet River."

As a "boot" with no previous combat experience in the war, Jay was viewed with some apprehension by his new teammates. "I hadn't proven myself yet," Jay later explained. "The old salts all thought CAG was going to hell. Here I was a boot straight from staging [from stateside], put right into a CAG unit. All the other guys had at least six months in country before being assigned to a CAG. We're gonna get killed keeping this boot alive, they said. But I gained their confidence. Hell, I was the second oldest one there."

As the new man on the team, Jay had to carry the radio, "because it was added weight and you were a prime target for the enemy."

Once he settled into the routine of the Marine team and the villagers who worked with them as PFs (Popular Force personnel), there were predictable ups and downs.

"On three or four occasions we had language problems with the PFs. The translation would be lost and somebody would get insulted, and before you knew it there'd be eight Marines on one side and twenty-five or thirty PFs on the other locked and loaded. I'd be in the middle trying to raise the actual [commanding officer] on the radio to ask what the hell to do."

For that matter, what were the CAPs themselves supposed to be doing in general? As explained by book editor Al Hemingway, the Marines in Vietnam went beyond their traditional combat role to become "innovators, paradoxically, in another field—pacification."

While the U.S. Army pursued its well-known Vietnam strategy of search and destroy, the Marines "began to develop plans to provide security for the villages and hamlets and to permanently oust communist guerrillas operating in their areas." Thus, the Marine CAPs "lived, ate, worked, and fought alongside their Vietnamese counterparts, the Popular and Regional Forces (PFs and RFs)." The goal was to establish a real bond between the Vietnamese and the Americans.

This was no Peace Corps mission for the Marines assigned to villages scattered about the countryside. Yes, they were there to make friends, but also to fight, to go out on night and day patrols, to root out any Viet Cong infiltrators among their PFs, even to go up against North Vietnamese Army troops coming through their respective areas.

In time, of course, Jay became a seasoned CAP veteran. In fact, in just three months he was second in seniority. "Everyone else had either been hit or rotated," he noted.

But things were going well for the moment. "We set up ambushes, usually made up of two or three Marines and six PFs. We had total control over our villages. We tried to stop any infiltration and had specific rules set up with the village chief. We told him explicitly that if anyone stepped out at night they were game. We ruled the roost in the hours of darkness."

Nighttime control was crucial because that was usually the time that "Charlie" (the Viet Cong) liked to operate, "and we were trying to take it away from him."

Jay and his fellow Marines didn't tell anyone exactly where their ambushes were to be set up. They used code names, such as "Grand

Central Junction" for a crossroads near the river. "Even our PFs didn't know what these names meant, because there could have been a Viet Cong agent among them. Who knew?"

Meanwhile, "Our combat was night after night," Jay wrote in his first-person chapter in *Our War Was Different*. "You just did it until you were killed, wounded, or rotated." Meanwhile, after two months in the field, Jay needed a break and went back to Quang Tri to get medication for his feet. "My clothes were rotting off and I weighed 139 pounds. I guess I was a true CAG Marine."

Naturally, he was soon back at his village post, where he learned the Viet Cong "had put a price on our heads." The villagers themselves "were so tired of the war they really didn't care who controlled things." They just wanted people to leave them alone. "Some of them shared their hootches, their food, their laughter, and their tears with us."

A key to safety was staying friendly with their children, Jay soon figured out. "As long as kids were around I felt comfortable, but if no kids or PFs showed up, I knew I was in for a long uneasy night."

After five months with the CAG/CAP duty assignment, Jay's career in the field abruptly ended. It was October 5, 1969. "You might say five is my unlucky number. I was wounded five months after landing in Vietnam, five days after getting promoted to lance corporal, five days after being assigned to another CAP unit, at five o'clock in the morning. I was hit five times, they got five out of seven of us, and I spent five months in the hospital. It took me a year to learn how to walk again."

By chance, it might have been Hemingway himself who on October 5 called in the Medevac helicopter that picked Jay up after his wounding at Dong Ha. "We figured out that it could have been me who radioed in his Medevac chopper," wrote Hemingway, while saying Jay's sense of humor got him "through some rough spots" in his Vietnam service.

In any case, once he was resettled back in the States, Jay wrote to get his records. "They told me they never heard of CAP."

He went on to say, "At our first reunion, some colonel spoke, saying that two-thirds of the people in the CAP wouldn't qualify to enter the Marine Corps today. Some of those boys didn't have high school diplomas. But we were good. We were damn good."

———

ADDITIONAL NOTE: ROCKY JAY, CO-OWNER OF A MEDICAL SUPPLY company in Abilene, Texas later in life, also said he once read "that out of the 5,000 Marines in CAG, we took 30 percent fatalities, had an 80 to 85 percent chance of getting wounded once, and a 50 percent chance of getting wounded twice." Despite such discouraging statistics, "many Marines extended their tours in CAP."

SELECT PERSONALITY
CAPTAIN BILL DABNEY

"It took a hell of a man even to ask for the hand of Virginia Puller, the daughter of General Lewis B. 'Chesty' Puller," once recalled a friend of Canadian-born William H. Dabney, "and a hell of a man to meet with his approval. Bill was that man."

And true, if anyone ever had entertained any doubts about Captain Bill Dabney's Marine Corps credentials, he certainly disproved any such doubts day after day on an obscure hill in South Vietnam overlooking the besieged Khe Sanh Combat Base.

For seventy-seven days (and nights), if a Medevac chopper landed…boom! Minutes—no, even seconds later, a mortar round landed. Stick your head out of a trench line…bang! You could be dead.

Indeed, on this hill overlooking besieged Khe Sanh in northern South Vietnam, the casualty rate was nearly 100 percent. And Capt. Bill Dabney was there the whole time, rallying his men, meeting every Medevac chopper, and warning the troops on the combat base itself of incoming rounds.

"He has had a round land close to him every day for the past three weeks," wrote his 105-millimeter howitzer officer Lieutenant Carlton Crenshaw at one point during the siege of Khe Sanh and its nearby top-of-the hills observation posts. Theirs was Hill 881S, and just to the north was a twin, 881N. Both came under constant fire from the invading North Vietnamese.

There was to be no relief ever coming by land and, when the weather closed in, as it often did, no help from the outside world even by air—no reinforcements, no supplies, no Medevacs.

"He is thirty-two years old and looks like he has aged five years up here on Hill 881," continued Crenshaw. At six foot four, Dabney offered the North Vietnamese Army (NVA) snipers an easy target, but "He also leads a magic life in terms of not being hit."

That fact really was remarkable, considering the casualty rates of Dabney's India and Mike Companies, Third Battalion, Twenty-Sixth Marines, atop Hill 881S. "He personally supervises every medical evacuation we have. He is there helping to direct the helos in. He gets stretcher-bearers moving the minute the wheels touch ground. When we get replacements or the return of our stretcher-bearers, he directs them immediately to a nearby trench because it is only a matter of seconds before a mortar round will land."

Keep in mind that during the seventy-seven days of siege, seven helicopters were shot down at Hill 881S. Forty-two men, all Marines or medical corpsmen, died there, and nearly two hundred were wounded, excluding aviation casualties.

As Dabney himself later said, his Marines "knew that if wounded, they would be evacuated to a medical facility only when and if the weather broke and the helicopters could fly—that there was little their corpsmen could provide save comfort and some morphine to ease their pain."

Not that Dabney and his men were helpless sitting ducks— it's true they were a target of the NVA massed all around—they also served as vital observers and defenders of the nearby, much larger Khe Sanh Combat Base.

From their vantage point, Dabney and his Marines could call down, or even themselves inflict, lethal showers of fire upon any of the enemy who appeared on the terrain below, whether by aircraft strikes, artillery, mortar rounds, or even small arms.

Ironically, the man who found himself in charge of Hill 881S in early 1967 was neither American-born nor a Marine officer from the start of his military career.

Born in New Brunswick, Canada, in 1934 to Hugh and Mary Dabney (she was from Virginia), he soon was living in the United States, where in 1953–1954 he briefly attended Yale University. He left the school and enlisted in the Marine Corps, notes Marine Corps historian Beth Crumley in a post for the Marine Corps Association.

"Upon graduation from recruit training, Dabney reported to the Third Marine Division on Okinawa…and was promptly put on mess duty for seventy-one consecutive days. Next assigned to a communication station, that was all he needed to make up his mind—he decided the Marine Corps would be his life, not as an enlisted man, but as an officer."

He was so impressed, he told Crumley, "by the dedication and competence of the officers I'd seen, and I thought, 'This would be a great way to spend a career.'"

Still, there were the usual hoops to jump through. He remained an enlisted Marine until 1957, when he was discharged as a sergeant. Then it was on to Virginia Military Institute (VMI) to earn his commission and college degree. In the interim he served in the Reserve's Hundredth Rifle Company.

It was at VMI that he met and married Virginia McClandish Puller. "Her father was also a VMI graduate and a Marine…perhaps the most famous Marine of all," notes Crumley.

By the time he was deployed to Vietnam in 1967 to serve as commander of India Company, Third Battalion, Twenty-Sixth Marines, Third Division, "the war was heating up in Northern I Corps." The Navy Seabees were extending and improving the air strip at Khe Sanh, located almost smack dab astride Route 9 leading into nearby Laos and even North Vietnam. NVA pressure on the combat base came and went all year, until really heavy fighting broke out around the base in early 1968 and the famous siege of Khe Sanh began.

Surprising to some, this situation was exactly what the high-level U.S. strategists wanted—to use the remote Khe Sanh base as sucker bait to draw the North Vietnamese invaders into an underpopulated killing zone, rather than have to fight them farther south in more complicated, more densely populated, sometimes even urbanized areas.

The strategy did draw in the North Vietnamese, but some of the fighting men assigned to carry out the plan resented being "used" as bait at the risk of their lives.

In any case, India and Mike 3/26, both of them rifle companies, were given the mission of occupying and defending Hill 881S. "Dabney's Marines made an overland march from Khe Sanh to the hill. From 27 December through 17 January, India Company patrolled the area aggressively, sometimes to the limit of the range of [their] attached 81-millimeter mortars (about 4,000 meters)."

But then, on January 18, a handful of Marines ran into an ambush by a platoon-size unit of the NVA, which turned out to be part of a full company, which in turn was part of the point battalion for two entire NVA divisions flooding into the area. Thus, the seventy-seven day siege was on for the Americans aboard four hilltop observation sites, as well as at the Khe Sanh Combat Base itself.

"The area erupted into firefights, artillery duels and close-in aerial bombing brought on by a Marine regiment [the Twenty-Sixth Marines] under siege," adds an account by R. R. Keene in *Leatherneck* Magazine in 2005. Dabney began his weeks atop Hill 881S with about 400 Marines and corpsmen, but as casualties ate into his troop complement, that total sometimes fell to as low as 250 men, *Leatherneck* also says. In addition to India and Mike companies, he also had with him two 81-millimeter mortars, two 106-millimeter recoilless rifles, and three 105-millimeter howitzers from the Thirteenth Marines (and their respective gunners).

With enemy rounds arriving on 881S right on the heels, so to speak, of the choppers coming and going, the Marine air and ground commanders devised a responsive tactic they called "Super Gaggle," Dabney himself once explained. "In the first four weeks of battle, six birds [choppers] were downed on Hall 881S alone, with a bunch of WIA (wounded in action) aircrews...We lost 100-plus KIA (killed in action) or WIA getting them in and out. In the seven weeks after Super Gaggle started, zero birds were downed...and we had perhaps twenty WIA and zero KIA during resupply. Wow!"

To set up Super Gaggle, the Marines registered all their mortars on known or even suspected anti-aircraft fire sites. Then, about ten minutes before expected chopper re-supply landings, his men would fire all mortars with white phosphorus rounds on the NVA anti-aircraft sites. Skyhawk A-4 attack jets would attack the marked sites with Zuni rocket rounds, and other aircraft would throw in cluster bomb units (CBUs), even 250-pound bombs and napalm on the sides of the hill. The last were intended "to discourage NVA who would lie on their backs and fire up into the bellies of birds with their AK47s," added Dabney.

The "gaggle" of scorching fire gave Marines on 881S about two minutes in which helicopters could "land, deliver, pick up [and] get out," he said. The tactic probably saved 150 to 200 more casualties and perhaps another half dozen helicopters.

Most of the time, the Marines on 881S were well dug in, even out of sight—*the deeper the better* was the constant watchword. But several Marines appeared twice a day, proud and bold, in full view—to raise and lower the American flag.

Except for their frequent air support, the men manning the hilltop outposts were chicks totally cut off from mother hen, that sprawling combat base just four miles away. But they were doing mother hen a great favor not only by calling in air strikes and shooting up the enemy themselves, but also by acting as an early warning system.

"From the hill, Marines could observe the NVA gunners shoot off their rockets, usually in sheaves of fifty firing simultaneously from several sites toward Khe Sanh," writes Keene. "This permitted Dabney's Marines to give the main base about a ten-second warning to sound the alarm and for the Marines there to take cover."

In the meantime, especially at night, Dabney and his men used their mortars and 106-millimeter recoilless rifles to fire on the NVA firing platforms they had noted during the day, often with satisfying secondary explosions resulting. The warriors of 881S were even known to pack large shell casings with their own excrement, add a carefully primed grenade before sealing the top, and then send the entire assemblage bouncing down their hillside into the laps of the NVA at the bottom of the steep hill.

They often heard the distant explosion when one of the casings hit something solid.

The long siege of Khe Sanh and its adjoining hills finally came to an end after seventy-seven days, with the NVA pulling back and seeking victories elsewhere. "The North Vietnamese, pummeled by artillery and air power, abandoned their siege." Keene writes in *Leatherneck*. "Khe Sanh had earned its place in American history."

So, of course, had Capt. Bill Dabney and the men with him, whom he called "awesome," and indeed so had many others who fought the Siege of Khe Sanh.

At a ceremony at VMI in April 2005, Dabney was belatedly awarded the Navy Cross for his leadership and bravery on Hill 881S. Typically modest about his role in the courageous, weeks-long stand, he indicated the handful of 881S survivors attending the ceremony and said: "I wear this decoration only symbolically as their commanding officer. It is these men who earned it."

———

ADDITIONAL NOTE: WHAT MORE NEEDS SAYING THAN THIS Presidential Unit Citation issued by Lyndon B. Johnson?

> For extraordinary heroism in action against North Vietnamese Army forces during the battle for Khe Sanh in the Republic of Vietnam from 20 January to 1 April 1968. Throughout this period, the Twenty-Sixth Marines (Reinforced) was assigned the mission of holding the vital Khe Sanh Combat Base and positions on Hills 881, 861-A, 558, and 950, which dominated strategic enemy approach routes into Northern 1 Corps. The Twenty-Sixth Marines was opposed by numerically superior forces—two North Vietnamese Army divisions, strongly reinforced with artillery, tank, anti-aircraft

artillery and rocket units. The enemy, deployed
to take advantage of short lines of communications, rugged mountainous terrain, jungle, and
adverse weather conditions, was determined
to destroy the Khe Sanh Combat Base in conjunction with large-scale offensive operations in
the two northern provinces of the Republic of
Vietnam. The Twenty-Sixth Marines, occupying a small but critical area, was daily subjected
to hundreds of rounds of intensive artillery,
mortar and rocket fire. In addition, fierce
ground attacks were conducted by the enemy
in an effort to penetrate the friendly positions.
Despite overwhelming odds, the Twenty-Sixth
Marines remained resolute and determined,
maintaining the integrity of its positions and
inflicting heavy losses on the enemy. When
monsoon weather greatly reduced air support
and compounded the problems of aerial resupply, the men of the Twenty-Sixth Marines stood
defiantly firm, sustained by their own professional esprit and high sense of duty. Through
their indomitable will, staunch endurance, and
resolute courage, the Twenty-Sixth Marines and
supporting units held the Khe Sanh Combat
Base. The actions of the Twenty-Sixth Marines
contributed substantially to the failure of
the Viet Cong and North Vietnamese Army
winter/spring offensive. The enemy forces were
denied the military and psychological victory
they so desperately sought. By their gallant fighting spirit and their countless individual acts of
heroism, the men of the Twenty-Sixth Marines

(Reinforced) established a record of illustrious courage and determination in keeping with the highest traditions of the Marine Corps and the United States Naval Service.

POW IN BLINK OF AN EYE

"ONCE CAPTURED, THERE IS NO COMPREHENDING WHAT GOES through your head," commented fifty-nine-year-old Walter W. Eckes at a 2005 ceremony at Camp Pendleton, California, honoring American prisoners of war and those missing in action. He knew, because decades beforehand, then a Marine lance corporal from New York City and a radio operator in Vietnam, he had been on a long hike back to his unit when three men in South Vietnamese Army (ARVN) uniforms came along on the road he had been following before sitting down to take a break.

As he greeted the men, two of them pointed their weapons at him.

Just a joke, he thought. Coming to his feet, he pushed one of the guns aside.

After all, they were allies. Weren't they?

Wrong. Not these three.

ARVN uniforms or not, they were Viet Cong—"Charlie"—in disguise. In seconds they had disarmed him, wrestled him to the ground, and tied him up, putting one rope around his neck and tying his arms elbow to elbow behind his back.

In the blink of an eye, he was a POW.

His capture was in May of 1966. A member of an artillery battery in the Third Marine Division's Twelfth Marines at the time, he had volunteered for a four-man forward observer team serving with the division's Ninth Marines, according to an account compiled by the online POWNetwork.com. Operating out of a hamlet twenty-five miles south-southwest of the big Da Nang military complex, his team routinely sent a man back to headquarters every two weeks or so to pick up their pay and incidental supplies. On May 9, that man was twenty-three-year-old Eckes.

After spending the night at headquarters, he set out the next morning on his return. For part of the way he cadged a ride on a truck, but it wasn't going to the same campsite. Dropped off at a juncture with a short, often booby-trapped road to his team's location, he decided to wait for a possible ride with some other vehicle headed for the same destination.

Thus, he was sitting on the side of the road "propped against a tree," when the three Vietnamese entered his life and changed it forever. They dragged him off by the neck rope, then turned him over to another group the next day. The second group of Viet Cong took him to a POW camp, parading him through villages on the way.

There he was happy to meet up with a fellow Marine, Sgt. James Dodson, of York, Pennsylvania, who had been captured three days before Eckes. "Dodson had been working with an engineers' group clearing roads when he went behind a hut and was knocked unconscious and captured," it seems.

Dodson also was a focus for enemy interrogators because he was black. As reported by *Scripps-Howard*'s Pulitzer-winning staff writer Jim Lucas later in 1966, the Viet Cong "segregated" Dodson from his white companion "in a mountain prison camp to preach…about the evils of segregation."

Why fight the white man's battles for him? they asked the twenty-one-year-old Dodson.

"When Sgt. Dodson remained silent, they asked: 'Do you like the way your people are being treated at home?'"

According to Dodson, he told them, "I approve to a certain extent. Some things aren't right, but many things are."

Eckes also went through the Viet Cong's attempts at indoctrination. "They told me [President Lyndon B.] Johnson and [Defense Secretary Robert] McNamara were imperialists and kept repeating that over and over," he related. "They said the president and McNamara weren't concerned with the little people fighting their war, but only in making money."

Their captors told the two Marines that they were "imperialist Yankee dogs." Dodson later said, "It seemed like the guy was angry when he said it, but then he grinned."

The Viet Cong "believe they're winning this war, and why shouldn't they? They made us listen to Radio Hanoi every day. They hear the same thing. If they're shooting down [an alleged] 200 Yankee planes a day— and Radio Hanoi tells them they are—they're not going to think anything else but in terms of winning."

Meanwhile, as May of 1966 faded into June, Eckes and Dodson were kept on the move. Outfitted with black pajamas, they were started northward, only to return to their first POW encampment after three days because of American military activity ahead. Two weeks later, they and their guards set off again, and after three or four days the two Marines were in bad physical shape. "Eckes lost his toenails due to a combination of the effects of poor health and exposure, having been required to wear 'Ho Chi Minh' sandals," according to POW Network. "The left side of his face was badly infected from insect bites, and his weight had dropped to 98 pounds."

At a stop one night, feeling he had endured all he could, Eckes talked to Dodson about trying to escape. He agreed they must make a break if they were to survive.

That very evening, as they shared a small meal of rice with three of their guards some distance from the rest of the Viet Cong party, their wardens carelessly left their weapons leaning against a tree about twenty feet away.

"I kept looking over there toward the carbines, trying to figure the distance, how quick I could jump over there," Dodson said later. "For a while I almost backed out of it."

Luckily, he didn't. Instead, he jumped up, raced to the tree, grabbed a carbine and whirled around to confront their three guards. "When I turned they were on their feet, but they still had had their rice dishes in their hands," he said. "I was scared, kind of shaking. They looked at me. I looked at them. Then they ran."

So did Eckes and Dodson run too, after grabbing a second carbine. Plunging into the surrounding jungle, they also kept a canteen and a few pieces of hard candy purloined from a Viet Cong pack. Thus "equipped," they were on the run for four days.

"The Viet Cong must have sent a search party out," said Dodson. "We could hear them all around. We stayed as quiet as we could. We'd decided earlier, though, we'd fight it out with them before they could capture us again. But I was so scared I thought they'd hear my heart beating."

Eckes said at least three Viet Cong walked within three feet of where he and Dodson were lying one time but didn't notice them. He also reported that they were chased in one village by residents wielding shovels, while in another the villagers gave them rice to eat.

Years later, Eckes told the Orange County (California) *Register* they slogged through quicksand and had to avoid attacks by water buffalo and wild boars. Finally, they came across a friendly outpost about twenty-five miles southwest of Da Nang and were reunited with their fellow Marines a short time later. Safe at last!

"If there is something that I took from my experience it is that whatever you take on, don't quit," Eckes also commented at the national POW/MIA commemoration he attended at Camp Pendleton in 2005.

———

ADDITIONAL NOTE: ECKES AND THE LATE DODSON WERE AMONG THE mere thirty-three Americans who successfully escaped from captivity in South Vietnam during the long Vietnam War, most of them during their first month as POWs, according to an online report by John N. Powers, author of the book *Bean Camp to Briar Patch: Life in the POW Camps of Korea and Vietnam*. He also reported no American POW ever escaped from custody in North Vietnam.

LAST MAN OUT

It wasn't the infantry, the artillery, or the aviation arm of the Marine Corps that ended the war in Vietnam, but rather the often unheralded embassy guards.

Four of them, in fact, were killed on the very day the last American fighting men and diplomats left Saigon, 'coptered away from the embassy rooftop that was defended to the last by the Marine Security Guards (MSG) Battalion.

Of that group, Master Gunnery Sergeant John J. Valdez, staff NCO in charge, was "the last Marine out," according to the dramatic story he related in *Leatherneck* magazine later the same year (September 1975).

As he reported, it had been obvious for the previous two weeks in April of 1975 "that the big exodus was on and the Viet Cong and North Vietnamese Army would settle for nothing short of uncondi-tional surrender." To defend the big six-story American embassy in Saigon, he had a complement of forty-five men, including five or six recently returned from duty at the now-closed American consulate in nearby Bien Hoa.

With the end of the war imminent and tensions mounting, he had to post his security guards at all four entrances and exits servicing the embassy grounds on Thong Nhut Boulevard. "Crowds gathered outside daily and Saigon police would begin breaking them up by midday," he wrote. "A mood of panic and a sense of fear of being left behind began to develop during the last week."

Meanwhile, embassy personnel in the processing section "suddenly realized that there had been a serous miscalculation of [the anticipated] American figures, which up to this time had been based on 7,000 Americans to be evacuated. It now seemed virtually impossible to esti-mate how many Americans were living in Saigon and nearby Bien Hoa."

Despite the guards at the entrances, many Vietnamese lacking proper documents for evacuation slipped into the embassy grounds.

A processing center was set up at the Tan Son Nhut Airport six miles out of town to ease the pressure on the embassy staff. "A simple affidavit form, which until then had taken weeks to obtain, was now fixed on the spot."

These developments came after Americans planning to leave South Vietnam discovered they couldn't easily obtain exit visas for their wives and children, "unless they were willing to pay bribes to Vietnamese officials, often running as high as $1,500." Furthermore, a Vietnamese marriage certificate—once available for just twenty dollars—now could cost two thousand dollars.

Clearly, it was a desperate moment. "We were concerned with evacuating Vietnamese who had worked for [the U.S. agencies] AID, USIS, and the embassy and who might be on the Communist enemies list." The consulate gate on the embassy grounds "became a nightmare, with desperate crowds looking for ways to escape, and local and military authorities trying to break up the lines."

Off the South Vietnamese coast, ships of the U.S. Seventh Fleet were preparing for the flood tide of refugees about to come—even in Washington, at the Pentagon and the White House, American officialdom knew the hour of defeat was but moments away. Saigon would fall to the surging Communist forces any day.

In Saigon itself, wrote Valdez, "American planes continuously evacuated Americans and Vietnamese from Tan Son Nhut," with no real interference from the North Vietnamese Army or Viet Cong "until the last two days prior to final evacuation." In fact, it was the South Vietnamese soldiers who "interfered with the evacuation buses that were either transporting evacuees or winding through the streets, picking up Americans at designated assembly points."

Meanwhile, Marines normally billeted at the Marine House in Saigon (in later years to become the Saigon Hotel) were being housed in the embassy itself or its "recreation" area that consisted of a swimming pool and snack bar, among other amenities. "Only a skeleton crew was left at the Marine House to prevent looting."

By now the guards at the embassy's four fates found it more and more difficult to keep them secure as the crowds increased or threatened to become "uncontrollable." Still, the civilians never appeared dangerous, just desperate as they begged to leave their country "or [to] get their children off to safety."

The real chaos set in on April 29, 1975, when the Communist forces shelled the airport, rendering the runways unusable for sizable fixed-wing aircraft. That's when the U.S. authorities realized they must fall back upon a risky helicopter airlift—the largest in world history, as events turned out. The same truth dawned upon the South Vietnamese, who proceeded to carry out both authorized and more than a few unauthorized "lone-wolf" pick-ups in their own choppers.

Before day's end on April 30, eighty to a hundred choppers belonging to the Marines, the U.S. Air Force, the South Vietnamese military, and the CIA's Air America fleet took part in Operation Frequent Wind. The operation rescued nearly ten thousand Americans and Vietnamese who otherwise would have been left to the mercies of the incoming Communist regime.

It's often forgotten that U.S. combat forces had already left Vietnam two years before, based on a ceasefire agreement with the North Vietnamese. South Vietnam had been left to its own devices, which obviously weren't enough. Still, a host of Americans remained: hundreds of civilians; the diplomatic mission headed by Ambassador Graham Martin; and the faithful Marine embassy guards, technically Company C, Marine Security Guard (MSG) Battalion.

The Communist shelling of Tan Son Nhut Air Base the morning of April 29, was the last act in the drama for all of them, noted *Newsweek* magazine online in 2015 on the fortieth anniversary of the embassy evacuation. The damage at Tan Son Nhut meant "the military situation had deteriorated too far to use Options One, Two, or Three, which were all based on transport planes flying out of Tan Son Nhut." That left only an Option Four, "the much riskier helicopter evacuation." Risky or not, it later would be "called the largest helicopter evacuation on record."

Newsweek correspondent Loren Jenkins, himself expecting evacuation, was on the embassy grounds that last day of April 30. Behind the fifteen-foot concrete wall, "an assortment of CIA agents, State Department volunteers, and security guards roamed the embassy grounds armed with an amazing variety of weapons," he noted. "Some carried grenade launchers, several toted antiquated submachine guns, and a few even had bone-handled hunting knives stuck in their belts. Marines barked orders into walkie-talkies."

Some of the Marines he saw were busy taking down "the giant tamarind tree in the rear parking lot to clear a landing zone for Jolly Green Giant helicopters."

Meanwhile, behind the parking lot in the swimming pool area, "several thousand Vietnamese waited with piles of suitcases and bundles of clothing." In the crowds he saw "at least three generals in uniform, assorted South Vietnamese senators, a former mayor of Saigon, the police chief, a fire chief and all of his firemen wearing their back-flap hats, and Vietnamese employees of the embassy and their families."

At one point on this chaotic day, Ambassador Graham Martin went out a back gate, unnoticed, and walked to his home three blocks away "to pack his bag and pick up his black poodle, Nitnoy." He, of course, had security guards with him.

As the evacuation wore into late afternoon, "two choppers brought in another fifty Marines to beef up the embassy defense perimeter."

The tension was building by now. "At the back gate, Marines were forced to use their rifle butts to knock back Vietnamese trying to scale the fence." Just after dark, a darting motorbike rider threw a grenade into the crowd at the front of the embassy. "There were many wounded, but nobody dared venture out to help them. In the darkened embassy lobby, Marines checked their pistols and unsheathed bayonets."

By mid-evening, the embassy was "almost deserted" of U.S. civilians. "Open doors revealed offices stripped of everything important."

Meanwhile, the time had come for Jenkins to report topside for his own evacuation. He mounted the back stairs to the sixth floor to await his chopper ride. "Finally, we heard the order, 'OK, let's go.' Just before I rushed aboard, I looked down toward the pool area. A couple of thousand Vietnamese were still waiting for their turn. Soon we were high over the Saigon River."

Out of the chopper's rear bay, he saw the night lights of the doomed city, receding fast.

Back at the embassy somewhat later that night, the last Marines slated for pickup from the same rooftop were busy locking chain-link gates to every other floor of the building, to slow up the Vietnamese crowds still desperate to leave. If the crowds reached the roof, the last Marines and their chopper rescuers would be overwhelmed.

"The men barricaded the rooftop door using heavy fire extinguishers and wall lockers and waited nervously as Vietnamese outside rammed a fire truck through an embassy entrance," notes Associated Press writer Margie Mason in a fortieth anniversary story on May 8, 2015, datelined Ho Chi Minh City instead of Saigon. It was about 5:00 a.m., but still dark, when Ambassador Martin and his party were lifted off the embassy roof. Then, not much else…

"As the sun came up, the remaining Marines realized they had been forgotten." Their radio signals wouldn't carry as far as the Seventh Fleet ships standing by offshore. "The last U.S. servicemen in Vietnam were stuck alone atop the embassy, hoping someone would realize they were there before the city fell to rapidly advancing Communist forces."

Several former Marines from that last day returned to Ho Chi Minh City forty years after the event. They stood at the former embassy—now the U.S. consulate—for the unveiling of a plaque dedicated to Marine Cpl. Charles McMahon and Marine Lance Cpl. Darwin Judge. Both had been killed in the final rocket attack on Tan Son Nhut on April 29, 1975, and were the last two of fifty-eight-thousand-plus Americans killed in the Vietnam War.

One of the visitors returning to the embassy in 2015, Sgt. Kevin Maloney of Hollywood, Florida, recalled the hours he spent that final day "going over the wall to help pull Americans and allies from other countries out of the mob and into the compound so they could be air-lifted." While hoisting them up, he also was beating back the Vietnamese. There just wouldn't be room for all.

Not long before, he had been driving a rescue bus through the city picking up lucky Americans designated for evacuation. Seeing a boy with light brown hair, "he shoved the kid and his mother into one of the front seats anyway, knowing that the child was most likely the son of a GI."

He often wondered if they made it out of the city and on to America.

Soon, though, it would be his own turn, and that of his fellow Marines.

"Once the Marines got word that they were to abandon their posts and prepare to evacuate, they moved up to the roof where they could see parts of the city burning," writes Mason. "Many had not slept in two or three days and were running only on adrenaline."

One Marine stood guard next to a small window "where Vietnamese who had forced their way inside and through all the locked gates to the stairwell were pressed."

An hour passed, and then two. Still, no choppers in sight.

"They literally forgot about us," said the MSG detachment's Master Sergeant Valdez in 2015, by then seventy-seven and living in Oceanside, California. On that April night decades before he admittedly was wondering what would happen next. For one thing, the parties who had shelled the nearby airport might also fire on the embassy rooftop, which offered no cover for the eighty or so men awaiting evacuation.

Finally, they heard the chop-chop of an approaching helicopter, then another…and another.

They hadn't been forgotten after all.

"They stripped off their flak jackets, helmets, and packs to save weight, and stuffed as many people as possible into the final birds that landed," wrote Mason.

With a final glance to make sure all his men were gone, "Valdez became the last man to board the last helicopter."

MIA FOR A TIME

Marine Captain Donald Gilbert Cook was so dedicated to training his fellow Marines on how to withstand captivity and interrogation by the enemy that he wrote a pamphlet about the experiences of Americans held prisoner during the Korean War. He studied Communist interrogation techniques. Not only that, he copied them in "interrogating" phony Marine "captives." Going even further to simulate grim reality, he wore a homemade Communist uniform for the training task, and had his wife Laurette draw lines on his face with her eyeliner to make him appear Asian. They say he "was an imposing spectacle to the 'captured' Marines," notes an online biography appearing on the website of the Navy's Arleigh Burke Class destroyer USS *Donald G. Cook.*

But the day came when he himself was captured and became a prisoner of the Viet Cong for three years.

The practice sessions were held in Hawaii before he was shipped out. The real thing, his own prisoner status, came in the field in Vietnam from December of 1964 to December of 1967.

All during that time, Marine Captain Donald Gilbert Cook, while himself suffering from malaria and malnutrition, encouraged, supported, and often inspired his fellow POWs by his sacrifices, even giving them his own paltry food surplus and hard-to-get medicine.

He was also classified as MIA all that time. Only later was it determined, based on his captors' reports, that he died in December of 1967. Still later, he was posthumously awarded the Medal of Honor as the first Marine in history to earn the Medal while held as a prisoner of war.

As fate would have it, he had been in Vietnam—as a volunteer—for less than three weeks when he was shot in the thigh in the Battle of Bien Gia, forty miles southeast of Saigon, on New Year's Eve of 1964. He passed out from loss of blood and woke up to find he was a prisoner of the Viet Cong, as the first Marine POW of the Vietnam War.

"The Viet Cong held Cook in a number of primitive jungle POW camps," writes biographer Marine Col. Donald L. Price (*The First Marine Captured in Vietnam: A Biography of Donald G. Cook*).

"For nearly three years, he led ten fellow POWs in captivity, always looking out for their health and welfare while complying with the spirit and intent of the U.S. Military Code of Conduct. From the outset of his captivity, Capt. Cook did not waver in accepting his leadership responsibilities. Within days, he served notice to his captors that he was the senior POW and, therefore, the legal spokesman for all the Americans held with him."

From the beginning, also, he was totally uncooperative with their captors. He was so tight-lipped about himself and his military background, they never found out he was a Marine, his fellow prisoners said later. The Viet Cong never realized he had developed some understanding of their language, either. "Cook's fellow POWs said their Marine leader seemed to have an uncanny ability to read their captors' minds and always was one step ahead of them, much to the enemy's aggravation."

He was absolutely zealous in taking care of his men, often to the point of self-sacrifice. "While hiking on rugged jungle trails from one prison camp to another, Cook sometimes carried the packs of weaker prisoners." He frequently shared his rations with ill or weaker POWs. He twice stared down would-be executioners threatening to shoot him on the spot. He at least once led a failed escape attempt.

Steeped in his Catholic faith, he told a threatening Viet Cong: "You can't kill me. Only God can decide when I will die." Another time he told a weakening fellow POW to keep walking, despite their mutual exhaustion. "You must carry on. If Apostle Paul walked to Rome, you and I can walk to Hanoi if necessary."

Meanwhile, after his capture, the Viet Cong had taken his group of prisoners northwest to camps in Viet Cong "territory" along the Cambodian border, but then moved back eastward when American B-52s began bombing the same sanctuary area. In the interim, among these forced marches, Cook contracted malaria. He also suffered from anemia and dysentery during the monsoon season, and while the captors and POWS hid out for a year or so in flooded low terrain.

All the while, adds biographer Price, "Cook and his men subsisted on a starvation diet of rice and fish. He demanded that the VC provide his men with medicine, vitamin supplements, and additional and better food. From time to time, Cook's demands paid off in the form of a pittance of vitamins and medicine, stale loaves of French bread, a few ducks, and a banana or two, but that was about it."

After Cook's three years of captivity under such conditions, he and his fellow POWs were being marched once more toward the Cambodian border and drier terrain when the heroic Marine finally weakened beyond bodily endurance. He died on or about December 8, the Viet Cong later reported.

To the end, "Rather than negotiate for his own release or better treatment," his Medal of Honor citation says, "he steadfastly frustrated attempts by the Viet Cong to break his indomitable spirit, and passed this same resolve on to the men whose well-being he so closely associated himself [with]. Knowing his refusals would prevent his release prior to the end of the war, and also knowing his chances for prolonged survival would be small in the event of continued refusal, he chose nevertheless to adhere to a Code of Conduct far above that which could be expected."

It would be years later, in April 1980, when Cook's two grown daughters finally went through the personal effects that had been shipped back to the family while he was still alive as a MIA/POW. They found a letter he had written to all four of his children and left behind in a briefcase when deployed to Vietnam. In it, he had said in part: "Do what is right and just, no matter what the personal cost."

Today, those very words of Col. Donald G. Cook (he was promoted in absentia) appear on a heavy—and shiny—brass plaque bolted just outside the destroyer USS *Cook*'s galley, where any sailor who wants his chow must pass by every day. "The plaque is shiny because the crew constantly rubs it for good luck when passing through the line to get their daily rations," writes biographer Price. "It is a firm tradition for every

Cook sailor to be familiar with Colonel Cook's story and be able to speak knowledgeably on a moment's notice about his courage."

VIETNAM POSTSCRIPT

HE WAS A PLATOON LEADER IN VIETNAM'S "BLOOD-SOAKED" (HIS description) An Hoa Basin sometimes also known as "Arizona Valley." He won the Navy Cross. He came back home with shrapnel still embedded in the back of his head and in a kidney.

Undeterred, he wrote bestselling books, he served as secretary of the Navy, and he became a U.S. Senator from Virginia. And for good measure, in 2015, he ran for the Democratic Party's nomination for president. This Marine was First Lieutenant James Webb.

Unsuccessful in the primaries that followed, low in the polls, he did make his own bit of presidential history by mentioning in a nationally televised Democratic primary debate that the enemy who had wounded him with a grenade wasn't "around right now to talk to."

He later pulled out of the Democratic race, but meanwhile many of the pundits and probably some of the onlooking American public were a bit shocked. Some of the media did zoom in.

Oh, horrors! In combat he killed one or more people? What do we think U. S. Grant, John F. Kennedy, Andrew Jackson—to say nothing of what Presidents Garfield, Hayes, Pierce, Eisenhower, Truman, George H. W. Bush, and Teddy Roosevelt—did in person or with the weaponry at their disposal during *their* times of war? For one, World War I artillery officer Truman dropped two atomic bombs on Japan to end World War II. His predecessor in office, Franklin D. Roosevelt, never himself a soldier but once an assistant secretary of the Navy, approved development of the same atomic weaponry.

What, in any case, was the situation that First Lieutenant James Webb faced in Vietnam one fateful day in 1969?

Engaged in a search and destroy mission on July 10 for Company D, First Battalion, Fifth Marines, his platoon came across a warren of "well-camouflaged" enemy bunkers "deep in hostile territory," according to his Navy Cross citation.

The bunkers appeared to be unoccupied, but of course, as those things often go, they were all three of them occupied after all.

Deploying his men in "defensive positions," Webb approached the first bunker. Suddenly, three Viet Cong insurgents armed with hand grenades jumped out—so close, he was able to take hold of one and then capture all three by brandishing his big .45-caliber pistol.

Their sudden appearance naturally meant there probably were more of the enemy lurking nearby. Accompanied by one of his men, Webb turned to the second bunker and "called for the enemy to surrender."

Silence…and then out came a grenade, "which detonated dangerously close to him."

He responded with a claymore mine at the bunker entrance, the explosion "accounting for two enemy casualties and disclosing the entrance to a tunnel."

Not yet satisfied with the results, Webb ignored the smoke and debris from the mine explosion, entered the tunnel, and "conducted a thorough search which yielded several items of equipment and numerous documents containing valuable intelligence data"—all this despite "the possibility of enemy soldiers hiding in the tunnel."

Still to be checked out was the third bunker in the Viet Cong complex. Webb approached "and was preparing to fire into it when the enemy threw another grenade."

This was the crucial moment when First Lieutenant Webb really earned his pay—and his Vietnam War wounds. The citation sums it up:

> Observing the grenade land dangerously close to his
> companion, First Lieutenant Webb simultaneously fired
> his weapon at the enemy, pushed the Marine [his com-
> panion] away from the grenade, and shielded him from

the explosion with his own body. Although sustaining painful fragmentation wounds from the explosion, he managed to throw a grenade into the aperture and completely destroy the remaining bunker.

In his memoir *I Heard My Country Calling*, Webb himself writes, "I was hit in the head, back, arm, and leg. The grenade's concussion lifted me in the air and threw me down a hill into the stream. I still carry shrapnel at the base of my skull and in one kidney from the blast." In addition, a quarter-sized fragment "scored the inside of my left knee and lodged against the bone of my lower leg..."

In an op-ed appearing in the *Washington Post* on October 15, 2015, Webb's son, Jim Webb, himself a former Marine infantryman, rushed to his father's defense by saying: "Yes, the man who threw the grenade isn't around anymore, but more importantly the man who my father shielded with his own body lived to see another day."

Accusing the American public of an "almost stunning level of ignorance...about war," the younger Webb also reflected on the "ridicule" aimed at his father in the wake of the "isn't around anymore" remark: "I can't help but imagine what these same people must think about the service of my own generation. In their eyes, did we simply spend some kind of twisted 'semester abroad' in a place [Iraq] with plenty of sand, but no ocean? Or conversely, do they ignorantly dismiss our experiences, as they have my father, as those of cold, callous killers?"

THE "MISTAKE" OF KHE SANH

HIS RANK AS A TOP MARINE GENERAL NOTWITHSTANDING, VICTOR Krulak was prepared to run the moment his chopper touched down on the flat ground of the Khe Sanh Combat Base during its days of intense siege early in 1968. "Jumping from a rolling helicopter and diving into a strip-side bunker while the aircraft got back in the air to avoid the inevitable 120-millimeter mortar reaction was standard procedure," he wrote later.

Also omnipresent were the mist, the dampness, the mud—"Khe Sanh's trademarks," he added in his book *First to Fight*. "The cluttered bunkers were redolent of the smell of dirty bodies. The men's faces were drawn, their eyes deeply shadowed, yet, incredibly enough, their sense of humor was as lively as ever."

He never forgot the hand-drawn sign by a two-man foxhole that said, "The rain in Laos falls mainly in the House," a take from the famous line in *My Fair Lady* about rain falling on the plains.

A plateau rising out of jungle and surrounded by several dominating hilltops, Khe Sanh knew about rain—eighty or so inches a year on average. It was so isolated it hardly "knew" anything else. In the 1930s, the area had been considered prime tiger-hunting territory.

But let Krulak describe it for himself: "Khe Sanh is in the far northwestern corner of South Vietnam, four miles from Laos, twelve miles south of the Demilitarized Zone [between North and South Vietnam] a way point on Route Coloniale No. 9, the winding road that joins the Vietnam coast with Savannakhet in Laos."

Hearing that Army Gen. Westmoreland, commander of all American operational forces in Vietnam, wanted to base a communications station of about thirty Marines near there in 1964, Krulak, then commander of all Pacific Fleet Marines, reacted. "When I studied the area on the map, it seemed a pretty remote place to hang a few Marine communicators out to dry," he wrote. "So I took an opportunity to inspect it."

What he found was "impressively wild," "ruggedly beautiful," and "definitely" remote.

"Precipitous, dark green mountains are covered with tangled liana, boulders, bushes, and thorn trees; a little coffee grows in the low ground, as does a lot of four-foot-high elephant grass and bamboo; there are a few villages."

All was located about forty miles inland from the coast...and in the middle, "rising out of the valley, is the flat Khe Sanh plateau, some three hundred feet above sea level, about a mile in length and a half mile wide."

All were subjected to "some of the most miserable weather in all of Vietnam."

All was only accessible on the ground by a "bad road" with twelve bridges, meaning the plateau was highly vulnerable to supply interruption on the ground, while the incessantly bad weather ruled out dependable air supply. Even so, the French had once built a 1,500-foot dirt airstrip on the plateau.

In addition to resupply considerations, it would be "a hard place to defend," because "hills, rising to altitudes of three thousand feet, look down on the airstrip just as top-row seats in a football stadium look down on the playing field."

It was here, despite the protests of Krulak and other Marine leaders, that Westmoreland and his advisers later decided there should be a major Marine combat base.

Krulak also wrote, "My responsibilities did not extend to the operational employment of the Marine forces in Vietnam—that was General Westmoreland's business. Even so, I never hesitated to give him my thoughts concerning his tactical use of Marines."

Because this time Krulak was *very* concerned about the proposed *major* use of his Marines at the remote Khe Sanh site, he arranged to meet with Westmoreland aboard the Army general's aircraft at Chu Lai airfield.

Krulak not only harbored doubts about the tactical goals behind deployment of his Marines, but he also questioned Westmoreland's overall strategy in conducting the war. "As he saw it, firepower was the classic answer—locate the enemy formations, fix them, then back off and beat them to death with air and artillery." This strategy was the same the French had used nearly two decades earlier at Dien Bien Phu against the Viet Minh insurgents—the Viet Cong's "older brother," so to speak. And the French had lost.

More immediately and on the tactical level, Krulak warned

Westmoreland at Chu Lai that "protracted occupation" of Khe Sanh would be "demanding," would require more than a single battalion of Marines, as originally proposed. He argued the airstrip could not be defended without occupying key hilltops around the plateau, requiring "at least" another battalion, plus "major" helicopter support.

Moreover, all such efforts would draw manpower and resources from the fight against the Communist insurgents in South Vietnam, where the pacification program carried out by Combined Action Platoons (teams based in villages) was having good effect. "I reminded General Westmoreland that every Marine tied to the Khe Sanh area would be one less involved in pacification of the critical coastal area where 95 percent of the people lived."

But the Army general defended his plan on grounds that it would be critical to monitoring enemy north-to-south movement, would be a block to enemy use of Route 9, could help intelligence-gathering in the area, would be an anchor for defense of the western end of the Demilitarized Zone, and could be a possible jumping-off place, "should his dream of an expedition into Laos to cut the Ho Chi Minh Trail ever be realized."

More pointedly, however, Westmoreland also defended his plan by saying "that he saw Khe Sanh as offering an excellent opportunity to tie down and destroy thousands of enemy soldiers."

In one word, his goal was attrition.

That is to say, build up the remote base as bait, lure the enemy close in—the enemy in this case would be the North Vietnamese regulars rather than the Viet Cong guerrillas—and destroy them with superior firepower.

Westmoreland's decision was firm. "Our discussion got nowhere. Although the Marine commanders involved were dead set against it, the Marines went to Khe Sanh."

Over the next year, as the buildup proceeded, it consumed "first one, then two, then three, and finally four battalions, reinforced with forty-one light and medium artillery pieces, direct fire weapons, and six tanks." Ultimately, six thousand men were committed to the Khe Sanh campaign, capped in the end by the seventy-seven-day siege of 1968 that captured worldwide headlines and became the "Chosin" of the Vietnam War for the Marines.

However, often forgotten is the preliminary effort it took to clear the surrounding hills of enemy occupiers from limestone caves, trenches, and bunkers dug into the hills for the three years beforehand. "The North Vietnamese units had to be thrown out. The result was the bitterest fighting of the entire Khe Sanh battle, perhaps the bitterest fighting of the entire war for the Marines."

As the Marine buildup progressed, the enemy was attracted, and in time Khe Sanh came under constant attack, and then under that close and costly siege.

"Day after trying day, the weather dominated the battle," noted Krulak. "It ruled out visual close air support, and it prevented helicopters from supplying the hill outposts or evacuating their casualties. Mortars and rockets churned up the main base and drove everyone underground, while the key hills were under continued close-quarters pressure. It was the hardest kind of fighting, valiantly and efficiently done."

But was the fighting well worth it in the end?

No, not in Krulak's view. The truth in the end, he said, was that, "with all the dirt and blood and fatigue and frustration and heroic sacrifice, it had done little to advance our cause toward victory."

He also pointed out that the North Vietnamese, with thousands of infiltrating soldiers at their disposal, never mounted a possibly overwhelming human-wave attack on the Marines at Khe Sanh. They never did poison or cut off the Khe Sanh water supply from a nearby river.

Meanwhile, the Khe Sanh campaign cost the enemy an estimated ten thousand casualties.

However, could it be that North Vietnamese General Vo Nguyen Giap, mastermind of the Viet Minh's battle against the Colonial French twenty years earlier, also had a form of attrition in mind in response to the Marine buildup at Khe Sanh? Didn't he once say, as noted by Krulak, "The primary emphasis [is] to draw American units into remote areas and thereby facilitate control of the population of the lowlands [along the coast]?"

Thus, Krulak's point: "In that sense, Khe Sanh cannot have meant more to Giap than a convenient mechanism for drawing the Americans away from the populated coastal area." Especially with his large-scale Tet offensive about to take place, it so happens.

More explicitly: "Giap, deciding that he had us firmly committed to the Khe Sanh plateau and to expending great resources there daily, felt able to shift at least half and perhaps more of his Khe Sanh forces to the great Tet offensive of February 1968. As a result, the spring saw Giap realizing the better parts of both worlds. He still had us tied down at Khe Sanh, diverted from pacification, expending a thousand tons of bombs plus hundreds of artillery and mortar rounds a day, and delivering two hundred tons of supplies a day by helicopters, by fixed-wing aircraft, and [by] air drop. Meanwhile, he was able to free at least three regiments to participate in the Tet attack on Hue."

With up to three divisions surrounding the remote combat base, why didn't the North Vietnamese ever mount a human-wave run at the defenses of the base itself? For their own strategic reasons, they simply didn't need to.

———

ADDITIONAL NOTE: KRULAK ALSO RECALLED HIS BRIEF AND BRUISING encounter with President Lyndon Baines Johnson in the Oval Office after a Vietnam visit in mid-1966. "What is it going to take to win?" LBJ asked.

Well aware that the Administration was loath to provoke the Soviet Union or Red China by bombing the North Vietnamese ports, Krulak launched into his view of how the war should be won. First, improve the quality of the South Vietnamese government; next, accelerate the training of the South Vietnamese armed forces.

"But most of all I told him we faced a self-defeating attritional cycle involving engagement with large and increasingly sophisticated North Vietnamese units. We had to stop the flow of war materials to those forces."

The President then asked if the air campaign against supply routes in North Vietnam was ineffective. He noted that "it amounted to as many as four to five hundred sorties a day."

To which Krulak replied, "for the most part we were attacking the wrong targets." In addition, "I told him that the only real answer was to stop the supplies, not when they were dispersed in the North Vietnam road system or when they got to the Ho Chi Minh Trail in Laos, but before they ever crossed the dock in Haiphong [North Vietnam]. Then I voiced the critical words, urging that we 'mine the ports, destroy the Haiphong dock area.'"

And that was it, end of conversation.

"As soon as he heard me speak of mining and unrestrained bombing of the ports, Mr. Johnson got to his feet, put his arm around my shoulder, and propelled me firmly toward the door."

MARINE WITH A SECRET

WOULD THE VIET CONG OR THE NORTH VIETNAMESE WILLINGLY have shot Walt Disney's little deer Bambi, even during wartime? Unknowingly, they did almost exactly that when they sent American Marine Donnie Dunagan to the rear with various wounds during his three tours of duty in Vietnam.

But the real fear for Dunagan was not so much the enemy; rather, it was that some fellow Marine might discover his secret connection with Bambi.

How could that be? After all, he had been a Marine from the time he enlisted in 1952 at age eighteen. He had been a Marine Corps drill instructor. He had seen combat in Vietnam, and he ascended into officer ranks to retire as a major in 1977.

Even after that, he wasn't going around boasting about the Bambi connection…nor about his Bronze Star and three Purple Hearts.

"I was blessed to be in a leadership role for twenty-five years, either in counterintelligence or training troops," he once told an interviewer. And if his men had ever found out about Bambi, he added, "They'd have ridden me out on a rail."

He could have also listed Boris Karloff, Bela Lugosi, Frankenstein, and Basil Rathbone in the same breath as Bambi, thanks to his brief career in Hollywood as a child actor.

Other Marines, before and after service, found their claim to fame as astronauts (John Glenn), writers (William Manchester), and ballplayers (Ted Williams), but only one—retired Major Donnie Donagan—could claim to have been the voice of Bambi in Disney's famous animated film *Bambi*.

The fact is, Dunagan once was a child actor, and his *was* the voice of Bambi in the Walt Disney animated film of that title.

Raised in near-poverty, he was discovered at a talent show in Memphis, Tennessee—dancing a jig with a boot-blackened paper bag as a hat, he won the $100 first prize. He was just six "when Walt Disney hired him to be the model and voice of the fawn in the 1942 animated classic," noted Bruce Westbrook in the *Houston Chronicle* of March 7, 2005. Dunagan then made eight movies as a child, added Westbrook. "They included 1939's *Son of Frankenstein* with Boris Karloff and *Tower of London* with Basil Rathbone. But his career ended when his family fractured. He wound up in boarding homes, then joined the military as a teen."

As Dunagan himself once explained (according to writer Xan Brooks in the *Manchester Guardian* of February 16, 2005), "all that money" he earned hurt the family—they couldn't handle it. "We'd gone from a one-room tenement to a house in Beverly Hills, and it was too much, too quick. The family just ruptured, and I was then farmed out to a bunch of people."

To the teenaged Dunagan, no longer a child star in Hollywood, a career in the military looked pretty darn good by comparison. "I adopted the Marines, and the Marines adopted me," he would say later.

Dunagan then "distinguished himself in the service," the *Houston Chronicle*'s Westbrook also related. "The curly-haired lad with the Southern drawl whom Karloff hoisted on a monster's shoulder became the youngest Marine drill instructor ever. A boxer and devoted Harley rider, Dunagan served three tours in Vietnam and was wounded several times."

But never did he disclose his "clean little secret."

After finally leaving the Marine Corps in 1977, "he worked in business and kept mum about his childhood stardom, even as fans scoured phone books for him." But then, in 2004, he was "outed" when "a casual comment at a San Angelo [Texas] banquet tipped off a local TV crew that they had a star in their midst."

Dunagan, by then seventy, and his wife Dana had moved to San Angelo "so his stepson could attend college there." Only then, with his secret finally out, "did we open the old boxes I'd sealed for fifty years, with newspaper clippings about my time in *Bambi*," he said.

All this came just in time to greet and take part in the release of a DVD of *Bambi*. "Dunagan appears in a featurette about the cast, then and now," added Westbrook. "He was always fond of the film and showed videocassettes of it to children whenever he could. Now he's getting DVD copies from Disney [the company] to give to orphanages." Next step for Dunagan was appearing at movie fan conventions "to meet admirers and sign autographs."

Commented Donna Lucas, copublisher of *Video Watchdog*, "His autograph hasn't been out there since he was four or five. This is the one of the last living people who worked with Karloff, and he's got an incredible memory."

Obviously no longer reluctant to have his secret finally "out there," Dunagan said, "I go down the street now, and when some old Marine who knew me yells, 'Hey, Major Bambi!' I love it to death."

═══════

ADDITIONAL NOTE: ANOTHER CHILD ENTERTAINER WITH MARINE Corps ties was Bob Bell, best known as Bozo the Clown, a favorite for twenty-five years out of Chicago's WGN-TV station and syndicated to nearly two hundred more television outlets nationwide.

Already a veteran actor, he managed to join the Marines in 1941 despite near-blindness in one eye by memorizing the eye charts. Quickly found out, he was given a medical discharge less than a year later, but then joined the Navy and served in the Pacific until 1946. "It'd take him three and a half hours to put his makeup on every day," said a grandson, professional baseball player Trevor Bell, in 2014. "He'd be up at 3:30 in the morning putting on his makeup and he did it for the kids, and that's all he did it for. He did it to lighten the kids' days, it was something that was totally selfless." Trevor was noted in the team locker room for the tattoos on his left shoulder and forearm of his grandfather, Bozo the Clown. Others have played Bozo as well, among them the NBC-TV *Today Show*'s weatherman Willard Scott, "but perhaps no city was as smitten with Bozo as Chicago," said the *Chicago Tribune,* reporting on Bell's death at age seventy-five in December 1997.

RESCUE MISSION ABORTED

ONE BY ONE, THE ANNIVERSARIES ROLL ON BY. "25 YEARS AGO: Hostages in Iran." (CBS-TV). "30 Years Ago, Iran Hostage Returned Home to Wisconsin." (*Milwaukee Journal Sentinel*). "Iran Hostage Family Still Haunted 35 Years Later" (*Las Vegas Review-Journal*).

Not all of the sixty-six original hostages, thirteen Marine embassy guards among them, still survive. But those who do will never forget that day at the American Embassy in Tehran, Iran. Or the 443 days that followed.

"Those early days of blindfolds and beatings and handcuffs and interrogations were anything but easy," said Kevin Hermening, who at age twenty-one back in 1979 was among the youngest of the thirteen Marines taken captive on November 4. In more recent years, he has been a financial consultant in Wausau, Wisconsin, an activist in local politics, and a motivational speaker about his experience as a hostage, notes the *Milwaukee Journal Sentinel.*

Staff Sgt. Mike Moeller was a "strapping six-foot-four" at the time, the *Las Vegas Journal Review* reports. "He said his physical presence did not spare him from being pushed over chairs and thrown around while handcuffed and blindfolded, and being tormented in other ways."

During the 444 days that most of the hostages (more than fifty) were kept in captivity by Iranian students and other militants, "the Marines and other hostages were subjected to abominable conditions and constant harassment from their captors," notes the Prisoner of War Medal awarded to Maj. Steve Kirtley, USMC (Ret.), and his fellow Marines.

Kirtley, more recently of McLean, Virginia, was then just twenty-one, six-foot-three, and a corporal. He had arrived on station at the Tehran embassy for his security-guard posting in August 1979. He was a volunteer, and well aware "the atmosphere was still tense in the Middle Eastern country."

Early in the year, Shah Mohammed Reza Pahlavi had fled a hard-line fundamentalist revolution in Iran, to be succeeded by the anti-American cleric Ayatollah Khomeini. That fall, the Iranians focused virulent anti-American rhetoric on the decision to allow the recently deposed shah, a longstanding American ally in the Middle East, to enter the United States for treatment of a life-threatening (and, as it turned out, terminal) bout with cancer.

"I wanted to be where the action was," Kirtley recalled in an interview with the Fredericksburg (Virginia) *Free-Lance Star* in 2001. "You don't join the Marine Corps for the great benefits, you join the Marine Corps to be a Marine."

As his Prisoner of War citation also notes, "The hostages were continuously used in several forms of propaganda such as being paraded in front of media cameras while blindfolded and hands tied behind their backs."

Even so, and "despite the harsh conditions," the Marines in the group "continuously provided an example for all other Americans to emulate through their adherence to the Code of Conduct and unfaltering esprit de corps." Thus, their motivation and positive attitude "throughout this ordeal provided many of the other hostages with the necessary leadership and courage to endure the captivity successfully."

While many Americans feel that Middle Eastern terrorists struck their first blow against the United States on September 11, 2001, with that day's terrorist attacks on the Pentagon and the World Trade Center, "others look back exactly a quarter-century ago, on November 4, 1979, when sixty-six Americans were taken hostage at the U.S. embassy in Iraq," noted CBS-TV news on November 4, 2004, the twenty-fifth anniversary of the hostage-taking.

In a like vein, Marine Corps guard and hostage Rodney "Rocky" Sickmann of St. Louis County, Missouri, commented, "The day they took us is the day they [the United States] should have started the war on terrorism."

As is well known, there would be no relief for most of the hostages until months later, as Ronald Reagan took over the presidency from Jimmy Carter. Motivational speaker Hermening, for one, hoped it was good news when he and other hostages were blindfolded, loaded onto buses and taken to the Tehran airport. "He knew it was good news," wrote Tom Tolan in the *Journal Sentinel*, "when seated on the bus, he smelled jet fuel and heard the big engines and a chanting crowd ('Death to America!' 'Yankee go home!') that [had] formed a gauntlet for the hostages between bus and plane. He sprinted up the ramp and got on the plane. It took off, and a cheer went up when the pilot announced they were out of Iranian air space."

But there was another anniversary that would be marked in the years that rolled on after the hostage-taking and the later release. In late April

1980, there was the abortive rescue attempt, Operation Eagle Claw, in which three Marine Corps and five Air Force members died when a helicopter rotor clipped the fuselage of a big EC-130 refueling tanker plane.

This heartrending disaster was not the only reason the rescue mission could not go forward. The fact was, the complex, multiple-services operation had been plagued with problems from the start. One was the very nature of the mission itself: a secretly planned and staged dash into a hostile country to find, gather up, and liberate more than fifty hostages held under unknown conditions.

According to the Helis helicopter history website, the planning for the "audacious" operation involved "all four U.S. Armed Services." The plan called for the participation of eight Navy RH-53D Sikorsky Sea Stallion helicopters fitted with mine detection and neutralizing devices and manned by Marine crews, plus twelve Air Force planes—gunships, refueling tanker aircraft, and cargo planes among them. In addition, U.S. Army Rangers would be among the Delta Force personnel taking part, while Navy aircraft carriers standing by in the Arabian Sea could provide fighter aircraft support if needed.

"The basic plan was to infiltrate the [Delta Force] operators into the country the night before the assault and get them to Tehran, and after the assault, bring them home." *Them* meaning the military personnel and the hostages.

Meanwhile, three cargo planes would land at a barren desert spot in Iran, presumably undetected, and offload some Delta Force men, air combat controllers, translators, and truck drivers. The eight choppers would fly to the same spot from the offshore carriers, while three Air Force fuel tankers would be waiting to refuel them on the ground at the desert rendezvous spot.

Once refueled, the choppers "would fly the task force to a spot near the outskirts of Tehran and meet up with agents already in the country who would lead the operators to a safe house to await the assault the next day." The helicopters, meanwhile, would go "hide" overnight at some predesignated, out-of-the way refuge, also in Iran.

Of course, all those complex maneuvers were only a start on the plan to rescue the hostages held in Tehran, far inside Iran's borders, with little intelligence available on them, their condition, or the defenses available to their captors.

On the second night, the big transport aircraft would fly back into Iran, presumably avoiding detection again for as long as possible, and deliver a group of U.S. Army Rangers at Iran's Manzariyeh Airfield. They were to seize and hold the facility until two C-141 transports could land and pick them up, plus the hostages.

Meanwhile, the Delta Force personnel would assault the embassy that same night, free the hostages, and take them to the eight choppers, by then waiting at a nearby soccer stadium. The choppers would fly them to the airfield held by the Rangers, where all would board the C-141 transports and fly out of Iran. The valuable helicopters would be destroyed on the ground before leaving, a small sacrifice in return for freeing the hostages.

At first, all seemed to go well. An entire month beforehand, a CIA plane had flown an Air Force combat controller (akin to an artillery spotter) to the isolated desert site, called "Desert One," to check out the area on a light dirt bike and to plant hidden landing lights, "to help guide the force in."

That preparation done successfully, came Night One of the rescue mission itself, with disaster looming for the carrier-borne choppers from the start. Ordered to fly into Iran territory at no higher than two hundred feet to avoid radar, they ran into a ground-hugging *haboob*, or dust storm, that obscured vision. "Two helicopters lost sight of the task force and landed out of action. Another had landed earlier when a warning light came on."

That meant three of the eight critically needed choppers were unavailable for the moment. The remaining five battled on against dust storms and high winds. To make matters worse, another "bird" suffered a malfunction and had to drop out. Meanwhile, the EC-130 tankers had arrived at the Desert One rendezvous point, and the first two choppers to drop back started up again. Now there were six approaching the meeting point, just enough to carry out the planned mission, assuming all else went perfectly.

Half the choppers arrived an hour late; the next three hovered down fifteen minutes later. But one of them had lost its primary hydraulic system—no way could it be used fully loaded for the planned assault on the distant embassy in Tehran.

With that realization, the mission was scrubbed right then and there. Five choppers by themselves would not be enough to carry out the plan, even if all else went off without a hitch.

In the meantime, another unexpected complication: out of the blue, an Iranian bus with a driver and about forty passengers appeared on a nearby dirt road. They had to be held immobile and incommunicado until all in the raiding party could leave.

Bad went to worse as, in the dark and kicking up its own obscuring dust cloud, a chopper "drifted" into a parked EC-130 tanker, the rotor slashing into the side of the fuel ship. Five Air Force personnel, including the pilot and the commander, plus three Marine crew members from the helicopter were fatally injured in the fireball that erupted.

All remaining personnel and serviceable aircraft were ordered out of there right away…after blowing up the choppers, of course.

However, in the confusion of caring for the wounded and dying, while also moving the remaining aircraft out of harm's way on the ground, the destruction order went astray. Five valuable helicopters were left behind and fell into the hands of the Iranians, together with any secret equipment or papers still on board.

In conjunction with a twenty-fifth anniversary ceremony in 2005 honoring the eight who died in the Eagle Claw mission, a Defense Department press release said that from the disaster "came the impetus for a new, stronger, more integrated military and special operations force."

The press release also noted Joint Staff Director (Air Force Lt. Gen.) Norton Schwartz's statement that the Desert One tragedy "propelled a generation, of which I am a part, to assure that America would never again repeat that searing, transforming experience of the twenty-fifth of April 1980."

According to Schwartz, also, "Never again would we be so unprepared, so ill-equipped, so entirely dependent on the skills [and] resourcefulness of our people, who, despite shortcomings in force cohesion, equipment, and external support, lifted off into the darkness with only one mission imperative: 'Bring Americans home.'"

Army Lt. Gen. William Boykin, a survivor of the aborted mission, was cited in the same press release as saying it was both the "greatest disappointment of my professional career" and one of the proudest moments of that same career. "None of us wanted to die, none of us expected to die, but we knew the risk," he said. "We knew that we were up against an entire nation with a force of barely 100 people."

The three Marines who died in the mission were Sgt. John D. Harvey, Cpl. George N. Holmes Jr., and Staff Sgt. Dewey L. Johnson.

PART IV
TWENTY-FIRST-CENTURY WARS

===============

In my three tours in combat as an infantry officer, I never saw one of them hesitate, or do anything other than lean into the fire and with no apparent fear of death or injury, take the fight to our enemies...when seconds seem like hours and it all becomes slow motion and fast forward at the same time, and the only rational act is to stop, get down, save himself. But they don't.

—Retired Marine Corps Gen. John F. Kelly at a Marine Corps birthday celebration in St. Louis, Missouri, November 2010, a day after learning his son, Marine Capt. Robert Kelly, was killed in Afghanistan. General Kelly retired in 2015 as commander of the U.S. Southern Command and was named President Donald Trump's secretary-designate of Homeland Security in late 2016.

CONGRATS, THE WAR IS OVER

For Marine Capt. Russell A. C. Sanborn, POW, the guard had surprising news. "Congratulations," he said. "The war is over."

Indeed, the high-tech "Nintendo War," drawing the largest ever U.S. Marine deployment up to the time, was just about over in one hundred hours. Ninety thousand Marines, including Marine fighter pilots like Sanborn, had done their job well, with a minimum of casualties. Of course, they had benefitted from the simultaneous support of the U.S. Air Force, the Army, the Navy, and quite a few foreign allies, including some from Saddam Hussein's neighboring Middle Eastern states.

For all, the focal point had been tiny, oil-rich Kuwait, invaded and occupied some six months before by six hundred thousand Iraqi troops, who literally raped and pillaged like barbarians of old.

While the recent ground phase of the Persian Gulf War against the Iraqi invaders lasted from February 24, 1991, to February 28, 1991, the Allied air war against the Iraqis had begun a bit earlier—on January 16, to be exact. Thus, Marine pilot Sanborn had met up with every fighter pilot's nightmare—being shot down behind enemy lines—the afternoon of February 9.

A member of the Marines' VMA-231 fighter squadron, normally based at Cherry Point, North Carolina, he was pushing along his supersonic Harrier jump jet on his second mission of the day, this time attacking Iraqi artillery emplacements in southern Kuwait. As he zoomed in on his first pass, his plane balked at releasing its ordnance—a computer "glitch."

Not yet too concerned, he came back around again, and this time it was "bombs away" as hoped.

Still, a problem loomed. Pulling "off target," he said later, he rolled his Harrier so he could look back and see where the bombs had hit. That's when he felt "this loud thump on my left side." He had no time to wonder what it was. "My plane immediately started spinning and inverting out of control."

He struggled a few seconds to recoup, but in vain.

The fire warning light came on, and he knew then "she was a goner." He would have to bail out right there, behind enemy lines, "every pilot's worst fear."

Yet there was no helping it. "So, I got myself into a good body position and pulled the handle to eject—and out I went."

Right decision, considering the circumstances…but the enemy would be waiting below. The Iraqis already had displayed obviously beaten-up Allied POWs on television, so Sanborn wasn't sure what to expect… except that it likely wouldn't be good.

"I was on the ground no more than ten minutes before the Iraqi welcoming committee reached me." They had rifles, he had a single pistol. "I was outmanned and outgunned. My heart was racing."

Retelling his own story in the 1991 book *Desert Storm*, Sanborn was deprived of his pistol and radio before he was taken to a bunker.

As one surprise, he met the Iraqi who had shot him down with a handheld SAM (surface-to-air missile). The obviously excited soldier rushed in, pointed at him, and shouted, "I shoot you down! I get two of you now!"

The newcomer took Sanborn's name tag and actually shook the American flyer's hand. "He had his arms over his shoulders, showing me that he had downed my plane with a handheld SAM," Sanborn related later.

That was it for a while, until dark that night, when his luck, along with his mild treatment, ran out. Blindfolded, hands tied behind his back, he was heaved into the back of a truck and taken who knows where.

At a stop, he was told to run a gauntlet of Iraqis who hit him with fists, sticks, and rifle butts. "For the last eighteen or nineteen days we had been bombing them," Sanborn related. "The guys I saw looked pretty tired and ragged. They needed somebody to vent their frustration against. And I happened to be the unlucky one. They screamed at me in Arabic and broken English. I fell down a couple times. They would quickly pick me up and push me forward."

Never losing consciousness, Sanborn went through two more gauntlets at different stops, and by the third was admittedly "hurting."

Next he had to endure a series of three interrogations over the next three days that were not entirely gentle, either.

"I devised a way to protect myself during interviews," he said. "Again, I was tied up and blindfolded. Whenever they picked my chin up, I knew they were going to hit me. So…I would tuck my chin in and roll my shoulders forward to protect my face as much as possible."

He also figured out that if the Iraqi interrogators pressed on him with one thumb, he could expect a blow coming from the opposite side. "If it was the left thumb, then I knew it was the right hand coming around to strike me."

After the interrogations, he was taken on a six-hour truck ride to Baghdad, for another brutal questioning period, then placed in a cell about ten feet by twelve feet in size with one small window. For a time, he and about twenty other Americans also being held captive there were able to communicate with each other in whispers.

But as punishment for talking, Sanborn was placed in a dark cell with no window. "The pilots were the bad boys anyway," he said. "The guards didn't like us—for obvious reasons. They were gruff and would shove, kick, or push us. We were never beaten by them, though."

In late February all the prisoners took joy in a new captive's report that the Allies had begun their ground attack on the Iraqis holding Kuwait captive. It was just days later when a guard approached Sanborn and said, "Congratulations, the war is over."

Unbelieving at first, Sanborn nonetheless could take hope from the fact that Baghdad wasn't bombed that night. The next day he was allowed to shave for the first time. A day later he enjoyed his first bath since he had arrived. Finally, he and the others were taken downtown in the Iraqi capital to the Al Rashid Hotel and turned over to the International Red Cross, whose personnel flew them to friendly Saudi Arabia.

"When we crossed the Saudi border and two F-15s pulled alongside of us as escorts," he said, "the whole plane just erupted in a loud chorus of cheers."

IN PURSUIT OF DREAMS
BY INGRID SMYER

FIRST AN ROTC CADET (ARMY, THAT IS) IN COLLEGE, THEN A POLICE officer, Vernice Armour got to thinking. She was already an accomplished young woman, but why stop there?

"I realized I could always be a cop," she said later. "But I [wouldn't] always have the chance to be a combat pilot." Moreover, she already had Marines in her blood—both her stepfather and a grandfather had been Marines.

And then the recruiter she visited pointed out a really historic goal that was just waiting for the right person to come along. If she could handle Officer Candidate School at Quantico Marine Base, and then flight school as well, she quite possibly could become America's first female African American combat pilot.

That's exactly what Vernice Armour did, and just in time to be deployed twice in combat, both times in Iraq, as pilot of a Marine Corps AH1 W SuperCobra attack helicopter.

As related by Marine Lance Cpl. Chelsea Flowers February 10, 2012, on *Marines Blog*, a very young Captain Armour not only dreamed of becoming a cop, "but more than that, she wanted to speak and be a role model." She had a first close look at the military as an Army ROTC cadet at her college, Middle Tennessee State University. While in ROTC, she saw a woman in a flight suit. "After that I became very interested in aviation," said Armour.

Soon she was a police officer in Nashville, Tennessee, a motorcycle cop at that, but she hadn't forgotten that woman in the flight suit. She was well aware too of her family's Marine Corps lineage. Grandfather William Holman, after all, had been a Montford Point Marine during World War II, one of those very first African Americans admitted into the previously all-white Marine Corps and trained, still separate, at the corner of Camp Lejeune, North Carolina, called Montford Point. In addition, her stepfather, Clarence Jackson, was a three-tour veteran of Vietnam, where he had served as a USMC sergeant.

Deciding on making the switch from law enforcement to military service, Armour naturally considered the Marine Corps first. "I always wanted to be in the Marine Corps," she said. "For me, it was the toughest. It was the biggest challenge."

That's when her Marine Corps Officer Selection Officer pointed out she could make history as the nation's first black female combat pilot—not only of the Marine Corps, but of any of the country's military services.

"I knew a lot would be riding on my shoulders," she admitted. "I knew it would be hard. I knew there was a potential that there could be biases out there as well about whether women deserve to be in the Marine Corps, or combat or flying in that platform."

"Regardless," adds Marine journalist Flowers in her blog, "in October 1988, Armour started her historical journey at Officer Candidate School on Marine Corps Base Quantico, Virginia, following OCS in 2001; Armour earned her gold wings and was stationed at Camp Pendleton [California] with Marine Light Attack Helicopter Squadron 169 as a AH1 W SuperCobra pilot."

Racial discrimination had not been a noticeable problem for her, Armour said. "There is friction all the time in different places," she explained. "Friction is natural. When I had friction with someone it could've been because I had short hair, I smiled in the morning, I could bench press more than them, I rode a motorcycle, or because I'm a woman, or because I'm black. But honestly, I didn't care because my number one goal was to focus on the mission and to be the best pilot I could be."

Meanwhile, with the terrorist attacks of September 11, 2001, she and her fellow pilots all "knew we would be going somewhere and—soon."

In her case, it would not be until February 2003. With "the reality of the situation" then beginning to sink in, Armour crossed the border from Kuwait into Iraq on her first combat deployment.

"It was so surreal because you're not shooting at cardboard [targets], you're not shooting at tires and wood," Armour told Flowers. "There were people on the ground, trying to take us out of the sky to kill us. It was a huge reality check. All the training came into sharp focus."

Naturally, Armour sometimes "wondered how she and her comrades would make it out of certain situations," Flowers adds in her blog, "but they never doubted that they would give it their all."

Or as Armour herself later summed up: "Marines don't settle. Failure's just not an option for us."

———

ADDITIONAL NOTE: ARMOUR WAS AGAIN DEPLOYED TO AL ASAD, IRAQ, in 2004 with the Eleventh Marine Expeditionary Unit, before separating from the Marine Corps in 2007 to pursue her dream of being a role model and motivational speaker. She published a motivational book, *Zero to Breakthrough: The 7-Step, Battle-Tested Method for Accomplishing Goals That Matter,* in 2011. In it, she relates that one night she had to borrow a friend's car on short notice to drive six hours the very next day to Nashville to take a once-a-year civil service test that might to qualify her for police training.

"Early the next morning I made the drive to Nashville, arrived on time for the afternoon test, took it, and not long after…found out I was eligible to enter the [police] Academy. I did—and within two years I was the first African American woman to be a Nashville motorcycle officer," she writes in her book.

"The effort it took to get to Nashville wasn't a big deal. Whatever I had to do, whatever it cost me was worth it, because my burning desire to become a cop trumped everything else at that time. I knew it was a great training ground for my ultimate purpose in life to help people."

Even in combat, she had felt her goal "was to be the best pilot I could up there in the air to protect and serve my brothers and sisters on the ground."

SELECT UNIT HISTORIES
"FIGHTING FIFTH" MARINES

The "Fighting Fifth" was first seen afloat aboard ship in the Caribbean as a possible intervention force, but only as a paper tiger, really. Having then disappeared until the American entry into World War I, the "Fighting Fifth" Regiment of the Marine Corps at this writing can boast more battle honors than any other regiment of the entire U.S. Marine Corps.

"The muddy trenches of France, the steamy jungles of Nicaragua, the fire-swept beaches of the Pacific, the frozen hills of Korea, the rice paddies of Vietnam, and the desert sands of the Persian Gulf are all familiar to the regiment," explained Lt. Col. Ronald Brown (USMC Ret.) in the *Marine Corps Gazette* in 2006.

The fact was, rather than just post a threat of intervention from shipboard, show up to display the flag, the Fifth Marines were called up to fight, again and again.

For instance, take the solid coral "island" Peleliu, with more than 6,500 casualties considered by many the worst of all World War II island-hopping stops the Marines made in the Pacific. Here (and at Okinawa) was born the well-known battlefield epic *With the Old Breed at Peleliu and Okinawa,* a moving, often horrifying memoir by E. B. Sledge, a mortarman with K Company, Third Battalion, Fifth Marines. The story of Peleliu also fostered the book *Brotherhood of Heroes: The Marines at Peleliu, 1944: the Bloodiest Battle of the Pacific War,* by Bill Sloan.

In Vietnam two decades later, notes Brown in the *Gazette*, "A common refrain at the First Marine Division [1stMarDiv] processing center at Da Nang in 1969 was, 'If you want action, join the Fifth Marines!'" Still another book, *13 Cent Killers: The 5th Marine Snipers in Vietnam* by John J. Culbertson, came out of the regiment's proud duty in Vietnam, where the Fifth Marine's Sniper Platoon was widely known and feared by the Viet Cong. Author Culbertson himself was a Fifth Marines sniper.

In all, the Fifth Marines fought at Belleau Wood in France; at Guadalcanal, Peliliu, and Okinawa in the Pacific; at Pusan, Inchon, and Chosin in Korea; in Vietnam; in Iraq; and in Afghanistan. Overall, too, "The Fifth Marines has been involved in more combat action in the past century than any other similar-sized military unit in the world," writes Brown.

Among the Fighting Fifth's major plaudits was Iraq, where, in the opening minutes of the 2003 campaign against the dictator Saddam Hussein, Fifth Marines would be "First to Fight" as spearhead for the First Marine Division. The Fifth Marines—reconstituted and enhanced for the moment as a regimental combat team, RCT-5, and boasting more than seven thousand personnel—was the first U.S. unit to breach the berms forming the border between friendly Kuwait and Iraq the night of March 20. The initial goal, quickly accomplished despite high winds and dust storms, was to secure the oil fields near Rumaylah before Hussain could destroy them.

"By dawn the next morning," writes Brown, "the regiment had consolidated and was ready to continue forward after processing hundreds of enemy prisoners." *Forward* meant rushing north, then east to join the assault on Baghdad itself while leaving behind a field of battle "strewn with destroyed and abandoned enemy armored vehicles."

On the road north—a four-lane expressway still under construction—the RCT-5 ran an unending "gauntlet of small-arms and rocket-propelled grenade (RPG) fire," usually from poorly organized irregulars. The Marines countered by dismounting from their armored assault vehicles (AAVs) to flank and attack, again and again. "Occasionally, dug-in tanks or unarmored technicals (civilian utility trucks mounting crew-served heavy weapons) were encountered. They were inevitably destroyed by tank or missile fire before they could do much damage."

Any Iraqi regular army units seen as a threat, even distantly, were kept at bay, and often decimated, by "unrelenting" airstrikes.

In addition, "the way north was prepared by long-range artillery fire as helicopter gunships prowled the skies in search of targets of opportunity"

As the Marine force neared Baghdad, the plan was to make a feint in one direction south of the city, but actually swing to the northeast onto Iraq's Route 27 at an elbow-like junction. "From there they would cross the Tigris River, then continue the attack on Baghdad using northbound Highway 6 before the surprised Iraqis could block the way."

As before in the same campaign, and indeed throughout, the hope was that when the Iraqis did respond to the unexpected maneuvers, "they would be crushed by America's overwhelming combined arms firepower."

Pressing forward by that plan, elements of the RCT-5 met tougher fighting on April 3 from the Iraqi Al Nida Republican Guards Division. And naturally, the Marines attacked. "Marine tanks led the way and provided suppressive fire as Marine Cobra gunships, Harrier jump jets, and Hornet attack jets buzzed overhead." With that kind of all-Marines support, plus covering fire from the 20-millimeter guns of their own AAVs, the dismounted Marine infantrymen slowly secured the approach roadstead and fought their way into the town harboring the enemy. By dusk they were clearing "block by block," despite the Republican Guard's stubborn resistance.

"This was the most significant battle between the Marines and conventional enemy forces of the war to that point," adds Brown.

Of course there would be more combat...much more. The very next day, April 4, the RCT-5 clashed with, and eventually overcame, several hundred foreign jihadists and surviving Al Nida fighters in what became the longest firefight of the campaign.

Next came more urban street fighting, in Baghdad itself, followed by seizure of Samarra Airfield. As American forces settled into their lengthy occupation of Iraq's capital city, the Fifth Marines transitioned to civil action duties, punctuated by patrolling against pockets of enemy holdouts. By July, Fifth Marines personnel were on their way back to home base in California.

Summing up their accomplishments, Brown writes that in one month of active combat the regiment had moved more than 350 miles, "spearheaded the longest overland combat movement in Marine Corps history," "liberated numerous villages and a children's prison," "captured two airfields," and rendered two Republican Guard divisions, as well as uncounted irregular forces, "incapable of organized resistance." In its 33 days of combat, the Fifth Marines suffered 12 killed and 126 seriously wounded.

As some compensation for those minor but still numbers, Fifth Marines members could go home with a presidential unit citation, the tenth in the history of the regiment—quite a record for an outfit that traces its beginnings to a paper phantom never engaged in combat.

FROM MARINE TO WARLORD

SOME MARINES, AS STATED, GO ON TO BECOME ASTRONAUTS, TO PLAY professional baseball, even to run for president. But one, a Marine reservist from California, went on to become a clan leader—some would say warlord—in his native Somalia.

Back in California, naturalized American citizen Hussein Mohamed Farah Aidid had been studying engineering part-time and working for the city of West Covina on mundane matters such as traffic counts, water maps, and computers before suddenly departing for his native land on the east African coast.

According to newspaper reports, he was born in Somalia in 1962 to one of strongman Mohamed Farah Aidid's four wives, who later moved with her fourteen-year-old son Hussein and five other children to Southern California. He lived there for the next sixteen years, graduated from Covina High School, became an American citizen, and joined the Marine Reserves as a corporal.

"I always wanted to be a Marine," Hussein once said. "You know how it is, watching Marine soldiers. I'm proud of my background and military discipline. Once a Marine, always a Marine."

He went through basic training the summer of 1987, James C. McKinley Jr. of the *New York Times* reported (August 12, 1996). He then "skipped active service" and went straight into the reserves as an artilleryman. "He was assigned as a corporal to Battery B, Fourteenth Marines in Pico Rivera, Calif."

He also began taking courses at Citrus College in Glendora, California, followed by civil engineering courses at the University of California at Long Beach, the *Times* added.

In the meantime, Hussein's native country in Africa had been struggling for years through drought; famine, with an estimated three hundred thousand dying of starvation; homelessness, and civil war among rival clans bidding for power—one of them led by Farah's father, General Aidid, head of the Habar Gidir clan.

In December of 1992, President George H. W. Bush sent the Marines into Mogadishu, the Somali capital, to help safeguard United Nations peacekeepers and shipments of food to the stricken country in Operation Restore Hope.

For the Americanized reservist in California, these events were still distant, until the day two Marine officers turned up at one of his engineering classes, interrupted, and told him he "was urgently needed in Somalia" as a translator. Reportedly, he was the only Marine who spoke the Somali language. Suddenly, for three weeks, Hussein was back in his homeland serving as an interpreter and liaison between the American forces and his own father. "But the relationship between the United Nations and General Aidid soured, and the Marines sent Mr. Farah home on January 5 [1993]."

Once again, he was back to a seemingly mundane life as a reservist, part-time student, and engineering department worker for the city of West Covina.

In Somalia, however, conditions went from bad to worse. In mid-1993 the Marine's father would become "evil personified in the United States and at the United Nations" for his role in the notorious "Black Hawk Down" incident depicted in the book and movie by that title.

As summarized in the *New York Times,* in addition to diverting food aid and relief supplies, Aidid's fighters had ambushed and killed twenty-four Pakistani peacekeepers. The United Nations placed a $25,000 price on his head. Eighteen American troops were killed trying to capture him. The nation was shocked by the televised image of the body of an American soldier being dragged through the streets of Mogadishu.

Seeing the images of the outrage on television news programs himself, the Somali immigrant reacted in horror, the *Los Angeles Times* reported in January 2007. "Hell is coming," Hussein recalled thinking. The deaths of the Americans as two Black Hawk helicopters crashed "[were] like a black hole in me," he said.

But now the Marines turned to him again. He was asked to send his father a letter asking for the release of a captured U.S. pilot. He said he didn't hesitate, reported the L.A. newspaper. "I felt almost as if I could have been in that conflict and died," he said.

However, in 1995, the younger Farah suddenly returned to Somalia on his own. As related by McKinley in the *New York Times*, his strongman father "took him under his wing and began grooming him for a top spot in the clan's military organization, diplomats and United Nations officials said." Not long after, as General Aidid's forces captured Baidoa in south-central Somalia, the son "was given a large role commanding the forces and got his first taste of combat, diplomats said." In midsummer of 1996, General Aidid was fatally wounded in "a battle for a neighborhood in southern Mogadishu."

To the surprise of many in Somalia, with the father gone, the former Marine and naturalized American citizen was elected the new leader of his father's clan in a closed meeting of its elders. Later, Farah emerged as a minister in a coalition government that followed his father's death.

In 2001, he still was leader of the Somali National Alliance (SNA) once headed by his warlord father, according to BBC News, but he didn't quite look the part. There was little about him "to remind anyone of the terror, anger, or respect aroused by his father," reported the BBC's Roger Hearing. In fact, "The clean-shaven, round-faced, thoughtful young man in a business suit looks ill at ease among the rusting tanks and machine-gun trucks that guard his headquarters."

Living in a "crumbling" white mansion in the Somali capital of Mogadishu that once was the last refuge of Somalia's former dictator Siad Barre, Hussein faced an uncertain political future. "Hussein objects to the term 'warlord,' but he is the most prominent among a handful of faction leaders who refuse to recognize the new interim Somali Government set up by a conference in Djibouti last August," BBC newsman Hearing added.

"The Somali people were never consulted," Hussein complained. "It was a project led by [Djibouti] President Gelle. It was not accepted. It was completely rejected."

He claimed he and other faction leaders still had the support of the people. "Our roots are the will of the people," he asserted, but the BBC reported that "to many Somalis, he is one of those standing in the way of a return to normalcy."

More than a year later, the *Washington Times* was reporting that

Hussein Farah was "a warlord in exile in Ethiopia." But he hoped "to return to his Somali clan and is inviting the United States to come back too, this time to root out suspected al Qaeda leaders in his homeland."

U.S. officials "don't quite know what to make of their ex-Marine," the *Washington Times* added. They remember the "harsh rhetoric" he often used his father's death at a rally in a Somali stadium celebrating the violence against Americans led by his late father.

"Despite that, U.S. officials don't think he's a foe. But they're not sure he's a friend. It's a dilemma characteristic of Somalia's chaos."

NO WINNERS HERE

THIS IS A REAL HORROR STORY. NO WINNERS...BUT IT *IS* A PART OF Marine Corps history.

It is a story of bravery, of sadness, of haunting uncertainty. Did Marine Sgt. Rafael Peralta deserve the Medal of Honor, or instead the Navy Cross that he was finally awarded posthumously? Did he, while fighting in Fallujah, Iraq, consciously pull the grenade into his body and thus smother the blast?

Or was it the final spasm of a terribly wounded, dying man?

Three U.S. defense secretaries in a row decided it was the latter and rejected the Marine Corps' recommendation that the Mexican-born sergeant be awarded the Medal of Honor.

For the better part of seven bitter years, his family refused to accept the esteemed, but still lower-ranking Navy Cross instead.

No winners here.

Everything about his fate just seems unfair. There he was, a young man born in Mexico City who moved to the United States to get away from the city's gang violence, and to attend school in San Diego, according to Jon Harper in the June 15, 2014, issue of *Stars and Stripes*.

"He enlisted in the Marine Corps in 2000 on the same day that he got his green card and later became an American citizen while on active duty," reported Harper.

Moreover, he loved his newly adopted country. "The U.S. Constitution, the Bill of Rights, and his Marine Corps graduation certificate—all neatly framed—adorned his bedroom wall at his family's home."

"Be proud of me, bro," he once wrote to younger brother Ricardo, "and be proud of being an American." (Ricardo later became a Marine himself.)

It wasn't long after he joined that Rafael Peralta was shipped out to Iraq as a member of the First Platoon, Company A, First Battalion, Third Marines, Regimental Combat Team 7, First Marine Division. Then, in late 2004, came the tough struggle for control of Fallujah, a major city in Iraq.

This was house-to-house urban warfare at its worst, and the day came when Sergeant Peralta volunteered for a house-clearing operation with "an undermanned squad of Marines." The very next morning, November 15, 2004, he and his squad members kicked in the door of a suspect house and burst in side.

It turned out to be a haven for insurgents, who of course exchanged fire with the Marines. "Peralta fell wounded. It was later determined that Peralta was likely hit by friendly fire." Just after he fell, a grenade tossed by the insurgents landed on the floor close to the stricken Marine's head.

Whatever really happened next is "the heart of the dispute over whether the fallen Marine deserves the Medal of Honor."

Five of the onlooking Marines later said he pulled the grenade into his body and smothered the explosion, likely sparing one or more of his fellow Marines from great harm or death. After reviewing the related documents and witness statements, Lt. Gen. Richard Natonski, commander of the First Marine Division at the time, recommended a posthumous Medal of Honor for Peralta.

However, a medical examiner who performed an autopsy on Peralta questioned whether the slain Marine could have pulled in the grenade consciously. "The head gunshot wound would have been immediately incapacitating and nearly instantly fatal," he explained in an email in April 2005, according to the *Stars and Stripes* account. He also said that "the shrapnel pattern on Peralta's body suggested that the grenade exploded 'a few feet' away from him."

Other medical personnel examining the autopsy report disagreed, saying perhaps Peralta really could have been able to pull in the grenade as a conscious act. In addition, the fuse from the grenade was found lodged in the victim's body armor, seeming to prove the grenade "did explode up against him."

In any case, as the nomination for the Medal of Honor made its way up the chain of command, the secretary of the Navy and then even Defense Secretary Robert Gates approved.

That is, until questions about the capability of the dying Peralta to make decisions or to control his movements also filtered to the top. Gates already had sent his recommendation on to the president, but now, he wrote in his memoir, *Duty: Memoir of a Secretary at War*, "I decided the only way to clear the air quietly was to ask a special panel to look into the allegation."

Consisting of a Medal of Honor recipient, a general officer with time spent in Iraq, a neurosurgeon, and a forensic pathologist, the panel "concluded unanimously that, with his wounds, Peralta could not have consciously pulled the grenade under him," Gates said. As a result, Gates wrote, "I had no choice but to withdraw my approval."

Both of his immediate successors in the Defense post, Leon Panetta and Chuck Hagel, also reviewed the case and came to the same conclusion. Panetta wrote Rep. Duncan D. Hunter, a Republican from the Marine's U.S. House district in California and himself veteran of the fighting in Fallujah, that the evidence in favor of the Medal failed to satisfy the "beyond-a-reasonable-doubt" criteria. And Hagel, issuing a press release on the issue, cited the "considerable medical and professional doubt" that Peralta could have acted consciously.

Ironically, the unfortunate Marine's posthumous Navy Cross citation assumes awareness on his part when it says that "with complete disregard for his own personal safety, Sergeant Peralta reached out and pulled the grenade to his body…"

Further complicating matters, two Marines who survived the fire-fight in Fallujah later said the story of his reaching for the grenade was made up by others in their squad. While still another Marine, Cpl. Robert Reynolds, told *Stars and Stripes*: "When I saw the grenade, I thought I was dead. Peralta swept it up underneath his body… I wouldn't be here today if he didn't do it."

Declaring the medical skeptics were "110 percent mistaken," Reynolds said Peralta "clearly deserves" the Medal of Honor. "I mean, there's Marines still alive today that he saved!"

Younger brother (and fellow Marine) Ricardo Peralta said the situation had been "really emotional" for the family, but added, "There's not a single decoration or medal that they can give him that will make us more proud. We're proud to the fullest."

Meanwhile, Congressman Hunter complained that the Department of Defense wasn't paying enough attention in general to the heroics of the men and women deployed in Iraq. "The Peralta case is representative of the lack of recognition by DOD of our combat men and women," he asserted.

In the same vein, Doug Sterner, chief archivist for the *Military Times* Hall of Valor website, complained that the total of "only" fifteen Medals of Honor awarded in the nation's various combats against terrorism up to 2015 "tells me how broken this [awards] system is."

Former Defense Secretary Gates seemed close to agreement when he wrote in his memoir: "Too few have been awarded in the wars in Iraq and Afghanistan, in which there have been so many heroic, selfless deeds. I once asked [former Army Chief of Staff Gen. Peter] Chiarelli why so few had been recommended. He said because medals had been passed out so freely in Vietnam, succeeding officers were determined to raise the bar. They had raised it too high, he thought."

This came after the Navy announced it would be naming a new destroyer the USS *Rafael Peralta* in honor of the Mexican-born Navy Cross winner.

In the meantime, the Peralta family's long insistence on the higher Medal of Honor finally ended as Marine Sergeant Rafael Peralta's mother Rosa—dabbing at tears, said the *Los Angeles Times*—accepted the lesser Navy Cross on behalf of her heroic son from Navy Secretary Ray Mabus at Camp Pendleton, California, in June 2015.

———

Additional Note: The debate among three Marines shooting the breeze at their outpost one day in Iraq was on how to smother an exploding hand grenade and yet survive. Cpl. Jason Dunham suggested covering it with the Kevlar helmet every Marine wore in combat.

Just weeks later, he had grim occasion to test his theory in person, and with no time for thought.

He probably saved the lives of two fellow Marines in the process, but he suffered fatal brain injuries. Thus, in 2004 he earned the first Medal of Honor granted an American infantryman since 1993, Michael M. Phillips reported in the *Wall Street Journal*. The award, presented to his parents by President George W. Bush, would be posthumous.

A corporal with the Seventh Marines (Reinforced) and Regimental Combat Team 7, Dunham was physically attacked by an unnamed "insurgent" in Karabilah, Iraq, on April 14, 2005. The Marine wrestled his assailant to the ground. As the same man released a grenade, Dunham alerted the men with him. He attempted to cover the grenade with his Kevlar helmet and his body, thus saving the lives of at least two Marine comrades. But he had suffered injuries that would take his life eight days later.

In October 2015, the Navy announced that it also would name a new U.S. destroyer the *Jason Dunham* in his honor, as well. And who knows, the day may come when the *Peralta* and the *Dunham* will sail together, two "Marines" reunited.

Another grenade-smothering Marine hero who could also be noted here: Pfc. Douglas E. Dickey from Rossburg, Ohio, fell upon an enemy grenade while fighting the Viet Cong in Vietnam in March of 1967, thus giving up his life to save fellow soldiers with him. His citation mentions only one grenade, but one of his companions later said he actually scooped a second grenade beneath his body, smiling and winking as he did so. That story, told by former Marine Jon Johnson of Sidney, Ohio, appeared in the January 2016 issue of *Military*.

NO LONGER DESK BOUND
BY INGRID SMYER

NO COMBAT *EVER* FOR WOMEN MARINES ALL THOSE YEARS BEFORE the Pentagon opened the door to combat roles for women in all the armed forces in late 2015?

Try telling that to Lance Cpl. Angelica Jimenez, almost killed in Iraq, June 25, 2005. Or to Gunny Sgt. Becky L. Morgan, one of the first Marines to serve in the liberation of Kuwait from Iraqi invasion in early 1990 (Desert Storm/Desert Shield). Or to Tracy Abernathy-Walden (rank unknown), who personally captured an Iraqi soldier during the latter operation.

Says Morgan on the *American Women in Uniform* website maintained by USAF Capt. Barbara Wilson (Ret.): "There have always been women in combat."

Morgan was a staff sergeant with Marine Air Control Group One (MACS 1) when it was deployed to the Persian Gulf for the short war in 1990 that liberated Kuwait. Despite warnings that the American military's host Arab countries would not take kindly to women filling so-called men's roles, Morgan went with her unit as its only military intelligence specialist.

"I donned my gear, my weapons, and a very concealing flak jacket," she said. "Ten days after the beginning of the war I was in country with my fellow Marines. I kept a low profile and did the job that I had trained with my unit for three years to do." She was one of the first women *in country* at the time, she says, but adds, "This passed without fanfare, without ceremony, and more women came."

Meanwhile, Abernathy-Walden was deployed from Beaufort, South Carolina, for the same Desert Storm/Desert Shield conflict with a unit of nearly five hundred men and exactly seventeen women. "Myself and five other women are among the 100 Marines that built the largest/longest runway in the history of organized military worldwide, and we did it twice!"

She gave no details on her capture of an Iraqi soldier, but also says of her deployment, "I had another Marine die in my arms, from nerve gas poisoning."

She alleges that her unit "took fire...a lot," but when the authorities passed out the U.S. Combat Medal, none of the unit's women received one, because women were not supposed to be in combat. Worse, the unit records "were changed to reflect only male Marines," she says.

As for Jimenez, she was yet another woman Marine subjected to combat conditions but a decade or so later, in Iraq. She was plain lucky, since three more women Marines were killed and eleven others wounded in the same combat incident that almost took her own life.

As a member of an all-female Marine unit assigned to search and question Iraqi women at security checkpoints near the frequently fought-over city of Fallujah, she and her companions were in a truck convoy the night of June 25, 2005, when a suicide bomber rammed his explosives-filled car into their vehicle.

Because the women Marines were not allowed to sleep overnight with their male comrades stationed at the checkpoints, "every day the women would be driven to and from an American base," reported Kristina Wong on ABC News. That made them "a visible target each time they hit the road. It was only a matter of time before their luck would run out, and that night, it did." For Jimenez, that meant months of hospitalization and rehabilitation for the burn injuries inflicted on her by the suicide bomber.

The further fact is, women supposedly deployed in supportive roles in the field, rather than straight-out combat, often can and will fall prey to combat injury or death anyway. Many American women from all services have died in Iraq and Afghanistan in the twenty-first century.

As Jimenez herself told ABC News, "Convoys are always dangerous, anything that involves going outside the base is dangerous…outside the base, those are all very much dangerous jobs."

The ABC News report by Wong also pointed out the Department of Defense acted in 1994 to adopt a combat exclusion policy prohibiting the assignment of women to any units below brigade level whose primary mission was direct ground combat. However, DOD spokesperson Eileen Lainez said the policy failed to "preclude women from being involved in ground combat."

Lainez also noted that in the warfare of recent years, specifically in Iraq and Afghanistan, there is not always a front line to go by.

Also interviewed was Afghanistan veteran Genevieve Chase, founder of American Women Veterans. She added: "In both Iraq and Afghanistan, female troops have worked from day one outside the wire. In war you do what you can. You can't withhold somebody because of their gender. If you are in charge of an aid station with three female medics, and this infantry unit needs another medic, you're sending them a medic."

As another detriment for women in the field, Chase noted that she served in the field along with men and carried the same weapons, but the 1994 DOD policy on women in combat kept her from having the same combat training as the infantrymen. "When women are attached to these ground infantry units, we are actually more vulnerable because we don't have the [same] level of training as the men we support," she said.

Then, too, when the Military Leadership Diversity Commission subsequently called for lifting the Pentagon ban on women in combat, the commission chairman, retired USAF Gen. Lester L. Lyles, said that ending the restriction would allow more qualified women to achieve higher leadership roles in the military. "Women serving in combat environments are being shot at, killed, and maimed," he also said, "but they're not getting the credit for being in combat arms."

A lot of issues here, both before and after the Pentagon's reversal of 2015, and not all of them resolved.

NOT-SO-LUCKY LIMA COMPANY

THE ONLY TROUBLE WITH BEING IN A CLOSELY BONDED RESERVE unit is the neighbors—those other guys and gals could be hometown neighbors, and if the unit goes down, that hits the hometown community hard…very hard.

That's what happened to Lima Company from the Columbus, Ohio, area in Iraq in 2005.

One minute—let's say January 2005—they were home doing their usual pursuits as teachers, lawyers, even college kids. The next—let's say, February—they were in refresher training in California. And finally— let's say, March—the same Lima Company was "part of the 1,000-strong Third Battalion, Twenty-Fifth Marines, Fourth Marine Division—3/25 in military lingo—and engaged in full-scale war," John Kiener and James Dao point out in the *New York Times* of August 7, 2005.

"The members of Lima Company are emblematic of the citizen soldiers who are bearing much of the weight of the fighting in Iraq," the pair added in the *Times*. "They were plucked from their daily routines as college students, office workers, and parents, and in a matter of months were facing down a rapidly shifting insurgency. Back at home, their relatives and friends are left deeply torn about the war and its toll on their families."

At home, too, the same citizen-soldiers "saw one another only occasionally, meeting for one weekend a month…and then going on drills for two weeks in the summer."

It's like that for reservists in the Navy, Army, Air Force, National Guard, and Air National Guard as well. "Stressed by the demands of the war, the military has had to rely heavily on reserve components like the

3/25," added the 2005 *Times* story. "Reservists make up about 35 percent of the American forces in Iraq, and the Marine Corps, which is the smallest fighting service, is particularly hard pressed."

The *Times* also said that of the 138,000 American troops in Iraq as of August 2005, hardly more than 23,000 were Marines...and yet they had made up more than 25 percent of the war's 1,820 Americans killed by the same date.

Lima Company was a rifle company, "mainly young Marines," noted Lt. Col. Kevin Rush from the Third Battalion headquarters staff. "They are the tip of the spear. And when you are at the tip, you are at the most dangerous part."

Even so, war or no war, Lima Company's first few weeks in Iraq "were so uneventful," said the *Times* writers, "that the company of about 160 Marines took on the name 'Lucky Lima.'"

Interestingly, the *Times* account also pointed out that they and their fellow Marines (as was often the case in Vietnam, as well) were "not fighting the way they were meant to." Added the *Times*, "They [the Marine Corps] are designed not as an army of occupation, but as a hard-hitting, light attack force that can seize and hold a beachhead until heavier forces arrive."

In the meantime, "Lucky Lima's" good fortunes were about to change in two separate and shocking blows—not only to the company and the battalion, but also to the community back home.

First, eight Lima members were killed in military operations in May. Bad enough, but then came the first week of August. "A horrific roadside explosion took the lives of fourteen Marines, including an entire squad of ten from Lima Company." Additionally, two days before that, six other Marines attached to the same battalion were killed in an ambush.

All told, forty-seven men from the battalion had been killed since May, Colonel Rush estimated. Twenty-three of them, according to Master Sgt. Stephen Walker, a Columbus police sergeant, were Lima Company members—neighbors back home, you might say.

What had happened? In May 2005, units of their Third Battalion took part in major operations along the so-called "Ho Chi Minh Trail" of Iraq, a "lawless corridor" in western Al Anbar Province suspected of serving as an infiltration route for fighters and supplies from Syria. The high death toll among the Ohio Marine reservists in August came during more sweeps against insurgents in the province—a toll clearly felt back home, where "From rural towns along the Ohio River to the crowded streets of Cleveland, Ohioans spontaneously lowered flags to half-staff and created makeshift memorials to commemorate the dead."

When the deaths among the full-time "regulars" fighting America's wars abroad are reported, in some way it's different. It's a statistic to many, and almost impersonal. Most don't know them personally. The regulars "come from all over the United States and serve on bases relatively isolated from the rest of the population," the *Times* writers remind us.

However, not so with the reservists. "Reserve units are more intimately entwined with local communities—training, working, and often living in the same town."

The shock and the grief of a casualty list are for a whole community to bear.

THE "TRUE WAR"

HE HAD A GUT FEELING THAT MORNING. "I KNEW WE WERE ABOUT to get hit." No particular reason, and not even a unique story…except that when it did happen to him, Jacob Schick, it was so very unique to him; it was the one and only time such a thing ever befell him, despite the fact that it did (and still does) happen to so many men and women in modern combat. Some die; the others often go home as the wounded. Their life goes on, but often as a struggle.

For many, the true war.

Jacob Schick lived in Bossier City, Louisiana, until moving to Texas at the age of twelve. He knew from age eight that he wanted to be a Marine.

A Marine grandfather had served in World War II, and an uncle then became a second generation Marine, writes Lance Cpl. David Staten. "Jacob signed up to enlist at the beginning of his senior year of high school in 2000 as a reservist. He went to boot camp a month after the September 11 attacks."

"I knew day one, when I stepped on the yellow footprints [at boot camp], that I was destined to be here at this moment in time," he later said.

Afterward came infantry school at Camp Pendleton, California, for training as a rifleman, followed by assignment to First Battalion, Twenty-Third Marines, and deployment to An Anbar Province in Iraq in 2004. "Before deployment, Schick thought he knew what teamwork and the 'one team, one fight' concept was all about, but he learned quickly he didn't. He fully grasped the idea through brotherhood, sacrifice, and suffering during his deployment in Iraq."

As Schick himself later explained, "The fact is, when we're at our highest high we're together, and when we're at our lowest low it's together. We did it as a family, as one unit. So I learned that I could depend [on] the Marine to my left and right no matter what."

Simply stated, "They are willing to die for me and I am willing to die for them. I think it goes without saying that is what makes us the best in the world."

In any case, as so often happens, then came the morning his unit received a reaction call. The night before had been busy, capturing two hostages and engaged in "a standoff that lasted well into the night."

His Marines had been sleeping for only half an hour—and he not at all—when they got the reaction call, writes Staten. "Schick went to where his Marines were sleeping and not quietly, but like a Marine, yelled and told them to get up and get ready because they had a mission."

Schick took a bomb blanket with him when he climbed into the driver's seat of the Humvee lead vehicle. "He put the bomb blanket down and had all his Marines put on their goggles, button up their neck protectors [and] groin protectors, and made sure their flak jackets were buttoned up before heading out."

He had that gut feeling; he just knew they were about to get hit.

"I was trying to do everything I could to make sure they were okay and to make me not a liar to nine Marines' families."

In just three minutes, they hit it: an improvised explosive device called a triple-stacked tank mine designed to blow up a tank. The front tire hit, and Schick went about thirty feet in the air after going through the top of the vehicle.

Never losing consciousness or going into shock, Schick remembers it all. "My left leg was broken with compound fractures, my right leg was broken, my foot was crushed, my left arm was broken with compound fractures, and one of my bones got blown out of my arm," he later told writer Michael Slenske of HBO's *Alive Day Memories: Home from Iraq*. He could also have added his collapsed lung and burn holes to the list of injuries.

Whatever the details, Schick apparently knew right away what had happened. "I was lying on the sand. I got blown from the Hummer. It pretty much blew up right beneath me."

Meanwhile, "His Marines started yelling his name and immediately got to him," adds Staten in his account. It took forty-two minutes, but a Black Hawk helicopter did arrive to pick him up. "During that time, Schick asked God to please not let his Marines see him die."

Indeed, Schick himself later told HBO's Slenske: "Everybody was just saying words of encouragement but I was pretty mad they were talking. They were just doing what Marines do. They were scared. I could tell by the look in their eyes they didn't think I was going to make it."

Carried first to a field hospital of tents, he was "put to sleep." He awoke in Recovery—his right leg below the knee gone, amputated.

His next stop was hospitalization in Germany, and then on to Walter Reed National Military Center in Bethesda, Maryland, where he was happy to see his family. "I remember thinking, 'I'm so relieved to be back in my country and so happy to be able to see my family again,'" he later said. "At that point in time, little did I know that my true war was about to begin."

This was a war he would be fighting as a new member of the great army of the wounded, not only Marines, but all services.

For his individual battle, Schick first spent three months at the Walter Reed facility, then another fifteen months at Brooke Army Medical Center in San Antonio, Texas. "Throughout his time in rehabilitation, Schick underwent forty-six operations [and] twenty-three blood transfusions and was diagnosed with post-traumatic stress disorder and traumatic brain injury," adds Staten's account of the young Marine's true war.

Schick had many tough lessons to learn along the way. Among them, the fact that physical wounds are one thing, but there are other wounds that "keep giving if you don't address them." Thus, "Physical pain reminds you that you are alive, but mental pain will test your will to stay that way."

His constant anguish came with a mix of painful thoughts. Anger was one source of his pain—he was angry not only at the enemy but also at himself, "because the guys he loved more than life itself were still in harm's way while he was disabled and dependent on an oxygen tank in a hospital bed." One could call it guilt, too.

Understandably, he felt helpless and then hopeless.

"He masked his depression through painkillers," adds Staten. He reached a point where he was just plain tired of fighting. "His soul was broken. He didn't answer phone calls, didn't talk to anyone including his doctor at the hospital. He started to increase doses of pills until he would pass out and continue the cycle for about three or four days."

He later said, "At that point I didn't care if I died or not."

However, others did. His fiancée, whom he had met at a hospital stop, took action and called his aunt. She flew to San Antonio to intervene, and with her help Schick didn't commit suicide. Yet, "he continued to abuse painkillers until late 2008." At one point Lauren, now his wife, told him, "The difference between you eating a bullet [and] living the way you are living now is time, but the outcome is the same. You're slowly killing yourself."

Luckily, the point got through. "Schick realized that he was not doing his Marines justice by the way he was living. He called his doctor in San

Antonio and told him he wanted to quit taking the medication. They started slowly weaning him off the drugs."

It wasn't easy. "I don't know what was worst, being blown up or coming off the drugs," he later said. "During that time when I was ultimately trying to better myself, I went through the hardest time. I've never been that ill in my life."

He again contemplated suicide "and told God he was done," adds Staten's account. "A couple of weeks later, though, Schick had detoxed to the point where he felt like had had never taken drugs before."

"I had won, but it was hell getting there," he said.

Still, there would be more steps to go. "For many who have suffered post-traumatic stress disorder and traumatic brain injury or any other forms of a mental impairment from bad experiences, it's hard for them to talk about," notes Staten. "Schick struggled with this for a long time. To him, talking about mental issues was not something he and many servicemembers did as warriors."

But the day came when his grandmother took him to her Rotary Club at Tyler, Texas, to speak about his experiences in his two wars, the one in Iraq and the other back home.

"I learned that telling my story was a way for me to heal, and that was a life-changing step for me," he said. "I [also] knew I was truly healing and truly starting to make strides in mental well-being when I started helping my fellow warriors." No mere platitudes, these were hard-earned realizations for Schick, who admittedly "had a lot of yelling matches with God and lost every one of them."

No longer a needy "soul-bleeder," he became a positive-thinking "soul feeder."

"For the warrior that can't hug their son, daughter, wife, husband, brother, or sister, or mom or dad again, I owe it to them," Schick said. "I owe it to them to live a magnificent life."

ADDITIONAL NOTE: IN RECENT YEARS, SCHICK HAS TAKEN PART IN THE nine-week rehab program offered by the Adaptive Training Foundation, "which uses modified training to empower athletes after the rehabilitation process," according to Staten. The ATF seeks to provide people with physical impairments the facilities and training needed to achieve movement and other health goals. Schick not only joined that group's governing board, he also became an advisory board member of 22kill, an organization that helps promote awareness of suicide prevention and related support for veterans. He also is a board member for the American War Heroes organization and a Warrior Training Specialist for the Center for Brain Health and Brain Performance Institute. Very obviously, he is dedicated to helping his fellow war veterans.

OBITUARY: FRANK E. PETERSEN JR.

A FUTURE THREE-STAR MARINE GENERAL, FRANK E. PETERSEN JR. was once arrested in California on suspicion of impersonating a lieutenant. Another time in Florida, he was ejected from a public bus for refusing to sit in the back. In Hawaii, he and his wife were denied permission to rent a house.

And yet, Frank E. Petersen Jr. persevered anyway, working his way right up to the top from his first days as a U.S. Navy seaman apprentice and electronics technician in 1950 to Naval Aviation cadet, to first black aviator in the Marine Corps, to first black brigadier general in the Marine Corps, to first black three-star general in Marine Corps history, to senior ranking aviator of all U.S. military services by the time of his retirement in 1988.

Along the same extraordinary route, Petersen was also the first black Marine to command units at all levels of Marine aviation, as he moved from squadron to wing and to air group commander.

Born in Topeka, Kansas, to a radio repairman and General Electric salesman father and a schoolteacher mother, Petersen was age nine at the time of the Pearl Harbor attack, December 7, 1941. At that young age, he didn't know what war was, but he already knew about racism. "I was scared," he once said, "but happy that it hadn't been black people who'd done it."

He had a sense of humor, too. His family, of course, always rooted for Joe Louis against a white opponent, because "where else but in the ring could a black man kick a white man's ass with impunity and walk away smiling with a pocket full of money."

As both a child and young military enlistee, even in pilot training, he kept running into racial rejection. The bus in Florida? They expected him to sit in the back with other black passengers. The rental home in Hawaii? The landlord later admitted turning him and his wife down because they were black.

Meanwhile, an instructor once flunked him in flight training and predicted he "would never fly," according his obituary in the *New York Times* of August 26, 2015. But he did earn his wings and he did fly— serving tours in Korea and Vietnam, he flew 350 combat missions, all told. On one of them, in Vietnam, 1968, his F-4 Phantom was shot down, but he bailed out safely.

In short time he would become the first black Marine "to command a fighter squadron (the famous Black Knights), an air group, and a major base," the *Times* adds in its obituary by Sam Roberts.

After thirty-eight years in military service, Petersen retired from the Corps in 1988 as a three-star lieutenant general. As Roberts also writes, "He was the senior ranking aviator in the Marine Corps and the Navy, commander of the Combat Development Command in Quantico, Virginia, and special assistant to the chief of staff. He was awarded the Distinguished Service Medal."

Back in 1969, he had been appointed a special assistant to the commandant for minority affairs. He sought to eradicate barriers facing recruits from different backgrounds.

The signs of racial progress can be subtle, Petersen once said. "As you go off base, look around. If you see a white kid and a black kid going off together to drink a beer, you know that you've achieved a degree of success."

In a 1998 autobiography written with J. Alfred Phelps, *Into the Tiger's Jaw: America's First Black Marine Aviator*, he noted racial relations in America had improved, "and the military, originally recalcitrant, had led the charge."

In the same book, Petersen stressed that the issues of promotions, job assignments and inappropriate punishments often were areas "where racism was likely to raise its ugly head," both in the past and even in more modern times.

Fellow black officers who followed the general up the chain of command in the Marines gave Petersen credit for the improved racial atmosphere. "The impact he had on the Marine Corps is more than can be put into words," Lt. Gen. Robert Coleman (Ret.), the second black general to reach three-star rank, told the *Marine Corps Times* in 2015.

That impact was "monumental," said Coleman, especially if you can think about "where he came from and what he had to go through." As Coleman further said, "He pulled, he pushed a lot of people just to make it, maybe not to be a captain, major, colonel, or general, but just to persevere."

He was "an inspiration to all those who followed in his footsteps," added retired Lt. Gen. Willie Williams in the obituary, yet another high-ranking black officer who emulated Petersen's upward climb into the Marine Corps hierarchy.

Petersen's impact was "extraordinary," Williams declared. "When you look at the history of the Marine Corps, once the services opened the door to desegregation, he was one of the first to step forward. His performance was truly top of the line. True performance is color blind: if you perform at the highest level, you're recognized for that, not as black or white, but as someone worthy to wear the stars."

General Petersen died at age eighty-three in his home at Stevensville, Maryland, of complications from lung cancer on August 28, 2015.

ADDITIONAL NOTE: IF FRANK PETERSEN WAS THE FIRST BLACK MARINE to reach general's rank, and there were no black Marines from the American Revolution to World War II, someone had to be the first African American recruit in 167 years. By most accounts, he was Howard P. Perry of Charlotte, North Carolina, a private from 1942 to 1944 who was assigned as a cook with the Fifty-First Defense Battalion, the first black outfit trained at Montford Point (page 200). He was the first recruit to arrive at the new training facility, it seems. On the other hand, Alfred Masters apparently was the first African American to *enlist* in the Marine Corps, when he did so at 12:01 a.m. June 1, 1942, at Oklahoma City. Meanwhile, there seems to be no argument that Edgar R. Huff became the Corps' first black NCO and Gilbert "Hashmark" Johnson the first black drill sergeant, both taken from the ranks at Montford Point.

In 2012, surviving members of the Montford Point Marines were awarded the Congressional Gold Medal, the nation's highest civilian honor, for their World War II service. Nearly thirteen thousand went into combat zones as Montford Point Marines, but barely three hundred still survived in 2012. Back in the 1940s, all would have been amazed not only by General Petersen's achievements as a Marine aviator and commander, but also by the fact that early in the twenty-first century a black general, Maj. Gen. Ronald Bailey, commanded the historic and vaunted First Marine Division.

SELECT PERSONALITY
LANCE CORPORAL SARAH RUDDER

BY INGRID SMYER

You can't put a good woman down, not when she's Lance Corporal Sarah Rudder, USMC (Ret.), indirect casualty of the 9/11 terrorist attacks on the World Trade Center and the Pentagon.

As living proof of that proposition, who was the winningest

competitor in the worldwide Invictus Games of 2016 for wounded warriors? None other than this former Marine, who came away with a total of seven medals in all—that total including the gold medal for the women's 100-meter dash. She won the foot race despite having lost the lower part of her left leg. She was helping to retrieve bodies and body parts from the damaged Pentagon when a concrete block crushed her foot.

She also won the women's lightweight power-lifting at the same Invictus Games of 2016, held in Orlando, Florida. She won gold or silver in rowing and swimming, as well.

Her silver medal in the 200-meter women's foot race came in dramatic style.

Just steps away from crossing the finish line first, she fell! Yet, after jumping to her feet to continue running, she still came in second, according to the ESPN Wide World of Sports Complex. "Receiving a standing ovation from the crowd, gold medal winner Marion Blot from France embraced her on the track," noted ESPN.

Said Rudder herself: "It's amazing. For me, it's the culmination of all the training and hard work and effort to get here."

She also was quoted as saying, "Sport saved my life. It showed me that I can do and be something, and that I can be a part of a community again."

Her performance at the Invictus Games, the creation of Britain's Prince Harry Windsor, was no onetime fluke. Just the year before, a Defense Department press release reported the "medically retired" Rudder won gold in the women's 50-meter and 100-meter freestyle swimming events and a silver in the women's 50-meter backstroke race in the 2015 Defense Department Warrior Games.

She also won a bronze in volleyball, a gold in the women's 100-meter dash on foot, and silvers in the women's shot put and discus throw.

The same press release explained that she had first hurt her left ankle in boot camp "and was on the path of healing when she re-injured it" as a result of the 9/11 terrorist attacks.

Rudder was serving at the Pentagon at the time, and she herself later explained: "I was put on a working party for search and rescue, and when I was pulling out non-survivors, I hurt my ankle again. I was running on adrenaline, and didn't feel anything at the time because I wanted to do as much as I could."

According to the DOD press release, "She underwent five surgeries and had pieces of bone tearing up the cartilage in her ankle, so doctors took cartilage from her knee and placed it in her ankle. She had metal rods put in, taken out, and so on, until the decision to remove her limb and give her a prosthetic leg."

That invasive surgery was in 2014, thirteen years after she suffered her crushing injuries.

The decision, she later said, gave her new freedom. "I feel like I can challenge myself again and be an athlete, but it's been a challenge to run on it," she admitted.

But she obviously learned to adapt…and more.

Don't discount "wounded warriors," she says. "We're still human, and we're pushing ourselves against other people who have the same injuries, because we are making ourselves feel whole and normal again."

Rudder, from Irvine, California, enlisted in the Marine Corps as an administrative specialist in July 2000. After leaving the Marine Corps due to her injuries, she earned bachelor's degrees in paralegal and criminal studies.

Obviously happy with her performance at the Invictus Games in 2016, she said, "It shows that just because I'm an amputee doesn't mean that I can't go out and put out my heart and soul on the track or any event that I can do."

THE PRESIDENT TELLS A STORY

IF ANY SINGLE MEDAL OF HONOR WINNER OF RECENT TIMES MIGHT be considered a bit more "gutsy" than his fellow winners, it could be Marine Sgt. Dakota Meyer of Marine Embedded Training Team 2–8 and Afghanistan fame.

As the story goes he told the White House to please call back during lunch-hour break, before saying to the president, let's have a beer together the day before Meyer's elaborate presentation ceremony at the White House.

In any case, Dakota Meyer was only the third American to win the Medal—and live—in the Iraq or Afghanistan wars of the twenty-first century. At age twenty-one, he also was one of the youngest American fighting man to earn the Medal in decades.

His story, as told by none other than President Barack Obama at the White House presentation, is all about the day Meyer went back into a killing zone five times in quick succession to rescue trapped, even fallen and dead comrades. As Obama began the story, just imagine it's minutes before dawn in Kunar Province, Afghanistan, on September 8, 2009: "A patrol of Afghan forces and their American trainers is on foot, making their way up a narrow valley, heading into a village to meet with elders."

Then, suddenly, the lights in the village of Ganjgal "go out." Gunfire erupts. It's a Taliban ambush.

"About a mile away [at a patrol rallying point], Dakota, who was then a corporal, and Staff Sergeant Juan Rodriguez-Chavez could hear the ambush over the radio. It was as if the whole valley was exploding. Taliban fighters were unleashing a firestorm from the hills, from the stone houses, even from the local school."

With the patrol pinned down and taking "ferocious" fire from three sides, "Men were being wounded and killed, and four Americans— Dakota's friends—were surrounded."

He and Sergeant Rodriguez-Chavez, a fellow Marine, asked permission to go in and help.

345

Four times, they asked.

Four times, permission denied. They were told it was too dangerous.

So what did they do? With four of their Embedded Team comrades trapped, along with two platoons of Afghan National Army and border police, that apparently was a no-brainer. They went in anyway.

"Juan jumped into a Humvee and took the wheel; Dakota climbed into the turret and manned the gun," Obama said. "They were defying orders, but they were doing what they thought was right. So they drove straight into the killing zone, Dakota's upper body and head exposed to a blizzard of fire from AK-47s and machine guns, from mortars and rocket-propelled grenades."

Bouncing down a terraced hillside in their gun truck, they first came upon wounded Afghan soldiers. Meyer jumped out and "loaded" each one into the vehicle, fully exposed to enemy fire the whole time. "They turned around and drove those wounded back to safety."

That was not the end. "Dakota and Juan would have been forgiven for not going back. But, as Dakota says, you don't leave anyone behind."

So, back they went—"back into the inferno."

Again it was Rodriguez-Chavez at the wheel, "swerving to avoid the explosions all around them." Again Dakota up in the turret—"when one gun jammed, grabbing another, going through gun after gun."

This second time they found more wounded Afghans, loaded them up—under fire again—and brought them back to safety.

The third trip brought another storm of fire, but now with "insurgents running right up to the Humvee," Obama related before a jammed crowd in the historic East Room at the White House, where Abigail Adams once hung the wash, where assassinated Presidents Lincoln and Kennedy had lain in state. Included were an estimated 120 Meyer family members; Embedded Training Team 2–8 members; previous Medal of Honor winners; members of Congress, including Senate Republican Majority Leader Mitch McConnell from Meyer's home state of Kentucky; Cabinet members; and military leaders, including Marine Corps Commandant Gen. James Amos.

All were there, as Obama said, "to pay tribute to an American who placed himself in the thick of the fight—again and again and again."

Obama also reminded his listeners this was "only the third time during the wars in Afghanistan and Iraq that a recipient of the Medal of Honor has been able to accept it in person."

The president drew a laugh when he related how before the presentation Meyer told the White House staff to call back during his lunch hour break at a construction job. The staff was calling, "so I could tell him that I'd approved this medal." The Marine Corps hero felt he couldn't take the call right then, because, he said, "If I don't work, I don't get paid."

The staff went along with his wishes and called him back at the appointed time. That's when Obama also got on the phone. "I told him the news, and then he went right back to work. That's the kind of guy he is. He also asked to have beer with me, which we were able to execute yesterday."

According to ABC News, they shared the beer on a patio just off the Oval Office the evening before the Medal presentation, a "White House brewed honey ale beer." As they chatted, the young veteran, now a civilian, asked Obama, "What would you do if you were 23 years old and in my shoes right now?"

"Get an education," the president had said, as Meyer himself related later in the same ABC segment. "You've got to have something you can fall back upon." He went on to say, "Don't make any rash decisions. Take your time."

But first would come the Medal presentation the very next day, September 15, 2011. At the White House, Obama went on with his story of Meyer's five trips into the inferno of fire in a small valley almost exactly two years before in distant Afghanistan.

On the third foray into the kill zone, Rodriguez-Chavez deliberately "wedged the Humvee right into the line of fire, using the vehicle as shield." This time it was a group of Americans, "some wounded," that desperately needed rescue. "With Dakota on the guns, they helped those Americans back to safety as well."

But the intrepid pair wasn't done yet. They still had not reached four of their team members. "Dakota was now wounded in the arm. Their vehicle was riddled with bullets and shrapnel. Dakota later confessed, 'I didn't think I was going to die. I knew I was.' But still they pushed on…"

Four times, then a fifth, they charged back into the fray, changing gun trucks and their machine guns a couple of times in the rescue operation. As Obama put it, they charged back into "the fury of that village, under fire that seemed to come from every window, every doorway, every alley."

That last time, they finally reached an ominously slumped group of four Americans. "Dakota jumped out. And he ran toward them. Drawing all those enemy guns on himself. Bullets kicking up the dirt all around him. He kept going until he came upon those four Americans, laying where they fell, together as one team."

Meyer and others who also braved the gunfire "knelt down, picked up their comrades and—through all the bullets, all the smoke, all the chaos—carried them out, one by one." Because, as Dakota says, "That's what you do for a brother.'"

The four dead were their own team members.

The President of the United States stopped his story-telling to identify the four Americans whose bodies Meyer and Company risked their own lives to retrieve, along with a badly wounded man still living.

"Dakota says he'll accept this medal in their name," Obama said. "So today, we remember the husband who loved the outdoors—Lieutenant Michael Johnson. The husband and father they called 'Gunny J'—Gunnery Sergeant Edwin Johnson. The determined Marine who fought to get on that team—Staff Sergeant Aaron Kenefick. The medic who gave his life tending to his teammates—Hospitalman Third Class James Layton. And a soldier wounded in that battle who never recovered—Sergeant First Class Kenneth Westbrook."

Winding up his presentation remarks on that somber note, Obama told young Meyer, "I know that you've grappled with the grief of that day; that you've said your efforts were somehow a 'failure' because your teammates didn't come home."

But not so, the president declared. "As your commander in chief, and on behalf of everyone here and all Americans, I want you to know it's quite the opposite. You did your duty, above and beyond, and you kept the faith with the highest traditions of the Marine Corps that you love."

In addition, Obama pointed out, "Because of your honor, thirty-six men are alive today." Not only that, "four fallen American heroes came home and—in the words of James Layton's mom—they could lay their sons to rest with dignity."

———

Additional Note: Marine Corps hero Dakota Meyer was born and raised in Columbia, Kentucky. He enlisted in the Marine Corps in 2006 after graduation from Green County High School and served in Iraq as a scout sniper before his posting to Afghanistan with Embedded Training Team 2–8. After co-authoring a book, *Into the Fire: A First-Hand Account of the Most Extraordinary Battle in the Afghan War*, with writer Bing West, he reappeared in the news in early 2015 with the announcement that he was engaged to Bristol Palin, daughter of former vice presidential candidate and Alaska Governor Sarah Palin. Two months later, their wedding plans were called off. But in mid-2016, they turned up married after all.

WOMEN IN COMBAT AUTHORIZED
By Ingrid Smyer

The headlines shouted their news: Marines Reignite Debate on Women in Combat! (*The Hill*, June 25, 2016) Marines Gear Up for Women in Combat, But Will They Sign Up? (*National Public Radio* online, March 28, 2016).

And yes, new debate, new issues, arose the moment the Pentagon reversed field late in 2015 to allow women of any military service to enter ground combat units with the men who had been there from day one. It was Defense Secretary Ash Carter who made the announcement in December, saying combat jobs would be open to women without exception.

The debate on the role of women in warfare quickly focused on the Marine Corps. With a total membership of 184,200 members as of early 2016, the Marines had been operating for years with the lowest percentage of women among all American military services: just 7 to 8 percent.

Given the spur of Carter's announcement, the Corps quickly aimed for 10 percent instead. "I've told them [his recruiters] that 10 percent is where we want to go, and they're working on it," Marine Corps Commandant Gen. Robert B. Neller told the *New York Times*. "Go recruit more women. Find them. They're out there."

But the *Times* headline told the back story also making news in the wake of the landmark Pentagon decision on women in combat: "…Marines Turn to High School Sports teams." (*New York Times*, August 13, 2016).

In brief, "the ladies" were not flocking to the recruiting stations by the thousands to sign up for newly opened combat roles in armor, artillery, or infantry. Furthermore, many of those who did sign up were failing the new physical tests required to undertake combat training.

Six out of seven women who took the new physical fitness tests failed them, the Associated Press reported in June 2016. The tests call upon them to run three miles in less than 24:51 minutes, lift a thirty-pound weight sixty times in succession, run half a mile in combat boots in less than 3:26 minutes, and to perform six pull-ups, among other demands.

Meanwhile, *National Public Radio* (NPR) reported the Marines completed ground combat training in 2015 for two hundred women as an experiment, but in the immediate aftermath none wanted to switch into infantry from their ongoing assignments "ranging from truck drivers to comptrollers to helicopter refuelers."

In the same report, NPR also cited the unhappy results when Marine Capt. Ray Kaster led an infantry company including women on a training exercise in the Mojave Desert. "Male and female Marines ran across the sand, shooting at pop-up targets," said NPR's David Gilkey. "It was part of the effort to see if women could make it in the unforgiving world of ground combat. Living in the dirt, carrying a pack weighing more than 100 pounds."

The unhappy result was that "the physical demands cost Kaster about half of the women in his company."

Kaster's explanation: "'The majority of those were injuries,' he says, citing hip and leg injuries, including fractures."

Calling the injury rates "very high," Kaster said, "There are absolutely female Marines out there that can do the job. The concern I have as a leader is how long can that be sustained?"

The outlook for women Marines in combat remained a hot topic on Capitol Hill in Washington as well. According to *The Hill*, the Marines were the only military branch to request some exemptions from Secretary Carter's announcement opening the doors to combat roles for women. The Marines Corps cited "a study it conducted that found mixed-gender combat units did not perform as well as male-only units," the Capitol Hill newspaper said.

One outspoken critic of the women-in-combat decision was Republican Rep. Duncan Hunter from California, the first Marine combat veteran from both Iraq and Afghanistan to reach the halls of Congress as a member. He said the fitness test results were no surprise. "This is what happens when you have a military decision made for political ends," he asserted. "Men and women are physically different."

He predicted it's just a matter of time before the physical standards are lowered to meet "purely political" goals.

On the other hand, Rep. Jackie Speier, a California Democrat, offered the alternate view that "it's important to make sure both men and women meet certain physical requirements before sending them into combat, but it's equally important that women be given the opportunity to pursue combat service careers."

Whatever the outcome of the Hunter-Speier argument, the Marines were in the meantime scrambling to meet the goal of raising their percentage of women to 10 percent, but at the same time, to find physically fit women. Thus, as the *Times* reported in August of 2016, "Marine recruiters are turning to high school girls' sports teams to find candidates who may be able to meet the corps' rigorous physical standards, including for the frontline combat jobs now open to women."

Major Gen. Paul Kennedy, leading the Corps' recruiting effort, male or female, told the *Times* that the Marines were mailing recruitment literature to thousands of high school girls for the first time. In addition, new advertising would show active-duty female Marines doing their jobs on the battlefield.

Commandant Neller himself acknowledged it still would be an "adjustment" for men in the Marines to have women join their units. "I think a lot of the talk is more just maybe they're nervous about the unknown," he said. "But there are some things we're going to have to work through."

With apparently few physically qualified women clamoring for combat roles, recruiting chief Kennedy articulated yet another task still ahead for the Marines: to show prospective women recruits "that it's not a good ol' boys club anymore when you talk about career issues." *Still* there are a lot of issues here, both before and after the Pentagon's reversal of 2015, and not all of them are resolved.

"MARINES GOOD!"

THE MARINES OF YORE WOULD NOT RECOGNIZE THIS HIGH-TECH war. Imagine a high aerostat balloon, plus a towering shaft implanted in the Afghanistan soil. Each is equipped with swiveling TV cameras, each remotely controlled from the ground, and each providing live video feeds. There's a COC (Combat Operations Center), where the feed is displayed on one or more screens. And soon pictured are the bad guys, perhaps four of five of them, out on the trails, usually around dusk, planting their IEDs (Improvised Explosive Devices) or EID (Electrically Initiated Devices).

This unique war is Marines against the four or five bad guys, and their IEDs.

Lieutenant Colonel Seth Folsom's "Cutting Edge Battalion" (Third Battalion, Seventh Regiment) and its 1,200 or so enlisted men and officers had only just begun a combat tour, 2011–2012, in Afghanistan's dangerous Sangin District. Two men had already lost legs or feet to IEDs, and one had been killed by an EID that blew up in his face while he was looking down. Yet another would lose both legs and an arm before he died under emergency medical treatment at a base hospital.

"The improvised explosive devices that littered Sangin's trails and alleys—and the hideous casualties they inflicted on my Marines—preoccupied my mind most of my waking hours," Folsom writes in his 2015 book, *Where Youth and Laughter Go: With the "Cutting Edge" in Afghanistan*. "Troubling visions of my men being evacuated with shattered and missing limbs clouded the few hours of sleep I got each night. Eventually sleep escaped me altogether… I often lay awake in the darkness, dwelling on the mounting casualties and struggling to find a solution to the buried bombs that were maiming my men."

Another of those would be Sergeant Kyle Garcia, who blew off his left leg below the knee when he stepped on an IED, then shouted "Stop!" to his patrol comrades when they rushed forward to help him.

Stop! because they themselves could step on other hidden IEDs.

"Sweep your way up here," he ordered while reaching for the tourniquet sleeve that all the Marines carried while on combat patrol.

"The Marines halted in their tracks and patiently advanced toward him, the flat search head of the point man's metal detector gliding rhythmically back and forth like a metronome," adds Folsom's account. Garcia assumed he was going to die, "but as he cinched the tourniquet around what remained of his leg, he calmly guided his men toward his position."

They reached the stricken sergeant safely enough. But after he was quickly carried away by a medical evacuation helicopter (he survived),

Folsom also notes his comrades found two more IEDs, both carefully placed "to target first responders." Thankfully, they had followed Garcia's warning to go slow. Thus, by "placing their safety above his own, Garcia averted further disaster among his men."

Naturally, Folsom was "heartsick" to hear of his battalion's latest casualty, but Garcia's "actions after he was wounded flabbergasted me," he writes. "*Where*, I thought in amazement, *do we get such men?*"

Not just Garcia, but so many of them who keep going out on patrol and other duties every day, knowing the risk.

Fewer than ten days later, the risk to responders, first or otherwise, really came home to roost. A mortar man in Folsom's Weapons Company lost his right leg when he stepped on a booby trap. As an EOD (Explosive Ordnance Disposal) team conducted a post-blast analysis, one of the EOD members "initiated a hidden secondary device that tore off both of his legs below the knee."

On the better days, the Marines and the high-tech weaponry at their disposal did take the war to the Taliban insurgents first. The Cutting Edge Battalion did have its Eyes in the Sky—sometimes a drone, sometimes the aerostat balloon, sometimes the tall shaft at a home base.

One day in October of 2011, Folsom was called into the COC because one of the battalion's out-flung companies had spotted "several armed individuals burying explosives and connecting the wiring and pressure plates to trigger the devices."

The balloon cameras had been swiveled to the scene. "I scanned the television screen in front of me."

"Any civilians around?"

The answer was no, "Area is clear."

"Roger that," Folsom said, giving the video screen one last look. "Attention in the COC: I have positive identification of hostile act and hostile intent."

His assembled COC staff began final coordination for a Hellfire missile strike from a Predator drone circling overhead. "Once the target was in the drone's crosshairs, the air officer looked at me.

"'*Fire,*' I said."

In moments the missile was on its way. "We watched the feed intently, but at the last second the crouching fighters dropped everything and took off running in all directions. An instant later the Hellfire detonated in a white flash where the men had squatted. The insurgents had done their homework. The noise of the missile leaving the rails had tipped them off, and they knew to bolt as soon as they heard it."

Was it considered a totally failed attack?

Maybe not, it seems. As the video feed widened, "we saw several figures load a limp human form into a waiting white Corolla. The automobile inserted itself into an organized procession of motorcycles and sped south on Route 611."

That's the way the Marine response often went, even when the bad guys were actually seen burying their booby traps. Usually, it would be two or three doing the work while a watcher or two kept an eye—and an ear—out for a possibly lethal response coming out of nowhere. It could be a missile strike, helicopter gunships, even jet fighters streaking in suddenly.

But so, so often, the results of the response by all the high tech and very expensive hardware were so meager.

Throughout his battalion's deployment, Folsom comments, "We would observe similar evacuations of wounded enemy personnel. Somehow a white Corolla or a motorcycle always turned up to extricate the wounded fighters from the battlefield."

Fighting back long distance against the IED-planters this way was frustrating for the Marines, especially when they saw the distant insurgent forms melt among obvious civilians. Attacking whenever there was a single civilian at risk was a strict no-no, not only for obvious humanitarian reasons but also because a dead civilian, accident or not, fostered resentment and more insurgents to deal with down the road.

Meager results notwithstanding, not all was lost on occasions like the October episode that Folsom describes. "The insurgency's consistent ability to recover its dead or wounded astounded us," he writes, "but despite our collective frustration the interdiction [that day] was not a complete failure. We had eliminated at least one bad guy, and early the next morning India Company launched a patrol to the strike scene to conduct a battle damage assessment (BDA). Once on scene, the Marines discovered six IEDs in mason jars daisy-chained together."

What could be Folsom's conclusion? "With that evening's interdiction I finally realized the only way we would remove the insurgents and the IEDs from the battlefield: one at a time."

And true, in twenty-first-century Afghanistan, rare were the set battles, the hot firefights.

Worse than merely discouraging, war was hell for the slain, the wounded, the loved ones back home, and of course their fellow Marines on the line doing their daily patrols.

Still, looking back later on his time in Afghanistan (he had served earlier in Iraq, as well), Folsom would recall one wintertime patrol in particular that "captured the full range of emotions during the seven months of heartache, joy, terror, and hope in Sangin."

Going out the gate at home base that chill morning, he and his Marines crossed over a "battered" concrete bridge already hit by IEDs three times but still standing. They passed a waiting throng of disheveled children who yelled, "Hey, Marine!" or "Fuck you, motherfucker!"

All too soon, while crossing a canal, they heard "the deep bass echo" of another IED explosion. Folsom and his companions waited for the casualty report that would come by radio.

Finally, it came in. Relief. The victim was a lance corporal who once had chided the colonel himself for stepping off a freshly "swept" pathway. The corporal had suffered only shrapnel wounds to his leg and hand.

On with the patrol.

"As the patrol competed its twisting route past a small village, the chill morning air thawed."

Ahead were four young boys taking turns flying a small kite.

This was surprising. When the Taliban began to rule Afghanistan, kite flying was forbidden.

Struck by the sight of four innocents simply playing, Folsom stopped to watch. "What could be more natural?" he thought. Four boys without a care, totally absorbed in who got the kite next. "They didn't stop to beg for chocolate or pens, they didn't hurl obscenities at us. And then I wondered what kind of life lay before them. Would a buried IED meant for the Marines obliterate one of them? Would crossfire between the insurgents and the Afghan forces gun one of them down? Would one of them—would *all* of them—finally run out of hope and join the ranks of the Taliban?"

None of the above, not just then.

As Folsom stood to leave, the children caught his stare. He stood still as they looked at him in his gear and body armor, "an armed, Kevlar-draped creature from anther civilization."

Then, "one by one they held their hands aloft and gave me the thumbs-up sign."

Hope redeemed!

"In that brief sanguine moment I had one thought, one hope: maybe they realized we were the reason they were able to fly their kite in the first place."

Finally came the icing on the cake. "'Marines good,' said one, grinning broadly. The others followed suit, calling in unison, 'Marines good!'"

BOOT CAMP CENTENNIAL

THE PLACE IS AN ISLAND FOUR MILES LONG AND THREE WIDE, WITH only 3,200 of its 8,000 acres on dry ground and barely 21 feet above sea level. It is surrounded by salty tidal marshes—mud flats when the tide is out—for as far as the eye can see, consisting of pluff mud famous for its suction power. Alligators live there, and in the waters beyond are sharks.

It offers no easy escape and few distractions.

Yet, the tidal marshes and their shimmering waters can be beautiful at times, glinting in the sun, even in moonlight, and lined as they are by palmetto trees, high aquatic grasses, or live oaks with dangling Spanish moss.

Once accessible only by boat, today the island is approached by a two-lane, three-mile causeway and bridge.

For more than a hundred years, this has been that place, dreaded by many, called Boot Camp; more formally known these days as the Marine Corps' East Coast recruit training facility at Parris Island, next to Port Royal, South Carolina.

It is also the Corps' oldest major base.

"The buildings have morphed over the years—from tents to Quonset huts, to modern brick barracks and stately historical landmarks—but Parris Island has remained a constant for Marines," writes Chief Warrant Officer Randy Gaddo, USMC (Ret.) in the October 2015 issue of *Leatherneck* magazine.

The Marine Corps celebrated 2015 as the Parris Island centennial because October 25, 1915, was the date upon which the recruit depot there was separated from an early officer's school "and was established as Marine Barracks, Port Royal, South Carolina, with the mission of training enlisted Marine recruits." (Meanwhile, West Coast recruits who had been trained at Mare Island Naval Shipyard, Vallejo, California, were shifted to San Diego for recruit training as of 1923.)

Back at the century-old Parris Island facility, for many years the young recruits arrived only by ferry from the Port Royal docks. The palmetto-lined causeway and bridge over Archer's Creek didn't come into existence until 1929, "ending an era of water transportation to the island," Gaddo noted. In another change, the recruits during the years 1915 to 1965 arrived by way of the tiny Yemassee (South Carolina) train station.

"I remember the chaos, the screaming and the doe-eyed look on every recruit's face as orders were being yelled out by the young non-coms waiting for us at the station," said Vietnam-era veteran Marine Mark Figroul in an interview cited by Gaddo.

"This was my first true glimpse of the Corps," said Figroul. "This is where it all began for myself and many others."

Another nostalgic memory came from retired Master Gunnery Sgt. George Hijar, of Wilmington, Delaware, who arrived at Yemassee at 6:30 a.m. one day in 1961. "They got us off at the train station and took us to a restaurant for a breakfast of scrambled eggs, bacon, and grits," he said. "I didn't even know what grits were, but I ate them. Then they put us on a bus for Parris Island. At the gate they stopped and a drill instructor got on. He didn't say anything; he just glared at us."

Hijar also recalled there were no yellow footprints greeting recruits inside the gates to Parris Island, as there are today. "The imprints in platoon formation with heels touching and feet at a 45-degree angle now mark the legendary place where the recruits got off the bus," Gaddo explains in *Leatherneck* magazine.

The yellow footprints came into existence in January 1965. "To this day, upon a recruit's arrival to Parris Island, they are ordered off of the bus, or van, and instructed to stand on the yellow footprints, where they get their first taste of recruit training with a speech from a receiving drill instructor," notes the Parris Island Centennial website.

As another distinction for the old Marine base—and onetime U.S. Navy facility—it is today the only place in the world where women are trained to be enlisted United States Marines. In related fact, a woman Marine, Brig. Gen. Loretta E. Reynolds, served in "command of the entire training depot and the Eastern Recruiting Region, [which is] responsible for finding young men and women east of the Mississippi River who have the mettle to be Marines," Gaddo also wrote. Reynolds was the Parris Island CO from 2013 to 2014.

"It is amazing what our recruiters and drill instructors can do with somebody who has the heart to be a Marine," she remarked before moving on to a new assignment at the Pentagon.

But then, that's what it says on the sign hanging across Boulevard de France, the main road on Parris Island, boldly and simply: "We Make Marines."

AND NEVER TO BE FORGOTTEN...

As double trouble for Marine Corps enemies, these two officer-veterans of World War II came from Vermont, started military life as U.S. Army privates, joined the Marine Corps, served in Nicaragua, won Navy Crosses for valor there, served in Shanghai with the vaunted Fourth Marines, and then led the Corps' first two Raider battalions in the fight against the Japanese on Guadalcanal.

One served as a police chief in Nicaragua and the other became commissioner of the Vermont State Police late in life. And each reached flag rank.

The oldest of the pair, **Evans F. Carlson**, was born in 1896 in Sydney, New York, but later, as a teenager, lived in Vermont. He ran away from home at age fourteen and joined the Army two years later. He remained in the Army through World War I, reaching the rank of captain in the field artillery and earning a Purple Heart.

His compatriot, **Merritt A. ("Red Mike") Edson**, was born in 1897 in Rutland, Vermont, but grew up in Chester. A college boy for two years and then a private with the Vermont National Guard (Army), he briefly was sent to duty on the Mexican border. Edson then became the first of the two to join the Marine Corps—as a reservist in 1917. Soon earning a commission, he was deployed to France with the Eleventh Marines, but too late to see combat in World War I.

Carlson, in the meantime, joined the Marines as a private in 1922 but also earned his commission soon after. He briefly attended naval flight school at Pensacola, Florida, as did his compatriot Edson, but neither one finished the training needed to become an authorized aviator.

Both were soon posted to Nicaragua, where Edson fought twelve engagements against the Sandino insurgents in 1928 and 1929 and earned a Silver Star for valor. Carlson, for his part, followed in 1930 to 1933, earning a Silver Star of his own and serving as chief of police with Nicaragua's *Guardia Nacional*. Each then spent time as an officer with the Fourth Marines in Shanghai, China, where each made it a point to observe Japanese tactics in their war against the Chinese.

Carlson, after first spending time with the Marine detachment assigned to President Franklin D. Roosevelt's "Little White House" at Warm Springs, Georgia, traveled for weeks in the late 1930s with Chinese Communist guerillas on foot and by horseback as they fought the Japanese. He came to know the Red Chinese leaders Mao Zedong and Zhou Enlai.

By now, Edson had spent quality time as an ordnance officer, plans and training officer, and as captain of the Marines' national rifle and pistol teams of the mid-1930s. He was assigned as commander of the First Battalion, Fifth Marines, and remained at the unit's helm as it was redesignated the Corps' First Separate Battalion shortly after Pearl Harbor and then, still early in 1942, as the First Marine Raider Battalion.

He won acclaim, along with a Gold Star in lieu of a second Navy Cross, when his Raiders and the Second Battalion, Fifth Marines, captured Tulagi in the British Solomons after two days of tough fighting in early August of 1942 as prelude to the First Marine Division's landing on nearby Guadalcanal. Not to be outdone, Carlson had been placed in command of the Corps' Second Raider Battalion by this time. Just before Pearl Harbor, he had briefly resigned from the Marines to write and lecture on his predictions that Japan was preparing for war beyond China's borders. Now, in mid-August of 1942, he led a raid—by rubber boats launched from submarines—on Japanese-held Makin Island with heavy casualties to both sides. He also earned a gold star in lieu of a second Navy Cross, in his case for "personally directing his forces" in the face of "intense fire of enemy ground troops and aerial bombing barrage." The same daring raid was described in his citation as "the first operation of this type ever conducted by United States forces."

Also awarded a Silver Star for the same action was Carlson's good friend, and the battalion's executive officer, **James Roosevelt**, son of President Roosevelt.

Next for both Raider battalion leaders Edson and Carlson would be the six-month battle to oust the Japanese from Guadalcanal, where Carlson would earn a third Navy Cross and Edson the esteemed Medal of Honor.

But this came after September of 1942, and the equally noteworthy heroics of Edson and his First Raider Battalion on Guadalcanal. Edson's "crowning glory and the battle for which he will be long remembered by Marines and a grateful American people was the defense of Lunga Ridge," notes his official online Marine Corps biography.

Edson's Raiders and two companies of the First Parachute Battalion had been sent to a ridge line south of the vital Henderson airfield, supposedly for a short rest out of the direct line of fire. On the night of September 13, however, the Japanese picked his ridge for a sudden and overwhelming attack that penetrated the left center of his line of resistance and forced a withdrawal to a reserve position. "Here approximately 800 Marines withstood the repeated assaults of more than 2,500 Japanese on the 'Bloody Ridge,' as it became known to the world."

To his own men, it always would be "Edson's Ridge," due to Edson's unflagging efforts all during the engagement to encourage his men, while repeatedly exposing himself to enemy fire. "By his astute leadership and gallant devotion to duty," says his Medal citation, "he enabled his men, despite severe losses, to cling tenaciously to their position on the vital ridge, thereby retaining command not only of the Guadalcanal airfield, but also of the First Division's entire offensive installations in the surrounding area."

Edson went on to serve as chief of staff for the Second Marine Division and the Fleet Marine Force, Pacific before retiring at age fifty as a major general after thirty years of military service. He next organized the Vermont State Police as the agency's first commissioner, then headed the National Rifle Association before dying, a suicide, in 1955.

Carlson, for his part, earned a third Navy Cross at Guadalcanal. He was noted for his Raider battalion's monthlong (November 4–December 4, 1942) "Long Patrol" behind Japanese lines that resulted in nearly five hundred of the enemy killed. Carlson, who had given the Marines their motivational term "Gung Ho," briefly returned to the United States from Guadalcanal for treatment of malaria and jaundice. He recuperated in time to serve with his fellow Marines in the battle to seize Tarawa and to suffer a wound in the invasion of Saipan while attempting to rescue an enlisted radio operator from a forward post.

In 1946, the lasting effects of his wound forced him into retirement with the rank of brigadier general. He died from heart disease just a year later. During the war years, he also had found time to serve as technical adviser for the 1943 movie, *Gung Ho! The Story of Carlson's Makin Island Raiders*.

Before war's end, the Marine Corps dropped its Raiders designation altogether, but not their proud legacy. By then, both the pioneering Carlson and Edson battalions and two sister battalions had been merged into a single First Raider Regiment. And now it would become the nucleus—a newborn Fourth Marines Regiment in place of the ill-fated Fourth that disappeared at the time of the General Wainwright's surrender of the Bataan Peninsula.

His Letter of Commendation from the commanding general, Fleet Marine Force, Pacific, cites this Marine's "meritorious and efficient performance of duty while serving with a Marine infantry battalion during operations against the enemy on Vella Lavella and Bougainville, British Solomon Islands, from 15 August to 15 December 1943, and on Iwo Jima, Volcano Islands, from 19 February to March 27 1945." But that doesn't nearly tell the whole story.

Private Ira Hamilton Hayes, a Pima Indian born and raised at the Gila River Indian Reservation of Arizona, certainly did serve in the cited fighting, but he was also one of the only three Marines who survived the second raising of the American flag over Mount Suribachi on Iwo Jima, the action that led to the iconic photograph that in turn led to the seventy-eight-foot-high sculpture that today is the Marine Corps War Memorial.

Hayes, born in 1923, left high school after two years to serve briefly in the Civilian Conservation Corps, a major tenet of the Roosevelt Administration's New Deal programs, then worked as a carpenter. He joined the Marine Corps Reserve in late August 1942, soon after the First Marine Division landed on Guadalcanal in the Solomons to fight the occupying Japanese forces on the tropical island.

After graduating from boot camp at San Diego, he was assigned to Parachute Training School at Camp Gillespie, California (named for early Marine Corps hero Archibald Gillespie). It was with the First Marine Parachute Regiment that he took part in the successful Marine battles to oust the Japanese from both Vella Lavella and Bougainville.

With the parachute units then disbanded and their personnel assimilated in other Marine forces, Hayes was assigned to the Twenty-Eighth Marines of the Fifth Marine Division, then training for further action in the Pacific. For Hayes, that would be the bloody battle for control of Iwo Jima. Fighting on the heavily defended island from D-Day, February 19, to March 26, 1945, he then was called to Washington to take part in events marking the publication of the iconic flag-raising photo, including a war bonds tour.

By now promoted to corporal, he later rejoined the Twenty-Eighth Marines as the regiment settled into occupation duty in Japan.

Famous for his role in the flag-raising, he appeared in the postwar movie *The Sands of Iwo Jima*. After Hayes's death in 1955, he was the subject of the Ballad of Ira Hayes, made popular in the 1960s by Johnny Cash and other singers. The ballad stressed his addiction to alcohol, which is considered the cause of his early death at the Indian reservation where he was born. Like so many other Marines of note, he is buried in Arlington National Cemetery, not far from the iconic Marine Memorial sculpture of the flag-raising he took part in.

———

NO MARINE AND FEW AMERICANS ARE UNAWARE OF THE MARINE Corps' great, sprawling base of 244 square miles on the North Carolina coast, Camp Lejeune. But who was its namesake? Many may wonder.

Any World War I veteran, if still living, could fill in that gap without a moment's thought: Marine Corps General **John A. Lejeune**, who took a combined division of Army and Marine Corps troops into battle in France for America's first large-scale combat test in the "Great War."

The night of September 12, 1918, would be jump-off time for the Allies' great Saint-Mihiel offensive. In addition, this would be "the first time he led his division into battle, the first time an American Marine commanded a division in combat, and the first time an American Army fought in Europe under an American CinC [commander in chief, meaning Army Gen. John J. Pershing, commander of the American Expeditionary Forces (AEF) in Europe]," notes Robert B. Asprey in the Marine Corps *Gazette* of April 1962.

Twelve additional divisions, for a total of three hundred thousand men, leaped forward that same night, but it was Major General Lejeune's Second Division that spearheaded the attack against "a massif the Germans had been fortifying for four years."

His combined Army and Marines division, adds Asprey, was "a hot outfit" that already had fought at Belleau Wood and at Soissons. "Its deeds were famous throughout France."

But there were uncertainties, too. For one, "its ranks had been twice decimated, and twice refilled." Thus, when Lejeune took command of the division in July of 1918, "he had to fit 8,000 replacements into the business of war, had to reshape and train and inspire the Division for the rugged fighting ahead."

Fortunately, the fifty-one-year-old general did not come to the task unprepared. An 1888 Naval Academy graduate raised on a struggling plantation in Louisiana, he had transferred to the Marines after two years of shipboard duty highlighted by his personal heroics in a shipwreck and hurricane at Samoa. At the time he joined the Corps, its entire personnel numbered only about two thousand officers and enlisted men.

Commanding the Marine detachment aboard the USS *Cincinnati*, he took part in the occupation of Puerto Rico during the Spanish-American War. In 1903, he took a battalion of Marines to Panama, then "a hell-hole of yellow fever, malaria, dysentery, and smallpox."

Two years later and already regarded as a "comer," a man to watch, he was in command of the Marine Barracks in Washington, DC. A lieutenant colonel by 1909, he was the first Marine officer admitted to the Army War College.

Taking command of the Advance Base Brigade at New Orleans, he led the brigade in the 1914 occupation of Veracruz, Mexico, before being placed in charge of the Marine Corps' first field aviation operations and organizing the Corps' first motorized unit.

Promoted to brigadier general in 1916, Lejeune took command of the Marine Barracks at Quantico in 1917, but persuaded his superiors to send him to the war in France in 1918 as head of the Fourth Marine Brigade.

The Second Division that he took over that same year not only starred in the Saint-Mihiel Offensive, but also in the Battle of Mount Blanc Ridge and in the Meuse-Argonne campaign that ended the war that fall.

In June 1920, after resuming command of the Quantico base, Lejeune was named Commandant of the Marine Corps.

He is credited during his tenure with fostering higher standards of professionalism for the Corps, with establishing the Marine Corps Schools at Quantico, and with strengthening the Corps' focus on the tactics and techniques needed for amphibious warfare, the hallmark of Marine operations in the Pacific during World War II.

Upon retirement from the Marines in 1937, he served as superintendent of the Virginia Military Institute (VMI) for the better part of eight years. He published a memoir, *Reminiscences of a Marine,* in 1930, and died in Baltimore in November 1942. Camp Lejeune in North Carolina is thus named in honor of an old-time Marine veteran fully capable of adapting to new situations presented by a modern world.

───

THE LIEUTENANT HAD MESSAGES TO DELIVER, MESSAGES FROM THE president himself. That meant traveling westward across Mexico before catching a ship bound for California, where he reached Navy Commodore John D. Sloat and Thomas Larkin, the U.S. consul based at Monterey. He then borrowed a horse to meet explorer John C. Fremont near the Oregon border.

Thus did New York City–born Marine **Archibald H. Gillespie,** carrying secret orders from President James K. Polk, become embroiled in the Mexican-American War and the confusion of battles that led to the U.S. acquisition of the future state of California. In quick order, Gillespie and Fremont, in June of 1846, took part in the Bear Flag Revolt, soon followed by the bloodless American occupation of San Diego and Los Angeles. As second in command of the California Battalion headed by Navy Commodore Robert F. Stockton, commander of the U.S. Pacific Squadron, Gillespie was next left in charge of Los Angeles, the future state's largest city. When he sought to impose martial law on its three thousand residents, the decision fostered a revolt by up to three hundred insurgent *Californios* against Gillespie and his thirty to forty men.

Forced to leave Los Angeles, Gillespie linked up with an Army force under Brig. Gen. Stephen W. Kearney for the ill-considered Battle of San Pasquel. The Army men, exhausted by their long trek to the battle site and stuck with poorly trained horses and mules as mounts, were routed when they failed to surprise the aroused *Californios* in the engagement.

Gillespie took part with a handful of his own men and shouted: "Rally men, for God's sake rally, show them a front, don't turn your backs. Face them, face them!"

They didn't, and Gillespie himself was speared in the back by an enemy lance, "making a severe gash open to the lungs," he later said. He was then charged by another enemy, who "dashed his lance at my face, struck and cutting my upper lip, broke a front tooth and threw me on my back, as his horse jumped over me."

However, three weeks later, a combined Army, Navy, and Marine force of about three hundred—a still impaired Gillespie among them as leader of the rear guard—took on the *Californios* again, this time alongside the San Gabriel River in attempt to regain control of Los Angeles.

Brushing aside the insurgent cannon fire, the Americans now routed the *Californios* with steady fire and attack by bayonet. Gillespie's own rear guard broke up an insurgent charge. On the very next day, January 9, 1847, it was Gillespie himself who had the honor of raising the Stars and Stripes over the city's Government House, notes Dick Camp in the December 2013 issue of *Leatherneck* magazine.

Three days later, "the *Californios* signed the Treaty of Cahuenga, ceding Upper California to the United States." Gillespie then returned to the east, "fighting Indians along the way." He was promoted to captain in early 1848, then brevetted to major "for his California services."

Gillespie retired from the Marine Corps in 1854 under threat of a court martial by an old Navy enemy before briefly serving in the Union Army during the American Civil War. He finished out his life in San Francisco, back in the very state he had helped to create.

GENERALS SMEDLEY DARLINGTON BUTLER AND DAVID MONROE **Shoup**, Marine Corps war heroes of distinctly different eras, probably wouldn't like to see themselves paired together, but the fact remains that each became known later in life for his distinctly critical views on U.S. war policies.

On occasion called the most decorated of Marines, Butler was one of only two Marines (the other was Sergeant Dan Daly) to be awarded the Medal of Honor for two separate actions. Shoup also earned the esteemed Medal for courageous action all his own.

Butler lied about his birth date (1881 in West Chester, Pennsylvania) to secure a second lieutenant's commission in the Marine Corps in 1898 at age sixteen. He missed action in the Spanish-American War and left the Marines in February 1899, but rejoined two months later, this time as a first lieutenant.

From then on, he was given plenty of action. First deployed to the Philippines to serve against rebel insurrectionists, he was suddenly thrown into the fight against the Chinese Boxers at both Tientsin and Peking in 1900. He not only distinguished himself in action there, but was twice wounded and quickly vaulted to captain's rank.

As a first taste of his considerable time to be spent in the so-called "Banana Wars" of Central America and the Caribbean, he led the Marines from the transport *Panther* in the rescue of a U.S. consul besieged by Honduran rebels in 1903. Soon a major in rank, Butler commanded a Marine battalion in Panama from 1909 to 1914, then was deployed with fellow Marines to quell a revolt in Corinto, Nicaragua.

His first Medal of Honor came from his leadership in the seizure of Veracruz, Mexico, in April of 1914. His second Medal of Honor followed his command the next year of a Marine detachment that captured the *caco* bandits' stronghold of Fort Rivière in Haiti. By now a Marine

Corps lieutenant colonel, he also organized and commanded the Haitian *gendarmerie* (police) force.

He missed combat action in World War I but was noted for his smooth command of the Camp Pontanezen debarkation base at Brest, France. Then taking over the Marine camp at Quantico, Virginia, as Brig. Gen. Butler, he oversaw its transformation from a wartime cantonment camp to a permanent Marine Corps base.

Taking a leave of absence from the Marine Corps in 1924 and 1925, he served as chief of the police and firemen in Philadelphia. His tough, sometimes prickly military style alienated his civilian hosts, and he returned to Marine duty in early 1926, this time to command the Marine Barracks at San Diego, California. He then led a Marine expeditionary force to China in 1927 in reaction to the so-called Nanking Incident, in which foreign nationals were being attacked. He was credited for use of considerable diplomatic skills in defusing tensions on the scene.

By now promoted to major general, as the first Marine to reach that rank, he was passed over for appointment as commandant in 1930, even though he was the senior general available. As if to prove he truly had not been in step with the nation's military leadership, he published the book *War Is a Racket* after retiring and making an unsuccessful bid for the U.S. Senate in the early 1930s.

Marine General David Monroe Shoup, on the other hand, did become commandant of the Marine Corps after proving himself both in battle and a series of key duty posts during his nearly forty years as a Marine. Among his postings was a term as inspector general of recruit training shortly after six Marine recruits were drowned at Parris Island in a nighttime punishment march. While defending the Corps' training methods in general, he said mass punishment of any kind could not be tolerated.

After his retirement as a four-star general in the early 1960s, Shoup was an outspoken critic of the American engagement in Vietnam. He said President Johnson's assertions that Vietnam was vital to U.S. interests were "pure, unadulterated poppycock." Another time, he declared that all of Southeast Asia was not worth a single American life, "as related to the present and future safety and freedom of this country."

In a 1968 interview, he went on record again, this time questioning the argument that four American presidents had made related commitments. "We never made commitments, legal or otherwise, to furnish combat-type forces to anyone," he contended. "Why can't we let people actually decide their own destiny?"

A Marine officer since 1926, Shoup had served with the Fourth Marines in Shanghai, China, and then at the American Legation in Peiping during the mid-1930s. He was afterwards posted to duty in Iceland until reassigned to combat duty in the South Pacific in the months after Pearl Harbor.

After stints as Operations and Training Officer for the Second Marine Division, he was posted as an observer both with the Marines on Guadalcanal and with the Army's Forty-Third Division on Rendova, New Georgia (where he was wounded). He led the Second Marines (regiment) as spearhead for the Marine landings on Betio and Tarawa late in November 1943, with the latter known ever since as one of the bloodiest battles the Marines fought in the entire Pacific.

This was where he earned his Medal of Honor, by "fearlessly" exposing himself to "relentless" artillery, machine-gun, and rifle fire coming his way from the entrenched Japanese defenders. With Shoup soon wounded in the leg by shrapnel, he and his men were stranded half a mile from their intended beachhead, his citation also says. Undeterred, he "gallantly led them [his men] across the fringing reefs to charge the heavily fortified island and reinforce our hard-pressed, thinly held lines."

Also seeing combat in the Marine landings on Saipan and Tinian Island, Shoup served as chief of staff of the Second Marine Division. In the post-war years, he was chief of staff of the First Marine Division; commandant of the Basic School at Quantico; fiscal director of the Corps; inspector general of the Corps; commander of the Third Marine Division; commander at Parris Island, and finally chief of staff for the entire Corps. At that point, in 1959, President Eisenhower ignored several senior generals to appoint Shoup commandant, whereupon three of his potential rivals for the post applied for retirement.

Typically, as outspoken leader of the Corps, he left one mark by ending the use of swagger sticks and another by forbidding the practice of escorting Marines convicted in court-martial proceedings off-base to the slow drumbeat of the Death March.

Remaining at the commandant post until his retirement in 1963, he died of heart disease in 1983, at his home in Alexandria, Virginia, at the age of seventy-eight.

———

THIS PROMISING MARINE NEVER MADE GENERAL...JUST ASTRONAUT, instead.

The late **John H. Glenn**, born and raised in New Concord, Ohio, grew up in a home that his parents used as a boardinghouse for students from nearby Muskingum College. "Surrounded by older students, encouraged by a father who liked to travel, and tutored by a devoted mother," says the John and Annie Glenn Historic website, "John developed an early interest in science, a fascination with flying, and a sense of patriotism that would define his adult life."

In that adult life, Glenn became a Marine pilot in time to fly fifty-nine combat missions in the F-4U Corsair fighter during World War II with Marine Fighter Squadron 155 in the Pacific's Marshall Islands. He then flew another sixty-three combat missions with Marine Fighter Squadron 311 during the Korean War, including twenty-seven flown as an exchange pilot with the U.S. Air Force in the F-86 Sabrejet.

In the last nine days of fighting in Korea, Glenn downed three Communist MIGs in combat along the Yalu River, notes his online National Aeronautics and Space Administration (NASA) biography. Overall, he earned six Distinguished Flying Crosses for his combat forays in both wars.

After Korea, he served as a test pilot for the Navy and Marine Corps. In 1957, as project officer for the F8U Crusader, Glenn set a new transcontinental speed record by flying the plane across the country, Los Angeles to New York, in three hours and twenty-three minutes.

Upon entering the nation's fledgling space program, he was selected to be one of NASA's first seven astronauts as part of Project Mercury. Still a Marine officer, Glenn flew the *Friendship 7* Project Mercury spacecraft around the world three times on February 20, 1962, as the first American to orbit the earth in space.

"Glenn's ride into space, a great technical accomplishment, held even greater significance for the country," notes the Glenn Historic website. "Having lagged behind the Soviet Union in the 'Space Race,' Americans saw the event as a political as well as scientific milestone. Across the country, they welcomed Glenn as a hero who had conquered the bounds of the earth and given new wings to America's spirit."

Glenn resigned from the space program in 1964 and retired from the Marine Corps with the rank of colonel in 1965. He planned to run for the U.S. Senate, but lest anyone think everything came easily to the former fighter pilot and astronaut, it was only on his third try that he was elected. First, an accident had forced him to withdraw from the Ohio Democratic Senate primary. Glenn then served as a business executive (vice president and president) with Royal Crown Cola until finally elected to the U.S. Senate from Ohio in 1974.

In the Senate, he "took a leading role in weapons control and government affairs," says the Glenn website. He served as chairman of the body's Government Affairs Committee for seven years. "Never far from the center of Democratic politics, he was a contender for the vice presidential nomination three times and ran in the Democratic primaries as a presidential candidate in 1984."

Announcing his retirement from the Senate in 1997—on the twenty-fifth anniversary of his orbital flight—John Glenn went back into space again in late 1998 at the age of seventy-seven. A member of the Space Shuttle *Discovery* crew at the invitation of NASA, he rocketed aloft this time as the oldest human ever to go into space. More recently, he and his wife Annie served as trustees of Muskingum College, their joint alma mater.

The nation mourned his passing when he died in a Columbus, Ohio, hospital on December 8, 2016, at the age of ninety-five.

———

PFC. GUY LOUIS "GABBY" GABALDON, A HISPANIC MARINE ALL OF five-foot-four in height, sought out Saipan's enemy-occupied caves, confronted pillboxes or pushed through the jungle brush, always alone and on self-appointed mission to bring in prisoners.

And he did bring in prisoners, about one thousand of them, usually without firing a single shot. On one day alone in July 1944, he brought in eight hundred Japanese as prisoners.

In his postwar memoir *Saipan: Suicide Island*, he explained: "Immediately after I landed on Saipan I decided I would go off into enemy territory to fight the war as I saw fit. I always worked alone, usually at night in the bush. I must have seen too many John Wayne movies, because what I was doing was suicidal."

Actually, there was some method behind his madness.

As noted by David Reyes in the August 31, 1998, *Los Angeles Times*, Gabaldon had learned snatches of Japanese as a child in the tough East L.A. neighborhoods.

"One of seven children growing up in a tiny house," wrote Reyes, "Gabaldon spent much of his time on the streets, where he was befriended by two Japanese-American brothers. Fascinated by their customs, he began spending time at their home and eventually moved in with them. He lived with his foster family for six years, learning their language and traditions, until the war broke out and they were sent to an internment camp. Gabaldon, then seventeen, joined the Marine Corps."

Years later, he told Reyes in a telephone interview from Saipan itself—he had settled there after the war—that in his first day of combat during the invasion of Saipan he had killed thirty-three Japanese soldiers, but then was "overcome with remorse."

After that, he drastically changed tactics. "He began going out alone and persuading Japanese soldiers to surrender to him, telling them they would be treated well, given food and water, and medical care."

As one "persuasion," "he would capture six soldiers at gunpoint but release three, telling them to spread the word about fair treatment as prisoners of war. He would release them with a warning: 'If they didn't come back, I would blast the hell of out the three left behind."

"It was a ruse, but it worked. That was how he managed to take 800 prisoners in a single day."

A private with the Second Marine Division at the time, he first was awarded the Silver Star for his exploits, but that award was later upgraded to the Navy Cross. "Working alone in front of the lines," the citation says in part, "he daringly entered enemy caves, pillboxes, buildings, and jungle brush, frequently in the face of hostile fire, and succeeded in not only obtaining vital military information, but in capturing well over 1,000 enemy civilians and troops."

A wound from machine-gun fire late in the campaign to seize Saipan ended his combat career, but he later operated seafood businesses both in Mexico and Saipan, according to his obituary on September 4, 2006, in the *New York Times.* His heroics became widely known after the war through the television program "This Is Your Life" and the Hollywood movie, *Hell to Eternity,* the obituary noted. He was an adviser to the film, "in which Richard Eyer portrayed him as a youngster and Jeffrey Hunter played him as a Marine."

Both before and after his death from heart disease in Old Town, Florida, there was a movement in the Latino community of his hometown Los Angeles to persuade the Pentagon to award Gabaldon the Medal of Honor for his exploits as the "Pied Piper of Saipan." But Gabaldon himself always said, "The heroes are still over there. Those who gave their all are the heroes."

WHO WOULD RANK AS THE MARINE CORPS' OUTSTANDING AIR ACE of World War II? Therein lies a tough choice between two amazing heroes: **Joseph Jacob Foss**, who shot down a known twenty-six Japanese aircraft in the South Pacific, or the "Black Sheep" Squadron's **Gregory "Pappy" Boyington**, who accounted for twenty-eight enemy planes... but not all on behalf of the Marine Corps.

Boyington was born in 1912 in Idaho, and first joined Marine Corps Aviation in 1936. By 1941 he was a flight instructor at the naval aviation training facility at Pensacola, Florida. With war already raging in China, however, he resigned in September that year to join the all-volunteer "Flying Tigers," led against the Japanese by Gen. Claire Chenault.

It was with the American Volunteer Group, more colorfully called the Flying Tigers, that Boyington shot down six Japanese fighters, a total that immediately made him an ace.

Returning to the Marines in 1942 with a reserve major's rank, he served quietly in administrative posts for some months in the Pacific, but in August 1943 he was finally given command of a squadron largely filled with replacement and inactivated pilots soon to be known as his "Black Sheep"—technically, Squadron 214—based much of the time at Espirito Santo in the New Hebrides.

Over eighty-four days of combat, "Pappy" Boyington and his pilots shot down ninety-eight Japanese aircraft in the central Solomons of the South Pacific, while shooting up another 130 caught on the ground. He and his "Black Sheep" became a wartime legend.

On his last day in the air, January 3, 1944, Boyington personally shot down three Japanese planes, bringing his total number of "kills" from both his Flying Tiger days and his Marine Corps exploits to twenty-eight. Of course, his twenty-two shoot-downs as a Marine in the Pacific redoubled his qualification as an ace, and more. He thus became the second highest scoring Marine Corps ace of the war, while his overall total of twenty-eight made him the fourth highest among all American pilots, worldwide.

With months still to go before war's end, he might well have added considerably to his "score," but on the very day he downed his last three enemy planes, he himself was shot down, strafed for two hours, and picked up by a Japanese submarine that took him all the way to Japan. His location and even his survival unknown for certain, he was promoted to lieutenant colonel and awarded the Medal of Honor in his absence of twenty months as a prisoner of the Japanese.

He returned home a legend soon after the Japanese surrender in 1945, conquered his alcohol demons after retiring from the Marine Corps as a colonel, and published a successful memoir in 1958, *Baa Baa Black Sheep*, later made into a popular movie.

Joseph Jacob Foss, on the other hand, made his mark as the top Marine Corps ace in the Pacific by downing twenty-six Japanese planes and again later in postwar public life as governor of his native South Dakota, first commissioner of the AFL (American Football League), head of the National Rifle Association, and host of his own outdoorsman television show.

Born in 1915 on a farm near Sioux Falls, South Dakota, and graduating from South Dakota University in 1940, Foss joined the Marines shortly after Pearl Harbor, earned his pilot's wings, and was deployed to the southwest Pacific with Fighter Squadron 121. A visit by aviation pioneer Charles Lindbergh at a nearby airport and a sightseeing ride in a Ford Tri-Motor during his youth had helped inspire his interest in flying. Now, in 1942, based at Henderson Field on Guadalcanal and usually flying the Grumman Wildcat, Foss and his fellow Marine pilots were charged with defending the same primitive airstrip and surrounding Marine facilities from repeated attacks by Japanese aircraft.

In just five weeks, October 9 to November 9, 1942, he personally shot down twenty-three Japanese aircraft. Not long after, on January 15, 1943, he scored three more, to bring his total to twenty-six, the highest Marine score for the entire Pacific campaign, as compared to Boyington's total of twenty-eight, which included his Flying Tiger sorties in China.

By the time Foss and his pilots downed seventy-two Japanese aircraft in all, they became known as "Joe's Flying Circus."

The total of twenty-six for Foss was the same as World War I American Ace Eddie Rickenbacker's otherwise unmatched twenty-six "kills"—but it's worth noting that four of Rickenbacker's downed enemy craft were mere observation balloons.

Totals aside, Foss would become widely known for one action in particular. On January 25, a large Japanese force of bombers and fighters approached Guadalcanal. Foss led a mixed group of only eleven or twelve F4F and P-38 fighters into the sky against the superior Japanese numbers, but held back on attacking the fighters—he thought the Japanese strategy was probably to engage his own planes while the bombers slipped past, unhindered, to give Henderson Field a real pasting.

With four of their bombers then shot down and their fighters beginning to run low on fuel, the Japanese turned back, as he had hoped. Henderson Field was saved one more time.

Similarly to Boyington—but with less severe consequences—Foss was also shot down one time. Left to fend for himself for five hours more than a hundred miles from home base in shark-infested waters, he was rescued by members of a Catholic mission from a nearby island who carried him to safety by canoe.

Another (happier) time, as his squadron's executive officer, Foss allowed a visiting civilian test pilot, Charles Lindbergh, his hero of old, to fly with the "Flying Circus" on strictly unauthorized combat sorties.

In May of 1943, Foss, by now a major in rank, was presented the Medal of Honor at the White House by President Roosevelt in person—*Life* magazine ran his image as its cover at the time of the morale-boosting presentation. He went on war bond tours and was treated for malaria. He also was awarded the Silver Star, the Bronze Star, and a Purple Heart for his wartime service.

Immediately after the war, he and a friend established the Joe Foss Flying Service in Sioux Falls with an eventual fleet of thirty-five aircraft.

He entered politics as a Republican state legislator in 1946 and, after a stint in Marine aviation training during the Korean War, was twice elected governor of South Dakota, in 1954 and 1956. He later ran for the U.S. House, but was defeated by future Democratic presidential nominee George McGovern.

In the meantime, he had helped organize the state's Air National Guard and served it as a squadron commander with the rank of brigadier general. In 1959, he was chosen as head of the newly formed AFL. He also hosted *The American Sportsman,* an ABC television hunting and fishing show.

Later, he hosted the syndicated TV show *The Outdoorsman: Joe Foss,* followed by his stint as president of the National Rifle Association (NRA). The outdoors show drew criticism from some environment and animal rights groups, and his time at the NRA (1988–1990) was marked by his statement that "all guns are good guns."

On the first day of 2003, Joe Foss died of cerebral bleeding in Scottsdale, Arizona, his home at the time. Former President George Herbert Walker Bush, himself a Navy aviator in World War II, said, "Joe Foss was not only my hero but the hero of every Marine and Navy pilot who served in the war."

———

Sad to say, another Marine of note, probably the most notorious of all time, was presidential assassin **Lee Harvey Oswald**.

Born to a recently widowed mother in New Orleans on October 18, 1939, he grew up a loner in a family always in financial straits. With no great accomplishments to his credit in school or out, he nonetheless had fantasies of himself as "the Commander" or as "a political prophet," according to the Warren Commission, the blue-ribbon panel appointed to investigate the circumstances of President John F. Kennedy's assassination in Dallas, Texas, by the same Lee Harvey Oswald. "He had a great hostility toward his environment, whatever it happened to be, which he expressed in striking and sometimes violent acts long before the assassination [in 1963]," says the Warren Commission report.

Charged with school truancy, Oswald was placed under psychiatric observation for nearly a month at a New York City Youth House at age thirteen in 1953. He was diagnosed as having "personality pattern disturbances with schizoid features and passive-aggressive tendencies." But he was not considered psychotic or potentially dangerous at the time, despite strong "paranoid overtones."

His doctors recommended that he be placed on probation and seek help through a child guidance clinic. Before Oswald could be forced to accept such help by the courts, however, he and his mother Marguerite moved back to New Orleans in January 1954. There, "Lee finished the ninth grade before he left school to work for a year."

Oswald apparently started reading about communism when he was about fifteen. "In the Marines, he evidenced a strong conviction as to the correctness of Marxist doctrine." But while he stated several times "that he was a Communist," he "apparently never joined any Communist Party."

He joined the Marine Corps in October 1956, at just barely seventeen, after trying to join a year earlier at age sixteen. His older brother Robert had joined the Marines three years before.

As was his pattern throughout his youth, the younger Oswald found it difficult to make friends. He was notably sloppy in appearance, challenged the authority of his superiors, and never rose above the rank of private. Deployed to Japan, he was court-martialed for drunkenly challenging a sergeant to a fight and, in another incident, for possession of an unauthorized pistol, "with which he had accidentally shot himself."

Soon after, and just short of his enlistment term, he was voluntarily transferred to the Marine Corps Reserve "under honorable" conditions, ostensibly to care for his mother after she was injured in an accident. He was then "undesirably" discharged from the Reserve "after it was learned he had defected to the Soviet Union."

He later wrote to then-Navy Secretary and later Texas Governor

John Connally in protest to the undesirable discharge, saying he would "employ all means to right this gross mistake or injustice."

Connally himself was later severely wounded in the shooting that resulted in President Kennedy's death. Yet, Oswald's Russian wife Marina "said that her husband did not say anything about Governor Connally after his [Oswald's] return to the United States."

According to the Warren Commission, also, "it does not appear that Oswald ever expressed any dissatisfaction of any kind with either the president or Governor Connally."

He did continue in efforts to reverse the discharge by petitioning the Navy Discharge Review Board, which declined to modify its decision "and so advised him in a letter dated July 1963." This was just months before the assassination in Dallas in November of that year.

Earlier in 1963, Oswald apparently fired a bullet into the home of Army Gen. Edwin Walker, whom he considered dangerously right-wing. The bullet was linked to Oswald's ammunition after the Kennedy assassination, as reported by the PBS television *Frontline* program "Who Was Lee Harvey Oswald?"

Concluding that Oswald "alone" was the assassin of John F. Kennedy, the Warren Commission said, "Oswald was profoundly alienated from the world in which he lived." And further: "His life was characterized by isolation, frustration, and failure. He had very few, if any, close relationships with other people and he appeared to have great difficulty in finding a meaningful place in the world. He was never satisfied with anything."

SELECT BIBLIOGRAPHY

PART I: EARLY WARS

Boyd, Julia. *A Dance with the Dragon: The Vanished World of Peking's Foreign Colony*. London: I. B. Tauris & Co. Ltd., 2012.

British Gazetteer and New Daily Advertiser. May 5, 1778.

Butler, Glen G. "The Boxer Rebellion: Coalition Expeditionary Operations in China." *Marine Corps Gazette* 87, no. 10 (October 2003).

Green, Israel. "The Capture of John Brown." *The North American Review* (1885): 564–578.

Johnson, Edward C. *Marine Corps Aviation: The Early Years, 1912–1940*. Washington, DC: History and Museums Division Headquarters, 1977.

Moskin, J. Robert. *The U.S. Marine Corps Story*. New York: Back Bay Books, 1992.

Nalty, Bernard C. "The Barrier Forts: A Battle, a Monument, and a Mythical Marine." *Marine Corps Historical Reference Series*, no. 2 (1962).

Offen, Lee G. *America's First Marines: Gooch's American Regiment, 1740–1742*. CreateSpace Independent Publishing Platform, 2011.

Offenbach, Jacques, composer. "The Marines' Hymn." Lyrics by Thomas Holcomb, 1942.

Peck, Pascal, to an officer on board U.S. Brig *Argus*. Naval History and Heritage Command. "Battle of Derna, 27 April 1805: Selected Naval Documents." Published December 9, 2015. https://www.history.navy.mil/research/library/online-reading-room/title-list-alphabetically/b/battle-of-derna-27-april-1805-selected-naval-documents.html.

Seitz, Don C. *Paul Jones: His Exploits in English Seas During 1778 to 1780*. New York: E. P. Dutton and Company, 1917.

Smith, Charles Richard and Charles H. Waterhouse. *The Marines in the Revolution: A Pictorial History*. Washington, DC: History and Museums Division Headquarters, 1975.

Sousa, John Philip. "Feast of the Monkeys." *Pipetown Sandy*. Indianapolis: Bobbs-Merrill Company Publishers, 1905.

Stevens, Paul Drew, ed. *Congressional Medal of Honor: The Names, the Deeds*. Forest Ranch, CA: Sharp & Dunnigan Publications, 1990.

Thomas, Emory M. *Bold Dragoon: The Life of J. E. B. Stuart*. Norman: University of Oklahoma Press, 1999.

Trapshooting Hall of Fame. "John Philip Sousa." Last modified 2012. www.traphof.org/Inductees/Sousa-John-Phillip.html.

U.S. Marines Virtual Birthplace Memorial. "First Lieutenant Presley Neville O'Bannon, USMC." www.usmarinesbirthplace.com/OBANNON.html.

Whitehaven and Western Lakeland. "John Paul Jones: The Raid on Whitehaven in 1778." Last modified August 8, 2012. http://www.whitehavenandwesternlakeland.co.uk/johnpauljones/raid.htm.

PART II: WORLD WARS

Berry, Henry. *Semper Fi, Mac: Living Memories of the U.S. Marines in WWII*. New York: William Morrow and Company, Inc., 1982.

Bevilacqua, Allan C. *The Way It Was: A Seabag Full of Marine Humor*. Phillips Publications, Inc., 2006.

Billison, Samuel. Lecture given at the McGuire Veterans Affairs Medical Center, Richmond, VA, November 2003.

Brand, Max. *Fighter Squadron at Guadalcanal.* Annapolis: U.S. Naval Institute Press, 1996.

Cage, Nicolas, Adam Beach, Peter Stormare, Mark Ruffalo, Christian Slater. *Windtalkers.* DVD. Directed by John Woo. Los Angeles: Lion Rock Productions, 2002.

"The China Marines." *History Detectives: Special Investigations.* PBS. http://www.pbs.org/opb/historydetectives/feature/the-china-marines/.

Cooper, Courtney Ryley, ed. *Dear Folks at Home: The Glorious Story of the United States Marines in France as Told by Their Letters from the Battlefield.* New York: Houghton Mifflin Company, 1919.

Coram, Robert. "The Bridge to the Beach." HistoryNet. Published September 30, 2010. www.historynet.com/the-bridge-to-the-beach.htm.

———. "Brute Krulak: The Most Important Marine." By Maureen Cavanaugh. KPBS (December 2010).

Crumley, Beth. "'Elizabeth Ford'—A Model T Truck in France." *The Huffington Post.* Last modified April 1, 2012. www.huffingtonpost.com/beth-crumley/blog-elizaberth-ford-a-mo_b_1244897.html.

Davis, Burke. *Marine! The Life of Chesty Puller.* New York: Bantam, 1991.

Henderson, F. P. "Roy S. Geiger: The First Air-Ground General." *Marine Corps Gazette* 79, no. 4 (April 1995).

Hewitt, Linda L. *Women Marines in World War I.* Washington, DC: History and Museum Division, 1974.

Hinds, Joseph. "JFK's Other PT Boat Rescue." *America in WWII* (February 2011): 53–57.

HistoryNet. "Battle of Wake Island." www.historynet.com/battle-of-wake-island.

Keene, R. R. "The Battle for Cuzco Well." *Leatherneck Magazine.* Originally published September 1998. https://www.mca-marines/org/leatherneck/battle-cuzco-well.

Korean War Educator. "Women (Military Personnel) in the Korean War." Last modified August 21, 2015. www.koreanwar-educator.org /topics/women_in_korea/women_in_korea.htm.

Krulak, Victor H. *First to Fight: An Inside View of the U.S. Marine Corps.* Annapolis: Bluejacket Books, 1984.

Lord, Walter. *Day of Infamy.* New York: Henry Holt and Company, 1957.

Martin, Douglas. "Obituary of Felix de Weldon." *The New York Times,* June 15, 2003.

Mason, John T., ed. *The Pacific War Remembered: An Oral History Collection.* Annapolis: Naval Institute Press, 1986.

McClellan, Edwin. *The United States Marine Corps in the World War.* Anderson, Angela, ed. Washington, DC: USMC History Division, 2015.

Morison, Samuel Eliot. *History of United States Naval Operations in World War II.* Vol. 3, *The Rising Sun in the Pacific.* Edison: Castle Books, 2001.

Moskin, J. Robert. *The U.S. Marine Corps Story.* New York: Back Bay Books, 1992.

Nalty, Bernard C. "The Right to Fight: African-American Marines in World War II." Marine Corps History and Museums Division. https://www.nps.gov/parkhistory/online_books/wapa/extContent /usmc/pcn-190-003132-00/sec3.htm.

Pendleton, Robert. "The Biography of Colonel Robert Watkinson Huntington." The Spanish American War Centennial Website. http://www.spanamwar.com/1stmarinehuntington.html.

Reinburg, J. Hunter. *Aerial Combat Escapades: A Pilot's Logbook.* Grand Canyon: GCBA Publishing, 1988.

Santelli, James S. *A Brief History of the 4th Marines.* Washington, DC: USMC Historical Division Headquarters, 1970.

———. *A Brief History of the 7th Marines.* Washington, DC: USMC Historical Division Headquarters, 1980.

Sherrod, Robert. "Marine Corps Aviation: The Early Days." *Marine Corps Gazette* 36, no. 5 (May 1952): 52–61.

Stremlow, Colonel Mary V. *Free a Marine to Fight: Women Marines in World War II.* USMC History & Museums Division.

Women Marines Association. "Women Marines in Vietnam." Published August 24, 2010. https://womenmarines.wordpress.com/2010/08/24/women-marines-in-vietnam/.

Zimmerman, Dwight Jon. "The Incredible Saga of OSS Col. Peter J. Ortiz in World War II." Defense Media Network. July 20, 2014. www.defensemedianetwork.com/stories/the-incredible-saga-of-col-peter-j-ortiz/.

PART III: WAR UPON WAR

Appleman, Roy E. *Escaping the Trap: The U.S. Army X Corps in Northeast Korea, 1950.* College Station, TX: Texas A&M University Press, 1990.

Brown, Ronald J. *Whirlybirds: U.S. Marine Helicopters in Korea.* Washington, DC: Marine Corps History and Museums Division, 2003.

Clayton, James D. *The Years of MacArthur*: Houghton Mifflin, 1970.

Collier, Peter. *Medal of Honor: Portraits of Valor Beyond the Call of Duty.* New York: Artisan, 2003.

Crumley, Beth. "In Memoriam: Colonel William H. Dabney." Marine Corps Association & Foundation. Published February 22, 2012. https://www.mca-marines.org/mcaf-blog/2012/02/22/memoriam-colonel-william-h-dabney.

Hemingway, Albert. *Our War Was Different: Marine Combined Action Platoons in Vietnam.* Annapolis: Naval Institute Press, 1994.

Hubbell, John G. "The Long Way Home." In *True Stories of Great Escapes*, edited by Charles Vernal. Pleasantville, NY: Reader's Digest, 1978.

Krulak, Victor H. *First to Fight: An Inside View of the U.S. Marine Corps.* Annapolis: Bluejacket Books, 1984.

MacArthur, Douglas. *Reminiscences.* Annapolis: Bluejacket Books, 2001.

MacDonald, James A. *The Problems of U.S. Marine Corps Prisoners of War in Korea.* Washington, DC: USMC History and Museums Division Headquarters, 1988.

Moskin, J. Robert. *The U.S. Marine Corps Story.* New York: Back Bay Books, 1992.

Powers, John N. *Bean Camp to Briar Patch: Life in the POW Camps of Korea and Vietnam.* Wittenberg: Cronin Publications, 2011.

Price, Donald L. *First Marine Capture in Vietnam: A Biography of Donald G. Cook.* Jefferson, NC: McFarland & Company, Inc., 2007.

Robinson, Stephen. "Bombed U.S. Warship Was Defended by Sailors with Unloaded Guns." *The Telegraph.* Published November 15, 2000.

Russ, Martin. *Breakout: The Chosin Reservoir Campaign, Korea 1950.* New York: Penguin, 1999.

Shettle, M. L. *United States Marine Corps Air Stations of World War II.* Schaertel Publishing Company, 2001.

Wagner, Robert. *POW: Americans in Enemy Hands.* Directed by Carol L. Fleisher. Homevision, 2000. Videocassette (VHS), 93 minutes.

Webb, James. *I Heard My Country Calling: A Memoir.* New York: Simon & Schuster, 2014.

PART IV: TWENTY-FIRST-CENTURY WARS

Armour, Vernice. *Zero to Breakthrough: The 7-Step, Battle-Tested Method for Accomplishing Goals that Matter.* New York: Gotham Books, 2011.

Collins, Shannon. DOD News, Defense Media Activity, U.S. Department of Defense. "Marine Pushes Through Pain to Win Warrior Games Gold." Published June 28, 2015. www.defense.gov/News/Article/Article/604918/marine-pushes-through-pain-to-win-warrior-games-gold.

Eckles, Norman. "Legendary Marine: Joe Foss." Marine Corps Association & Foundation. Published October 9, 2013. https://www.mca-marines.org/leatherneck/legendary-marine-joe-foss.

Folsom, Seth W. B. *Where Youth and Laughter Go: With "The Cutting Edge" in Afghanistan.* Annapolis: Naval Institute Press, 2015.

Gates, Robert M. *Duty: Memoirs of a Secretary at War.* New York: Alfred A. Knopf, 2014.

Invictus Games. "I AM Spotlight: Sarah Rudder, USA, a Real Life Super-woman." Published May 10, 2016. www.invictusgames2016.org/2016/05/spotlight-sarah-rudder-usa-real-life-superwoman/.

Petersen, Frank E. with Joseph A. Phelps. *Into the Tiger's Jaw: America's First Black Marine Aviator.* Annapolis: Naval Institute Press, 1998.

Roberts, Sam. "Obituary of Frank E. Petersen Jr." *The New York Times,* August 26, 2015.

United States Marine Corps History Division. "Colonel Gregory Boy-ington." https://www.usmcu.edu/?q=node/1568.

INDEX

W

X

Y